LAW, MYSTERY, AND THE HUMANITIES:
COLLECTED ESSAYS

Law, Mystery, and the Humanities

Collected Essays

Edited by Logan Atkinson and Diana Majury

UNIVERSITY OF TORONTO PRESS
Toronto Buffalo London

Toronto Buffalo London
www.utppublishing.com
Printed in Canada

ISBN 978-0-8020-9001-0

Printed on acid-free paper

Library and Archives Canada Cataloguing in Publication

Law, mystery, and the humanities : collected essays / edited by Logan Atkinson and Diana Majury.

Includes bibliographical references.
ISBN 978-0-8020-9001-0

1. Law. 2. Humanities. I. Atkinson, Logan, 1954–. II. Majury, Diana, 1952–.

K487.C8L425 2008 340′.115 C2008-902583-0

University of Toronto Press acknowledges the financial assistance to its publishing program of the Canada Council for the Arts and the Ontario Arts Council.

University of Toronto Press acknowledges the financial support for its publishing activities of the Government of Canada through the Book Publishing Industry Development Program (BPIDP).

Contents

Acknowledgments

This book, no doubt like many of its ilk, was born of a multitude of stimulating and eclectic conversations among colleagues, conversations ranging across several years and generated in many venues, academic and otherwise. During the course of these discussions, we discovered that our apparently varied interests in fields beyond our home discipline of law – in history, literature, philosophy, religion, language, cultural studies – actually functioned to bring us closer together and enabled us to escape the confines of law into (what was to us) the more heady terrain of the humanities. We began to recognize more fully what we share and to engage with some of the larger, more esoteric questions that we saw as both connecting and moving beyond the humanities and beyond the law. Our conversations were animated, intense, and fun, and to a large degree we experienced them as liberating. We had discovered an exciting intellectual space, transcendent of disciplinary restrictions, a space in which our curiosity could be allowed free rein.

This book is one of several products of that excitement. The Canadian Initiative in Law, Culture & the Humanities, founded and based in the Department of Law at Carleton University, an initiative still in its infancy in early 2008, is another. In October 2005, and again in October 2007, a small group of colleagues in the Department of Law hosted a conference in which scholars from across Canada and elsewhere explored many interdisciplinary themes. Participants in the conferences have shown great patience with our efforts to establish the Initiative and demonstrated their enthusiasm clearly with remarkable, stimulating scholarly presentations, some of the products of which are published in this book. We want to thank Neil Sargent, our colleague in the Department of Law, for his commitment and his exceptional contributions, to the Initiative and especially with respect to this book, and Sheryl Hamilton, Canada Research Chair in Communication, Law and Governance at Carleton, for her leadership and her vision for the Initiative.

None of this work would be possible without a nurturing environment in our academic home, the Department of Law and Faculty of Public Affairs at Carleton University. We are very fortunate to be surrounded by encouraging and supportive colleagues and leaders, themselves scholars who understand the urgent desire to explore and express one's curiosity, however tentative that expression might first be. In this respect, our thanks go out to Dean Katherine Graham of the Faculty of Public Affairs, and Professor Peter Swan, Chair of the Department of Law, for the faith they have shown, both in this book and in the Initiative.

We wish to thank Solandia of Aeclectic Tarot, the artist whose rendition of the Magician tarot card appears on the cover of this book. Solandia was extremely generous and gracious in responding to a request from complete strangers asking for permission to use her artwork. For us, her work perfectly captures the mood and the mystery of our book. We want to thank as well the editorial team at the University of Toronto Press, especially Virgil Duff, Executive Editor, for their encouragement, patience, and wise counsel as the publishing process unfolded.

The contributors to this book have been a delight to work with. Each of them shares our excitement at being involved in what must ultimately be termed an intellectual experiment, and each has gladly allowed their work to be integrated into a larger, somewhat enigmatic whole. The enthusiasm with which they produced drafts and re-drafts, and the patience they demonstrated in addressing editorial and critical responses, shows a commitment to both the process by which recondite collections of essays are put together and the intellectual journey out of which new ideas might emerge. We thank each of them for their loyalty to the project, for their participation, and for their remarkable contributions.

LAW, MYSTERY, AND THE HUMANITIES: COLLECTED ESSAYS

1 Points of Convergence: Law, Mystery, and the Humanities

DIANA MAJURY AND LOGAN ATKINSON

In May 2006 it was widely reported that one of life's most persistent puzzles had finally been solved. It turns out that the egg really did precede the chicken. According to John Brookfield of the University of Nottingham, the resolution of this problem resides in evolutionary genetics. The DNA of the living organism inside the eggshell would have been the same as that of the chicken that ultimately emerged, meaning the egg was the first member of the species. Brookfield's conclusions were supported by David Papineau of King's College London and Charles Bourns, chair of the trade group 'Great British Chicken.'[1]

It is likely that the suggestion of a solution to this intriguing problem of order and causation was met with a measure of regret in scholarly circles, stemming not necessarily from a secret hope that the chicken would emerge the victor, but rather from the loss of mystery that successful research can represent. The enduring perplexities generated by a host of (to this point) unanswerable questions are possibly the most important motivators in scholarly work, such that if we were successful in answering these questions, there would not be much of interest left to do. The conclusions of Professor Brookfield, therefore, symbolize the potential for ultimately satisfying our curiosity as a species, making further questioning little more than intellectual self-absorption.

However, many of us resist the linear, scientific answer. While literally about chickens and eggs, this question has engaged us because it is also about more fundamental questions, those pertaining to the (inter)relationship between linearity and circularity, between creation and creator, and our own ambivalent relationship with dichotomy. The 'egg' answer resolves none of these questions; it does not even address them and is thus deeply unsatisfying, ineffectual as an 'answer' for many of us. We may be living in an age that craves certainty, that is, an age of destabilizing uncertainty in which the proliferation of violence and war, the widening gap between rich and poor, the preventable but ongoing deterioration of the environment, and a pervasive sense of randomness and arbitrariness make us desperate for answers, reasons, and causes. But the answers and reasons proffered (such as simplistic characterizations of good and evil) are inevitably unsatisfying and reductionist and ultimately unhelpful. Historically, the humanities have risen to prominence in such times of certainty-craving uncertainty, to remind us of the fundamental nature of these questions, to encourage us to eschew easy answers, and to assure us that uncertainty and unknowability are neither inherently bad nor inherently good. They simply are. There is for many of us a comfort, as well as an excitement, in embracing the mystery and in struggling with the unanswerable questions and tensions that are the inevitable result. Our desire is to expand knowledge and to further understanding, rather than to reach a definitive end point.

The persistence of mystery (that is, the insatiable urge to ask questions that defy our abilities to provide an answer) binds humans together as a species. Indeed, Bernard Lonergan suggested that unending curiosity is one of the obvious characteristics that distinguishes the human species from other species in the world. In his comparison of the 'ways of knowing' of a kitten and a human being, Lonergan pointed out the experiential basis of the kitten's behaviour, without the need for the intervention of intelligence or reflection. In the case of the human, however, experience supplies nothing more than 'materials for questions,' questions that serve as the foundation for 'concepts, suppositions, definitions, postulates, hypotheses, theories.' As Lonergan concluded, '[a]nimals have no epistemological problems,'[2] whereas '[m]an's unrestricted desire to know is mated to a limited capacity to attain knowledge ... The fact is that the range of possible questions is larger than the range of possible answers.'[3]

In commenting on Lonergan's philosophy, Hugo A. Meynell wrote that '[t]he human mind is characterised by an unrestricted desire to understand, which is never to be entirely satisfied until no more questions remain to be asked. But in fact further questions always confront the human mind and its understanding, which as a consequence are in a perpetual state of development.'[4] Building on this position, it is our observation that it is not simply a matter of endless 'further questions,' but also the apparently irresolvable nature of particular questions that is shared across human experience, despite political, cultural, linguistic, religious, and other differences of historical contingency. It is not merely the urge to ask questions and the role this urge plays in allowing us to identify the 'perpetual state of development' of the human mind; it is the apparently universal attraction to mystery that binds us together.

It is in the humanities (philosophy, the arts, literature, history, and often religion) where the allure of shared mystery is perhaps most central, if sometimes obscure. The problems of metaphysics, aesthetics, ethics, epistemology, and logic inhabit the humanities like a skeleton, often taken for granted, but somehow holding the whole thing together. It is our fantasy that the answers to these problems are just waiting to burst forth in some sort of revealed splendour while at the same time we know that answers might well prove to be anticlimactic and disappointing. The most that we really want is new insight and further intriguing questions. It is the speculative anticipation of that splendour of discovery, together with the joy in the exploration, the fascination with the puzzle, the tentative and partial answers, and the ensuing raging debates, that fosters great research and creativity in the humanities. In contrast to the 'logical speculation' criticized by John Ralston Saul as the basis of false absolutes,[5] this is speculation born of wonder and imagination. We see thematic patterns inside particular disciplines and across the humanities that demonstrate this speculative wonder over and over again. The tension between individual realization and the duty to others, the need to understand and claim authenticity, the constant battle between reason and emotion, the apparent incompatibility between universality and contingency, the idea of 'the self' juxtaposed with the problem of (religious, political, social) alienation and 'the other,' the desire for agreement counterbalanced by the creative importance of dissent, the persistence of suffering, the existence and possible experience of God, the hope captured in faith and the promise of transcendence – these are themes that raise the unanswerable questions of the humanities, the ones that generate many of our most beautiful and important texts. The result is a conversation (perhaps timeless) among scholars and artists in the humanities, in which speculation is shared, explored, debated, denied, then celebrated, dismissed or extended, forever generating new images, fresh metaphors, novel interpretations, and innovative philosophies.

Our goal in this collection of essays is to explore law's relevance in this conversation that has long taken place across the humanities. Our focus will be the identification of possible points of convergence between the humanities and law by considering the position of law with respect to some of the central themes explored in the humanities. As Linda Myrsiades has reminded us, the separation of knowledge into fields of greater and greater specialization is a relatively recent phenomenon in historical terms, emerging only in the eighteenth century to transform the academy from a place for the pursuit of 'the holistic view of knowledge' to a more segregated world of multiple disciplines. Interdisciplinarity, Myrsiades suggests, can be considered as an attempt to reintegrate knowledges generated in otherwise separate disciplinary locales, such that the 'boundaries are busted and disciplinary paradigms are subordinated to the interests of a particular issue.'[6] Focused questions, then, are conceived of as transcending particular disciplinary confinements, and the insights of the separate disciplines are knit together so as to accomplish, it is hoped, something new. It is our ambition, in this collection of essays, to recognize the centrality of a certain group of issues or questions in the disciplines commonly called 'the humanities,' and to explore the potential of law to contribute to an expanded understanding of those issues. In turn, we recognize the interactive nature of that exploration, whereby in looking at law's potential contribution we are necessarily also looking at the ways in which law has been influenced by these larger themes and questions.

This book ought not to be read as an attempt to claim or reclaim law as an art, nor to distance it from the disciplines grouped under the science umbrella. We believe law shares a great deal with both the humanities and the sciences, and we believe that the humanities and the sciences share a great deal with each other. Indeed, the 'big questions' that appear to endure across history and across cultures may be the motivation, at some deep level at least, for all fundamental intellectual struggles, such that the humanities and the sciences represent but different methodological orientations to the same ultimate set of questions.[7] Law, we want to suggest, is a hybrid discipline, involving a great deal of the creativity and beauty in both form and substance commonly recognized as characteristic of literature and the arts,[8] but also containing elements of the systematic problem-solving techniques at the heart of physics and chemistry.[9] Law students (and others) continue to debate the proper positioning of law in the academy, teasing out its characteristics, emphasizing now this and now that, in what may be in many ways a Sisyphean attempt to distance law from one intellectual tradition while claiming it for the other. It is not our intent to engage in that debate through this book.

A developing tradition in 'law and humanities' scholarship appears to be centred on continuing curiosity about law as a (first) social and (more recently) cultural phenomenon. These scholars ask what we might learn about law by approaching it through themes or orientations or methods ordinarily explored or put to use in the humanities or in cultural studies. Perhaps one by-product of the idea of law as the object of humanities-inspired curiosity is the attempt to position law inside the humanities, typified one might suggest in the work of James Boyd White. Indeed, Austin Sarat and Thomas R. Kearns have said that '[i]n a series of books and articles dating back to 1973, White has led the effort to rescue law from the technocrats and secure for it a place as a humanistic discipline.'[10] For example, in his text *The Legal Imagination*, White urged law students to consider the law first as an art, and not as a science or a social science, so as to free them as lawyers from subservience to rules, and instead to instil in them the idea of rules as the basis for creative thought and argument.[11]

White moved beyond this initial attempt to understand law more fully by thinking of it in literary terms, effectively reversing the process so as to use law to think more fully about literature. According to White's own reflections,[12] his work *When Words Lose Their Meaning: Constitutions and Reconstitutions of Language, Character, and Community*[13] constitutes an invitation to think of literature as law, concentrating perhaps on its discursive characteristics as ethically or politically significant. Ultimately, one might consider *When Words Lose Their Meaning* as a study of the way in which law reconstitutes community through language, with the penultimate chapter of the book exploring the possibility of law as central to a culture defined by the ways in which authority is distributed and power expressed. Read this way, the book is 'about' law, framed in the context of enduring questions or issues, and functions in many ways as instructive to lawyers and judges on their rhetorical ethical responsibilities.

White and other law and humanities scholars opened the door to a more transcendent interdisciplinarity, that is, an interdisciplinarity transcendent of the narrow issues that tend to preoccupy scholars in law and in other disciplines as well. In *Justice as Translation: An Essay in Cultural and Legal Criticism*, White resisted the image of the university as a collection of separate 'fields' and criticized the attempts at interdisciplinarity through what he referred to as 'territorial spread or conquest.'[14] Instead, he anticipated the sort of interdisciplinarity suggested by Myrsiades.[15]

> Suppose, then, we were to think of our minds as minds, and our selves as engaged with the perpetual questions: How to think? What to think? What to say and how to say it? ... How are we to talk about, how imagine, what we are doing when we talk to each other across these lines? If you think of 'fields' not as terrains or machines, but as communities of discourse, groups of people defined by their willingness to talk in certain ways, the question becomes: what kind of relationships can we establish among these various ways of talking, and the communities they define? In so doing, what larger community can we create?[16]

What we see in White's later work is the beginning of a project to isolate characteristics of law (its arguably unique use of language, for example) that have the potential to combine with insights in the humanities to create a fresh understanding of human relationships.

Contemporary cultural analysis, or cultural studies, has been and continues to be used profitably to deepen our understanding of the nature of law as a sociocultural phenomenon. Consider some of the important work that has recently been done in this respect, including Austin Sarat and Jonathan Simon's edited collection *Cultural Analysis, Cultural Studies, and the Law: Moving beyond Legal Realism*.[17] The collection reflects the idea that a cultural study of law has a reciprocal effect, widening our understanding of both culture and law. In a sense, then, something new and possibly transcendent of both cultural studies and law does emerge from that analysis, but the imagery of conquest is too close to the warnings from White referred to above to give us any real comfort that the movement to cultural analysis and cultural studies is offering up a fresh approach to interdisciplinarity itself. Indeed, Sarat and Simon actually invoke this territorial imagery in their introduction to the collection, suggesting that 'perhaps a cultural analysis/cultural studies of law will help expand the terrain of learning about law,' although their apparent expansionary ambition is tempered somewhat by a suggestion that such an analysis could foster 'the development of new understandings of the self's relation to the social.'[18] But at some point, if an 'issues-based' interdisciplinarity is to become a reality, we must explicitly ask questions independently of disciplinary allegiances, and allow those questions to generate innovative thought whether from one disciplinary locale or another.

Despite the announcement of a solution to the chicken-and-egg conundrum, we think that mystery will endure and will persist in providing the underlying impetus for much of the conversation taking place across the humanities. Law's participation in that conversation must be something more than a happy by-product of our curiosity about law. In this book, we identify a set of four large issues – rationality, dissent, suffering, and transcendence – for exploration, and ponder the extent to which insights from law might yield new ground for reflection on those issues. The issues that we have isolated are four among a countless number, albeit four that, in our view, resonate through history, literature, and philosophy. The issues are pervasive, and they are ones on which a great deal of debate has taken place across the humanities and throughout Western literary culture, with little certainty and less agreement. Therefore, the most that can be done in a small volume is, first, tentative, both in the selection of the issues to be considered (an admittedly arbitrary exercise) and in the extent to which those issues might be explored, and, second, speculative, both in the opening assumption that law may have something of significance to say and in the attempt to isolate points of convergence between law and the humanities that may seem tenuous or insignificant or banal to some. This book ought to be read as one that simply raises possibilities – possibilities (it is hoped) that will stimulate ongoing interdisciplinary scholarly conversations about law's contributions and law's role.

The book opens with four chapters on law and rationality. The significance of reason in human experience is constantly under scrutiny in literature and philosophy, at times functioning as the fundamental benchmark against which all thought is evaluated, and at other times acting as a restraint on creative thought and action, becoming the source of much of the disenchantment in our lives. Reason is often considered the key element in human progress, equated with 'the art of thinking,' as if structured, logical thought is the only form of thinking with any value. David Kelley's fine textbook on logic begins with the words 'This is a book about thinking. It is a book about *how* to think,'[19] as if forms of thought other than the logical are somehow of lesser value or should be suppressed, certainly for specific, named purposes. As is well recognized in philosophy, much of the structure of (certainly) Western culture is founded on the assumption that human beings behave rationally, that rational behaviour is connected to our individual self-interest, and that self-interested action is inherent in who we are.[20] This is arguably the principal legacy of the great thinkers of the Enlightenment. Reason defines us in this tradition more clearly than anything else, giving rise to economic rationalism and scientism as dominant ideologies of modernity. Non-rational behaviour, then, becomes marginalized and discredited, labelled in literature as deviant or hysterical, dark and dangerous, dismissed as a threat to the possibility of establishing truth.[21]

But the predominance of reason in modern life has not been without its important detractors. Arthur Koestler famously argued that 'the Age of Enlightenment, culminating in the French Revolution, was a decisive turning-point in the history of man. It was dramatised by Robespierre's symbolic gesture of deposing god and enthroning the Goddess of Reason in the vacant chair. She proved to be a dismal failure.'[22] He went on to point out some of the fallacies in the commitment to reason, including the idea that reason could somehow subdue 'the dark passions' and 'the beast within us' that lay at the centre of much nineteenth-century anxiety,[23] arguing ultimately that the dual character of human intelligence (reason/faith or intellect/emotion) is a disorder, a flaw in our composition.[24]

Feminist and critical race scholars have provided extensive critiques of the dominance of reason, as well as of the gendered and racialized construction of reason.[25] Others in philosophy have attempted to soften the hard edge of critical reason by introducing the mollifying potential of empathy and imagination. Rather than positing a distinct separation of reason from other faculties, in the tradition of Koestler's critique, some thinkers are suggesting that the exercise of cognitive capabilities is actually a composite of the use of reason and other qualities and ought to be recognized as such, in the interest of overcoming the biases inherent in the institutional and, more thoroughly, sociocultural commitment to reason. John Ralston Saul's *On Equilibrium* is a study of the potential in recognizing the multiple co-operative qualities in human thought and therefore action.[26] Delores Gallo has written that '[r]eflection suggests that all feelings are not by nature more weak, transitory, or capricious than rational thought ... Further, the specific emotions, often called the altruistic emotions or empathy, may actually have a positive effect on reasoned judgment in a variety of contexts.'[27] And so the issue is joined.

It is central to law's mythology that law is a thoroughly coherent, ordered endeavour. This claim is one key to law's authority in modern contexts, the idea that law is a purely rational, disinterested observer of history, transcendent of the machinations of political actors, necessarily independent even of the pleas of morality. Much of the traditionally recognized appeal of the law is this very rational independence, whereby the emotional and the sympathetic are brushed aside as inappropriate, as evidence of weakness, in favour of the strict objectivity of the dogma known as the rule of law.[28] Of course, law's mythology, in particular this claim to an unshakeable rationality, has been the subject of repeated attacks in legal scholarship, including among several others the legal realist movement of the early twentieth century, the critical legal studies initiative of the late twentieth century, and contemporary feminist and critical race scholarship. But perhaps out of a need to maintain the appearance of impartiality as a quality deemed equivalent to justice, the law seems to soldier on as if nothing were wrong.

Given law's experience of fundamental critique from multiple quarters of what is perhaps its core value, it may be that law has something special to contribute to deliberations about the nature and significance of human rationality generally in the humanities. To set the stage for such an enquiry, Neil Sargent opens our collection with his chapter 'Murder and Mayhem in Legal Method: or, the Strange Case of Sherlock Holmes v. Sam Spade,' an assessment of detective fiction's contradictory representations of law as the practice of reason bringing order to disorder and law as an irrational contributor to disorder. Sargent compares the formal detective novels in the English tradition of Agatha Christie, Sir Arthur Conan Doyle, and others with the 'hard-boiled' stories of American authors Raymond Chandler and Dashiell Hammett. Central to this comparison is an analysis of the 'ways of knowing' of the detective in each genre, the purely rational, disinterested calm of Holmes on the one hand, the reckless, impulsive engagement of Spade on the other. Competing interpretations of law are captured in this comparison of epistemologies, symbolized in the tension between the idea of law as the absolutely objective arbiter of truth and the suspicion that law may very well be implicated as a reified participant in the crime itself.

Sargent's comparative study motivates what for traditional lawyers (and others enchanted by law's self-image) may be an awkward epiphany, that is, that law may suffer from the self-same anxieties at work in other humanistic disciplines. Is human progress reducible to the rational, such that law, as the actual source of 'beneficent rationality' leading to truth, is the last stand against chaos and violence? Or, just as likely, are the corrupting forces of the non-rational so powerful that even what appears to be our most ordered of institutions is contaminated? Do we live in a world where everything is certain, or where nothing (even, or perhaps especially, law) is certain? If we cannot rely on the law as our anchor in this chaotic place, then must we necessarily abandon all hope of being anchored at all? Does exposing the illusion of the rationality of law, thought to be so unshakeably and fundamentally rational, unsettle the whole concept of rationality?

It is vital to acknowledge nevertheless, as Sargent does at the end of his essay, that our real-world experience with law has a pragmatic urgency that cannot be avoided, an urgency captured most completely in the trial. This is something that perhaps separates law's attempted rationality from anything similar emerging in studies of the human mind and behaviour in literature or philosophy. That is, at some point the law (the methods of proof, the application of rules), flawed and mythological as its claim to objectivity is exposed to be, must *decide* – liable or not, guilty or not, insane or not, responsible or not. At some point, even recognizing the frailties of law's claims to objective truth, we must *act*, thus raising some of the same implications raised by John Ralston Saul in his lament about the role of 'logical speculation' in leading to false absolutes.[29] We construct a reality based on assumptions about logic and rationality we know cannot be accurate all of the time and are at best only ever partial, but we cling to these assumptions (through the well-recognized rules of evidence, for example) as our best foundation for justice, deluding ourselves into thinking that they *must* be true. It may be, then, that law, supported by pragmatic necessity, stands as the last defence against creeping indeterminacy, despite the epistemological weaknesses we recognize must be there.

In legal contexts at least, human decisions must yet be defensible as rational decisions, even while the possibility of certainty in that respect is more and more elusive. Rationality in this context involves the imposition of a privileged, but partial, tenuous, and value-imbued mode of understanding. In her chapter 'Analytic Philosophy and the Interpretation of Constitutional Rights,' Sophia Moreau investigates this problem in a more specific and more overtly legal context, that is, in the difficulty experienced in enriching constitutional decision making with analytical tools from philosophy. She opens her essay by summarizing some of the methods central to philosophical analysis, including the honest recognition (highly relevant to law's concerns) that the possibility of an authoritative (that is, objectively valid) interpretation of concepts or rules (or texts at all, for that matter) is a very slim one indeed. Instead, Moreau suggests, philosophical analysis considers *possible* interpretations, based on the recognition of shared values and beliefs and language. Philosophical analysis, then, evidently not always motivated by the same pragmatic necessities driving law, is more patient, perhaps more democratic than law, allowing for a range of interpretative possibilities without the need to position them relative to a presumed rational heritage before acknowledging their potential applicability.

The 'ordinary language philosophy' Moreau describes involves the dissection and delineation of multiple, different meanings and the exploration of the assumptions and values that might underlie the adoption of one meaning over another. This is a method shared by many authors in this book, even though the method is not explicitly drawn from philosophy. Responses to the big questions posed as themes for this book very much depend on values and beliefs, and in exploring the questions one is necessarily exposing and debating assumptions, beliefs, and values. It is thus that we end up looking very directly at belief and faith and values in the last chapter of the book. Moreau's discussion of resistance to such exploration in the constitutional context and the possible rationales for it could be applied to many of the discussions that follow in later chapters.

The resistance of constitutional law to assistance from philosophy is puzzling, suggests Moreau, given that other branches of law have profited quite nicely from philosophical analysis. Moreau systematically introduces and dismisses a variety of possible objections to this interdisciplinary sharing, leaving no obvious explanation for the intractability of constitutional law. The philosophical insistence on exploring possibilities, of course, does not lead to any sort of certainty, and that may be sufficient to frighten away decision makers, who, after all, are faced with that persistent pragmatic necessity, suggested in Sargent's paper and called 'forcing the issue' by Moreau (borrowing from Bernard Williams). And yet, as Moreau suggests, there is something honest about pursuit of the *best* outcome, as opposed to the dogmatically correct one, implying for us a type of reconciliation between competing epistemological claims. In effect, the application of philosophical analysis of the sort Moreau describes leads to what we might term a 'soft rationalism,' that is, a decision-making method that answers the pragmatic necessity while acknowledging the fallibility of rules. In turn, this is potentially instructive across the tense boundary between chronic scepticism and the commitment to reason, awkwardly coexisting, as they do, in the modern condition.

While Moreau's chapter focuses our attention on a specific problem of interdisciplinarity with an eye to the emergence of a less strictly rules-bound epistemology, Alain Papaux explores this same tension by taking us on a sweeping survey of the interrelationship between legal theory and the philosophy of science through Western history, using the environment as the point of reference. His chapter 'Nature: From Philosophy of Science to Legal Theory ... and Back?' centres on the significance of dualisms emerging in modernity on the strength of Cartesian philosophy, that is, the 'subject/object distinction,' the 'reason/emotion' dichotomy, perhaps 'fact and opinion,' even 'science and the humanities.' In science, early conventions posited a natural world, governed by determinate rules, separate and distinct from humankind, thus raising a dualism represented on the one hand by the unchangeable essence of the law of gravity, for example, and on the other hand by the experience of humankind itself. In legal theory, this chronic dualism is manifested in the conceptual separation between the essence of law (its transcendence and immutability) and the substantive character of law as expressed in its application to specific cases. Therefore, in early modernity at least, both law and science theorize a knowable, predictable, and unchangeable essence, quite separate and apart and unaffected by the day-to-day experiences of the human being.

In science, however, it became apparent as modernity progressed that the human being did wield power sufficient to interfere with nature's unfolding. The presumed immutability of the laws of nature was shaken through the successes of an interventionist, even dominating, human. Nature's powers could be harnessed, controlled, directed to human ends, if not completely then at least in very significant ways, such that the lines of demarcation by which the dualism was recognizable, by which the separation between subject and object was knowable and maintainable, were blurred and, ultimately, in many senses erased. Along with the realization of the impact of humans on nature came recognition that knowing was a process of interpretation rather than a revelation of truth. Accordingly, in legal theory, suspicions began to be raised about the role of the judge as translator of law's essence to real-world application. This dualism, understood to be as characteristic of law as of science, started to collapse with growing focus on the idea of the judge as interpreter and of law as subjective and essentially political. In both law and science, then, early modern Cartesian assumptions about the ordering of those worlds were replaced with a growing scepticism about truth and the possibility of objective disinterest. Uncertainty, multiple causes and effects, and interrelationship become the contexts within which science and law are forced to function, and these themes, as we have already seen and will continue to see, are reflected throughout the chapters of this book.

Papaux argues that the separate but conceptually related experiences of law and science connect in the contemporary environmental crisis. He characterizes our awakening to the environmental threat as a message from nature itself, a strike back against the species that would arrogate to itself the presumed controlling power. With this awakening comes a new conceptualization, that is, a final rejection of Cartesian dualism and a final recognition of the inseparability of humankind and nature at large. The result is what Papaux refers to as a 'regime of co-belonging,' of mutual interaction, of symbiosis. At the same time, Papaux says, law has evolved to acknowledge the indispensable function of the interpreter (the judge) in rendering necessarily commensurable that which, until recently, has been considered to be quite distinct. The judge 'gives voice' to the law, thereby creating another regime of co-belonging, unifying the essence of law with the concrete world of cases.

Papaux's analysis of the general sweep of the history of legal theory and the philosophy of science provides a conclusion similar to the observations of Moreau in her study of the particular epistemology of formal judicial reasoning. For both, there is a necessary recognition of the weakness of dogmatic legal rationality in the face of an honest assessment of the significance (or potential) of interpretation in formal legal applications. Moreau cautiously suggests an innovative epistemology, free of the constraints of hard rational justifications, open to possibilities, to more holistic judgment, to a search for the best result. Papaux's revelation that what was once considered immutable in law has been rendered comparable and shiftable through the process of judicial interpretation lends weight to Moreau's suggestion that what is considered not comparable is not necessarily so. Papaux's chapter leads to a generalization about the erasure of those dualisms that have functioned as conceptual control in our thinking and creativity since

Descartes, leading in turn to a consideration of unity, 'co-belonging,' as the inevitable consequence of our evolution in this respect. Both imagine a breaking through. This imagined breakthrough and possible synthesis is one that many of the contributors to this book explore, through very different means and described in very different ways, representing the ongoing dialectic of these fundamental issues.

In the final chapter of the opening section of the book, Rémi Samson offers reflection on rationality and the persistence of the idea of objective form and essence in philosophy, using Chomskyan linguistics and the legal positivism of H.L.A. Hart as the foundation of his comparative analysis. Samson's essay, 'Language and Law as Objects of Scientific Study,' explores the underlying rational structure that supports both disciplines and the related criticisms to which each has been subject as a way to expose their foundational assumptions and values and to further more fundamental critical thinking. In the case of language, Samson explains, Chomsky argues for an innate language faculty, defined by a set of rules about language that always exists in advance of particular languages. The formality of language, then, captured in Chomsky's idea of a 'universal grammar,' functions as the immutable structure already familiar to us through Papaux's summary of Cartesian dualisms, existing like nature (in our early understanding at least), independent of human interference. Form precedes and survives substantive application intact. In the case of Hart's positivism, an elaborate typology of abstract categories exists and continues with the same disinterest, allowing for the classification and interpretation of particular rules without threat to the nature of the categories themselves. In a remarkable similarity to language as theorized by Chomsky, the laws that result from human activity can have no bearing on the a priori quality, the essence, of Hart's typology.[30] Apparently, Cartesian dualism survives in both Chomskyan linguistics and the positive law of H.L.A. Hart.

Both of the theoretical thrusts summarized by Samson emerged (virtually concurrently) after the middle of the twentieth century, when evolution towards the breakthrough identified generally by Papaux and suggested in a more specific context by Moreau was well under way. As a result, critics of both Hart and Chomsky suggest that their theories are philosophically anachronistic in important respects. In an age when philosophy is moving further and further away from the possibility of transcendent truth separate from either experience or science (as demystifying as that appears to be),[31] Hart and Chomsky assert immutable, ahistorical essences that have little (if any) connection to either.[32] And despite the challenges levelled against them, Samson points out that both Hart's legal positivism and Chomsky's universal grammar have their staying power, raising a host of further questions (similar to those generated by Sargent's and Moreau's chapters) about our need to cling to the possibility of transcendent truth in the face of mounting evidence to the contrary. In this sense, a traditional perspective on the possibility of the absolute actually takes on the profile of dissent. Just as the paradigm shift that Papaux traces contains echoes of the precursors to Cartesian reason (law etymologically as discussion and science as relation), rationality and essentialism may be poised for a comeback in some new guise.

Thus, despite this apparent reversal of roles for the critical and the traditional, it is perhaps the persistence of a belief in the formal (the presumed essence) in philosophy and the arts, and certainly in law, that has led to some of the most innovative dissent to which we have been witness over the course of modernity. By 'dissent' we mean something more than political dissent, although we mean to include that too.[33] But further than that, we intend to capture the idea that resistance to the imposition of form (or a priori categories, or structures the shape of which are beyond debate), held out as rational, disinterested and given, is the fuel for much of the most dramatic change that has taken place across the humanistic disciplines in the post-Enlightenment world. The potential re-emergence of immutable form in some new guise is part of this dialectic of dissent and resistance becoming dominance and status quo, and vice versa. This is dissent broadly conceptualized, and it is the focus of the second section of the book. In terms of the persistent questions that we want to suggest have the potential to form the foundation of interdisciplinarity in the humanities and law, dissent (understood broadly) generates tensions between the desire for freedom on the one hand and the urge (sometimes arguably the need) to control on the other. Dissent raises debate about toleration and suppression in religion, in the arts, and across political and moral philosophy, revealed through insistence on the status quo and the equally insistent claim to do things differently.

As is well recognized, the power of dissent to effect change is not to be underestimated. The enormous Western migrations of the seventeenth and eighteenth centuries, for example, are attributable in large measure to the 'problem' of religious dissent, most notably perhaps through the revocation of the Edict of Nantes by Louis XIV of France in 1685 (by which the 'dissenting' Huguenots were forced to flee in vast numbers) and through the tribulations of the English throughout the seventeenth century, culminating (in formal terms at least) with the Toleration Act of 1689. The literature of this period is consumed with the relationship among religious dissent (that is, the refusal to be bound by the formal requirements of the state church and an insistence on the freedom to worship in one's own way), toleration, and the exigencies of socio-political life. Daniel Defoe, among many others, made his early reputation through continued attacks on the constraints of formalism in this respect, actually serving time in the pillory for his satirical condemnation of the High Church titled 'The Shortest Way with the Dissenters.'[34]

In the fine arts, dissent, playing upon these same tensions, emerged in the urge to escape classical formalism, an urge that gained momentum through the nineteenth century and into the twentieth, perhaps culminating in the music of John Cage[35] and the repetitive images of commodification generated by Andy Warhol.[36] In this case, the dogma to be overcome was a classical tradition recognized most fully by a belief in the representation of classical values in art, by a commitment to the ideal in both form and content, and by a conviction that 'art is governed by rules which are determined by reason. Beauty, which is one form of truth, must depend on some system of measurement and proportion.'[37] In other words, in classical art we find something similar to the essences referred to by Papaux as inherent in early modern philosophies of science and law, formal rules unchanged by particular interpretations and applications but (certainly in the case of art) to which those particulars must strive to conform. The dissenters' rejection of the concept of ideal form released artists from creative constraints and revealed the possibilities inherent in a marriage of form and artistic expression, perhaps a 'regime of co-belonging' and mutual interaction consistent with Papaux's analysis. As Kandinsky wrote, '[f]rom the point of view of the inner need, no limitation must be made. The artist may use any form which his expression demands; for his inner impulse must find suitable outward expression.'[38]

In at least two important respects, law has had a particularly interesting relationship with dissent. First, in the English common-law tradition at least, law has apparently devised a way to appropriate dissent, to allow it a unique and relatively undisruptive place in the formal, rational structures that support the process of judging. Second, law has the role of controlling, and ideally eradicating, extra-legal dissent. Thus law is responsible for either taming or eliminating dissent. As we shall see, the understanding of these two forms of dissent addressed by law are very different, at least on the surface.

Generally speaking (of course there are exceptions), judicial dissent is understood not as the voice of the other, the non-conformist, but rather as an alternative yet essentially unconvincing interpretation of reason, as mildly threatening as that may be to a discipline founded on the presumed immutability of principle. The dissent in common law judging is a controlled dissent, a dissent that can lead to change only through either the intervention of the legislature or a continued and ultimately successful appeal to supplant one rational response with another. In other words, change in this legal model occurs only through the application of formal processes, rather than through their rejection (as happened in the examples of the arts and religious dissent referred to above).

In their chapter 'I Beg to Differ: Interdisciplinary Questions about Law, Language, and Dissent,' Marie-Claire Belleau and Rebecca Johnson investigate the qualitative character of judicial dissent with a similar conceptualization in mind, suggesting that judicial dissent often resides in what they describe as 'noetic space.' 'Noetic space' is a term coined by Amsterdam and Bruner to describe a place where reason meets imagination and emotion for the purpose of pushing the boundaries of what is considered doable in a way that involves and persuades the reader. Not to be overlooked, of course, is the fact that the dissenting judgment, as imaginative and passionate as it may be, is nevertheless produced by a judge in an official capacity, giving it an air of authority despite its being in the minority on a particular issue at a particular moment. But the dissenting judge (in pushing to enlist and persuade) may be less constrained by the strict demands of reason, thereby providing an opportunity for a convergence of imagination, reason, and authority that is seldom as freely adopted in the majority position.

Belleau and Johnson's interpretation of the character of judicial dissent may in effect provide an opening for the exploration of an epistemology consistent with that imagined by Moreau in her chapter. Judicial dissent, flourishing in a space that combines the rational and the imaginative, has more freedom to focus on the possible and less restraint in exploring alternatives than is found in the space reserved for the rational and right (read, doctrinally correct) result.[39] In an odd twist, then, the mechanism designed by law to allow dissent controlled expression actually liberates the judge to enlist emotion and imagination while yet retaining judicial authority. Dissent, conceptualized as an expression of rejection of the formal, then, emerges in law as a hybrid of conformity, managed resistance, and creative challenge to the status quo, both in form and content, ultimately closer to the artistic dissent described by Kandinsky than one might initially have considered.

The second way in which law has a significant relationship with dissent lies in law's policing responsibilities. Dissent that is not contained within and by law, as in the example of judicial dissent, is considered to offend against the public good. It is law's job to suppress this extralegal dissent, that is, to establish a regime of controls to be exerted in defence of that public good. Of course, these are state-sanctioned, state-enforced controls involving consequences (fines, imprisonment, even death in some jurisdictions) quite different from those that might result from the attempt to impose controls in other humanistic disciplines (artistic ostracism, for example). Key to understanding this responsibility in law relative to our conceptualization of dissent is to recognize that, in the legal arena, the dissenter (almost always) interprets his or her behaviour as consistent with the public good that law is intended to defend. In other words, the form (or essence) of the good is agreed, but the performance of the good is contested. This means, in turn, that the contest is fought over competing interpretations, rather than over an absolute rejection of a particular formality sought to be imposed on the dissenter.

It is dissent fostered through competing interpretations of the public good and played out through law's attempt to eradicate the dissenting voices that serves as the focus in Barry Wright's chapter, 'Imagining Sedition: Law and the Emerging Public Sphere in Upper Canada, c. 1798–1828.' Of particular interest to Wright is the attempted suppression of dissenting voices heard through the growing reform presses in Upper Canada during the tumultuous decades leading up to the rebellion of 1837. At issue was the manner in which the English constitution was to be experienced in Upper Canada, whether through the dominating and arguably self-serving, essentially oppressive interpretation sought to be imposed by the political élite (the 'Family Compact'), or through the 'reform' interpretation expressed through popular challenges to the dominance of the élite itself. The Family Compact, enjoying the power and place necessary to enlist law in defence of its interpretation of constitutional right, initiated a series of prosecutions to silence dissent through allegations of sedition and like offences. Some of these charges were superficially successful; many of them withered in the attempt.

In Wright's summary of some of the leading Upper Canadian prosecutions during this period, it is particularly telling that defence representatives insisted on a rigid interpretation and application of the constitution just as vehemently as did the prosecution. Strictly speaking, then, it was not resistance to the imposition of order and the rule of law generally that drove dissent, but rather the perceived political manipulation of principle, agreed on all fronts to be immutable. It was in large part fear that drove the heavy-handed response to the dissent. According to Wright, the Family Compact's anxiety about the growth of reform presses was bred of an imagined connection between criticism and the potential for revolution. The suppression of dissenting voices was doomed to fail once that connection was exposed as self-serving and inconsistent with constitutional principle. As a result, dissent actually grew in the wake of continued, desperate attempts to suppress a formal interpretation of the constitution inconsistent with the continued domination of political life by the élite. As Wright points out, the Upper Canadian dissenters' refusal to be bullied into submission actually contributed to the creation of the conditions necessary to bring about wholesale constitutional change in Upper Canada, effectively succeeding in supplanting one ideology with another.

It is likely the manipulation of law for political ends, illustrated so thoroughly in the examples related in Wright's chapter, which spelled the beginning of the end for the mythology of law constructed on the presumed ahistorical, immutable character of legal principle. A detached, disinterested, transcendent law is beyond reproach; there can be no legitimate dissent from law when law is truth. However, a demythologized law is a social institution, open to criticism, correction, and perhaps even resistance. Dissent then becomes a rational alternative rather than an hysterical departure, and any attempt to enlist law to suppress dissent becomes subject to the most critical scrutiny possible, political as that enlistment must be. The idea of law as an instrument for the promotion of particular ideologies, then, raises the prospect of law as an active, engaged contributor to the consequences of the implementation of those ideologies. Such consequences would include the very suffering experienced by those who, in expressing their dissent, feel the full power of state-supported legal sanction,[40] as well as the suffering of those who are disadvantaged or harmed by the ideological fallout or its implications.

It is law's participation in suffering that forms the focus of the third section of our collection. Human suffering is a preoccupation in the humanities, forming arguably the single most dominant theme in literature, and at least one observable motif in religion, history, and the fine arts. The nature of suffering, its meaning and character, its inexplicability, its justification, its tragedy – all of these problems contribute to a rich tradition of exploration in the humanities that claims as its lineage some of the most poignant texts of the ancient world and, indeed, of the entire cultural canon, certainly in the West. In the Old Testament, for example, we find the ancient exemplars of suffering, emerging in Abraham's awful journey to sacrifice his son in answer to God's command,[41] and captured by the miseries of Job as his faith was tested by the most unspeakable tragedies.[42] These stories, among many others, have formed the basis of an interrogation of suffering by scholars that has endured throughout the history of philosophy and literature. Kierkegaard's *Fear and Trembling*, for example, draws on Abraham's experience to develop an analysis of suffering central to his concept of faith.[43] Dostoyevsky's *Crime and Punishment* chronicles the self-inflicted suffering of a felon consumed by guilt.[44] Defoe's *A Journal of the Plague Year*[45] and *Due Preparations for the Plague, as Well for Soul as Body*,[46] explore the ineffaceable tragedy of epidemic disease, interpreted by sufferers to be God's wrath inflicted as punishment for an impure life. In the twentieth century, Sartre's *Nausea*[47] and Kafka's *Diaries*[48] investigate the connection between suffering and the production of history and literature. Much of contemporary feminist literature and literature by people of colour exposes the suffering of those who have experienced domination, exploitation, exclusion, and marginalization in their lives.[49] The exploration of human suffering in the humanities is deep and complex, multidimensional and thorough, transcending genres and disciplines in a continual search for meaning where, it must be concluded, little can be found.

While idealists may cling to the hope that law has the potential to relieve (even cure) suffering of particular types (perhaps as a tool for the elimination of crime or the reversal of environmental degradation), it is law's complicity in suffering that attracts the most critical attention. Primarily, this is a political question, involving both the inertia implicated in law's failure to live up to its promise and law's instrumentality in the actual creation and perpetuation of suffering. Further, the central role played by judges in the interpretation and application of law that results in the routine infliction of suffering on those who appear before the courts is a stark example of the intimate relationship between law and suffering.[50] The reality of law's role in these respects is disheartening, to say the least, generating something like grief and anger in fiction and poetry over and over again.

In Brenda Carr Vellino's chapter, 'Human Rights Poetry as Ethical Tribunal: Bodies and Bystanders in Margaret Atwood's "Footnote to the Amnesty Report on Torture,"' we see an analysis of the way in which poetry, pursued through a genre Vellino calls 'witness poetry,' can be used simultaneously to critique law, to offer an alternative to law, and to mobilize for legal change. Witness poetry is a form of testimonial that intertwines reason, emotion, and rhetoric of the body to explore the suffering of victims of torture. The poem itself becomes an ethical tribunal before which the reader is induced both to empathize with the tortured body and to feel its pain, while at the same time recognizing his or her possible complicity in and responsibility for creating that suffering. This is a powerful combination of the aesthetic and the ethical/political, one having the potential to cast law in the darkest light imaginable and thus also the potential to inspire its readers to demand change.

As Vellino points out, witness poetry has true reform possibilities, functioning as the 'conscience of law' and generating a widening public awareness of injustice similar to that generated by Upper Canada's reform presses in the history related by Wright in his chapter. But witness poetry itself is more akin to the noetic space described by Belleau and Johnson. Its combination of reason, emotion, and imagination pushes the reader to the boundary of what is possible. The reader connects with the sufferer in an intimate and vivid way that elicits both compassion and agency. As Vellino argues, witness poetry thus operates as a representational auxiliary to law, making advocacy for law reform not only thinkable but inescapable.

However, the reaction of the bystander to suffering is never assured, even in response to the most graphic of aesthetic appeals. It is when we move beyond the 'mere bystander' to a direct consideration of the sufferer that the response is arguably more predictable. It is law's role in facilitating particular responses in the sufferer that forms the focus in Diana Majury's chapter, 'Who Do We Blame for Blame? Moving beyond the Fiction of Blame in *The Sweet Hereafter*.' Majury describes what she refers to as a 'culture of facile blame,' that is, a predictable, widespread response to suffering whether it be generated by injustice (the perpetration of recognizable legal wrongs) or by simple misfortune. That response is the assignment of blame – blame that is burdened with the impossible task of catharsis that, in some symbolic way at least, is intended to vindicate and heal the sufferer. It is law's function to encourage blaming, to actually facilitate the process by which the sufferer stands up and finds fault so as to relieve the feelings of helplessness and complicity that often accompany the position of victim.

The role of law described here is opposite to the role of witness poetry described by Vellino. Whereas the role of witness poetry is to extend the experience of suffering in order to acknowledge and accept collective responsibility, in Majury's assessment law is deployed so as to assist sufferers in divesting themselves of their pain. In effect, law's job is to transfer suffering, relieving the victim by providing a vehicle through which the blameworthy are made to feel the effects of their wrongful acts. Suffering then resides where it ought to, at the source of the injustice. So long as law is successful in this respect, then our general need is met, that is, to construct an understanding of suffering that somehow overcomes the jarring incomprehensibility of the 'meaningless victim.' However, as Majury points out, law is a guarantor neither of success nor of the linear causation that this transfer model implies. As prerequisites to catharsis, both criminal conviction and the assignment of civil liability can be elusive. Perhaps even more disturbing is the realization that a successful prosecution or victorious civil suit does not necessarily result in the transfer of suffering considered necessary, in popular constructions at least, to retributive justice. Despite the presence of suffering and of victims, there may be no perpetrator, no wrongdoer who deserves to absorb the suffering. And suffering may simply not be transferable; it may only be capable of expansion. Law thus may simply increase the suffering rather than facilitate its transfer. Nevertheless, law is the instrument we use in constructing a more noble sufferer, providing a mechanism by which the victim might fight back by finding fault.

Majury concludes by posing the possibility of a transformed understanding of suffering, one that enlists all of us in sharing pain and fault, suffering and blame, one that moves beyond the easy finger pointing that thrives through law's encouragement, and one that transcends the confrontational to establish a new community of shared responsibility. This is an attempt consistent with much recent analysis, according to which our understanding of suffering is culturally and historically contingent.[51] As a community, we manage the inevitability of suffering by constructing it as innocent, or noble, or sacrificial, or futile. We search for explanations, and then devise a taxonomy of suffering that allows us to compartmentalize and, it is hoped, understand the consequences in at least some small degree. We come to terms with suffering, and move on. The blaming process explored by Majury is one way in which that taxonomic ordering is accomplished, and one way in which law can participate in the ordering. The imagined community of shared responsibility is another.

In Logan Atkinson's chapter, '"Our Woe ... Our Great Distress": Law, Literature, and Suffering during the Great Plague of London, 1665,' this exploration of law's role in a conceptualization of suffering is extended to include a disruptive role for law, a role that reasserts and participates in the unanswerable injustice of suffering. Relying on polemical literature produced during the plague by clergy and medical professionals, Atkinson analyses discourses critical of law's participation in creating and perhaps exacerbating the conditions suffered by the sick. Tough restrictions on mobility, the cruel separation of families, the employment of horrible symbols of death and disease (the red cross painted on the homes of the sick, the guard armed with the dreadful halberd stationed outside every afflicted house) – these regulatory measures stigmatized the sick, highlighted their pain and fear, made a terrifying crisis of public health also a personal nightmare of isolation.

Critics of the regulatory framework struggled in vain to understand the place of this sort of individual suffering in their contemporary world view. None of the conventional explanations answered their exasperation with law as a participant in the suffering of the sick. Law was intended to assist in the accomplishment of justice; this law punished the sick without justification. Suffering must be construed as admirably stoic or virtuous, perhaps as a sacrifice for the sake of the health of the wider community; the inefficacy of law made this suffering vacant and unnecessary. In the end, sympathetic critics were compelled to plead with officials for either change in the law or a relaxation in enforcement, in effect arguing for law's withdrawal so as to re-establish conventional explanations of suffering. For medical professionals, suffering as a consequence of injury or disease was explainable and treatable. For clergy, suffering as a consequence of God's disapproval was equally explainable, and treatable through reconciliation and ultimately transcendence. For both, law's participation was a disruption that interfered with both their ministrations and their rationales.

The possibility of transcendence that plays a critical role in Majury's reconceptualization of the relationship among suffering, blame, and law also figured prominently in coming to terms with suffering during the Great Plague. In the latter, clergy exhorted the sick to overcome physical pain and emotional distress by focusing on hope and the possibility of reconciliation with God, that is, to transcend their material existence with faith. In the former, the superficiality of ordinary human experience in facilitating blame through law is rejected for a more meaningful community-wide assumption of responsibility, effectively transcending vengeance with understanding. As depicted by Vellino, the transcendence of understanding can be induced through witness poetry, leading similarly to community responsibility and action. The idea of transcendence contemplates both surpassing the physical with the spiritual and overcoming the banalities of normal experience with something exceptional. Transcendence forms the focus of the fourth and final section of our book.

In the humanities, it is arguable that the possibility of transcendence is conflated with the possibility of truth, such that the successful search for any moral, rational, theological, or artistic truth would represent the final step towards leaving the mundane behind. Each of these intellectual trajectories, however, tends to claim special insight, unique access to truth and special keys to transcendence, leading inevitably to the fracturing of the disciplines in early modernity referred to by Linda Myrsiades.[52] In the age of humanism, then, we find growing scepticism about the possibility of divine truth, but an equally growing disenchantment with the search for perfection based on a universal human morality or purely rational order. The transcendence imagined through utopian literature in the tradition of Plato's *Republic*[53] and More's *Utopia*[54] suffers its counterpoint in the 'dystopian' tradition of Orwell's *Nineteen Eighty-Four*,[55] Atwood's *The Handmaid's Tale*,[56] and Zamiatin's *We*,[57] illustrating the essential conflict between a deep faith in human potential and immanent despair. Further, while the abandonment of ideal form in the fine arts can be credited with freeing artists to explore their creativity more fully, it also leads inevitably to the possibility that, in absolute terms, perhaps music does not exist at all. In law, the rejection of the notion that truth resides in immutable legal principle leads to a crisis of authority, a realization that law is not partly, but *merely*, political. Across the humanistic disciplines, the idea that transcendence resides in truth may relegate hope to the old-fashioned, based as both must be on an assumption about the possibility of the absolute that is largely rejected in this postmodern era. We are left, then, with nothing more than nostalgia and existential anxiety.

It is the attempt to reconcile these competing patterns that forms the focus in M.H. Ogilvie's chapter, 'The Strange Gospel and a Common Law: The Reconciling Word to a Fragmented World.' Ogilvie's principal question, central to the themes of this book, is whether theology and law have anything to say to each other in a postmodern world where the search for divine truth is dismissed as anachronistic and where even law, clinging to its claim as the light of reason in a very dark place, is deconstructed as at best little more than the handmaid of special interest and at worst as itself a contributor to the darkness. Her question takes her to a review of the claims of radical orthodoxy, a theology that embraces postmodernism for its attack on the culture of reason and for its reliance on narrative as a potential source for a more nuanced understanding of truth. From this perspective, the Christian narrative is arguably a metanarrative that posits peace and reconciliation as the only viable alternatives to the violent nihilism of postmodernity that, otherwise, appears inevitable. Radical orthodoxy reminds us that theology has always promoted thoughtful moral deliberation, and as such has traditionally exerted a profound influence on the doctrinal content of Western legal systems. In thus reclaiming theology as a spiritual rather than a rational pursuit, radical orthodoxy represents a dramatic alternative to the uninhibited and dangerously self-centred licence of postmodernity, such that theology may hold the key to the continuation of culture at all.

Radical orthodoxy is comfortable with the recognition that human reason is weak, being unable to cope with unending curiosity about truth and transcendence, and that Scripture itself is subject to the same contests of interpretation that afflict all texts in postmodernity. Neither reason nor Scripture alone can deliver certainty. It is the struggle with this difficulty that leads radical orthodoxy to argue that truth lies in community, the community of those who share particular interpretations about the meaning and significance of Scripture. This leads to a reassertion of the traditional role of the Church, but it also leads necessarily to a leap of faith about the truth of any particular interpretation, including the radical orthodox interpretation. In the absence of rational argument, there is no alternative basis on which radical orthodoxy can demand adherence. Ultimately, then, radical orthodoxy is undone by the same hermeneutic challenges that stifle law, and as a result it is unable to reclaim with any conviction a position of influence in the secular legal world.

It may be that the inability of radical orthodoxy to cling to and then survive the scrutiny of postmodernism symbolizes something of great significance for us. Radical orthodoxy sounds like a last attempt at reintegrating the sacred and the secular, which in turn represents the enduring appeal of questions about human nature, the spiritual, and the possibility of transcendence itself. The idea with which we began this introductory chapter, that our unending preoccupation with mystery binds us together as a species, may suffer a final blow with the argument from postmodernism on which radical orthodoxy ultimately stumbles. The unanswerable questions of the humanities are just that – unanswerable. Our continual searching is hopeless and futile, nothing more than busywork, whether law is integrated into the conversation about those questions or not. When the shared experience of our curiosity is debunked as mere play, then the nihilism described by Ogilvie as inherent in postmodernism is, in fact, the inevitable result. Reason is overrated and flawed, dissent will simply be absorbed into the status quo, suffering is assured and meaningless, transcendence is a pipedream.

As threatening as postmodernism seems, the project must be to reinstate curiosity and mystery for the sake of community. The mandate must be to preserve belief in the possibility of transcendence (whether this be ultimate or merely temporary) while living in a world where postmodernism appears to have laid everything to waste. It is this mandate that is undertaken by Clinton Timothy Curle in his chapter, 'The Re-enchantment of the World? Max Weber, Ernst Troeltsch, and Human Rights.' Curle is searching for a provisional compromise that will break through the impasse between spirit and nature that constrains modern society. He finds the possibility of a synthesis between law, politics, and religion in the spiritual aspirations of the contemporary human rights project grounded by their focus on political action. This is an evolving, changing compromise in which the elements exist in tension, rather than in conflict, with each being reinvented in response to the other.

Curle begins his search by recognizing that our insistence on a culture of human rights in the post-Enlightenment era is itself based on faith, that is, on a language of authority that is shrouded in mystery. Human rights discourse flourishes in the postmodern world of disengaged self-interest and radical secularism, but subtly denies the premises of postmodernism through the vagueness of its language of individual value and dignity and its focus on collectivity. In a postmodern, nihilistic world, many of us nevertheless cling to a discourse of human rights, the truth of which cannot be established on any foundation except through an appeal to belief and fundamental, perhaps universal, values. In this respect, law and religion have something profound to share, something both immanent and transcendent. It is a matter of reconciling the sacred and the secular through a sharing of faith and mystery that holds the key to a 're-enchantment of the world.'

Drawing on Troeltsch, Curle argues that the historical coexistence of the sacred and the secular was founded on compromise, the integration of the spirituality of religion with the mundane. But in modernity the traditional expressions of this compromise (natural law, for example) have been abandoned for the secularism of science, which, as Papaux and Samson elucidated, has itself been subject to extensive critique. If we are to escape the perpetual see-saw between relativism and universality, we must integrate the two. A new compromise must be found to ensure the continued relevance of religion. It is in the discourse of human rights that the possibility of such a compromise emerges, enlisting as it does concepts of human value and respect also inherent in the Christian ethic. Both discourses posit human dignity as central in ethical terms; both are founded on authority that is demonstrable only through faith. Postmodern scepticism and disenchantment are challenged by human rights discourse, a discourse that seems particularly well suited to survive deconstruction. The vision of fundamental human rights opens up the possibility of a reintroduction of the life of the spirit, through its focus on human freedom and personality, unity and sympathy, both emanating from and challenging contemporary politics in a dialectic process. This human rights-based synthesis of the spiritual and the political possibly offers a way out of the impasse of the traditional Cartesian dualism described so powerfully under the rubric of rationality in the first part of this book. The possibilities for change and growth, for the uniting of perceived opposites, for certain uncertainty, and for re-enchantment that Curle pursues in this final chapter reflect the understanding of mystery that informs this whole book. It is the mystery of adventure and enquiry in the face of unknowability. For us, as contributors to this volume, this mystery is where law and the humanities converge.

In a postmodern world, the relevance of Bernard Lonergan's reflection on human curiosity as a unique and binding human characteristic is in some jeopardy.[58] As it turns out, and as both Ogilvie and Curle suggest, the most urgent question may not reside in one or the other of the enduring mysteries of the humanities, but rather in the viability of mystery at all. As a unifying force, then, mystery is in trouble, and it may ultimately fall to the humanities to keep curiosity alive in a world where the age-old conundrum of the chicken and the egg is reduced to a question of the egg's DNA. We began this chapter with speculation that law has something of significance to say about those enduring questions, the ones that in historical terms at least seem to capture our curiosity in enduring ways. We hope that this book will be read as a valiant first attempt to investigate the merit of such speculation. In the discussions presented in this book, law has not been given its usual role of answering questions and passing judgment. Instead, law has been asked to engage in dialogue with the humanities, sometimes contributing complexity, sometimes asking parallel questions, and sometimes offering a divergent perspective. If nothing else, we believe that there are significant points of convergence to be explored.

It is the energy and excitement triggered by the questions that have engaged us in this project. It is our hope that the perspective law brings to the exploration of the limits of human rationality, the worries of human dissent, the apparent inevitability of suffering, and the intellectual challenge of transcendence will at least muddy the waters sufficiently to allow for mystery to become popular again.

NOTES

1 Alan Hamilton, 'Two Philosophers and a Farmer Cracked an Age-Old Conundrum,' *Times* (London), 26 May 2006, 5. This story was picked up by presses around the world, including the *Ottawa Citizen*, 26 May 2006, final edition, A6.

2 Bernard Lonergan, *Insight: A Study of Human Understanding* (New York: Philosophical Library, 1965), 252–3.

3 *Ibid.*, 639. However, in the spirit of Lonergan, some will question if and how we can definitively determine the existence or not of animal epistemology. Perhaps it is simply human arrogance or our own epistemological limitations that have us ascribe unmediated experience to animals and intelligent, reflective thought processes to ourselves.

4 Hugo A. Meynell, *An Introduction to the Philosophy of Bernard Lonergan*, 2nd ed. (Toronto: University of Toronto Press, 1991), 132.

5 John Ralston Saul, *On Equilibrium* (Toronto: Penguin Books, 2002), 270.

6 Linda Myrsiades, 'Un-Disciplining Literature: Literature, Law, and Culture,' in *Un-Disciplining Literature: Literature, Law, and Culture*, ed. Kostas Myrsiades and Linda Myrsiades, 1–20 (New York: Peter Lang, 1999), 1, 2.

7 For an exploration of this possibility, see Stephen Jay Gould, *The Hedgehog, the Fox, and the Magister's Pox: Mending the Gap between Science and the Humanities* (New York: Harmony Books, 2003).

8 See, for example, Adam Gearey, *Law and Aesthetics* (Portland, OR: Hart, 2001) for a study of the relationship between law's aesthetic appeal and its moral content.

9 We do not mean to suggest that the methodological similarities between science and law are at all obvious, nor that they are understood fully and without controversy. See Wai Chee Dimock, 'Rules of Law, Laws of Science,' in *Cultural Analysis, Cultural Studies, and the Law: Moving Beyond Legal Realism*, ed. Austin Sarat and Jonathan Simon, 220–44 (Durham, NC: Duke University Press, 2003). We simply mean to point out that at least the modern practices of law and science seem to converge in the minds of their practitioners from time to time, which, in effect, is enough to make the connection real notwithstanding our occasional scepticism about the validity of the convergence. See Tal Golan, *Laws of Men and Laws of Nature: The History of Scientific Expert Testimony in England and America* (Cambridge, MA: Harvard University Press, 2004). See also the short section by Martin P. Golding, 'Discovery and Justification in Science and Law, ' in *Legal Reasoning* (Peterborough, ON: Broadview Press, 2001), 2–3.

10 Austin Sarat and Thomas R. Kearns, editorial introduction to *The Rhetoric of Law*, ed. Sarat and Kearns, 1–28 (Ann Arbor: The University of Michigan Press, 1994), 7.

11 James Boyd White, *The Legal Imagination: Studies in the Nature of Legal Thought and Expression* (Boston: Little, Brown, 1973), xxxiv–xxxv.

12 See James Boyd White, *Justice as Translation: An Essay in Cultural and Legal Criticism* (Chicago: University of Chicago Press, 1990), 18–19.

13 James Boyd White, *When Words Lose Their Meaning: Constitutions and Reconstitutions of Language, Character, and Community* (Chicago: University of Chicago Press, 1984).

14 *Ibid.*, 15.

15 *Supra* note 6.

16 *Supra* note 12 at 16.

17 Austin Sarat and Jonathan Simon, eds., *Cultural Analysis, Cultural Studies, and the Law: Moving Beyond Legal Realism*, *supra* note 9.

18 Austin Sarat and Jonathan Simon, 'Cultural Analysis, Cultural Studies, and the Situation of Legal Scholarship,' in *ibid.*, 1–34 at 10.

19 David Kelley, *The Art of Reasoning*, 2nd ed. (New York: W.W. Norton, 1994), 1.

20 See, for example, Michael Oakeshott, *Rationalism in Politics and Other Essays* (London: Methuen, 1962).

21 Many great works in fiction explore the tension between the rational and the non-rational (if not hysterical). Charlotte Brontë, *Jane Eyre*, ed. Q.D. Leavis (London: Penguin Classics, 1985), first published in 1847, is one example. Wilkie Collins, *Armadale*, ed. Catherine Peters (Oxford: Oxford World Classics, 1991), serialized in 1864 and first published in book form in 1866, is another. In twentieth-century fiction, consider Jean Toomer, *Cane* (New York: Harper and Row, 1969), first published in 1923.

22 Arthur Koestler, *The Ghost in the Machine* (London: Arkana Books, 1989), 256. Koestler's book was first published in 1967. John Ralston Saul's *Voltaire's Bastards: The Dictatorship of Reason in the West* (Toronto: Viking Books, 1992) is perhaps exemplary of later attacks. More specifically, recent criticisms have shown the ways in which our deference to the rational has contributed to the expansion of particular social problems. Is logic gendered, for example? See Andrea Nye, *Words of Power: A Feminist Reading of the History of Logic* (New York: Routledge, 1990).

23 Koestler, *ibid.*

24 *Ibid.*, 259.

25 See, for example, the writing of Derrick Bell, in particular *Faces at the Bottom of the Well: The Permanence of Racism* (New York: Basic Books, 1992); the writing of Catharine MacKinnon, in particular *Feminism Unmodified: Discourses on Life and Law* (Cambridge, MA: Harvard University Press, 1987); the writing of Sherene Razack, in particular *Looking White People In the Eye: Gender, Race and Culture in Courtrooms and Classrooms* (Toronto: University of Toronto Press, 1998); and the writing of Patricia Williams, in particular *The Alchemy of Race and Rights* (Cambridge, MA: Harvard University Press, 1991).

26 *Supra* note 5.

27 Delores Gallo, 'Educating for Empathy, Reason, and Imagination,' in *Re-Thinking Reason: New Perspectives in Critical Thinking*, ed. Kerry S. Walters, 43–60 (Albany: State University of New York Press, 1994) 44. For a thorough study of the relationship between reason and emotion with a par-

ticular focus on the requirements of justice, see Martha Nussbaum, *Poetic Justice: The Literary Imagination and Public Life* (Boston: Beacon Press, 1995). Particularly relevant to Gallo's observations is 'Rational Emotions,' chapter 3 of *Poetic Justice*, Nussbaum, 53–78.

28 This tendency in formal legal settings is perhaps best captured in the law of evidence, by which until very recently only evidence of certain sorts, demonstrated to be evidence through accepted procedures, could be accepted as helpful in the search for truth in the trial. Evidence based on modes of proof outside of traditionally recognized legal forms of proof, perhaps story-telling or artistic expression, has always been rejected as unacceptable in a legal forum, not simply as a matter of the relative weight of that evidence, but as a matter of its very qualitative character *as* evidence in the pursuit of truth. On occasion in recent years, such strict observance of rules of evidentiary validity has been relaxed, but only in exceptional circumstances. See, for example, Mary Richardson, Joan Sherman, and Michael Gismondi, *Winning Back the Words: Confronting Experts in an Environmental Public Hearing* (Toronto: Garamond Press, 1993).

29 *Supra* note 5. For an exploration of the implications of the relationship between law's pragmatic necessity and the imposition of violence through judicial interpretation, see Robert Cover, 'Violence and the Word,' Yale L.J. 95, no. 8 (July 1986), 1601–29.

30 H.L.A. Hart, *The Concept of Law* (Oxford: Clarendon Press, 1961). Samson refers to the Oxford University Press edition of 1994.

31 See George Steiner, *Nostalgia for the Absolute* (Toronto: CBC Massey Lectures Series, 1974).

32 Arguably, this is so despite attempts to position Chomsky's theory of language relative to the biology of the human brain, something that it has been impossible to demonstrate with any degree of comfort. See, generally, J. Lyons, *Chomsky* (New York: Penguin Books, 1978).

33 For a thorough study of political dissent in a post-9/11 world, see Austin Sarat, ed., *Dissent in Dangerous Times* (Ann Arbor: University of Michigan Press, 2005).

34 Daniel Defoe, 'The Shortest Way with the Dissenters,' in *The True-Born Englishman and Other Writings*, ed. P.N Furbank and W.R. Owens, 132–45 (London: Penguin Books, 1997). 'The Shortest Way with the Dissenters' was first published in 1702, and it caused such an outcry (especially among those who had read Defoe literally rather than satirically) that Defoe was condemned to spend time in prison and the pillory as a result. Defoe wrote widely on dissent, and some of his most important works in

this respect are repeated in *The True-Born Englishman and Other Writings*. See 'An Enquiry into the Occasional Conformity of Dissenters,' 114–31, and 'A Dialogue between a Dissenter and the Observator,' 150–69, among others.

35 Among Cage's most intriguing works are the chamber music composition *4'33"* (intended to be a silent piece for any instrument or combination of instruments) and the piece for solo piano *0'0"* (apparently to be performed in any way by anyone). Cage's entry in *The Concise Oxford Dictionary of Music* says '[t]he particular elements of Cage's *avant-garde* outlook are: use of any kind of environmental sounds or noises; use of "chance," as in *Music of Changes* where the selection process involves tossing a coin; abandonment of formal structures; use of silence.' See Michael Kennedy, ed., *The Concise Oxford Dictionary of Music*, 3rd ed. (Oxford: Oxford University Press, 1985), *s.v.* 'Cage, John.'

36 See Richard Brilliant's assessment of Warhol's work in *Portraiture* (Cambridge, MA: Harvard University Press, 1991).

37 Michael Greenhalgh, *The Classical Tradition in Art: From the Fall of the Roman Empire to the Time of Ingres* (New York: Harper and Row, 1978), 11.

38 Wassily Kandinsky, *Concerning the Spiritual in Art*, trans. M.T.H. Sadler (New York: Dover, 1977), 35. First published in German in 1911 and in English in 1914.

39 For a particularly expressive example of the freedom to explore alternatives in the dissenting judgment, see Madame Justice Bertha Wilson's dissent in *Frame v. Smith* [1987] 2 S.C.R. 99, in which Judge Wilson canvassed the entire range of possibilities in tort law in an effort to find a cause of action for an ultimately unsuccessful plaintiff.

40 This is one of the themes explored in Austin Sarat's edited collection, *Dissent in Dangerous Times*, *supra* note 33.

41 Abraham's trial is related in Gen. 22:1–18. the *Bible*.

42 Job's sufferings are detailed in the Book of Job.

43 Søren Kierkegaard, *Fear and Trembling*, trans. Alastair Hannay (London: Penguin Books, 1985). First published in 1843.

44 Fyodor Dostoyevsky, *Crime and Punishment*, trans. David Magarshack (London: Penguin Books, 1951). First published in 1866.

45 Daniel Defoe, *A Journal of the Plague Year* (London: Routledge, 1980). First published in 1722.

46 Daniel Defoe, *Due Preparations for the Plague, as Well for Soul as Body*, ed. Logan Atkinson (Ottawa: Penumbra Press, 2003). First published in 1722.

47 Jean-Paul Sartre, *Nausea*, ed. Lloyd Alexander (New York: New Directions, 1964).

48 Franz Kafka, *Diaries*, ed. Max Brod, trans. Joseph Kresh and Martin Greenberg (New York: Schocken Books, 1948–49).

49 Some of the classics in this rich body of literature include Margaret Atwood, *The Handmaid's Tale* (Toronto: McClelland and Stewart, 1985); Ralph Ellison, *Invisible Man* (New York: Random House, 1952); Langston Hughes, *The Panther & the Lash: Poems of Our Times* (New York: Knopf, 1967); Zora Neale Hurston, *Their Eyes Were Watching God* (New York: Perennial, 1990), first published in 1937; Toni Morrison, *Beloved* (New York: Knopf, 1987); and Alice Walker, *The Color Purple* (New York: Harcourt Brace Jovanovich, 1982).

50 Cover, *supra* note 29.

51 Joseph A. Amato is a leading proponent of this view. See his *Victims and Values: A History and A Theory of Suffering* (New York: Greenwood Press, 1990).

52 *Supra* note 6.

53 Plato, *Republic*, trans. Robin Waterfield (Oxford: Oxford University Press, 1993).

54 Sir Thomas More, *Utopia*, ed. and trans. Robert M. Adams (New York: W.W. Norton, 1975). First published in 1515.

55 George Orwell, *Nineteen Eighty-Four* (London: Penguin, 1973). First published in 1949.

56 Margaret Atwood, *supra* note 49.

57 Evgenii Ivanovich Zamiatin, *We*, trans. Gregory Zilboorg (New York: Dutton Books, 1952).

58 *Supra* notes 2, 3, and 4.

PART ONE

Rationality

2 Murder and Mayhem in Legal Method: or, the Strange Case of Sherlock Holmes v. Sam Spade

NEIL C. SARGENT

Introduction

This chapter sets out to explore some possible connections between the literary universe inhabited by fictional detectives and the more practical world inhabited by lawyers. No claim is made that literary texts produced by writers of detective fiction should be read in the same way as legal texts produced by legislators and lawyers. For present purposes I will adopt Posner's view that legal and literary texts have different functions and are produced for different audiences, and thus should be read or interpreted differently.[1] Instead, the chapter focuses on the ways in which fictional accounts of law provide a literary mirror in which we can see particular images of 'the legal' reflected in the text. From prime-time crime dramas on television to Dickens's literary exposé of the workings of the English Courts of Chancery in *Bleak House*, or from the practice of divorce by wife sale in Hardy's *The Mayor of Casterbridge* to the racialized character of the jury system in *To Kill a Mockingbird*, the fictionalized representation of law often provides a powerful account of the political and social dimensions of the law in operation, as well as the ways in which law works in the popular imagination.

One such literary space in which we confront the popular image of law is within the genre of detective fiction. In a significant way, the whole genre is drenched in law. Indeed, at least one commentator on the history of the detective novel has observed that the modern detective story only comes into existence with the establishment of centralized police forces and systematic methods of criminal investigation in the nineteenth century.[2] We might almost say that detective fiction is written in the shadow of the law. First of all, the nature of the mystery often involves the suspected commission of a crime, most notoriously, of course, the crime of murder, which can be seen in detective fiction terms as the ideal crime. Similarly, the authority of the detective, even if a private investigator or an amateur sleuth, is ultimately derived from law, since the process of resolving the mystery, of uncovering the criminal and establishing how and why he or she committed the crime, must be done in a manner that satisfies the canons of proof and evidence required by law. It may be permissible for the reader to guess at the murderer's identity, but it is never permissible for the detective. Law thus establishes the determinants of truth that are at the core of the detective novel. Finally, of course, it is law that not only defines the crime but also disposes of the body of the criminal, at least if they are still alive at the end of the last chapter, and the detective does not exercise his or her prerogative of mercy. So law permeates the whole structure of the narrative and implicitly regulates the motivations and actions of the protagonists.

But if law is always present in the detective story, it does not always bear the same popular image. In the classic 'armchair' detective story,[3] exemplified by the fictional cases of Sherlock Holmes or Hercule Poirot, law typically appears garbed in the robes of beneficent rationality. The definition of crime, the method of detection, and the authority of law's claims to justice are alike secured by a positivist epistemology in which the neutrality of the observer, the distinction between subject and object, and the possibility of obtaining unmediated access to objective reality are taken for granted and unquestioned. Grounded in rationality, in this fictionalized world it is as unthinkable to question law's claims to justice, to certainty, and to truth as it is to ask whether Sherlock Holmes could be wrong.

And yet in the fictionalized world of *The Maltese Falcon* a very different set of epistemological assumptions about the nature of law and the role of the detective is apparent.[4] Here the positivist certainty of Sherlock Holmes has been replaced by the sceptical realism of Sam Spade. The subject-object distinction that is the basis for positivist scientific method has now been brought into question, with the realization that the observer always acts upon that which is being observed, whether consciously or otherwise.[5] So the canons of truth and certainty under which the detective must operate have to be radically revised. It follows from this that Sherlock Holmes's reliance on close observation and analytical reasoning to solve the mystery may no longer be adequate to the task in hand. Instead, in the hard-boiled school of detective fiction the detective's active intervention into the narrative by following up a lead or in provoking further action becomes as important to the solution of the mystery as the reasoning process of the detective in the classical detective story.[6]

This chapter will seek to examine the manner in which the representation of law in the hard-boiled detective story differs from that in the classical armchair murder mystery, not only in terms of the moral status of the detective, but also in terms of the conditions of epistemological uncertainty under which the detective must now operate. It will be suggested that law's claims to stability, to justice, and to truth are brought into question in the hard-boiled detective story in a way that differs significantly from the popular image of law in the classical detective story. The chapter will examine the moral landscape of the mystery, the place of law in the narrative, and the ways in which the loss of certainty is both revealed by and reflective of the narrative standpoint of the detective in the hard-boiled mystery story.

The Study of Detective Fiction as a Literary Genre

Why study the representation of law in detective fiction? After all, detective fiction is eminently forgettable. That is one of its most salient characteristics as a literary genre. It has few or no pretensions to high literary art. Once you have read one, you have read them all. What can we expect to find that will deepen our understanding of the nature of law or the psychology of crime and punishment from the study of detective novels? Why not focus instead on the more interesting dialogic encounter between competing legal narratives in works such as *Crime and Punishment*, *The Trial*, *Billy Budd*, or *The Merchant of Venice*, or a myriad of other canonical literary texts, rather than in the more prosaic world of Agatha Christie or Raymond Chandler?

My answer to this is that the representation of the legal in a detective story is not so much an effect of a deliberate choice on the part of the author as it is an essential structural component of the narrative. The narrative has no choice but to represent the legal, in order to be recognizable as a detective story. And this applies even in those instances, such as Agatha Christie's *And Then There Were None*, in which the author appears to violate the conventions of the detective story genre by providing no detective and no possibility for the arrest of the guilty party. In this famous story, it is precisely law's inability to bring the murder victims to justice that provides the motive for the murderer (a retired judge, known for his lack of sympathy on the bench) to take the law into his own hands and do the law's retributive work for it. So there is an implicit representation of law's authority, its claims to truth, and its imperative demands for justice embedded in the narrative, even while the narrative appears to be outside the terrain of law altogether.[7]

Representations of the legal thus function as an integral element of the narrative structure of the text, part of the implicit contract between author and reader that goes into the making of a detective story as such an eminently 'readable' text.[8] What makes a particular kind of text 'readable' in the sense being used here by Porter is that both author and reader implicitly agree upon the narrative conventions that go into the construction of the text. Porter observes that any literary work can be viewed as a cultural artefact that comes with implied instructions for its use.[9] Literary genres such as the detective story (or a spy story, or a western, or a historical romance) tend to come with even more precise instructions for use on the part of the reader. 'Genres are essentially contracts between a writer and his readers; or rather they are literary *institutions*, which like other institutions of social life, are based on tacit agreements or contracts.'[10]

Porter suggests that an experienced reader is able to infer the terms of the contract governing the reader's prospective interaction with the text 'from the signs constituted by a cover, a title, an author, or the silhouette of a recurring character on the jacket. The names Doyle, Christie or Simenon, especially when accompanied at the entrance to a text by those signifiers which identify a familiar fictional character ... guarantee the terms of the agreement. Such devices may also be seen as the equivalent of the indicators that, in speech-act theory, furnish the frame of reference and thus enable an utterance to be understood by a listener.'[11]

The most formulaic articulation of this implicit contract between reader and writer was actually laid down as a set of rules for aspiring detective-story writers to follow by Monsignor Ronald Knox of the Detection Club of London, during the so-called Golden Age of detective fiction during the twenties and thirties.[12] As Symons points out, these rules were understood not as a set of commandments governing the production of a certain form of literary work, but as rules for a game played between writer and reader.[13] In this literary game, the writer sets a task for the reader, to unravel a mystery that the writer has constructed, but in competition with a fictional detective whose function in the narrative is to organize the clues interspersed within the text, differentiate between the false clues and the important clues, and so unravel the mystery.[14] The reader's task is essentially to pit his or her wits against the detective and try to reach the correct conclusion before the detective does. At the same time, the reader also sets a task for the writer, to construct a mystery that can be solved using the information concealed within the narrative, without either cheating or losing the reader's attention. There must be no happenstance, no artfully contrived coincidences, no concealment of vital clues. The solution to the mystery must be found through a logical chain of reasoning, in which all the essential facts are tied together, all false clues are eliminated, and a solution reached that is uncompromising and complete, perfect in every way.[15]

The focus of the 'rules' was thus on 'playing fair' by the reader, and ensuring that the reader has a 'sporting chance' to solve the mystery.[16] All must be logical and rational from beginning to end. There must be no metaphysical solutions. Even the most gothic, the most mysterious crime must be susceptible of rational explanation. The mythical hound of the Baskervilles is revealed as just that, a myth, an artifice created by the real villain to obscure his true purpose. Nor should the crime be committed by a sinister foreigner or an exotic stranger. The exotic explanation must always be the false one. The crime must be rational at its core, in its planning, in its execution, and in its discovery by the detective, who acts as an agent of rationality in the narrative.

Pity the poor murderer, then, who is set a task as impossible as that of the author – to conceive and carry out a perfect crime, but in conditions under which it is impermissible to conceal or destroy all the evidence, to rely on luck or the paranormal, or even to murder across rigidly defined class or ethnic lines. The murderer must at all times be a rational instrumentalist thinker, who conceives plans and executes them and seeks to avoid the consequences of discovery and investigation. The ideal murderer should never act recklessly or impulsively, but should always act calmly and deliberately, taking advantage when opportunity presents itself. This is why the murder should never be committed by a member of the servant classes, like James the under-gardener (who has always held a grudge against the Baskervilles), because in a pinch James the under-gardener is likely to act impulsively rather than rationally. And to apply rational, deductive logic to a crime that was committed impulsively would be to risk obtaining an irrational or absurd result, which would violate the implicit terms of the contract between reader and writer.

Needless to say, these strict narrative conventions of the Golden Age detective story were ridiculed by the 'hard-boiled' writers of detective fiction such as Hammett and Chandler, and by critics such as Edmund Wilson.[17] But in taking the detective novel out of the Victorian drawing room and dropping it in the alley,[18] Hammett and Chandler and their followers were not only injecting more 'realism' into the detective novel, but also self-consciously creating their own set of narrative conventions for the production and consumption of hard-boiled detective stories as a particular kind of literary work – conventions that are every bit as religiously adhered to by many contemporary crime writers and television producers as were the detective club rules of the Golden Age writers of detective fiction in the twenties and thirties.

We will have more to say about the narrative conventions governing the intervention of the detective and the conditions of truth that govern the resolution of the mystery in these two types of detective fiction later in the chapter. But in the best traditions of armchair detection, it would be proper to defer this discussion until we have had a closer look at the scene of the crime, and learned all that there is to know about the moral significance of the mystery, the identity of the victim, and how he or she came to be in this precise location in the first place.

The Scene of the Crime

Imagine the scene. We are in a small hotel in a New England village, or a fishing lodge in Algonquin Park, travelling with a group of sea-kayaking eco-tourists. At breakfast one of the guests fails to appear to join in the day's activities. At first no one is suspicious. But then one of the guides discovers that one of the sea-kayaks is missing. Could Jane Protheroe, the thirty-something stockbroker with the broken heart, have gone out alone in the kayak without telling anyone? If so, why was she not wearing her custom-made life jacket, which was found in her room? Or did something else happen? Could she have been murdered? But if so, how, and why, and by whom? The questions keep multiplying as the guests look around nervously, suspicion and fear growing in their hearts, and the one question that will not go away – who will be next?

We are immediately in a very familiar scene. The setting may have changed from the Golden Age country vicarage, and the characters may have been updated slightly. The murder victim, Jane Protheroe, now works as a stockbroker, not as a secretary. And the detective, who, curiously enough, happens to be one of the guests, is no longer required to be asexual, independently wealthy, and on terms of social equality with the upper classes (although these are still desirable traits among armchair detectives to this day).[19] In most other respects, however, we could still be in Miss Marple's drawing room at St Mary Mead. It would not surprise us to learn that Jane Protheroe is her niece or grand-niece, or that our detective has a highly developed analytical mind, and is an avid connoisseur of the *New York Times* crossword.

Now imagine a very different scene. We are in a seedy area of downtown Toronto, or Montreal, or Chicago, where office rents are cheap, and the pimps and the pushers ply their trade in the alleys between vacant buildings. There is a fly buzzing in the outer office, and through the screened window the traffic on King and Spadina can be heard faintly from two blocks away. Outside the window there is a Chevy Malibu with big fins and rust on its wheel rims, and a couple of winos arguing over a bottle of cheap booze. If there is a secretary she is probably on the phone talking to her girlfriend while painting her nails. There is a knock on the outer door, and in walks the prospective client, dressed a little too elegantly for this part of town, and with a story to match.

Once again, we are in very familiar literary terrain. But now we have left the orderly world of the armchair murder mystery far behind. The visual background to the narrative is provided by the evening news, with its televised images of chaos, violence and depravity down the mean streets of the city. Against this background of murder and mayhem, our detective sits with his or her feet on the desk, a cigarette hanging from a lower lip, and a world-weary scepticism about every story ever heard from a would-be client.

What do these narrative settings have to tell us about the kind of mystery we are being asked to solve? Clearly, they tell us quite a lot. The setting of the mystery, what Porter calls 'the landscape of detection,' establishes boundaries for the narrative. Boundaries are never purely descriptive; they are also prescriptive – they establish expectations on the part of both reader and writer as to what can be included (or excluded) within the narrative. Within the classic armchair detective story the artfully constructed and spatially confined setting is central to the narrative conventions of the formula, in that it limits the scope of suspects and locations, and the time frame within which the crime could have been committed.[20] After examining all the witnesses, our detective deduces that it could not have been Colonel Mustard in the drawing room with the blunt instrument, because at the time of the murder, Colonel Mustard was in fact making love (in a figurative sense, of course) to Professor French's wife, Mildred, and this was observed by the chambermaid, Alice, who failed to say anything for fear of getting in trouble with her employer, who insists on complete discretion for all of her guests. In other words, a closed spatial and temporal environment establishes the necessary conditions for those breathless feats of deductive logic on which the detective relies to solve the crime.

At another level, too, the setting of the mystery plays an important part in establishing the moral confines of the narrative, the evocation of a particular place in which the crime was committed, and the social meanings captured in the relationship between landscape and crime.[21] Porter points out that in the classic armchair mystery, the relationship between landscape and crime is often ironic.[22] The body is found in the library, where no bodies should be found. Auden captures this nicely when he says that '[t]he corpse must shock not only because it is a corpse but also because, even for a corpse, it is shockingly out of place.'[23] In the hard-boiled variant of the detective story, however, the corpse does not shock because it is out of place. Instead, it is the place that shocks.[24] The body is simply an addendum, a visual accessory to the place, which somehow makes it more complete in its depravity.

The setting of the mystery is thus key to understanding the moral significance of the mystery, and much of the pleasure derived by the reader from its resolution.[25] With respect to the classical detective story, Auden suggests that the narrative setting should follow certain prescriptions.[26] First of all, it should be a closed society, so that the possibility of an outsider committing the crime is foreclosed. Secondly, it should be a closely related society, so that all the characters are known to one another, and therefore all are potentially suspect. Thirdly, it must appear to be 'an innocent society in a state of grace,' in which 'there is no need of the law, no contradiction between aesthetic individual and ethical universal, and in which murder, therefore, is the unheard of act which precipitates a crisis.'[27] The crime occurs; all are suspect, because the crime reveals that some member has fallen from a state of grace. So the task of the detective is to unravel the mystery, reveal the nature of the evil within, and so exorcize it from the community by the act of revealing the identity of the murderer, who is then symbolically removed from the garden, a state of innocence regained.[28]

Auden further suggests that the writer is wise to choose a closed society with an elaborate ritual (religious or academic communities and upper-class weekend house parties being preferred instances), and to work the ritual into the narrative. A ritual, he observes, '[i]s a sign of harmony between the aesthetic [the individual] and the ethical [the community] in which body and mind, individual will and general laws, are not in conflict. The murderer uses his knowledge of the ritual to commit the crime and can be caught only by someone who acquires an equal or superior familiarity with it.'[29] This essay was originally published in 1948, just after the Second World War. But we can still see the relevance of this observation in the Morse narratives and in many of the Adam Dalgleish mysteries written by P.D. James.

What is the role of social conflict within this seemingly harmonious social order? Social conflict is banished from the narrative, conveniently kept to the margins. There is no hint of a society in crisis.[30] We only discover the conflicts seething under the surface, once the detective has been called in to investigate the crime. As the detective investigates the mystery, he or she finds that the contradiction between aesthetic desire and ethical imperative is far more widespread than at first appears. All are suspect. All conceal within their breasts the hidden desire for murder, the secret wish to violate the ethical universal in pursuit of individual gain, or lust, or envy, or any of the other deadly sins. The task of the detective, then, is to determine which among the members of the community has acted on this hidden desire, has stepped over the invisible Rubicon that separates those who restrain their desires and stay within the moral order of the community and those who give way to their desires, and thus transgress the ethical boundaries of community life.

The detective thus acts as an agent of the collective conscience of the community, since without this intervention there is a risk that crime will go unpunished, and that evil, once entered into the 'great good place,' will corrupt all that is within it. Consequently, the law always wears a benevolent guise within the armchair murder mystery. Law's authority is never called into question, any more than the authority of the detective can be called into question. (We will deal with the detective's method later in the chapter.) The institutional agents of the law may be bumbling idiots, which is why the gifted amateur is often called upon to intervene. But their integrity as agents of the law, as official representatives of the ethical universal, as Auden might put it, is never called into doubt.

What if this were not so? What if the official agents of the law were also corrupt or suspect? We have only to ask the question to reveal law's profound *innocence* in the classic armchair murder mystery. Law is never complicit in the commission of the crime, only in its solution. Likewise, the official face of the law, from the local police detective sergeant to the local magistrate, all the way up to Commander Adam Dalgleish or the chief constable of the county, is equally innocent of the crime, and concerned only with its resolution. There is, in short, no conflict between the aesthetic and the ethical within the breast of the law. The conflict resides within the breast of the individual, not in the breast of the community. Law is therefore as innocent as the society whose values it expresses and protects. If authority can ever be called truly innocent, it surely is in the classic form of the armchair murder mystery. Indeed, I would suggest that it is the very innocence of authority in the armchair detective story that is one of its most comforting features, one of the primary sources of pleasure in the narrative.[31]

What happens when we change the scenario, when we move from the genteel middle- or upper-class world of the armchair detective story, to the milieu of the hard-boiled detective narrative? To use Auden's imagery once again, we have now left Eden. It is not the Great Good Place in which the crime is committed, but the Great Bad Place.[32] Often the location of the crime is the city, represented as an urban wasteland in which all kinds of vice and corruption may grow unchecked.[33] Is this a society in an innocent state of grace? Clearly it is not. No one is innocent, not even the detective, and least of all the law.

How should we understand the nature of the mystery and the task of the detective if the society is no longer innocent? In the urban landscape of the hard-boiled detective story, down the mean streets of San Francisco or Los Angeles, or 'Poisonville,'[34] there is no presumed congruence between aesthetic individual and ethical universal. As Porter puts it, the humane moral order of the Great House has been symbolically replaced by the moral corruption of the Sternwood mansion.[35] General Sternwood in *The Big Sleep* says of his two daughters that they are like all the Sternwoods, they have no more sense of morality than a cat.[36] Individual desire runs unchecked. A gambler and extortionist like Eddie Mars can operate outside of the purview of the law because he has friends in the DA's office, or down at the police precinct. Geiger, whose blackmail attempt on General Sternwood initiates Marlowe's entry into the narrative, openly runs an illicit bookstore dealing in pornographic material on a main boulevard of the city.

It is no longer a society with any semblance of normative cohesion. And yet, all of a sudden, law is everywhere, though never shown, it must be admitted, in a very good light. In Auden's idyllic scene, the law is conspicuous for its absence – 'a society where there is no need of the law' – precisely because there is no contradiction between aesthetic individual and ethical universal. Individuals self-regulate themselves in accordance with the ethical universal. Only when individuals violate the normative consensus and act on illegal or illicit desires is the law called upon to intervene. And then for a while all are forced to live in its shadow, until the disorder is resolved and the law can retire.

But in Marlowe's Hollywood, no one can be relied on to self-regulate themselves in accordance with the ethical imperative. So the law is called on to intervene even before the crime is committed. Sexual desire is not regulated through the institution of heterosexual marriage, but through laws prohibiting the public sale of indecent material. Indeed, the incapacity of marriage to regulate sexual desire is demonstrated not only in Carmen Sternwood's unregulated sexual behaviour, but also in Vivien Sternwood's casual marriage to the missing Rusty Regan.

In this state of normative disorder, the aesthetic individual is always potentially at war with the ethical universal. There are none of the formal elements of tragedy in the narrative, with the catharsis coming in the moment of revelation, of revealed guilt, that produces the restoration of order.[37] In the urban wasteland inhabited by Sam Spade and Philip Marlowe innocence can never be restored, even by the resolution of the mystery.[38] It is not so much that the sinful motives of lust and greed have been banished from the narrative. Clearly, they have not. It is just that these sinful motives are no longer located primarily in the breast of the individual, but now reside, as it were, in the institutions of society as a whole, in the mayor's office, and down at the police precinct, where Eddie Mars has pull.

In these circumstances, the detective can no longer act as an agent of the collective conscience of the community, since the community no longer has a collective conscience. Even the retributive function of law has lost much of its moral force, given the absence of any sense of shared moral purpose that could provide an ethical foundation for law. Here law is no longer equated with innocence, or justice with moral virtue. Instead, law has become corrupted by the very forces of disorder that it sets out to police and contain. In a nice poetic irony, it is precisely the normative conflicts generated by law's attempts to regulate and prohibit certain forms of 'undesirable' social behaviour that generate much of the narrative tension and motives for murder in the hard-boiled detective story. In seeking to impose its vision of moral order on a community that lacks any normative cohesion, law thus becomes a source of the very disorder that the detective is called upon to investigate.

Narrative Standpoint and Method

Having looked at the moral landscape in which the mystery takes place, and how this influences our view of the task of the detective, it may be useful to turn our attention to the question of method and the narrative standpoint of the detective. Porter provides a very suggestive analogy between the art of literary detection and the task of the literary critic. 'A novel,' he observes, 'like a corpse, is approached by professionals as an enigma requiring a solution. It, too, is assumed to be in need of a mediating intelligence if its true story is to be told. A critic, and every reader by virtue of the fact that he is engaged in the act of reading a literary work is ipso facto a critic, seeks to solve the crime/problem of the novel's meaning by collating all the material as it is furnished to him in its sequence of time. And he organizes and reorganizes his theory of that material in light of the continual flow of evidence that is the text right up to the denouement.'[39]

If a novel can be approached like a corpse, as 'an enigma requiring a solution,' then it follows that a crime can also be approached in the same way as a novel, as a text in need of an interpretation. And indeed, Porter observes that 'the detective behaves like a well-trained critic to the extent that he also (re)constructs a whole out of more or less disparate material for the purpose of conferring a meaning.'[40]

This image of the detective as an interpreter of texts rather than as an investigator of facts opens up a number of suggestive questions about the interpretive standpoint adopted by the detective towards the mystery, and the interpretive strategy or method by which he or she approaches the task of interpretation.[41] Is it the detective as reader who confers meaning on the text through the very process of organizing and selecting from among the disparate materials that together constitute the text of the mystery, as reader-response criticism and deconstruction would suggest? Or is the true meaning of the crime already inscribed within the text, awaiting only the omniscient intelligence of a Holmes, or a Morse, or a Poirot to reveal its true secrets?

In the armchair detective story, of course, it is the latter approach that predominates. The detective stands outside the mystery in need of an interpretation, and approaches the task of interpretation as one of revealing the hidden strands of meaning located within the text. Like any other text, the mystery is susceptible to a variety of competing interpretations; and the task of the detective in the formal detective story is to select the correct interpretive strategy that will enable him or her to identify the real meaning of the mystery, to eliminate all the false or misleading narratives contained within the text, and so to arrive at the truth at last. In the end, the detective gives us a reading of the text that unravels its various narrative strands; clarifies the motive, means, and opportunity that are at the heart of the crime, and thus enable its author to be identified; provides us with a glimpse of the reasoning process by which the detective was able to arrive at this solution; and invites us, as readers, to compare our reading of the text with that of the detective.

In order to accomplish this task, however, the detective has to adopt a standpoint of critical detachment towards all of the information that is presented to him or her in the course of the investigation. The detective must be sceptical of every piece of information, every fact, every motive, every soliciting sign, unless and until it can be verified for its truth content. No item of information is too small to be significant. Likewise, nothing that appears obvious should be taken for granted. Most of all, as Poirot and Holmes both emphasize to their respective counterparts, Hastings and Watson, nothing that appears at first glance to be incongruous or inconsistent should be ignored. The solution to the mystery lies in making sense of the apparently inexplicable, in revealing the hidden pattern that lies concealed beneath the most banal or innocuous details.

In the formal detective story, the standpoint of the narrator is the objective voice of the detective, or better yet, once removed even from this, we hear the narrative as related to us by the detective's intimate friend, who has privileged access to the same information as our detective, but without being privy to the detective's internal reasoning process.[42] Watching Holmes in action, through the adoring but uncomprehending eyes of Watson (who is himself trained as a doctor, but who never recognizes Holmes's method in his own training in diagnosing and treating disease), we observe Holmes briefing the Baker Street Irregulars, sending off telegrams, the contents of which we are not privy to, following up lines of enquiry that often seem totally peripheral to the task at hand, the results of which are often as spectacular as they are unexpected. Here we see the natural scientist at work, who seeks to apply the scientific method to the study of crime; always formulating, testing, and refining hypotheses until he arrives at the truth.[43] Moreover, the evidence and the chain of reasoning, when finally revealed, prove compelling. We are forced to admit the mastery of Holmes's method over the material facts of the crime or the mystery.

One or two observations are in order about this method.[44] Despite the apparent openness of the application of Holmes's method – the locations range from the gothic confines of Copper Beeches and Baskerville Hall to the opium dens of East End London – the conditions for the application of this method are in fact always controlled. First, the detective is always instantly aware of the true nature of the puzzle that has to be solved, and the right line of enquiry that must be followed.[45] Watson and Hastings and the police may blunder along in the dark, unsure about what it is they are searching for. But the true detective will always appreciate the real gravity of the mystery from the instant it is presented to him or her, no matter how trivial or absurd the matter may appear to be on its surface.

Second, the number of possible solutions to the mystery is always finite.[46] Once again, we as readers may be off on some speculative wild goose chase, because we do not know the true nature of the mystery that must be solved. But the detective does, and thus can already eliminate some of our more far-fetched notions about the crime, because they could not possibly be relevant to the true nature of the puzzle that must be solved.

In this context, Bonfantini and Proni liken the task of literary detection to that of de-encryption of a coded message.[47] The code breakers begin from the premise that there is no process of encryption that cannot be de-encrypted, no code that cannot be broken. All that is required is that the code breakers take infinite pains to check every possible mode of encryption that is known to them, eliminating all those that do not yield useful experimental results, until they have decoded the correct message. As these commentators observe, this is also how Holmes describes his own method to Watson.[48] The mystery always involves a hidden code encrypted by the murderer. The task of the detective is to observe the coded message and to decipher it to discover its hidden meaning. The bloodstain found at the scene of the crime, the wife who leaves her husband's hat unbrushed before he goes out of the house – all these are hidden messages that can be decoded easily enough by one who takes pains to practise the art of reasoning backwards from effects to their causes, rather than the more commonplace skill of reasoning forward from cause to effect.[49]

Finally, there is the element that provides the key to Holmes's whole method, the claim that for every effect there is but one cause; that among all the possible hypotheses that suggest themselves to explain the mystery, there is only one correct solution that is capable of explaining all the relevant facts, of tying together all the disparate narrative strands of the mystery. In order to arrive at this correct solution the detective must rely only on the techniques of observation, abduction (or inference), and deduction.[50] Above all, the detective must never guess, or seek to create hypotheses that are not suggested by the facts available to the detective. ('It is a capital mistake to theorize before you have all the evidence. It biases the judgment.'[51]) Nor should the detective ignore even the most trifling detail that may be relevant to deciphering the hidden message left behind by the murderer.[52] Remember that the correct solution is that which ties together *all* of the facts, even the most trivial or inconvenient ones. Consequently, by eliminating all of the hypotheses that cannot explain all of the facts, the detective finally arrives at the only possible solution that can. Or, as Holmes succinctly puts it, 'when you have eliminated the impossible, whatever remains, however improbable, must be the truth.'[53]

But if these are the methodological assumptions underpinning the formal detective story, what can we say about the canons of truth and method that animate the action-oriented approach of Sam Spade or Philip Marlowe? Here, it is not truth but scepticism that prevails. Scepticism not only about motives and dates, times and alibis, and whether it really was Mr Ogilthorp who purchased the strychnine from the chemist's shop at 6.00 p.m. on Monday;[54] but more worryingly, scepticism about the very possibility of truth at all. We are never quite so sure about what is an effect and what is its cause. Actions often appear to take place without prior intentions, so it is impossible to discern the mind of the murderer behind them. Consequently, any detective who depends for his success on the power of reasoning backwards from effects to their causes is likely to find himself on the wrong end of a bullet before the end of chapter 3.

We do not even enter into the narrative with a first initiating action, such as the arrival of the guests at the college dinner, or the discovery of the body in the library.[55] Instead, the narrative commences at an arbitrary point, in the midst of an action sequence that has already commenced. In *The Maltese Falcon*, the Fat Man and Joel Cairo have already chased Brigid O'Shaughnessy from Istanbul to San Francisco before Sam Spade enters into the action.[56] Consequently, he is not even aware of the real nature of the mystery he is called upon to resolve until later in the narrative. There is no longer a single author who encodes the mystery and initiates the action. Instead, the script, or the code, or the action is still being written as the detective intervenes.[57] In these circumstances, the detective does not have the luxury of adopting a standpoint of critical detachment towards the protagonists in the mystery. He or she is too busy being lied to, beaten up, threatened by the police, or sent down dark alleys in pursuit of leads to step outside of the action in order to critically examine clues for their hidden meaning.[58]

The implications of this shift in the detective's relation to the mystery can also be seen in the narrative standpoint of the detective. Typically the standpoint of the narrator in the hard-boiled detective story is the first-person singular. We 'hear' the inner voice of the detective narrating the action, and his or her observations on the narrative. According to Porter, this question of narrative standpoint, or what he refers to as the language of detection, can be viewed as predominantly a literary device that mediates the reader's relationship with the text. This use of the first-person singular tends to narrow the gap between reader and the action described in the narrative, and thus to create a sense of immediacy in the reader, a heightened sense of emotional intensity.[59] The narrative is consumed by the reader in the present tense, so to speak, so that the reader feels vicariously present with the detective in the abandoned stone yard when she stumbles across the mangled body of her informant, crushed under a monstrous slab of rough-cut marble.

This literary device, however, also reveals quite a lot about the methodological conventions that are at work in the narrative. One of the cardinal principles of the Holmesian method is that the detective as observer should never interfere with the evidence found at the crime scene, lest the truth content of the data found at the crime scene be contaminated by the presence of the detective. We instantly visualize Holmes whipping out his magnifying glass, pacing out measurements, looking at mud stains, cigar ash, footprints, bicycle tracks. All these disparate items of data have their stories to tell, their part of the puzzle to explicate. But while observing, measuring, recording, and drawing inferences from all this data, it never occurs to us to imagine that the mud could have been brought by Holmes himself from his walk on the South Downs the day before; or that the curious pattern of the blood on the wall could have been made by Holmes accidentally brushing the still wet bloodstain with his sleeve. Watson, yes, we can imagine this of him. Inspector Gregson also, although he is one of the few good men down at the Yard. But Holmes, never. It is unthinkable. All the wondrous chains of inferences that so delight us would collapse in an instant if it turned out that the distinction between observer and observed on which the whole method of observation, abduction, and deduction rests was invalid.

But what of Sam Spade and Philip Marlowe and all the legions of hard-boiled literary detectives who followed in their wake? In chapter 2 of *The Maltese Falcon,* Spade does not even bother to examine the dead body of his partner Miles Archer, before leaving to pursue his investigation. He learns all that he needs to know about how Miles was killed from the police, whose business it is to examine the physical evidence. In so doing he violates Holmes's rule that the detective must never take anything at face value; all information should be treated sceptically until tested or independently verified by the detective him- or herself. Worse, Spade himself relies on this second-hand information in browbeating Brigid O'Shaughnessy into confessing that she killed Miles in chapter 20 of the book. How do we as readers know that Miles was killed close up, without even reaching for his gun? We do not know. We were never at the crime scene. We also have to take Police Sergeant Tom Polhaus's word for it.

And if Sam Spade wilfully disregards the distinction between object and observer on which Holmes's whole method rests, what are we to make of Philip Marlowe in *The Big Sleep,* whose first action on discovering the dead body of Geiger (in chapter 7) is to remove the naked and unconscious body of Carmen Sternwood from the crime scene and alter the physical evidence to make it appear she was never there. Not only does this make Marlowe an accessory after the fact, or at the very least guilty of failing to report a murder, but his actions also materially affect what we might call the truth content of the physical evidence revealed at the crime scene. How is Marlowe to get at the truth of the murder, when his actions as an independent investigator in the employ of General Sternwood compromise his objectivity in such a crucial manner?

In the world according to Sherlock Holmes, once the criminal is uncovered, the mystery solved, the motive, opportunity, and modus operandi of the murderer revealed, there is no more room for doubt. All other possibilities have been eliminated and the murderer stands revealed before us. But in Sam Spade's fictional universe we can never know anything with certainty. We do not even know who killed Miles Archer, Spade's partner, in *The Maltese Falcon*. We think that Miles was killed by Brigid O'Shaughnessy, because she confessed to the murder, and because it is more likely than any other possible explanation. It is unlikely that Miles would have let down his guard and let himself be shot at such close range by another gunman without even reaching for his own gun. So it was probably a woman, because Miles, unlike Spade, was always a sucker for a broad. Who else, then, but Brigid O'Shaughnessy, since she had left the hotel with Formby, and we know that Miles was already attracted to her? But we are never told how she obtained Formby's gun, or even why she shot Miles.

Is this enough to prove Brigid O'Shaughnessy's guilt? Manifestly it is not. According to the same logic, it could have been Spade himself who shot Miles, since Miles is unlikely to have been suspicious of Spade, and Spade knew where Miles was likely to be that evening. Moreover, Spade does not have an alibi. We know that he was awoken with the news that Miles had been shot. But we do not know where he was all evening. He could have followed Formby from the hotel, obtained his gun, shot Miles and then Formby, and pinned the whole crime on Brigid O'Shaughnessy in order to save his own neck. The police lieutenant certainly thinks Spade had the motive, the means, and the opportunity to have killed Miles, and thus considers him a suspect. The lieutenant may have been bluffing in order to get Spade to reveal the names of the other suspects in the case. But how do we know that Spade was not using the mystery of the Maltese Falcon as a way of getting rid of a business and sexual rival? There is nothing in the physical evidence that rules this possibility out of contention. It is just less likely than the alternative explanation, that Brigid killed Miles.

The irony is that in confronting Brigid O'Shaughnessy with the 'truth' that it must have been she who lured Miles Archer to his death,

Spade is using the very process of reasoning analytically from effects to their causes that Holmes relies on in the famous story of *Silver Blaze*, when the identity of the miscreant who removed Silver Blaze from his stable is revealed through the curious fact that the dog did not bark in the night. In Holmes's case this inference provides the missing link in the chain of reasoning that ties together all the other known facts concerning the horse's disappearance, and thus provides incontrovertible evidence that the horse was removed by its trainer, John Straker, in an attempt to disable the horse from running in the Wessex Cup.[60]

In Spade's case, despite the use of Holmes's method, we are still left with a nagging feeling of doubt. Nothing is ever quite what it seems. In the end, Brigid's confession that she killed Miles is all that prevents him from being implicated in the crime. But her confession was arguably forced out of her at gunpoint, in circumstances in which Spade had a clear conflict of interest. His 'solution' to the mystery of who killed Miles Archer is thus inherently suspect because of his own involvement as a protagonist in the mystery. The closer we examine the methods used in getting at the truth of this murder, the further we appear to be from the truth.

My point is not to try to establish that Lieutenant Dundy was right, and that it should really be Sam Spade who goes to the electric chair instead of Brigid O'Shaughnessy. Rather, the point is to try to show that the linear notions of causality underpinning the Holmesian method are no longer applicable within the world of the hard-boiled private eye. Above all, the claim that for every effect there is but one cause – that there can be only one solution capable of explaining all the relevant facts – is belied by the denouement of *The Maltese Falcon*, in which we are left with at least two[61] competing narratives or solutions to the crime, each of which can be logically defended in terms of its capacity to fit all the known 'facts' about the mystery.

Moreover, I would argue that this is not just a function of poor plotting by the author or the slipshod methods of the detectives, but is indicative of a more fundamental shift in the epistemological conditions under which the detective must now operate. As we have seen, even the conventions of time and space are deployed differently in the narrative. The physical setting in which the mystery takes place is no longer closed, but open. The time sequence in which the action takes place is not presented as a linear sequence in which the meaning of events can be fixed in accordance with the precise time at which they took place. Instead, we are now living in a post-Einstein universe, in which time and space are relative, and the standpoint of the observer always exercises an influence on that which is being observed.[62]

It follows from this that the meaning of the facts or events that the detective relies on to construct a theory about the truth of the mystery is not already inscribed in the events or the data themselves. The facts do not speak for themselves, but depend on the vantage point of the observer. As this vantage point changes, then so, too, does the truth content of the facts.[63] There is no standpoint of critical detachment, no Archimedian (or Holmesian) point, from which secure objective knowledge about the mystery can be obtained. The detective, like the reader, is always *actively* engaged as a protagonist in the creation of knowledge about the crime.[64]

The truth value of any proposition, then, appears to be as much a function of the interpretive standpoint adopted by the observer as it does of any inherent attribute or truth content in the proposition itself. In the hard-boiled detective novel, the implications of possible observer bias are made very clear to us as readers from the outset, in the narrative positioning of the detective towards the other protagonists in the mystery, and in the dubious motives presented even by the official police. In the conventional or armchair detective novel, the implications of observer bias are concealed from the reader by the narrative distancing of both detective and reader from the sequence of events that constitute the mystery, and by the conventions of causality and method that are at work in the text.[65]

When we extend this discussion of truth and method from the realm of detective fiction back to the so-called 'real world' of law, we find that the significance of interpretive standpoint, and the possibility of observer bias are built into the very warp and weft of the criminal trial process itself. The trial is structured not as an experimental laboratory in which truth claims are tested by scientifically rigorous methods of enquiry by impartial observers, but as a contest over truth between two legal adversaries with radically different interests in the outcome. Far from being objective truth seekers, the main protagonists in this struggle are assumed to be self-interested advocates in their own cause, with as much interest in suppressing evidence that may contradict their legal position at the trial as in having it come to light. Moreover, the judge is not expected to take an active part in the fact-finding process, but to leave it to the litigants, in consultation with their lawyers, to determine what kinds of evidence or proof to introduce in support of their respective claims.[66]

Consequently, there is no objective mechanism by which truth claims can be tested within the structure of the adversarial trial process. Instead, the truth content of any given factual narrative presented in the course of a trial is left to be tested by the very legal adversary who has the most personal interest in discrediting it. In this contest over truth, it is assumed that each protagonist will be motivated to try to discredit or to destabilize the truth claims of the other side, and therefore will do all within their power, within the limits set by the rules of evidence and procedure governing the trial, to challenge the reliability of the truth claims made by the other side. The quality of the evidence presented before the court is thus presumed to be directly related to the self-interestedness of the participants in trying to convince the trier of fact of the persuasiveness of their own truth claims. Bias is used to counteract bias; self-interestedness, ironically, is deployed in pursuit of truth.[67]

The very structure of legal fact finding within the criminal trial – based as it is on the requirement of proof beyond a reasonable doubt – thus admits of the possibility that the evidence presented against an accused person may be biased, may be incomplete, may be just plain untrue. Evidence could have been falsified or adjusted to make it look like it was the accused who was present at the scene of the crime at the crucial time, and no one else. Evidence exculpating the accused could have been conveniently lost in order to make the prosecution's case against the accused look more compelling. The accused might be browbeaten into making a confession in order to protect someone else from being implicated in the crime. We may not believe that Sherlock Holmes or Jessica Fletcher are capable of this. But I defy any reader of *The Maltese Falcon* to look me in the eye and state categorically that Lieutenant Dundy is not capable of stitching up a suspect in order to get a conviction. Spade certainly believes this, which is why he works so hard to get Brigid to confess that she killed Miles. And while I hate to admit it, I think the same could be said of every writer of formal detective stories who ever lived. Agatha Christie made her whole career as a detective novelist out of stitching up unlikely suspects. The only reason we do not like to admit this is because we are so passionately fond of the idea of the Great Detective and the marriage between Rationality and Truth that the Great Detective seems to exemplify.[68]

If we look back at the confession scene in *The Maltese Falcon* from this perspective, it is the adversarial nature of the confrontation between Spade and Brigid O'Shaughnessy that immediately catches the eye. Once again we are presented with a contest over truth involving two protagonists, both of whom have a direct personal interest in the outcome. In this struggle, we can clearly see the possibilities for abuse and observer bias. While the conversation takes place in private, both parties seek to present their narrative in such a way as to persuade an external decision maker, in this case the police, of their essential innocence in the events that have defined the mystery. We see power employed in an attempt to gain strategic or tactical advantage, in a way that is typically concealed within the formal detective novel. In this contest over truth, there are likely to be no clear winners, at least in the terms that we have come to expect from Holmes and Poirot. But at least we are able to identify the loser, in this case Brigid, who will now be handed over to the unwelcome attentions of the police, together with Spade's narrative of her involvement in the mystery. Whether this narrative will stand up to hostile cross-examination in the courtroom we do not know. But our task as readers is now done. The rest we can leave to the lawyers.

Now compare this scene with the typical denouement in a Sherlock Holmes mystery, or any of Hercule Poirot's celebrated cases, when the detective finally 'outs' the guilty suspect, after demonstrating how and why the crime must have been committed. Faced with the implacable reasoning process of the detective, the accused can only deny his or her guilt, or try to explain it; the accused is never given the right to challenge the detective, or to question the detective's motives, methods, or conclusions. It is as if the accused were to be involved in a trial scene in which only the prosecution is given the right to present evidence, the verdict is not open to appeal, and the accused is not given the right to a defence lawyer. What is concealed from the reader is precisely the fact that the detective has the upper hand, and that power is deployed in the pursuit of 'truth' in ways that could prove extremely prejudicial to one who is falsely accused. Yet we, as readers, cheerfully participate in this authorial sleight of hand and put down the book with a pleasant sense that justice has been done, and that truth has once again triumphed over uncertainty, little thinking that Sherlock Holmes, or Inspector Morse, or even, good heavens, Miss Marple, could ever have sent the wrong suspect to the gallows.

Conclusion

In this chapter, I have tried to show that the representation of law within the formal detective story depends on a twin pairing of justice with authority, and truth with reason, both of which pairings are contested and destabilized in the hard-boiled detective story. In the latter, we are invited to confront the fact that the pursuit of justice and the preservation of authority may often prove to be mutually incompatible objectives, such that the detective is often caught in a very contradictory relationship towards his or her own task. In the same way, the hard-boiled detective novel also forces us to confront the unwelcome realization that our truth claims should always be tempered with doubt, and that reason alone can never lead us to the truth about human behaviour. Instead, the detective lives in a world of uncertain motives, in which truth claims often depend on the standpoint of the knower, so the detective's notions of truth and certainty have to be adapted to fit the measure of the times.

I want to leave the last word on this subject to Justice Oliver Wendell Holmes Jr, who is far better qualified to comment on the workings of the common law than I. Like his great literary namesake Sherlock, Justice Holmes was obviously a keen student of the science of criminology, and the associated art of detection. But unlike his celebrated literary cousin, Justice Holmes was no fan of the deductive method. Commenting strictly off the record, but obviously with Holmesian maxims of detection in mind, he observed, '[T]he life of the law has not been logic; it has been experience.'[69]

NOTES

1 Richard Posner, *Law and Literature: A Misunderstood Relation*, rev. ed. (Cambridge, MA: Harvard University Press, 1998); see, generally, Dennis R. Klink, *The Word of the Law. Approaches to Legal Discourse* (Ottawa: Carleton University Press, 1992), 133–43. For the contrary view, see James Boyd White, 'The Judicial Opinion and the Poem: Ways of Reading, Ways of Life' (1984) 82 Mich. L. Rev. 16–69; James Boyd White, *Heracles Bow: Essays on the Rhetoric and Poetics of the Law* (Madison: University of Wisconsin Press, 1985); Sanford Levinson, 'Law as Literature,' in *Interpreting Law and Literature: A Hermeneutic Reader*, ed. S. Levinson and M. Mailloux, (Evanston, IL: Northwestern University Press, 1988); Robin West, 'Jurisprudence as Narrative: An Aesthetic Analysis of Modern Legal Theory' (1985) 60 N.Y.U. L. Rev. 145–211; Peter Brooks, 'The Law as Narrative and as Rhetoric,' in *Law's Stories. Narrative and Rhetoric in the Law*, ed. Peter Brooks and Paul Gewirtz, 14–22 (New Haven, CT: Yale University Press, 1996).

2 E.M. Wrong, introduction to *Crime and Detection* (Oxford: Oxford University Press, 1926), x. See also Dorothy L. Sayers, 'The Omnibus of Crime,' in *Detective Fiction*, ed. Robin W. Winks, 53–83 (Englewood Cliffs, NJ: Prentice-Hall, 1980), at 55, 56.

3 So-called because of Watson's incredulous response to Holmes's claim that he could logically deduce the answer to many mysteries on which he was consulted without ever leaving his rooms in Baker Street. It is only in cases in which there were 'some considerable points of interest' that Holmes could be induced to bestir himself into action. See Sir Arthur Conan Doyle, 'A Study in Scarlet,' in *The Celebrated Cases of Sherlock Holmes*, 547–622 (London: Octopus Books Limited, 1981), at 558.

4 William W. Stowe, 'From Semiotics to Hermeneutics: Modes of Detection in Doyle and Chandler,' in *The Poetics of Murder*, ed. Glenn W. Most and William W. Stowe, 366–83 (San Diego: Harcourt Brace Jovanovich, 1983), at 373–9.

5 *Ibid.*, 374.

6 Glenn W. Most, 'The Hippocratic Smile: John le Carré and the Traditions of the Detective Novel,' in Most and Stowe, *supra* note 4, 341–65, at 347.

7 Contrariwise, as Alice would say, Christie's equally well-known *Murder on the Orient Express*, provides a different variant on a similar theme. Once again it is law's insistent demand for knowledge and proof, and its inability to differentiate between morally justified violence and morally unjustified violence, that provides the motivation for all the passengers to take part in the retributive killing on the train, as well as the detective's willingness to thwart the law's demands for justice once he has uncovered the real 'truth' of the crime.

8 Dennis Porter, *The Pursuit of Crime: Art and Ideology in Detective Fiction* (New Haven, CT: Yale University Press, 1981), 82–5.

9 *Ibid.*, 83.

10 Frederic Jameson, 'Magical Narrative: Romance as Genre,' *New Literary History* 7, no. 1 (1975): 135–63 at 135, quoted in Porter, *ibid.*, 84. Italics in original. See also Tzvetan Todorov, *The Poetics of Prose* (Oxford: Basil Blackwell, 1977), at 43.

11 Porter, *supra* note 8 at 84–5.

12 Knox's Ten Commandments are listed in A.E. Murch, *The Development of the Detective Novel* (London: Peter Owen, 1968), at 225, as follows:

(1) The criminal must be mentioned early on, not just brought in at the end.

(2) The puzzle must be solved rationally, not by 'supernatural causes.'

(3) No more than one secret room or passage to be used.

(4) No 'undiscovered' or 'undetectable' poisons.
(5) No sinister foreigners, particularly chinamen.
(6) The puzzle must not be solved by a lucky accident.
(7) The detective must not have committed the crime himself.
(8) Nor must he conceal clues or reasons for his deductions.
(9) A 'Watson' if such a character is used, must not conceal his opinions.
(10) There is a special veto against using identical twins or 'doubles.'

See also Julian Symons, *Bloody Murder*, rev. ed. (New York: Viking Press, 1985) at 13 and 93; Porter, *supra* note 8 at 85; and Howard Haycraft, *Murder for Pleasure: The Life and Times of the Detective Story* (New York: Biblo and Tannen, 1968) at 225.

13 Symons, *ibid.*, 93; Haycraft, *ibid.*

14 Jacques Barzun, 'Detection and the Literary Art,' in Winks, *supra* note 2 at 15–24; Dorothy L. Sayers, 'Aristotle on Detective Fiction,' in Winks, *supra* note 2, 25–34; Roger Caillous, 'The Detective Novel as Game,' in Most and Stowe, *supra* note 4 at 1–12.

15 Sayers, *ibid.*; Caillous, *ibid.*

16 Haycraft, *supra* note 12.

17 Edmund Wilson, 'Who Cares Who Killed Roger Ackroyd?' in Winks, *supra* note 2 at 35–40.

18 Raymond Chandler, *The Simple Art of Murder* (New York: Vintage Books, 1988), 14.

19 Symons, *supra* note 12 at 138.

20 John G. Cawelti, *Adventure, Mystery and Romance: Formula Stories as Art and Popular Culture* (Chicago: University of Chicago Press, 1976), 97; George Grella, 'Murder and Manners: The Formal Detective Novel,' in *Dimensions of Detective Fiction*, ed. Larry N. Landrum, Pat Browne and Ray B. Browne, 37–57 (Bowling Green, OH: Popular Press, 1976), at 47.

21 Porter, *supra* note 8 at 189 and 190; Cawelti, *ibid.*, 97.

22 Porter, *supra* note 8 at 193.

23 W.H. Auden, 'The Guilty Vicarage,' in Winks, *supra* note 2, 15–24 at 19.

24 Porter, *supra* note 8 at 197.

25 Porter, *supra* note 8 at 195; Grella, *supra* note 20 at 41.

26 Auden, *supra* note 23 at 17 and 18.

27 *Ibid.*, 18.

28 Cawelti, *supra* note 20 at 97; Grella, *supra* note 20 at 47 and 53.

29 Auden, *supra* note 23 at 18.

30 Porter, *supra* note 8 at 195; Grella, *supra* note 20 at 56; Symons, *supra* note 12 at 96; Peter J. Rabinowitz, 'Rats behind the Wainscoting: Politics, Con-

vention, and Chandler's *The Big Sleep*,' *Texas Studies in Literature and Language* 22, no. 2 (Summer 1980): 224–45, at 227.

31 Rabinowitz, *ibid*., 228 and 231. See also Cawelti, *supra* note 20, 90. Grella, *supra* note 20 at 41 and 49, suggests that the formal detective novel should be seen as a comedy of manners, in which both victim and criminal are seen as social undesirables, whose removal 'insures the continued happiness of those remaining.' The victim as social undesirable is removed through the intervention of the criminal, while the criminal as social undesirable is removed through the intervention of the detective.

32 George Grella, 'The Hard-Boiled Detective Novel,' in Winks, *supra* note 2 at 112.

33 Cawelti, *supra* note 20, 155; Liahna K. Babener, 'Raymond Chandler's City of Lies,' in *Los Angeles in Fiction*, ed. David Fine, 109–31 (Albuquerque: University of New Mexico Press, 1984); Paul Skenazy, 'Behind the Territory Ahead,' in Fine, *ibid*., 85–107, 95, 97.

34 The reference is to the town of Personville in Hammett's novel *Red Harvest*, in *Dashiell Hammett: Five Complete Novels* (New York: Avenel Books, 1980).

35 Porter, *supra* note 8 at 198.

36 Raymond Chandler, *The Big Sleep* (New York: Vintage Books, 1992), 13.

37 Auden, *supra* note 23 at 16 and 24; Sayers, *supra* note 14 at 26 and 27; Rabinowitz, *supra* note 30 at 228.

38 Grella, *supra* note 32 at 111; Edward Margolies, *Which Way Did He Go?* (New York: Holmes and Meier, 1982), 221 and 229; Rabinowitz, *supra* note 30 at 231.

39 Porter, *supra* note 8 at 226.

40 *Ibid*.

41 *Ibid*., 229.

42 See Cawelti, *supra* note 20 at 83 and 84, for an interesting discussion of this narrative standpoint.

43 Porter, *supra* note 8 at 225; D.F. Rauber, 'Sherlock Holmes and Nero Wolfe: The Role of the "Great Detective" in Intellectual History,' in Landrum, Browne, and Browne, *supra* note 20, 89–96, at 89; Massimo A. Bonfantini and Giampaolo Proni, 'To Guess or Not to Guess?' in *The Sign of Three*, ed. Umberto Eco and Thomas A. Sebeok, 119–134 (Bloomington: Indiana University Press, 1985) at 123–8.

44 For an interesting comparison of Holmes's application of the hypothetico-deductive approach to the art of detection and C.S. Peirce's discussion of 'abduction,' see Thomas A. Sebeok and Jean Umiker-Sebeok, 'You Know My Method: A Juxtaposition of Charles S. Peirce and Sherlock Holmes,'

in Eco and Sebeok, *ibid.*, 11–54; also Marcello Truzzi, 'Sherlock Holmes. Applied Social Psychologist,' in Eco and Sebeok, *ibid.*, at 55–80.

45 Cawelti, *supra* note 20 at 83.

46 As an illustration of this point, Miss Marple, in *The Murder at the Vicarage*, remarks that she can think of at least (but no more than) seven possible solutions to the murder. It only remains to eliminate six of these seven possibilities and we will have identified our murderer! Agatha Christie, *Murder at the Vicarage* (New York: Berkley Books, 1984), 63.

47 Bonfantini and Proni, *supra* note 43 at 128.

48 Doyle, 'A Study in Scarlet,' *supra* note 3 at 566. Cited in Bonfantini and Proni, *supra* note 43 at 125.

49 Bonfantini and Proni, *supra* note 43 at 127; Sebeok and Umiker-Sebeok, *supra* note 44 at 39; Doyle, 'A Study in Scarlet,' *supra* note 3 at 619; Stowe, *supra* note 4 at 368.

50 Sebeok and Umiker-Sebeok, *supra* note 44; Bonfantini and Proni, *supra* note 43 at 123–5.

51 Doyle, 'A Study in Scarlet,' *supra* note 3 at 562. For a discussion of the role of 'guessing' in Holmes' method, see Sebeok and Umiker-Sebeok, *supra* note 44 at 23–4, 38, 44; Bonfanitini and Proni, *supra* note 43.

52 Sebeok and Umiker-Sebeok, *supra* note 44 at 22–3; Heta Pyrhonen, *Mayhem and Murder: Narrative and Moral Problems in the Detective Story* (Toronto: University of Toronto Press, 1999), 67.

53 Sir Arthur Conan Doyle, 'The Sign of Four,' in *The Celebrated Cases of Sherlock Holmes*, *supra* note 3 at 648.

54 Agatha Christie, *The Mysterious Affair at Styles* (Glasgow: Collins, 1989).

55 Todorov, *supra* note 10 at 47.

56 Rabinowitz, *supra* note 30 at 162, comments, '[T]o the extent that there *is* a story, it is a story of a search without a beginning. More important, the search is a search without an ending, except the promise of endless deferral.'

57 Pyrhonen, *supra* note 52 at 113.

58 Most, *supra* note 6 at 347.

59 Porter, *supra* note 8 at 137–42.

60 Sir Arthur Conan Doyle, 'Silver Blaze,' in *The Celebrated Cases of Sherlock Holmes*, *supra* note 3 at 211 and 214.

61 And possibly more, for instance, that it was Miles's wife, Ida, who shot Miles, so that she could run away with Spade.

62 Stowe, *supra* note 4 at 373 and 374.

63 Pyrhonen, *supra* note 52 at 124 and 125.

64 *Ibid.*, 114.

65 Once again, Agatha Christie, by violating the conventions of narrative distancing between narrator and reader in her novel *The Murder of Roger Ackroyd*, demonstrates the exception that proves the rule.

66 Neil Brooks, 'The Judge and the Adversary System,' in *The Canadian Judiciary*, ed. Allen Linden, 89–133 (Toronto: Osgoode Hall Law School, York University, 1976).

67 In defence of this curiously self-interested attitude towards truth, the American evidence scholar Wigmore called the adversarial trial process the greatest engine for producing truth ever invented. See Brooks, *ibid.*, at 131, note 99.

68 Porter, *supra* note 8 at 224–5; Sayers, *supra* note 14 at 53. See also Sebeok and Umiker-Sebeok, *supra* note 44 at 11–23; and Marcello Truzzi, 'Sherlock Holmes, Applied Social Psychologist,' in Eco and Sebeok, *supra* note 43 at 55–80.

69 Oliver Wendell Holmes Jr, *The Common Law*, ed. Mark DeWolfe Howe (Boston: Little, Brown, 1963), 1.

3 Analytic Philosophy and the Interpretation of Constitutional Rights

SOPHIA MOREAU[1]

Analytic philosophy has been used in many areas of Anglo-American law to help clarify the content and the implications of the legal concepts central to these areas. As early as the 1950s, Herbert Hart and Tony Honoré argued that the type of philosophical analysis that was central to the school of philosophy known as 'ordinary language philosophy' could shed light on the concept of causation as it is used in tort law and criminal law.[2] Hart and Honoré tried to show, in particular, that a clear and detailed examination of the uses to which we put the concept of causation in ordinary speech would reveal that causal questions are distinct both from questions of policy and from questions of responsibility. Since then, a more modest type of philosophical analysis that grew out of ordinary language philosophy and that many now term 'analytic philosophy' has influenced many areas of the law. The aim of analytic philosophy is still, in part, to clarify the content of our concepts and to make explicit the assumptions and implications of the doctrines that employ them. But unlike ordinary language philosophy, it does not treat certain ways of understanding these concepts as authoritative just because they reflect an allegedly 'ordinary' usage. Rather, it aims to separate out and discuss in some detail the different possible interpretations of a particular concept; to consider the logical implications of each of these interpretations; and, where the context is a legal one, to lay bare the consequences for legal doctrines of adopting one particular interpretation of a concept over another. In order to do this, analytic philosophy looks beyond facts about our language, to facts about what we believe and what we value. Its methods include attempting to separate out and delineate very precisely the different meanings that we might give to a particular legal term; exploring the assumptions or value judgments that might lead us to prefer one interpretation over another; and assessing the different logical implications, for particular doctrines, of adopting one meaning of a given term rather than another.[3] It aims thereby to help us make a more informed choice about which meanings are most appropriate in a particular legal context. Many of the central concepts of tort law have been subjected to such analyses. Torts theorists have reflected, for instance, on different understandings of the objective standard of care in negligence law, and the ways in which these different understandings are supported by different views of interpersonal responsibility; and on what it is to own the consequences of one's actions and whether strict liability offences can be adequately understood and justified simply by combining ideas about ownership of actions with ideas of causation.[4] Likewise, discussions in the law of property and, most recently, the law of intellectual property have drawn on philosophical analyses of what it is to have property in an object and what valuable interests this can serve.[5] Also, our understanding of basic components of the criminal law has been shaped by analyses of the nature of agency and the nature of punishment, as well as consideration of when and why we can justifiably be held responsible for, and justifiably be punished for, expressions of our agency.[6]

In the face of these many legal uses of analytic philosophy, it is striking that the interpretation of constitutional rights has proceeded largely in isolation from it. Courts and constitutional law scholars have certainly engaged in detailed reasoning about the interests and values that underlie constitutional rights. But it is rare to find them using the type of abstract conceptual analysis that is used within analytic philosophy, and rare to find analytic philosophers writing on constitutional law.[7] Of course, many analytic philosophers have discussed the higher-order methodological question of what approach courts ought to follow when interpreting constitutional rights – of whether, for instance, the court's task is to locate the intent of the framers, or to find the interpretation that will best safeguard the process that allows the contemporary public to have their voices heard, or to affirm the answer that best accords with the values that underlie our constitutions or the very ideal of a liberal democracy. But analytic philosophers and their methods have not, in the same way, influenced our interpretation of particular constitutional rights themselves. They have not played a significant role in shaping our understanding of the scope of these rights or the interests they protect.

For instance, although analytic philosophers have engaged in rich debates amongst themselves about what general principles of distributive justice legislatures should adopt in order to treat citizens as equals, they have not similarly engaged with the question of how courts ought to interpret constitutionalized equality rights;[8] nor have courts or scholars concerned with these constitutional questions used detailed conceptual analyses to enquire into the different possible ways of conceptualizing the interests that are protected by principles of equality. Indeed, much of the scholarship on Canada's equality rights has been written from the perspective of a particular disadvantaged group within society, with the goal not of elaborating a general account of equality rights but rather of foregrounding the real needs and concerns of this group and the ways in which our current approach to equality fails to consider them.[9] And the scholarship and case law that does focus specifically on the nature of equality often speaks quite generally of the oppression of disadvantaged groups, stereotyping, prejudice, and loss of dignity, as though all were self-evidently examples of harm to the same interest.[10] It does not clearly explore what exactly this interest might be, whether it is in fact the same interest that is affected by each of these unfair exclusions, and if not, whether the different interests affected are all properly understood as protected by equality rights.[11]

Why is it that these questions about the nature of equality rights have not been probed in detail, either in legal scholarship or in the relevant case law? And why is it that the same seems to be true of other constitutional rights? Is there reason to think that in some or most cases concerning the content and scope of particular constitutional rights, the type of analysis that analytic philosophy offers is not helpful? Is there reason to think, more strongly, that it is not just unhelpful but positively inappropriate for courts to engage in this type of analysis when determining the scope of constitutional rights? In this paper, I shall explore three different sorts of concerns that might draw us towards this conclusion. I shall try to show that none of them offers a legitimate reason for thinking that we should reject the type of philosophical analysis offered to us by analytic philosophy as a means of elucidating the various possible interpretations of a particular constitutional right. (For the sake of brevity, I shall hereafter refer to the type of philosophical analysis employed by analytic philosophy simply as 'philosophical analysis.' I shall do this simply for the sake of brevity; I do not mean to imply that analytic philosophy has a monopoly on philosophical reasoning.)

Before turning to the three concerns, however, I want to address one much simpler objection to the use of philosophical analysis in constitutional argument. One might object that, of course, philosophical analysis is inappropriate as a tool for clarifying the proper extent of a given constitutional right. This is because we cannot determine the scope of a particular right (or, in the Canadian context, cannot ascertain whether an action that violates this right is nevertheless justifiable under section 1 of the *Canadian Charter of Rights and Freedoms*)[12] without engaging in a complex exercise of balancing the interests protected by this right against broader social goals. And surely the question of what the relevant goals are, and of what the right balance is, are political questions. That is to say, they require detailed evidence from the social sciences about the *particular* circumstances that are at issue, not highly abstract conceptual analyses. And they can be settled only by a *decision* about which interests ought to be protected, not by observations about our concepts or observations about abstract values embedded in the *Charter*. Philosophical analysis, then, can appear both to provide the wrong type of information – it is too abstract, not sufficiently focused on the particulars of the case – and to be the wrong type of activity – it only allows us to report on the various interests that we might protect, whereas constitutional rights adjudication requires judges to make a decision about which interests we should protect.[13]

This objection rests on an overly simple picture of philosophical analysis, as well as a contestable view of the nature of adjudication. It is certainly true that we require a great deal of social-science evidence in many cases involving constitutional rights, so that we can learn about the particular social problems that the government action was intended to rectify, and about whether there were alternative actions that would have intruded less on the claimant's rights, and just how much less they would have intruded. But we also need a clear sense of what the protected interests of the claimant involve, how far they require protection, and what their importance is, relative to the importance of the interests underlying the government action. Philosophical analysis can certainly be sufficiently attentive to the particulars of the case to assist us in answering these questions. There is no one level of abstraction or generality that philosophical analysis must operate at: it can incorporate as much detail as is necessary, given the case at hand. Moreover, we need not accept the simple dichotomy presupposed by the objection, between adjudication that involves 'political decisions' and adjudication that simply reveals values embedded in pre-existing law or in the *Charter*. We can acknowledge that judges do make decisions about which interests merit protection and to what extent, when they ask such questions as whether a law's beneficial effects are proportionate to its deleterious effects on the claimant; yet we can at the same time recognize that such decisions are constrained and guided both by the *Charter* and by the values and principles that have been recognized in past case law. We need not think of these decisions as 'political' in the sense that they are pure reflections of the decision maker's personal policy judgment, unconstrained in the same ways that a legislator's judgment can be unconstrained. Rather, they are guided by the principles laid out in past case law, and in the Constitution. And precisely because they are so guided, they are capable of benefiting from the kind of informed, detailed examination of the relevant legal values and principles that philosophical analysis can provide.[14]

I turn now to three more complex views of why, in constitutional argument, philosophical analysis might seem inappropriate.

1. Constitutional Law 'Forces the Issue,' but Philosophical Analysis May Leave It Open

When a rights claimant challenges government action as contrary to her rights, the court is obliged to resolve the issue one way or the other, provided of course that the rights claimant has legal standing to bring a claim. Does the claimant's interest fall into the protected sphere of a certain constitutional right, or not? Was the right violated, or not? These are questions that the court has to answer. Indeed, it has a legal obligation to answer them, and this obligation is arguably an aspect of the rule of law.[15] In some cases, however, philosophical analysis may lead us to the view that neither the claimant's position nor the government's position is stronger than the other. When this occurs, then, to borrow a phrase from the philosopher Bernard Williams, law 'forces the issue' relative to philosophy.[16] The law forces us to come down in favour of one position or the other; but philosophical analysis provides no basis for doing so.

How exactly might such circumstances arise? And do they arise frequently? I shall consider three ways in which they might arise.

Firstly, in some cases, the interest grounding the claimant's constitutional right and the wider social interest promoted by the challenged governmental action seem to be what philosophers call 'incomparable.'[17] When two interests are incomparable, neither is more nor less important then the other. But this is not because they are of equal value. It is because they are incapable of being compared. This means not merely that it is very difficult to compare them, but, more strongly, that they cannot even in principle be weighed or balanced against each other. We can assess whether each, on its own, has value for us, and what sort of value each has. We can even compare each of them separately with other interests. But we cannot compare them with each other.[18]

Consider, as a possible example of such incomparability, the two interests at issue in the case of *Newfoundland (Treasury Board) v. Newfoundland and Labrador Assn. of Public and Private Employees (N.A.P.E.)*.[19] The union claimant in this case alleged that the government had discriminated against female employees and denied them the equal dignity guaranteed by the equality rights in section 15 of the *Charter,* because it decided to defer their pay equity for a further three years. The government, however, faced a serious financial crisis at this time and claimed that the pay equity deferral was simply a justifiable part of a larger program of cutbacks that were necessary to preserve the fiscal health and credibility of the province. The case therefore pitted women's interest in the equal protection of their dignity against the pressing need to maintain a government's fiscal health. From the standpoint of philosophical analysis, we might well conclude that these two interests are incommensurable. A person's interest in being treated with dignity is an interest in having her intrinsic, unconditional, and incomparable worth as a human being respected; and this type of worth is, by definition, incomparable with anything else.[20] How could we then compare it with a fiscal goal, even one as important and urgent as restoring the province's international fiscal credibility?

Although this apparent incomparability does not pose a problem for the Court's section 15 analysis, it does pose a problem at the stage of section 1 analysis. At the stage of section 15 analysis, the Court is not engaged in comparing violations of dignity with any other value or goal, precisely because it is the purpose of this stage of analysis to determine whether a violation of dignity has occurred. So the possible incomparability of dignity with the fiscal goal is not a problem at this stage of the analysis. However, once the Court finds (as it did in this case) that the claimant's dignity has been infringed, the Court seems to face a difficulty in determining whether this violation is justifiable under section 1. For the final branch of the proportionality test of section 1 requires courts to assess whether the salutary effects of the legislation as a whole are proportional to its deleterious effects, and in particular the deleterious effects on the claimant's rights. And this requires just the sort of comparison of interests that, in the case of the two sets of interests at issue in *N.A.P.E.*, it seems impossible to make.

Interestingly, in *N.A.P.E.* the Supreme Court did not attempt such a comparison: it discussed the other branches of the proportionality test in detail, but omitted the fourth stage of the test and simply never engaged in a wholesale comparison of the pressing fiscal goals of the province with the deleterious effects on the claimants' dignity. It may be that this is the correct approach for a court to take in cases of apparent incomparability: courts should simply drop the final branch of the proportionality test in such cases, and assume that as long as the legislation satisfies the other branches of the proportionality test, then it withstands scrutiny and is justifiable as a reasonable limit on the right, under section 1.[21] Alternatively, however, courts might hold that if the fourth branch of section 1 cannot be applied because the interests in question are incomparable, the legislation *cannot* be saved under section 1. This would be a less deferential solution, placing the interests of the claimant above the needs of the government in situations where there is no answer to the question of which is more weighty. What is important for our purposes, however, is that both solutions represent a purely pragmatic compromise, made necessary by the fact that the Court has an obligation to decide the case. For in such cases, it appears that law 'forces the issue' relative to philosophical analysis: the latter seems to tell us that there cannot be a comparison of the interests in question, but courts have an obligation to reach a decision on the case.

The *N.A.P.E.* case has shown us both what it is for interests to be incomparable and one way in which their incomparability can result in legal cases 'forcing the issue' relative to philosophical analysis. When the claimant's interest and the broader social interests served by the challenged legislation are incomparable, then philosophical analysis provides us with no basis on which to answer the final question of the proportionality test under section 1. It leaves us with no basis to determine whether as a whole the legislation does more good than harm. But importantly, there are other respects in which incomparability can affect *Charter* analysis and result in law forcing the issue relative to philosophical analysis. Some rights in the *Canadian Charter* –

and indeed, all rights in the bills of rights of other countries, such as the United States – have a qualification stemming from other constitutional values built directly into them. The rights extend only as far as is compatible with protection of these other constitutional values. Section 7 of the *Canadian Charter*, for instance, which protects 'life, liberty and security of the person,' does so only as far as is consistent with 'principles of fundamental justice.' Section 8 guarantees security from searches and seizures, but only those that are 'unreasonable.' And the equality rights in section 15, likewise, have been interpreted in such a way as to build a qualification into them: they have been read as protecting against *discriminatory* denials of opportunities or benefits, and whether a denial is discriminatory depends in part on the purpose of the denial, and whether it is fair or non-demeaning to deny someone this particular opportunity or benefit in order to achieve that purpose.[22]

To see how the balancing of interests within particular rights can also lead, in cases of incomparability, to the law forcing the issue relative to philosophical analysis, consider the case of *Rodriguez v. British Columbia (A.G.)*, [1993] 3 S.C.R. 519. Sue Rodriguez challenged the prohibition on assisted suicide as being, among other things, a violation of her right to liberty and security of the person under section 7, because it robbed her of control over what would happen to her body while she was alive and robbed her of the ability to implement fundamental personal decisions concerning the last stages of her life. Sopinka J., writing for the majority of the Court, accepted that the law impinged upon her interest in security of the person, but held that in determining whether it was nevertheless justifiable, as being in accordance with 'principles of fundamental justice,' it was appropriate to balance these individual interests against the wider set of interests that the law aimed to protect. Quoting McLachlin J. in *Cunningham v. Canada*, [1993] 2 S.C.R. 143, he insisted: 'The principles of fundamental justice are concerned not only with the interest of the person who claims his liberty has been limited, but with the protection of society. Fundamental justice requires that a fair balance be struck between these interests.'[23] Sopinka J. went on to assert that the social interests involved here – namely, the interests of vulnerable citizens in being protected against potential abuses of assisted suicide, and the interest of society as a whole in preserving the sanctity of life – outweighed Sue Rodriguez's personal interests in having control over her body and control over the end of her life. But philosophical analysis of these interests might lead us to think differently. Can we really compare a person's interest in having control over what happens to her body during her lifetime, an interest which Sopinka J. himself deemed crucial to a person's autonomy, with the equally important but very different interest in protecting vulnerable citizens from medical abuses, an interest that is crucial to their autonomy, but in a very different way? If not, then this is another example of a case in which law forces the issue, relative to philosophical analysis.

We have been considering one type of reason why constitutional law may force the issue relative to philosophical analysis, namely, because some cases involve interests that are incomparable, and yet the law must nevertheless make a decision on whether legislation that impinges on one of these interests in order to protect the other is justifiable. But there are also at least two other, very different reasons why philosophical analysis may not be determinative even though the law forces us to make a decision.

In some cases, there are two legal frameworks or two sets of legal principles that could be used to decide a question of constitutional rights, such as principles of private law, on the one hand, and principles of constitutional law, on the other. Each set of principles covers the field entirely, in the sense that it could, on its own, provide us with sufficient reason to decide the case in favour of one party or the other. In such cases, we may from the standpoint of philosophical analysis have no better reason to choose one set of principles over the other.[24] And yet the court must choose. Consider, for instance, cases in which a striking union has been engaging in secondary picketing; a lower court issues an injunction prohibiting some or all of this picketing on the grounds that it constitutes a nuisance, and this injunction is challenged in an appellate court.[25] The appellate court faces a choice as to how to construe the challenge. Is it best understood within the framework of constitutional law? That is, should the appellate court treat the injunction as an act of one branch of the government, and construe the union's challenge as a constitutional challenge to this government act, on the grounds that it violates the union's constitutional right to picket? Or, alternatively, does private law form the relevant framework for the challenge? If so, the issue is whether the lower court was right on the question of whether nuisance law, when informed by *Charter* values, supports the granting of an injunction in this case. Although the values underlying the right to picket can enter into this latter, private law analysis, it is possible that they will have less force against competing values than they would if the issue were framed as a matter of constitutional rights.[26] It therefore matters which framework a court adopts. But philosophical analysis may not help us settle this question.

There is also a further way in which philosophical analysis may not settle a question for us, even though the law requires that it be settled. Suppose that, unlike the cases we have just considered above, the case before us is clearly amenable only to public law analysis. So it is clear from the outset which set of legal principles we are to use. It is nevertheless true that, in our application of these principles, we can start from any one of a number of very different claims about the purpose of the right in question or the purpose of the challenged government action. Differences in the claims made about these core aspects of the analysis are a quite common cause of dissent within the court, and philosophical analysis may have little to say about how we are to decide between these claims, or at least, how we are to decide between the more fundamental assumptions that underlie them. One case that demonstrates this quite visibly is *Sauvé v. Canada (Chief Electoral Officer)*, [2002] 3 S.C.R. 519, which concerned the constitutionality of provisions that removed the voting rights of prisoners with sentences of two years or more. Both the majority and the dissent agreed that the right to vote exists to ensure that all citizens view legislation as something that they could reasonably consent to. And they agreed that this matters because it matters that citizens' dignity be respected, and it is only citizens who are bound solely by laws that they could reasonably consent to that are treated with dignity. The majority, however, held that citizens can only reasonably consent to legislation when they have had an *actual* opportunity to vote for it. In their view, the purpose of the right to vote was to provide this actual opportunity, and thereby to ensure that citizens were treated with dignity. Hence, it was irrational for the state to attempt to take the vote away from prisoners in the name of promoting responsibility and dignity among citizens. The dissent denied this. They held that a further crucial aspect of treating citizens with dignity is holding them publicly responsible for the consequences of their choices. Hence, they saw the restriction on voting rights as quite consistent with dignified treatment, and with the legislation's avowed purpose of promoting a sense of dignity and responsibility among citizens.

It seems unlikely that philosophical analysis of what is involved in treating citizens with dignity and promoting civic responsibility could help us resolve the dilemma here. It might indeed help clarify the details of each of these two sets of assumptions about what dignity and responsibility require, and by clarifying them, and their implications, it might place us in a more informed position to decide between them. It might even provide reasons for thinking that we should reject certain views completely, as inadequately justified. But it may not be able to settle the question of which basic assumptions we are to start with, that is, which assumptions we are to ground our various claims upon and treat as fundamental posits.

We have now considered a number of cases in which law forces the issue, whereas philosophical analysis is silent. We looked at these cases in the hope of finding a legitimate reason why philosophical analysis might be thought inappropriate in constitutional argument. However, all that these cases have demonstrated is that philosophical analysis often cannot *settle* the legal issue for us. Philosophical analysis is silent on certain questions, and it may be silent on the ultimate soundness of the assumptions from which we begin. But this does not mean that it cannot legitimately be invoked to shed light on the competing interests concerned, or to reveal the extent to which each requires protection, or to clarify the implications of attempting to protect them in one way or another. We have not yet seen any reason to think that it is inappropriate to invoke such analysis at all.

2. When Philosophical Analysis Resolves an Issue, but the Law Should Not Adopt All of that Analysis

In the previous section, we considered several ways in which constitutional law may 'force the issue' relative to philosophical analysis. But what about cases of the reverse type? That is, cases in which philosophical analysis leads us conclusively to a result through certain premises, but courts may wish, in their judgments, not to explicitly invoke some of these premises, or not to spell out the full content of the legal principles that these premises support, or not to narrow the set of basic assumptions that could be used to justify the premises. Such cases, too, might give us reason for thinking that philosophical analysis is sometimes inappropriate in constitutional argument.

Let us first consider cases in which the reasons for not wishing to import all of the elements of a certain philosophical analysis are *pragmatic*. It is possible that in order to secure judicial unanimity (or a majority), an appellate court may decide not to articulate the full extent of a particular legal principle explicitly in the judgment, or it may be silent on the question of which of a number of basic assumptions underlies its arguments about the purpose of a certain right or of the challenged legislation. A certain silence and open-endedness, then, may sometimes be necessary in order to secure judicial support. Moreover, a further pragmatic reason for leaving certain premises or assumptions unsaid might arise in cases involving a doctrine or a legal principle that is still in the early stages of being conceptualized. In such a case, a court might decide not to expound on the various components of the doctrine as fully as it might, on the grounds that if it did so too broadly, this might lead to misconceptions or confusion in the lower courts, while if it did so too narrowly, it might close the door to valuable legal developments in the future. In such circumstances, a pragmatic strategy might be not to attempt to spell out the principle or doctrine beyond a few comments that provide a general, but not overly broad, picture of the doctrine or principle and how it operates in the case at bar.

One example of a case in which the Canadian Supreme Court may have adopted this pragmatic strategy is the *Reference Re: Secession of Quebec,* which concerned whether the Canadian Constitution permitted the unilateral secession of Quebec.[27] The Court decided this case by appealing to what it called the 'fundamental and organizing principles of the constitution.'[28] These principles, the Court said, help to justify, and give a sense of purpose to, the structure of our government, the various provisions of the written constitution, and our constitutional conventions. The Court appealed to four principles, which it described as 'federalism, democracy, constitutionalism and the rule of law, and respect for minority rights' (para. 49). Significantly, the Court claimed that, far from merely aiding in the interpretation of the constitution, these principles could impose significant limits on government action.[29] However, throughout the judgment these principles remained quite generally stated, and capable of a number of different interpretations. Although the Court discussed the history of Canadian federalism, democracy, respect for the rule of law, and respect for minorities in detail, at no point did the Court attempt to pin down exactly what it meant by these principles, or which theory of federalism or democracy or the rule of law it was endorsing. Nor did it specify in detail the argument that takes us from these general concepts to the substantive obligations that they were held to place upon the provincial governments, namely, the obligation not to secede without negotiation, and to negotiate in good faith. And finally, the Court did not go on to discuss the other types of circumstances in which such unwritten principles could successfully be invoked to constrain government action. One way of understanding these silences is as necessary pragmatic elements in judicial decision making: it was much more prudent to limit the discussion of these potentially vast principles, in order at once to limit the risk of misinterpretation and yet not close off opportunities for future legal developments.

Such pragmatic decisions may seem of limited use to us, in our search for whether there is indeed a legitimate basis for excluding philosophical analysis from constitutional argument. For they suggest, not that philosophical analysis is unhelpful or illegitimate in reasoning about constitutional law, but simply that the results of philosophical analysis should sometimes not ultimately be spelled out in the judgment itself, for pragmatic reasons.

There are also, however, at least two deep *theoretical* reasons for thinking that certain elements of philosophical analysis are inappropriate in cases involving constitutional rights. Firstly, our constitutional rights are not simply a collection of independent rights. They are intended to form a coherent whole, as the basis for a liberal democracy. And as such, the full content and extent of any given constitutional right could never, even in principle, be spelled out in isolation from consideration of each of the other rights, and from the various circumstances in which each of the rights may be claimed. So, insofar as philosophical analysis purports to look at particular rights individually, in isolation from others, and in light only of a certain limited set of circumstances, it cannot provide a sufficient description of the right. It will certainly tell us something about the right in question – about the interests it protects, and the implications of protecting them in certain ways. But we cannot simply import into legal analysis all of the details of the picture of the right that this philosophical analysis has given us.

The second theoretical reason for thinking that not all aspects of a philosophical analysis of a particular constitutional right can legitimately be incorporated into legal argument arises from a certain ideal of legal legitimacy. According to the view of legal legitimacy defended by John Rawls and broadly accepted by political theorists, constitutional essentials such as a given set of constitutional rights are legitimate only if is possible for each citizen to endorse them, and see them as fully justified, from within his or her own set of basic personal convictions (or, as Rawls terms it, his or her own 'comprehensive doctrine,' which includes an individual's fundamental beliefs about what makes life valuable and how it should be lived).[30] Of course, these convictions must themselves be consistent with the ideal of respect for others' dignity and equal treatment of others. But assuming that a person's set of basic convictions meets this condition, it must be possible for her to accept them and also consistently accept her country's set of constitutional rights, indeed, even to use these convictions as a basis for justifying these constitutional rights. Although Rawls was not himself concerned with drawing out the implications of this view for adjudication, it seems to have at least one significant implication. It suggests that when a judge discusses the content or extent of a particular constitutional right, he should limit himself to stating those assumptions and premises that can be endorsed from a variety of 'comprehensive doctrines,' even if philosophical analysis suggests that there are certain further assumptions or implications that form a part of the argument, ones that would not necessarily be acceptable to all reasonable citizens from their own personal perspectives.

We have now located two sound theoretical reasons for thinking that some elements of philosophical analysis may be inappropriate in constitutional argument. However, these reasons do not support the wholesale exclusion of philosophical analysis from constitutional argument. All they suggest is that we must be cautious in importing certain assumptions or premises from the philosophical analysis into legal argument. They do not imply that such analysis can never serve a legitimate clarificatory function.

There is, however, a further concern with importing philosophical analysis into the analysis of constitutional rights. It is rooted in a somewhat different conception of legitimacy than that discussed above, which, if correct, may imply that philosophical analysis *is* simply inappropriate, in constitutional argument. I turn to this concern in the next section.

3. Worries over the Legitimacy of Judicial Review of Legislation

Many of us harbour concerns about the legitimacy of judges striking down legislation on the basis of a philosophical account of a certain constitutional right, or an account that depends crucially on certain philosophical distinctions. Candidates for American judicial positions commonly avow that they will not strike down legislation like 'philosopher-kings,' or that, as Learned Hand famously wrote, it would be unacceptable for society 'to be ruled by a bevy of Platonic guardians.'[31] But what does this mean, exactly, and why do we have this concern?

The concern seems to stem from a more general worry about the legitimacy of judicial review of legislation. In constitutional rights adjudication, the issue of how unelected judges can issue decisions that legitimately bind us seems to present itself with particular urgency, in a way that it does not in other areas of judge-made law, for instance, tort law, or contract law. This is partly, of course, because although unelected judges do determine our rights and obligations in these other areas of law, the legislature can always enact a law to change the common law; and if it does, judicial decision making cannot trump this legislation. So if a judge were to delineate our rights and obligations in these other areas of law in a manner that the public deemed unjust, then it would, at least in theory, be possible for the legislature to rectify the matter, and no judge would have the authority to dispute this. By contrast, the *Canadian Charter of Rights and Freedoms* gives judges the power to strike down legislation; so when it is a matter of constitutional rights litigation, the principles laid down by unelected judges can trump those decided upon by the legislature. The subject matter of constitutional rights litigation also contributes to the urgency with which the problem of legitimacy is raised. Although tort law and contract law make use of state power, their subject matter is the private rights of citizens as against each other; so what judges are deciding, when they interpret these areas of the law, is first and foremost the limits of citizens' powers over each other, and only in an indirect way the limits of the state's power over the individual. Constitutional rights, however, directly concern the permissible exercises of the state's coercive force over the individual; indeed, the question of how far a given constitutional right extends is just the question of whether the state can legitimately exercise coercive force over individuals to do x or y, or to prevent them from receiving x or y. Because questions of constitutional rights directly determine the limits of the state's coercive power over the individual, it is particularly important to ensure that these decisions are made in a manner that is legitimate. Hence the question that preoccupies so many theorists: how is it that unelected judges can legitimately decide such questions? And is there a certain method they might use, which might confer legitimacy on their decisions? If there is, then it may seem that it cannot be one that involves appealing to philosophical analysis. But why is this? There are, I believe, two quite separate concerns that might lead us to think so.

The first is that if judges simply looked to philosophical accounts of such concepts as equal treatment, or freedom of religion, or freedom of speech, they might end up appealing to ideas that were not sufficiently rooted in the constitutional text or case law history, and that therefore did not accurately reflect the context in which the right was to be interpreted. Worse still, judges might simply use the opportunity to invoke philosophical analysis as an invitation to import their personal moral views into their judgments.[32]

While this is a valid concern, it is a concern with the abuse of philosophical analysis in constitutional argument, not a concern with the proper use of it. It is possible to invoke philosophical analysis in a manner that is sensitive to the details of the text and to the particular features of the context in which the particular right is invoked. And it is possible to separate the question of which values are appropriate in the interpretation of a legal right from the question of which values one believes should be promoted, as a matter of interpersonal moral interaction. This first concern, therefore, does not show that philosophical analysis would necessarily present a problem for the legitimacy of legal decisions employing it.

The second concern, however, might. One might hold, as Jeremy Waldron has argued, that the only way in which judges can legitimately decide constitutional rights cases is by giving some independent weight to the views of the legislature on interpretive questions, even if these views are not in accordance with what the judges deem to be the correct conceptual analysis of the rights in question.[33] In Waldron's view, judges cannot decide constitutional cases as though they were simply interpreting the text and the values underlying the Constitution, on their own. They must, in their interpretation, give some authority to the legislature's various interpretations of the constitutional right at issue, as evidenced through the challenged legislation and related pieces of legislation. Judges need not treat the legislature's view as fully authoritative, otherwise they could not ever strike down legislation. But they must give some weight to it, even if it conflicts with what appears to be the most relevant philosophical analysis of the interests in question.

One difficulty with this proposal is that it is unclear that it is always possible for judges to give some weight to a legislature's interpretation of a particular right, without simply deferring to the legislature's interpretation. This is because it is not always possible to weigh and balance different interpretations in such a way that the resulting interpretation reflects some of the principles foregrounded by each of them. In some cases, interpretations may simply clash: the judiciary may believe that the most plausible interpretation of a right, the one that best accords with the text or with the values underlying the Constitution, is one that is inconsistent with the legislature's interpretation. How, in such a case, are they to give 'some' weight to the legislature's interpretation, short of completely deferring to it? If I am right that this is a problem, then this proposal may collapse into a directive to defer to the legislature, at which point it is no longer a theory of legitimate judicial review, but rather the claim that there can be no such thing.

A more important problem, however, is that this proposal rests on a highly controversial conception of legitimacy. It assumes that the judiciary can legitimately strike down legislation only if it does so for reasons that have (at least in part) been endorsed by a democratically elected legislature. In other words, a legal body can issue binding directives only if it acts on views that the people themselves endorse. This is a rather literal understanding of 'democracy.' But there are others, notably the conception of democracy that has been defended by Ronald Dworkin.[34] On Dworkin's view, what makes any kind of state action democratic is not the literal fact of its having been endorsed by the people, but rather the fact that it respects the values that we aim to preserve by having a democracy, the values that form the very purpose of our erecting democratic institutions, such as respect for all citizens' equality, a desire to ensure that all have certain specific liberties, and so on. As long as judicial decisions accord with, and attempt to protect, these values, then they are sufficiently 'democratic' to be legitimate, regardless of whether they actually accord with the views of the legislature.

I cannot, in this space, attempt to defend this value-based conception of democracy and democratic legitimacy over the more literal approach sketched earlier. But it suffices, for our purposes, to note that it poses a viable alternative to the literal approach, and also that it seems to make better sense of the purposes for which we have democratic institutions. If we adopt the value-based conception of democratic legitimacy, then we will not conclude that judicial decisions in constitutional rights cases are illegitimate if they appeal to philosophical analyses of the rights in question and give no weight to the views of the legislature on matters of interpretation. As long as the courts' analyses accord with the values that underlie our democratic institutions, they will have democratic legitimacy.

I have now explored a number of concerns that might lead us to think that philosophical analysis has no place in legal argument over constitutional rights. I have tried to show that all of these concerns can be adequately addressed. Whether philosophical analysis will ultimately prove helpful to us, of course, can only be demonstrated in practice, through its application to particular constitutional rights. But it is time that more theorists and judges began to consider invoking it. For it might give us increased clarity concerning the full extent of the interests that our rights could protect and, in the process, the ability to extend constitutional protection to those who seem unfairly to fall through the cracks of our current tests for the violation of particular constitutional rights.

NOTES

1 I am grateful to Logan Atkinson, Diana Majury, Arthur Ripstein, Lorraine Weinrib, and the participants in the October 2005 Symposium on Law, Culture and the Humanities at Carleton University for helpful comments on earlier versions of the paper.

2 H.L.A. Hart and Tony Honoré, *Causation in the Law* (Oxford: Clarendon Press, 1959).

3 This is not offered as an exhaustive list of techniques used within analytic philosophy. It is simply a list of certain common techniques that I believe most analytic philosophers would acknowledge as part of their method of analysis. Because the nature and ultimate purpose of analytic philosophy is itself the subject of considerable philosophical disagreement, I shall not attempt here to offer a single comprehensive definition of philosophical analysis and its methods. Instead, I have pointed to several relatively uncontroversial aims and features; and I hope that this brief general description, along with the specific examples discussed throughout the paper, will give readers a sufficient sense of the discipline. It is also worth mentioning that I am not claiming here (nor do the arguments of my paper presuppose) that these methods of analysis are *exclusive* to philosophy. It is generally true, I think, that philosophy encourages us to pursue conceptual clarification and the elucidation of assumptions and logical relations between claims in more detail than do other disciplines;

but many other disciplines also draw on such methods, and my arguments do not deny this.

4 See, for example, Ernest Weinrib, *The Idea of Private Law* (Cambridge, MA: Harvard University Press, 1995); Arthur Ripstein, *Equality, Responsibility and the Law* (Cambridge: Cambridge University Press, 1999); John Gardner, 'Wrongs and Faults,' in *Appraising Strict Liability*, ed. A.P. Simester, 51 (Oxford: Oxford University Press, 2005); Stephen Perry, 'The Impossibility of General Strict Liability' (1988) 1 Can.J.L.&Juris. 147; Stephen Perry 'Responsibility for Outcomes, Risk, and the Law of Torts,' in *Philosophy and the Law of Torts*, 72, ed. Gerald Postema. Cambridge: Cambridge University Press, 2001); Mayo Moran, *Rethinking the Reasonable Person* (Oxford: Oxford University Press, 2003).

5 For instance, Jeremy Waldron, *The Right to Private Property*; Margaret Jane Radin, *Reinterpreting Property* (Chicago: University of Chicago Press, 1993); Mark Rose, *Authors and Owners: The Invention of Copyright* (Cambridge, MA: Harvard University Press, 1993); Mark Rose, 'The Author as Proprietor: Donaldson v. Becket and the Genealogy of Modern Authorship' in *Of Authors and Origins: Essays on Copyright Law*, ed. Brad Sherman and Alain Strowell (Oxford: Clarendon Press, 1994), 23; Justin Hughes, 'The Philosophy of Intellectual Property' (1988) 77 Georgetown L.J. 287; Alfred C. Yen, 'Restoring the Natural Law: Copyright as Labor and Possession' (1990) 51 Ohio State L.J. 517; Alfred C. Yen, 'The Interdisciplinary Future of Copyright Theory,' in *The Construction of Authorship: Textual Appropriation in Law and Literature*, ed. Martha Woodmansee and Peter Jaszi (Durham, NC: Duke University Press, 1994) 159; and Wendy Gordon, 'A Property Right in Self-Expression: Equality and Individualism in the Natural Law of Intellectual Property' (1993) 102 Yale L.J. 1533.

6 See George Fletcher, *Rethinking Criminal Law* (Boston: Little, Brown, 1979); Alan Brudner, 'Agency and Welfare in the Penal Law,' in *Action and Value in Criminal Law*, ed. S. Shute, J. Gardner and J. Horder (Oxford: Clarendon Press, 1993), 21; Alan Brudner, 'Owning Outcomes: On Intervening Causes, Thin Skulls, and Fault-Undifferentiated Crimes' (1998) 11 Can.J.L.&Juris. 89; John Gardner, 'The Gist of Excuses,' (1997) Buffalo Criminal L.J. 1, 575.

7 I wish to emphasize here that I am not denying that many other types of reasoning, or other types of philosophy, are often used in the interpretation of constitutional rights. Seminal work has been done on constitutional rights, for instance, by feminist scholars such as Drucilla Cornell, Patricia Williams, Frances Olsen, Carol Smart, Katherine O'Donovan, Anne Phillips, and Nicola Lacey, many of whose writings can broadly be

termed 'philosophical.' My concern is with the absence of the particular kind of philosophical analysis that is known as 'analytic philosophy.'

8 For examples of philosophical writings on equality that are concerned with what it is for legislatures to treat individuals as equals, see Elizabeth S. Anderson, 'What Is the Point of Equality?' (1999) 109 Ethics 287; Richard J. Arneson, 'Equality and Equal Opportunity for Welfare' (1989) 56 Phil.Stud. 77; Arneson, 'Equality of Opportunity Defended and Recanted' (1999) 7. J.Pol.Phil. 488; G.A. Cohen, 'On the Currency of Egalitarian Justice' (1989) 99 Ethics 906; Ronald Dworkin, *Sovereign Virtue: The Theory and Practice of Equality* (Cambridge, MA: Harvard University Press, 2000); Ronald Dworkin, 'Sovereign Virtue Revisited' (2002) 113 Ethics 55; Thomas Nagel, *Equality and Partiality* (New York: Oxford University Press, 1991); Thomas M. Scanlon, 'The Diversity of Objections to Inequality' (Lindley Lecture, University of Kansas, 22 February 1996) (Lawrence: Department of Philosophy, University of Kansas, 1997); Amartya Sen, *Inequality Reexamined* (Cambridge, MA: Harvard University Press, 1992).

9 For some prominent examples, see D. Majury, 'Equality and Discrimination according to the Supreme Court of Canada' (1990–1) 4 C.J.W.L. 407; C. Stychin, 'Essential Rights and Contested Identities: Sexual Orientation and Equality Rights Jurisprudence in Canada' (1995) 8 Can.J.L.&Juris. 49; D. Lepofsky, 'A Report Card on the Charter's Guarantee of Equality to Persons with Disabilities After 10 Years – What Progress? What Prospects?' (1997) 7 Natl.J.Const.L. 263.

10 A classic example is the description of the purpose of equality rights in *Law v. Canada* [1999] 1 S.C.R. 497. Iacobucci J. endorsed MacIntyre J.'s earlier claim that equality rights were 'a guarantee against the evil of oppression,' and then went on to assert that these rights aimed 'to prevent the violation of essential human dignity and freedom through the imposition of disadvantage, stereotyping, or political or social prejudice' (paras 42 and 51, respectively). And he defined human dignity as 'personal autonomy and self-determination ... physical and psychological integrity and empowerment.' This general characterisation melds together a vast array of possible understandings of the interests protected by equality rights, as did the test for violations of equality rights that Iacobucci J. went on to propose.

11 However, for academic literature that does try to probe these questions using philosophical analysis, see Denise Reaume, 'Discrimination and Dignity' (2003) 63 Louisiana Law Revew; and my own attempt to apply philosophical analysis to equality rights in 'The Wrongs of Unequal Treatment' (2004) 54 U.T.L.J. 291.

12 See the *Canadian Charter of Rights and Freedoms,* Part I of the *Constitution Act*, 1982, being Schedule B to the Canada Act 1982 (UK), 1982, c.11, s.1.

13 The view of judicial decision-making that underlies this objection is put forward by, among others, Hutchinson and Monahan in 'Democracy and the Rule of Law,' in *The Rule of Law: Ideal or Ideology* (Oxford: Carswell, 1987) at 121. Hutchinson and Monahan of course regard it as problematic that judges must make such political decisions when engaging in constitutional adjudication; indeed, they view judicial review with suspicion precisely because they believe that it forces judges to make political decisions, even though judges cannot legitimately speak for the people. However, they believe that this is the only accurate way of conceptualizing what judges must do when they engage in judicial review. For an alternative conception of judicial decision making, see my response to the objection, as well as the literature cited in note 13.

14 For a detailed defence of this understanding of judicial decision making, see Ronald Dworkin, *Freedom's Law: The Moral Reading of the American Constitution* (Cambridge, MA: Harvard University Press, 1996), and *Law's Empire* (Cambridge, MA: Harvard University Press, 1986).

15 See Timothy Endicott, 'The Impossibility of the Rule of Law,' (1999) 19 O.J.L.S. 1 at 14; and Aileen Kavanagh, 'The Elusive Divide between Interpretation and Legislation Under the Human Rights Act 1998' (2004) 24 O.J.L.S. 259, at 265.

16 Bernard Williams, 'What Has Philosophy to Learn from Tort Law?' in *Philosophical Foundations of Tort Law*, ed. David G. Owen (Oxford: Clarendon Press, 1995) 487 at 490.

17 For helpful philosophical accounts of incomparability, see Joseph Raz, *The Morality of Freedom* (Oxford: Clarendon Press, 1986), ch. 13; Bernard Williams, 'Conflict of Values,' in *Moral Luck* (Cambridge: Cambridge University Press, 1981), 79–80; and Ruth Chang's introduction to *Incommensurability, Incomparability and Practical Reason* (Cambridge, MA: Harvard University Press, 1997). Some philosophers, including Raz and Williams, use the term 'incommensurability' to mean what I have called 'incomparability.' However, because there is some controversy among philosophers as to whether incommensurability really is equivalent to incomparability (for a persuasive argument on this point, see Chang's introduction), I have framed my discussion in terms of 'incomparability.'

18 The aforegoing remarks are offered only as an explanation of what incomparability is, not as a defence of the claim that there are indeed incomparable values. I hope that the case examples I go on to discuss provide plausible candidates for incomparable values, if such exist; but it

is not my aim here to defend the claim that they do exist. Those who think they do not exist will obviously hold that the alleged presence of incomparable values is not a good reason for thinking that philosophical analysis is inadequate; but I hope to show, more strongly, that *even if* we assume that some values are incomparable, this is *still* not a good reason for thinking that philosophical analysis has no place in such discussions.

19 [2004] 3 S.C.R. 381.

20 See Immanuel Kant, *Groundwork for the Metaphysics of Morals,* trans. James W. Ellington (Indianapolis: Hackett, 1993), at s. II, 436.

21 Interestingly, it is quite often the case, in Canadian Charter litigation, that courts simply overlook the final branch of the proportionality test. They hold legislation to be justifiable as long as the purpose is pressing and substantial, the means rationally connected to the broader social interests that the legislation aims to promote, and the means impairing the right no more than is reasonably necessary. It may be that the fourth branch of the proportionality test has dropped out simply because courts have become increasingly deferential. But it might also be the case that it has been eliminated precisely because there are many cases in which the competing interests seem to courts to be incomparable, and hence the kind of comparison required by this fourth branch of the test simply cannot, in the courts' view, often be performed.

22 Though note that the two goods being compared in the case of s.15 internal balancing are (i) the wider purpose of the legislation and (ii) the good whose denial allegedy amounts to a failure to respect dignity, such as equal pay, or access to marriage. So the issue with respect to s.15 analysis is not the same as the one that we dealt with above in the NAPE case, concerning the impossibility of ever comparing denials of dignity with other social goals. That is not the issue here, because at the stage of s.15 analysis, it has not yet been established whether there was a denial of dignity in the first place. If an issue of incommensurability arises in s.15 analysis, then, it must be because the *other* goods are incommensurable – e.g., J's receiving equal pay vs. preserving the province's fiscal health, or L's being able to marry vs. preserving the traditional institution of marriage.

23 For discussion of the courts' increasing use of balancing in s.7 and incorporation into s.7 of the very types of balancing normally undertaken in s.1, see T. Singleton, 'The Principles of Fundamental Justice, Societal Interests and Section 1 of the Charter' (1995) 74 Can. Bar. Rev. 446; S. Wexler and C. Jones, 'The Charter's Burdens: The Return to the "Presumption of Validity" in Section 7 of the Canadian Charter of Rights and

Freedoms' (1999) 10 Const. Forum 31. See also *Suresh v.Canada (Minister of Citizenship and Immigration)*, [2002] 1 S.C.R. 3, at 32, where the Supreme Court explicitly states that s.7 analysis involves a 'proportionality' test.

24 Although this of course depends on one's theory of the relationship between private and public law.

25 See, for instance, *R.W.D.S.U., Local 558 v. Pepsi-Cola Canada*, [2002] 1 S.C.R. 156.

26 This is arguably what occurred in the Supreme Court's judgment in *Pepsi-Cola, ibid*. Here, the Court assumed without argument that the correct way to frame the issue was as a matter of private law. And it concluded that secondary picketing is generally lawful unless it involves 'tortious or criminal conduct.' Because this formulation provides no detailed guidance as to when picketing becomes tortious, it has the potential to be read in an extremely narrow way.

27 [1998] 2 S.C.R. 217 at para 32. What follows is speculation only, for the purposes of illustrating the type of case that I have in mind; I make no claim to be presenting the actual motives of the Court on this occasion.

28 For other cases in which the Supreme Court has relied extensively on unwritten constitutional principles, see *Reference re Remuneration of Judges of the Provincial Court of Prince Edward Island*, [1997] 3 S.C.R. 3; and *Reference re Manitoba Language Rights*, [1985] 1 S.C.R. 721. For discussion of the Court's approach to these principles, see D. Gibson, 'Constitutional Vibes: Reflections on the Secession Reference and the Unwritten Constitution' (1999) 11 Nat'l J.Const.L. 49; Jean Leclair, 'Canada's Unfathomable Unwritten Constitutional Principles' (2002) Queen's L.J. 389.

29 Though interestingly, the Court suggested that these limits are not judicially enforceable, and that should the obligations to which these principles give rise (e.g., Quebec's obligation not to secede prior to negotiation, and the other provinces' obligations to negotiate in good faith) be violated, the sanctions would be left to the electorate, and to the international community. See para. 102.

30 See *A Theory of Justice* (Cambridge, MA: Harvard University Press, 1971); *Political Liberalism* (New York: Columbia University Press, 1993); and *Collected Papers* (Cambridge, MA: Harvard University Press, 1999).

31 Learned Hand, 'The Bill of Rights,' Holmes Lectures delivered at Harvard University, 1958, at 70.

32 This worry – both about judges appealing to independent ideas and about judges invoking their personal moral beliefs – seems to be what prompts politicians and judges alike to warn against turning the judiciary into 'philosopher-kings.' In the public mind, at least, philosophers

seem to be perceived as people who appeal to independent, idiosyncratic ideas; hence, to think of a judge as a philosopher-king is to think of him as someone who invokes his own independent idea of justice instead of the letter of the law. See, for instance, a speech from the High Court of Australia in 2001, in which the Court emphasizes that judges are not 'free to act as philosopher-king bound by no principle except the dictates of his or her individual (and perhaps idiosyncratic) sense of justice' (Reply to the Honourable Ruth Bader Ginsburg, 'Remarks on Judicial Independence: The Situation of the U.S. Federal Judiciary,' Melbourne, 1 February 2001).

33 Jeremy Waldron, *Law and Disagreement* (Oxford: Oxford University Press, 2001). Christopher Manfredi has also defended such a view in the Canadian context: see 'Judicial Power and the Charter: Reflections on the Activism Debate,' (2004) 53 U.N.B. L.J. 185 and 'The Life of a Metaphor: Dialogue in the Supreme Court, 1998–2003,' (2004) 23 Sup.Ct. L.Rev. (2d) 105.

34 See particularly *Freedom's Law: The Moral Reading of the Constitution* (Cambridge, MA: Harvard University Press, 1996), and also *Law's Empire* (Cambridge, MA: Harvard University Press, 1986).

4 Nature: From Philosophy of Science to Legal Theory ... and Back?

ALAIN PAPAUX[1]

Opening: Intimacy between Law and Science and Cross-Feeding

It all started on the banks of the Nile. Measuring the land, delimiting plots whose boundaries had been washed out by the floods of the Nile, such was the work of applied geometry carried out by land surveyors known as harpedonaptes (official geometricians of sorts at the service of Pharaoh). In so doing, they 'de-termined' (in the proper sense of setting a *term*, an end, a boundary) property and thereby established everyone's rights by distributing and alloting them (according to 'distributive justice') to each. The scientist (at the time) and the jurist-scribe-geometrician thus combined in a single individual.

This intimacy between law and science continued in the Greek cities. From the rhetor-jurist's judicial 'case' (*causa*) to the scientist's 'causality' to the 'evidence,' that is, the universally recognized means of making a fact 'relevant' for a given argument; these borrowed notions flowed *from* law to science. The intimacy, however, began to wane and the distance between them to increase as scientific activity drew attention out of the city, all of nature in fact being found outside of the city, 'beyond the walls.' Through his very activity, the scientist became a misfit, and besides his exclusion was a matter for *trial* – Galileo's trial was by no means *exceptional* in the history of science, but rather *exemplary*, for us modern and contemporary people. It made explicit the autonomy of the individual with respect to the institution using familiar and hence overdetermined means.

We shall therefore begin the following journey with what is most immediately known to us, that is, modern thought and its dualisms claiming to separate in absolute terms Object from Subject, objectivity from value judgment, fact from opinion, the natural sciences from the humanities. Yet the humanities were never guaranteed to be *sciences* and natural sciences are no longer entirely sure to be safe from subjectivity or value judgments, and are thus exposed to the possibility of a certain dialogue with 'culture' (a less academic term for 'humanities').

This possibility for a (rekindled?) collaboration between the natural sciences and the humanities becomes even a necessity under the pressure of environmental questions that have in a sense cancelled the distance that Modernity had attempted to wedge between nature and culture. By polluting nature, we pollute ourselves; Object and Subject blend together. That is why the present outline of the mutual influence of the philosophy of science and legal theory will be carried out with reference to the environment in each of the two parts of this paper.

First (Part 1) we will ask ourselves what became of nature in modern thought, which has primarily evolved out of science after it rendered nature homogeneous and mathematically expressible. Modern thought *analysed* nature in terms of force (efficient causality), as illustrated by the *law* of gravity, that is, in terms of power or *potestas*. It analysed nature in a unique and 'mono-logical' way. And as mankind gradually became more powerful than silent nature, it overtook it. Jurists copied this model by 'translating' *potestas* into powers, and hence rights, which may be *deduced* from a few principles (laws), thus ensuring definite and predictable conclusions, following the example of scientists.[2]

Dualisms dominate this period, notably by separating Objects from Subjects into absolute and irreductible poles of reality. While theoretical philosophy (natural sciences) and practical philosophy (social sciences) are separate, the latter attempts to borrow from the former its methods and ways of reasoning – a mimetic enterprise called 'positivism.' But nature, by means of the environment, ends up proving the artificiality of these dichotomies (part 2). Pollution forces people (Subjects) to realize that the natural milieu (Objects) is very closely connected to them, through a symbiotic *relationship*.

Part 2 addresses the thinking behind this relationship or relational philosophy. Contemporary sciences have relativized the separation Object/Subject. They are now aware that nature (Object) must be *provoked* in order to be known, and that this requires the mediation of a Subject and his instruments. Moreover, scientists know that their theories are merely hypotheses and that their results are uncertain in light of, notably, excess complexity. The intellectual activity of *interpretation* thus takes hold in science. The distance between Object and Subject, so distinctive of Modernity, shrinks. Collaboration between the natural sciences and the social sciences seems once again possible.

Contemporary legal epistemology is undoubtedly ready to vehemently reject dualisms, the most emblematic of which is law versus application. Jurisdiction (i.e., the activity of saying the law) does not boil down to a calculation or a syllogism, but operates through the mediation of a Subject, typically a judge, who makes the law speak *on account of* a case, and *interprets* it *thanks to* and *within* this case.

The common matrix of interpretation, necessary in the face of uncertainty, gets its most manifest and most shared relevance from the precautionary principle. Nature and culture – singularly western and highly polluting – cooperate so that the earth may remain *inhabitable*, so that it may be the habitat, namely, that viable and indispensable part of nature that a culture needs in order to develop. Law becomes (again) a *measure* in the face of immoderation, *delimitation* in the face of technological unlimitedness, in other words, a type of law whose conception is based on the 'relationship to,' the 'measure of.' By bringing to the foreground and updating the ancient notion of prudence (another word for 'precaution'), namely, a judgment or decision made in a situation of uncertainty, legal epistemology presents the hard sciences with ways to overcome dualisms yet without submitting to the arbitrariness of subjectivity too quickly reduced to irrationality, and offers them the possibility of rediscovering their own origins. The term 'science' comes from the Latin *scire* – to slice, to split, to decide, and even to decree!

Let us go back to modern times and their humanism, which through the Renaissance, and subsequently the Enlightenment, asserted the increasing autonomy of the individual with respect to institutions. The effect of such autonomy was notably a change of the status of nature within the framework of science. Nature was no longer studied as a *creation* of an omnipotent god, but in and for itself, as having its own value.

Such a change did not occur abruptly, as a result of one person or one discovery, as T. Kuhn has demonstrated. All 'revolutions' arise out of the thickness of time. Perhaps this is due to the fact that we are never dealing with pure realities or intrinsically *homogeneous* data. If this were the case, then we would observe radical departures from, and the immediate discarding of, an entire theoretical corpus in favour of a new body of principles and hypotheses – ones that are often not ready and not even conceived when the 'crucial experiment' comes to open a new paradigm. The existence of resistance, the production of ad hoc hypotheses to 'save' a theory on the way to falsification, and more simply the rivalry between various schools or scientific models are evidence of the extent to which subjectivity and tradition press on so-called objective science. Contemporary epistemology has established on the one hand that facts are *developed* and built, and on the other that theories are always only models, hence generalizations, and that they must, according to Popper, allow for their invalidation by a competing theory, lest they operate as an ideology. In short, reality as apprehended by science is a mix of objectivity and subjectivity, a blend of Object and Subject, both of which collaborate in the *act* of cognition (see part 2): all we ever know are hybrids.

Although *contemporary* science is clearly aware that it is operating with mixes – nature is no longer 'simply' observed but provoked by means of instruments (i.e., 'artifices' or artefacts) – *modern* science, as conceived since Galileo, was thought of as being *pure*, unmixed, perfectly objective, safe from any mediation by the Subject. This is evidenced by Galileo's motto recorded in 1623 in the *Saggiatore*: 'Nature is written in mathematical language.' The metaphor of the 'Great Book of Nature' is much owed to the Christian religion within which Galileo was raised and lived. In fact, medieval sciences examined natural phenomena to the extent that they bore witness to the work of the Creator; nature was thought of as a book written by His hand. Far from pure science, cut off from any cultural (and hence religious) influence, we discover a Galileo protected by powerful noblemen and benefiting from the clergy's very high-level protection, including that of the Pope, for a great portion of his career. Science and politics are thus not impervious to each other, which is yet another example of hybridity.[3]

Thus, even if the question of nature was henceforth posed in and for itself, which amounted to affirming the autonomy of *human* thought against the dependence of God's *creature*, there is no head-on opposition, as Popper subtly noted with respect to the position of the Church, but rather a power struggle. That a theory of the daily movement of the sun contradicted a passage in the Old Testament (Joshua 10:12ff.) was by no means conclusive in the eyes of the Church; it was rather that the interpretation produced by the 'free thinkers' (should they prove successful) would lead to the decline of the faith and of the authority of religion. Indeed, the thinkers saw in the success of science a proof of the human capacity to discover the secrets of the world without the help of divine revelation.

This dose of autonomy with respect to the divine enabled Galileo to assert a logic specific to science and free of any cultural influence and of any mediation by subjectivity. This logic was summed up in a so-called resolutive-compositive approach, which was illustrated by the discovery of the law of falling bodies. On the one hand, the *decomposition* or *resolution* of a phenomenon, such as *movement* or *fall of objects* in its simplest phases, allows us to determine the relations that underlie it (e.g., speed, space, time, etc.). On the other, the *constitution* or *composition* of the observed phenomenon allows us to formulate the *principle* or *law* that governs it, the mathematical expression of its *constitutive relations*.

Yet this approach is not pure in reality. It *mixes* or *combines* the data of observation and experimentation with their mathematical measurement in order to formulate laws that govern the observed phenomena. We are therefore dealing with a mixture of induction (i.e., a bottom-up, pragmatic, rather Aristotelian approach) and deduction (i.e., a top-down, idealist, rather Platonic approach, which is itself also characterized by the prevalence of mathematics, which notably underpin the quest for universal laws).

Natural phenomena are so mixed, so heterogeneous ('hetero-genēs,' i.e., involving different kinds), that by confining himself to one unique point of view on his object, Galileo found it very difficult to account for them using a single pure and homogeneous model: 'Simultaneously acquiring theoretical and practical mathematics, in the tradition of Archimedes and Aristotle's qualitative physics, initiates him to what later becomes the fundamental dilemma of his world system: A vast organism driven by anthropomorphic qualities, or a rigorously mathematically-structured machine?'[4] He did not attempt to develop an epistemology of mixture.

It is indeed difficult to think about mixture or hybridity, given how seductive the univocal conception of reality appears to be. It is as though the latter responds to a quasi-natural inclination towards a closed, simple, and thereby *controllable* world. However: 'There is great danger, though, in taking this unity of a supreme intelligence as being already fulfilled and, through a dire reversal, to yield to lazy reason [...] which leads us to take the final perfection for the real foundation of reality.'[5] Thus are overturned a priori systems of thought, namely, those which posit their Ideas irrespective of any experience (hence top-down), in the manner of Cartesian idealism. This overturning is of utmost importance to the civil lawyer, whose dominant philosophy is taken to emulate the methodological approaches of natural sciences, which are conceived as pure and certain, a mimicry that appears increasingly artificial: 'Moreover, [...] many problems in legal theory and legal practice are linked to the underlying philosophical concepts of rationality in these theories and practices. The logico-deductive approach of Cartesian thinking in continental European legal theory and practice over the last two centuries has recently been more and more under attack from several sides. As an alternative, argumentation and discourse theories have been developed in legal theory.'[6]

As such, it is necessary to bear in mind the Cartesian conception of science in order to understand modern legalism, which is meant to be the imitation by jurists of the methodological approach of sciences thought of as pure (part 1). We will then be able to make apparent (part 2) the overturnings of the legalistic model that were brought about by the emergence of the problem of the environment in law that is, nature that is neither truly a Subject (of law) nor merely an Object any longer, but a *mix* of both. We shall see that law has always operated with hybrids and that, from the start, many of its figures, who have been revitalized thanks to environmental law, could bring some light to contemporary hard sciences, which are in fact facing Subjet-Object hybrids, culture-nature mixes, and questions of mixture with which they are hardly familiar.

At first blush, based on the writings of the authors cited, this thesis is consistent with European philosophical and judicial culture. With respect to the philosophical tradition within which the argument is developed, although authors such as Serres, Latour, and Popper make it *formally* European, it bears mentioning that each made a career in the Anglosaxon world. For earlier authors (e.g., Aristotle, Duns Scotus, Hobbes), they naturally belong to Western thought as such. The biggest difference between American philosophy and European philosophy, which is readily reflected here, resides in the lack of reference to 'analytical philosophy.' In seeking to expunge any metaphysical considerations from science, analytical philosophy has in fact some of the characteristics of the dualistic *modern* mindset we have portrayed. So that, this study should by no means be seen as Eurocentric, even though our subject is not at all about ordinary language, which is the touchstone of analytical philosophy.

The homogeneity we will discuss (part 1) is thus a metaphysical homogeneity, for example, about our ways of dealing with reality and not merely a shared culture gained in the course of praxis in a particular place. From the perspective of cultural practices, Europe and North America should not be confused, and Canada represents a complex blend of both cultures. Yet our study aims to shed light on something else, namely, deeper structures of thought (of the *Weltanschauungen* type) stemming from scientific positivism and known in the humanities in the form of scientisms, notably a reading of social realities carried out by imitating the methodologies of natural science. This imitation has led to a homogeneous conception of reality common to the West, whether it be in Europe or North America, since it comes as much from modern thought as from modern science, both of which these regions share.

Only the selected legal theory could appear exotic for a North American audience of common-law lawyers. The clear separation (to the point of dualism) between the norm and its application makes no sense for legal systems of common law, which is essentially characterized by casuistry, that is, an inductive, bottom-up approach to law. Inversely, the civil-law lawyer operates, or rather thinks he or she operates, starting from general and abstract standards and then going down to the case; in other words, an elaborate and applied top-down approach to law. The consequences of the interrelation acknowledged nowadays between the Subject and the Object, or between human beings and nature in the area of the environment, in the form of a revaluation of the application, or practice (law in action), of law in relation to the legal text (law in the books), are certainly less novel for the common-law lawyer than for the civil-law lawyer. It should be noted, however, that the precautionary principle is translated everywhere in the form of a general and abstract norm or rule, which raises the question about the essential or accidental value of its application. In this context, the notion of interpretation and that of constructing commensurability between cases and principle, which we will show to be at the heart of legal epistemology, concerns all jurists, regardless of their tradition. This relevance is preserved and even reinforced with respect to the ultimate goal of this study, which is to 'overturn' (all things considered) the scientist imitation of the *Rechtswissenschaft* by showing that the epistemology of natural science has much to learn from the humanities, notably on the importance of interpretation in the establishment of 'fact,' of the shift from the particular to the general, and more widely on a type of thought that is essentially relation-based.

1. The Modern Era: 'Polar' Philosophy and Dualisms for Monological and Certain Knowledge

1.1. *Philosophy of 'Modern' Sciences: Monological Knowledge, Homogeneity*

No one perhaps has better captured the spirit of modernity than Descartes. While Galileo was working without a philosophical system, mixing induction and deduction in the practice of science, Descartes himself also intended to express nature mathematically but based on a well-defined metaphysical conception of reality and of human cognition. As such, the Cartesian methodology exerted a tremendous influence on modern science, and the Cartesian mindset, often a very inaccurate caricature of his thinking, quickly invaded all the realms of knowledge, including law. Descartes was convinced of the simplicity and univocity[7] of the world. Realities can be broken down into smaller entities until you reach ultimate simple entities, which correspond to 'clear and evident' and indivisible ideas. In philosophical terminology, the word 'analytical' refers to this type of reductionist thinking, where the whole is but the sum of its parts. On this basis, Descartes was able to write his famous *Discourse on the Method*, literally on *the* method, in other words one *sole* method, a single one for all sciences, contrary to Aristotle, who claimed that each specific realm of thought was organized according to its own 'epistemology.'

In order to achieve this, he reduced nature to a homogeneous, orderly, and determinist world, within which only one kind of causality was valid, in short, a *monological*[8] conception of reality. All these features could only fascinate jurists, who adapted them in the world of practical philosophy (i.e., politics, ethics, and law) in the form of legalism, which also seeks to capture in a few laws the whole of reality.

1.1.1. A homogeneous reality. The mathematical texture of Cartesian thinking commanded, by its very nature, a philosophy of univocity, a homogenized reality that it conceived (constructed) out of and thanks to the notion of the 'clear and distinct idea.' Founded on 'evidence,'[9] the Cartesian approach could claim a uniqueness of perspective of the world, hence *the* (same) method being valid for all areas of knowledge.

The steadfastness shown by Descartes came from his believing to have reached the *essences* (or 'simple natures').[10] This is shown clearly in the *Meditations* with the discovery of two *evident*, *simple*, and *ultimate* realities: the *res cogitans* or thinking substance, and the *res extensa* or extended substance, two absolutely distinct (and even irreconcilable) orders of reality. This dualism would give structure to all of modernity, marked throughout since then with radical dichotomies that Reason is no longer able to contain ('con-tenere'),[11] leaving pairs of fields, each term of which seems univocal, having *absolutely* distinct components but very problematic *links*, such as body/soul, natural sciences/social sciences, fact/law, form/substance, law/application, text/interpretation, etc.

The famous passage of the piece of wax in the Second Meditation illustrates the 'essentialist' conception of the world according to Descartes, namely, the accidental[12] or secondary nature of *existence* in *connection* with the single – and the only authentic – system of reference of the *essence*. The melting of the wax piece makes all its qualities noted by means of the senses disappear (smell, colour, shape, size, etc.), except for its extension, which remains beyond doubt. *Epistemologically* speaking, we can only truly (i.e., clearly and distinctly) know the *idea of the object* and not the object itself – the concrete object. The origins of knowledge, be they innate or a priori ideas of Reason, matter little here. Going from the idea to the thing is so difficult, so uncertain – how indeed do you guarantee the commensurability between the idea and the concrete thing? – that Descartes needed to resort to the supreme authority of divine truth. Later, God having fallen, He will be replaced with another figure, another *deus ex machina* – Kant's Transcendental Subject, Hegel's Spirit of the world, Laplace's Demon, etc. Its function will always be to guarantee the correspondence, outside of and before any practical experience, between ideas (cognition or 'thinking substance' or *res cogitans*, i.e., the point of view of the soul or the mind) and perceivable data ('extended substance' or *res extensa*, i.e., point of view of the body).

The *purity* of cognition is a fundamental principle of Cartesian epistemology and more generally of any idealism. The *existence* (as opposed to *essence*, which is known through cognition) of bodies seems to be provided by sensitive knowledge, which may nevertheless be manipulated by the malicious deceiver (a sort of deceitful god). That is why Descartes repeatedly asserted that the senses deceive us. It was therefore impossible to achieve authentic knowledge starting from concrete objects existing in the here and now, namely from an inductive (bottom-up) approach. The indirect nature of the knowledge of *existence*, of embodied, concrete things, revealed the secondary, *acci-*

dental nature of *existence* (by the fact of *existing*) with respect to essence. Existence itself had to be intellectually conceived (hence produced by cognition) as being 'clear and evident' before being able to be declared as *existing*.

Hence there was no doubt that essence *is* (could *be*), regardless of any existence, and that, accordingly, it is the ultimate object of thought. The links between *univocity* and *absolute abstraction* – *absolute* in the genuine sense of 'separate from,' then of 'independent from,' and finally of 'a priori' – asserted themselves at the core of idealism. In other words, *idealism* was expressed as *essentialism*, or a type of thinking that established the primacy of essence and, correlatively, the discredit of existence, of concrete things, of *pragmata*.[13]

Indeed, were there to remain only one point of view in order to preserve univocity and its requirement of 'clarity and distinctness,' it could only be that of the essence, since anything else is marked by contingency, stricken by adulteration. Essence, on the contrary, is defined as what 'sub-sists,' what remains unaltered by change and hence that upon which the mind can depend in order to authentically think the world with utmost certainty. By seeking to reduce the plurality of perspectives of the intelligibility of reality to unity, to a single kind of causality, the metaphysics of univocity instituted quite naturally the point of view of essence, of form (or *eidos* or *idea*, from whence *idealism*), of scientific *law*, to the detriment of a perspective of intelligibility based on existence, on occurrences, on *pragmata*. This marked the birth of the very spirit of legalist-type legal positivism in which the law occupied all the space, leaving as secondary, as a question of detail, its application to concrete cases.[14]

1.1.2. How to homogenize reality: The monological discourse of power-potestas. The example of the piece of wax showed that the extension (*res extensa*) was the 'essence' of external objects. This extension, because of its very nature, lets itself be entirely expressed mathematically. The homogenization of reality removes the need for many kinds of causes. In order to explain this now *homogeneous* ('homo-genēs,' i.e., involving the same kind – from the Greek '*genēs*' = kind or genus [itself, incidentally, from the Latin '*genus*' = birth, race, stock]) nature, a single *kind* of cause is sufficient. This is contrary to Aristotelian thinking, which apprehended reality with the four classic kinds of causes. This plurality was indispensable, for Aristotle, in order to account for the change, the 'becoming,' that characterizes nature, namely, going from state X to state Y through the simple passage of time, a state 'other' than the first, as when a child *becomes* an adult.

Aristotle summed up his doctrine of plurality of kinds of causes in the *caricatured* example of the statue (see *Metaphysics* I, 3, 983a): 1) the *formal* cause – what the statue represents, its form or what the Greeks termed *eidos*, which led to *idea* (hence idealism)[15] and thus the idea it incarnates – in short, and approximatively so, its *essence*; 2) the *material* cause, the 'matter' or 'substratum' – that out of which the thing considered is made, be it wood, bronze, etc.; 3) the *efficient* cause ('the source of the change,' the execution) – the force or power used by the sculptor to produce the statue; 4) the '*final* cause'– the purpose (*telos*, which gives 'teleologic') for which the artist summons up his power (his *potestas* or efficient cause) and creates his sculpture, and relative to which the other three kinds of causes arrange themselves. The notion of *causality* according to Aristotle is therefore intrinsically polysemic.

Many factors explain why modernity favoured the efficient cause over the other three. We will outline the most relevant ones for the present purposes.

The advent of the *individual* in political terms, of the *singular* in logical or cognitive terms – two aspects of the same reality – steered thinking towards what is particular or 'unique' *in* each person. Medieval Franciscan thinking had an important role in this development. Because the Christian God is a *person* and the Bible speaks to God's creature as a *person* and not as a *citizen* (i.e., as belonging first and foremost to the group), the Franciscan Duns Scotus (c. 1266–1308) claimed, quite consistently with faith, that there was an *immediate understanding* of the *singular*, of the *individual qua individual*, thanks to intuition. For Aristotle and Thomas Aquinas, science, on the contrary, developed on the level of the general, of kinds, of 'natures' (nature of man, of the universe, of the city, etc.) and not on that of individuals. For the Franciscans, these natures seemed like screens, products of Aristotelian intellectualism with no great use to God's creature for whom only the love of the Creator and of his neighbour is important. In short, for Scotus, the singular, the individual moved firmly to the forefront. *Nominalism*, thematized by another Franciscan, William of Ockham, amplified this thinking in the areas of knowledge, politics, and law, claiming that only singulars *exist*,[16] a focus which placed 'non-finalized'[17] will at the heart of practical philosophy.

Franciscan doctrine, in fact, established the primacy of will over reason – the two traditional faculties of the soul – because it gave love a central role in the life of God's creature, love which equals an emminently *personal* sentiment. Love, indeed, is a matter of will and not reason. And isn't reason by its very nature impersonal?[18] The pre-eminence of non-finalized will can claim to adhere to the noblest model: divine omnipotence, easily recognizable in the Decalogue, where there are precisely *commandments* to be found. The civil lawyer will recognize here the origin of his conception of law: obligations dictated by a superior capable of imposing them on his 'subjects,' elements that can be found written not only in Hobbes, for instance, but in all manuals of contemporary continental law.

These different notions – 'person,' non-finalized will, efficient cause (*potestas*) – hinged on the notion of the freedom of God and of the creature. The omnipotence of God was safeguarded, it was thought, only if no final cause could be imposed on Him 'by nature.' Everything must always be possible for Him, in every time and place. He would not 'suffer' any natural inclination. The same held true for God's creature. If man, by his very nature, tends towards an *end* (final cause, *telos*, purpose) of his own, then he is no longer a free being, and since he cannot *choose*, he can no longer be held responsible for his actions, particularly before God. In order to protect these two freedoms from what was later called 'Greco-Arabic necessitarism' – thus termed because Aristotelianism came back to Europe through the Arabic philosophers – in 1277, Étienne Tempier, bishop of Paris, condemned some often misunderstood theses by the Dominican Thomas Aquinas because of the final natural cause, thereby reinforcing will, which had become *infinite*, i.e., 'in-finite' or without 'end,' not naturally finalized.

This was the inception of the definition of freedom as understood by the moderns, freedom as being the absence of external obstacles, or choice none of whose terms prevails per se upon the others. Jurists reflected the *modern* definition of freedom in the central notion that is continental rights: 'subjective rights,' i.e., the prerogatives of the sovereign individual. The most famous of these prerogatives is undoubtedly the *subjective* right to property as defined in the Napoleonic Code at section 544: 'right to enjoy and dispose of things in the most absolute manner.' It is a subjective right 'understood as personal power to act. Here, will makes all of law; for is will not legitimate, so the thinking goes, from the moment it is assimilated to freedom?'[19]

Once the final cause was dismissed, reality was explained by means of the efficient cause exclusively. The world was viewed in terms of *potestas*, by showing consideration for the *omnipotence* (i.e., all the *potes-*

tas) of God and the omnipotence of non-finalized human will in the realms that God left at man's disposal, and by laying the foundation for the physical world, interpreted as an interplay of multiple forces.

These *forces*, many though they may be, are nevertheless 'homogeneous,' for they all come under the efficient cause and can also be measured. Homogeneous and measurable, they enabled the mathematization of nature, renewed science, opened up the realm of techno-sciences to man, and in general left a profound mark on practical *modern* philosophy, particularly in law. Henceforth the interest would be on the *how* and no longer on the *why*, on the means and no longer on the end, on the efficient cause and no longer on the final cause.

The homogenization of reality entailed an unprecedented cognitive consequence. *Commensurability* – the fact of two entities having the same measure (i.e., 'com-mensurable') – was a *given*. It no longer needed to be constructed. It did not constitute a problem since it was in a sense a priori, innate. From this flowed certainty, guaranteed notably by calculation. Inspired by this model, jurists for their part would substitute the *Rechtswissenschaft* (legal *science*) for the *ars juris*, the *syllogism* (or calculation) for the *judgment*.

1.1.3. Physics homogenized by power or force-potestas. It is not difficult to explain that modern science is permeated by forces, since we are so accustomed to this. Science found its emblematic expression in Newton's *mechanics*, an interplay of forces regulated (*regula* or rule in Latin) by one law, namely, that of the *force* of gravity, valid for all eternity, impervious to any historicity. Simply knowing the initial (and contingent or 'accidental,' i.e., that which could have been otherwise) conditions of the moving body is enough to be able to predict (foresee) its trajectory at any point in time, as much in the past as in the future.

Nature, being homogeneous, became 'legalistic' (subject to *laws* or *regula*), deterministic, and rendered the very notion of 'point of view' useless, since its laws were shielded from observer, place, and time. There were single, universal, and eternal laws, according to the same qualities as those given to Reason. These properties led to *certainty*. *Modern* science was in pursuit of truth and not only likelihood or relevance, both of which entail a finality, a certain point of view.

All of these considerations can be summed up in logical terms in the notions of *objectivity* of scientific knowledge and *neutrality* of the observer. The experimenter plays no part in the knowledge of the natural phenomenon which he only observes *as it is in itself*. Neither the context nor the subject are relevant. *Constitutive* ambivalence of reality (as in the mix, the hybrid) no longer exists, nor does any *constitutive* collaboration between the Subject and the Object in the *act of cognition*. Even the texture of reality is conceived as being univocal and transparent. This led quite logically, on many occasions, to the announcement of the 'end of physics,' as did Lord Kelvin, for instance, at the end of the nineteenth century, shortly before the famous 1905 articles of a certain A. Einstein.

Science corresponded adequately to the analytical paradigm, as Kant had characterized this term, and which can be schematically summed up in the following formula: the whole is always but the sum of its parts. No emergent quality can exist. Nature cannot experience qualitative leaps; the whole cannot display properties that are not to be found in its parts. The efficient causes can be added or subtracted but never extended beyond the given, 'efficient,' kind.

*1.2. The Law Homogenized by Power as Law-*potestas

Modern Continental law has been, since its beginnings dating back notably to the second Spanish scholasticism (Suarez in particular) and to modern natural law (from Grotius to Hobbes and Pufendorf in particular), structured around the binomial will/efficient cause, which in practical philosophy (*praxis*) is expressed by the *commandment* on the part of the superior – of 'power' precisely – and by (modern) *freedom* on the part of the individual. In both cases we are dealing with the same type of causality: efficient cause.

This is evidenced by the description of the constituting elements of the law according to Hobbes, an emblematic description of the modern conception, namely, a voluntarist conception of the law whose constituting elements according to *De Corpore* (Part I, ch. 6, § 6–7) are 'covenant' and 'power of coercion,' the latter analysed as 'the transferring of every man's right of resistance against him, to whom he hath transferred the power of coercion' since 'the wills of most men are governed only by fear, and where there is no power of coercion, there is no fear, the wills of most men will follow their passions of covetousness, lust, anger, and the like, to the breaking of those covenants.'[20]

If the more *powerful* (*potestas*) of the two has dominance over the other, in practice the State over the individual,[21] it is because they operate on the same level, one being *quantitatively* better equipped with power, with might – it can compel its opposite – than the other. Do we not in fact refer to the police as a *force*?

Legal praxis became homogenized as a result of a cause of the same type as that which governed natural science. In natural science force prevailed, *potestas*, which is power in the sense of mechanical or electrical forces. But *potestas* was also associated with power in the sense of authority, influence, control, or, as explained by Hobbes, who was an advocate of the mechanistic model of society (conceived as a machine), the prerogative of the powerful. It is therefore not surprising then to see how the philosophy of law undertook to imitate science, an imitation that was expressly advocated notably by the school of modern natural law and further underscored by the adoption of the mechanistic model in the social sciences.[22]

Another notion marking the transition between natural and social sciences is known all too well to require any lengthy development here. This is the notion of *law*, whose ambiguity was so skilfully maintained – by the seventeenth- and eighteenth-century theorists of law in particular – with the *analogous* (only) notion used in science, which enabled jurists to turn its aura of precision and achievement to their advantage. They also appropriated *certainty* by means of what is posited because it is mastered, and mastered because it is posited (positive law), mainly *laws*. This naturally led to the structuring of the law into *systems* – not in the recent sense used in systemics but according to the model of Euclid's Elements – which begot *codes*, manners of pulling together social realities algorithmically, it was thought, just as physical laws condensed natural realities by means of simple mathematical formulae. This subsequently gave rise to the belief in *Rechtswissenschaft* (legal science).

Laws now filled the core of Continental legal thinking. Cases, namely concrete situations or even occurrences, only provided a means of *clarifying* them, in the same way that initial conditions gave concrete expression to a given trajectory of a moving object, which is perfectly predictable within the framework of the laws of physics. Cases appeared to be as *accidental* as the initial *contingent* conditions. It was thus beyond their ability to have a retroactive effect on the law to change it. *Existence* cannot undo *essence*.

Indeed all the figures of legal logic attest to this subjection of occurrences to the law. We enter a deterministic, specifically *legalistic*, universe. For starters, there is the exclusivity given to formal sources[23] over material sources, and among formal sources, the recognized prevalence of statute law over custom, case law, and doctrine, the latter two often not accepted as a source of law but simply qualified as being 'authorities' or 'auxiliary instruments' of law. The concept of 'legalism' expresses this reduction of the law to (merely) laws.

It is easy to see already that the *application* of the law would be shown little consideration, since the 'accident' does not influence the essence of things. In Continental law terms, practical cases have no incidence on the law. We need only call attention to the quite marginal status of *equity* marked by its qualifications of *contra legem* (against the law) and *praeter legem* (beside the law), in which statute law appears to be law's centre of gravity. And if one is to accept equity *infra legem* (within the laws), if only to be able to go beyond the intrinsic *incommensurability* of laws as being *general and abstract* and of the case as being *singular and concrete*, one only accepts it in the framework of a philosophy of interpretation for which the operation of *interpretation* remains accidental. In searching for the equivalent of an algorithm as is known in natural science, legal philosophers espoused the deterministic a priori of the *single meaning* ('uni-vocity') of any text. Thus the ancillary value of interpretation in comprehension. Only 'pathological' texts require interpretation, that is to say those that do not immediately deliver *their* single and clear meaning. *Comprehension* normally operates without the need for any *interpretation*, as *THE objective* meaning residing in the text is revealed as though by itself to the neutral reader-observer. Any potential difficulties of comprehension are cleared up by the faithful application of interpretative *methods*. The univocal legal text is meant to be in law the counterpart of the mathematical formulation of natural law. The *objective* judge and the *neutral* observer alike clarify the law on the *occasion* of a case but do not interpret it strictly speaking since the law is clear per se and context-proof.

It would take decades for judges to be recognized as having a 'creative' or 'normative' power.[24] They remained the 'mouth of the law,' simply *stating* it as in the Exegetical School of the early days of the Napoleonic Code. And the reasoning expressed in their decisions scarcely extended beyond syllogism, a deductive succession of a major premise (the law), a minor premise (the situation to be judged), and the conclusion, the pronouncement, stemming automatically and mechanically from them. All the epistemological problems of *applying* the law were erased. How do you choose the major premise if several are available? How do you use interpretative *methods* when no criteria allow these methods to be organized into a hierarchy? How do you overcome the incommensurability of the law (general and abstract) with the case (unique and concrete), other than by designating this move by the terms 'to subsume,' which, at best, *describes* this move but never explains it?

Why did these epistemological questions not come up? Because it was about finding above and beyond the accidents that are represented by the cases, the essence of the law or the legal category. The occurrences were only notable in as much as they participated in the category (which 'subsumption' indicates), in the *eidos* (idea). All the singularities that exceeded the imitation, the trait-by-trait correspondence, were eliminated, which all but amounts to the definition of homogeneity or of a priori commensurability, the proof of it being the absence of the retroactive effect of occurrences on the law.

1.3. Nature Enslaved by Man's Power

Nature conceived as inert, homogeneous, expressed mathematically was thus given to the control of anyone who knew its laws, a domination which is not only theoretical but also ontological. In fact, in keeping with the Cartesian mind-body dualism, man, owing to his intellectual (and spiritual) faculties, was placed *above* and not *within* nature. He would therefore hold legitimate dominion over it, called on to become its master and owner, as a certain reading of the biblical message enjoined him to do.

But no sooner had it severed its total dependence upon divine omnipotence, nature, now considered for itself by science, fell under a new domination.

Being constituted by forces alone, efficient causes alone, nature offered itself entirely to anyone who could manage to channel them and thereby turn out to be more powerful than it. The techno-sciences would relentlessly devote themselves to this. No matter; nature did not have any meaning in and of itself. Besides, teleological considerations of final cause no longer held.

Thanks notably to the Cartesian dualism and to the criterion of clear and distinct ideas, the modern era gained a simple reality, consisting of Subjects on the one hand and Objects on the other, without compenetration, without hybrids, without mixture. But the disqualification of the body, reduced to a machine, would entail human boundlessness with respect to nature, since man had lost his intimate connection with matter. And what is boundlessness if not an aspect of the 'in-finite' (i.e., not finalized) will of man, who does not even ask himself the question of the commensurability between himself and nature, since these are two different realities, *res cogitans* or thinking substance *versus res extensa* or extended substance? These two irreconcilable[25] poles would guide modern thinking towards 'polar' philosophies and leave in the dark the problem of the links between these poles, hence of their commensurability. Otherness never proves to be constitutive of the individual or the singular, as reflected by the Cartesian *cogito*.

Nature, through the environmental issue, would rebel. She would break this modern solipsism and force a dialogue with man. By making him 'her' *symbiont*, she compelled him to think of her in the framework of a philosophy of relation. Subject and Object now cooperate. That is the major teaching of the contemporary era.

2. The Contemporary Era: The Rise of a Philosophy of Relationship

If the *relativization* – hence also and especially the fact of being *relative to* and therefore in a *relation* – of the Subject/Object distinction marks the contemporary era, epistemology must face the question of commensurability, more specifically of its *construction*. It is about this development that social sciences can give hard sciences food for thought, notably through legal thinking in the area of the environment.

Nature in law is in fact not an object like the others. The development of 'world-objects' ['artefacts that have at least one global-scale dimension (such as time, space, speed, or energy)'[26]] led to a profound change in our relationship with nature 'which was long ago our master and of late our slave, always in all cases our host, and now our symbiont.'[27] Such a relationship makes it unsuitable to posit poles whereby each would live quite autonomously. By polluting nature, we pollute ourselves. This sets a regime of 'co-belonging,' better yet of 'inter-determination,' and thwarts the epistemological scope of the Subject vs. Object distinction. If our control – and often today our loss of control – makes nature an Object, that is to say our Subject, in the genuine sense of subjected or subdued by subjection, the feedback of nature on our own conditions of existence makes us in turn the Subject (of subjection) of the environment, in other words the Object of nature.

Nature no longer *environs* us. She constitutes our *milieu*, that *within* which we live. Philosophical thinking is thus redirected towards *rela-*

tionship considered metaphysically as being prime. The poles are in principle thought of as ends of the relation, and in this sense a result of it while being indispensable to it. Contemporary physics has also adopted this 'relational' frame of mind: 'Everything in the end takes place as though the relations between objects became more important than the objects themselves.'[28]

2.1. *Philosophy of Contemporary Sciences: A Time of Uncertainty*

People were able to start thinking of nature as their *milieu*, their *symbiont*, from the moment, notably, when the *modern* dualism of *Subject vs. Object* was abandoned, first with thermodynamics, which reintroduced historicity to natural phenomena, then with quantum physics, which made the Subject and the Object *interdependent* in the very act of cognition.

Consequently 'confusion' (to fuse together, to blend) became of primary importance. Blends, mixtures, hybrids became our data. Science has discarded raw facts, pure facts whose existence is perfectly impervious to our 'observations.' Today, it develops in a rational and experimental dialogue *between* Subject and Object in that the experiment does not presuppose a single faithful observation of facts as they present themselves, nor a single quest for empirical connections between phenomena. Experimentation requires much more. It requires an interaction between theory and practical manipulation, which implies a real strategy, namely, that a natural process becomes inspected as a possible key to a theoretical hypothesis. And it is as such that this process is then prepared, purified, before being interrogated in the language of this theory, as the famous works of I. Prigogine and I. Stengers illustrate.

Only if *interrogated* does nature respond, and only human *choice* questions her: selection of viewpoints, of measuring scales, of levels of energy used, amount and allocation of grants, partnerships with industry, with other countries, institutionalized partnerships or non-institutionalized ones, etc. Mixture once more, hybrids yet again. Natural sciences are indeed human, which certainly accounts for their having some uncertainty and the need to thematize the relationships *between* hard and social sciences, particularly their commensurability.

However, their ambivalence also stems from *internal* reasons. A *fundamental* ambivalence resides in their principles and laws. For instance, Gödel's theorem on the intrinsic limits of the notions of proof and coherence, starting with and including fully given objects as mathematics. Or Heisenberg's relations of uncertainty (more precisely 'indetermination') by virtue of which science itself 'conceals' from us, by the very fact of measurement – albeit accurate measurement – an aspect of reality (atomic reality, as it happens), the existence of which it furthermore demonstrates. Or even Schrödinger's cat, which illustrates a *constitutive measurement* of the phenomenon to be 'observed' itself, in this way introducing a share of subjectivity (absence or presence of an 'observer') into quantum theory. And the dual nature of particles. Also it has been long since the 'genetic code' was no longer a *code* in the strict linguistic sense. Historicity, for its part, also instils a rather strong dose of uncertainty into scientific thought. The theory of relativity, even by its very title, offers itself completely to a logic of relation. Not only is time not independent of space, but the space-time continuum does not constitute a framework (a form) within which matter falls, it displays some materiality itself, notably in that it deforms: a 'form' that is also characterized by the typical attributes of matter or of energy, thus breaking the traditional dualisms.

In all these cases, we are not only faced with a plurality of types of causes but are also unable to thoroughly divide their respective effects on the phenomenon under examination. Univocity, certainty, Cartesian 'clarity and distinctiveness' no longer hold. More precisely, they appear as the result of a certain *interpretation* of reality that culminates in physics: 'Never had another science to such extent required another specific discipline, interpretation, in order to be understood and applied. By its very nature, quantum physics examines the relation between the world and its representation.'[29]

Without going into the debate generated by the problems of conceiving this relation – authentic conflicts of *interpretation* – it should be stressed that none of the considered hypotheses is based on an analytical conception of reality, on ontological dualisms, namely, the paradigm of the 'complicated' (*versus* 'complex').

Another certainty of contemporary sciences consists in dismissing absolute truth and ontological certainty, as emerges from such figures as falsification and trial and error. Such thinking involves uncertainty for sure. Reality appears to be woven with a multitude of heterogeneous, coexisting, even self-codetermining aspects, whose causes, they themselves therefore heterogeneous as well, have a retroactive effect on each other according to processes so complex – such as 'emergent properties,' which cannot be accounted for by the *analysis* of the components at the root of the phenomenon – that man has to admit his finiteness.

Now, social sciences, including law and in particular environmental law, are accustomed to the intrinsic collaboration of Subject-Object and to the *interpretive*, better yet *hermeneutic*, dimension of reality, and consequently to the absence of absolute truth, beyond any point of view. W. Dilthey, at the end of the nineteenth century, distinguished *erklären* (to explain causally) from *verstehen* (to understand a meaning) in order to characterize the natural sciences/social sciences dualism (*Naturwissenschaften* and *Geisteswissenschaften*, to be exact). Today, all human activity is permeated with interpretation-*verstehen*, including *erklären*. Is this not the most recent manifestation of one of Aristotle's most complex cognitive structures, one which a philosophical tradition would call 'transcendental relation'?

2.2. *Contemporary Theory of Law: The Hybrid 'Juris-diction' at the Heart of Law through the Unity of the Written Law (Object) and the Interpreter (Subject)*

The notion of 'transcendental relation' attempts to capture a reality that refers to another by everything which makes it be itself (constitutes it itself). Such a reality is therefore completely pervaded with relativity (in the sense of 'relative to'). It characterizes, ontologically speaking, the *constituting principles* that form the structure of the particular reality, such as essence *and* existence, matter *and* form, faculties *and* actions. It binds two realities with one another in that it penetrates, goes right through (*transcendit*) and imbibes (*imbibit*) both together in reciprocity.

Aristotle had considered this relation on the cognitive level as well, as the instrinsic collaboration of the Subject (intellect) and the Object (intelligible) in the act of cognition: 'the activity of the sensible object and that of the sense is one and the same activity'; 'the soul is in a way all existing things; for existing things are either sensible or thinkable, and knowledge is in a way what is knowable, and sensation is in a way what is sensible' as mentioned in *De anima* (425 b 25–27; 431 b 21–23).[30] Subject and Object are therefore no longer separate in the *act* of cognition. They are 'reciprocal and total' causes whereby each is the cause of the causality *in act* of the other.

We have shown elsewhere[31] that this relation also holds in law for its main operation, which is qualification, because only such a close collaboration, namely, the *constitutive* activity of the interpreter in the construction of the meaning of the legal *text*, enables the initial incommensurability of the *general-abstract* law with the *singular-concrete* case to be made commensurable. Law, in fact, does not speak by itself. The all too common expression 'the law *says* that' is only ever a metaphor. It is always incumbent on a subject in the flesh, notably the judge, to 'give voice' to the law, to bring alive the code that only amounts to paper and ink, which, in the West, has been given the form of so-called 'Latin' characters. For jurisdiction is clearly the '*juris-dictio*,' the 'saying the law,' which common lawyers know well. This intimacy (transcendental relation) between law *as applied* and the case is at the core of any legal reasoning through the rule of precedent (*stare decisis*) according to which a case 'is' law, that is, it becomes a model for future occurrences that jurists, and the judge as a last resort, will consider as being *analogous* to this 'model' case, more specifically known as *leading case*. This is how civil lawyers operate, after having spent several years in law faculties learning the 'textbook cases' of each legal category that has been formulated in an abstract manner in their manuals, namely, the jurisprudence that supreme courts have ruled to be the most typical and the most relevant to this or that article of law. The written law cannot be understood without the 'professional' reader that is the jurist having such a culture (i.e., being educated in this way). This is proven by the fact that non-jurists do not have any great deal of understanding of these codes. Not surprisingly, they lack many years of experience, training, know-how and *practice*.[32]

This intimate unity of 'text-reader' reflects the spirit of the hermeneutics of H.-G. Gadamer, which was dedicated to 'understanding' (a text, a law, for instance) conceived as a single operation of the mind inextricably *blending* 'comprehension-interpretation-application.' It also reflects the semiotics of U. Eco, which deal quite particularly with the retroactive effects – hence a circular, non-linear causality, a relational rather than polar philosophy – of pragmatics on semantics (and grammar in the broad sense). He also showed in particular the determining role of the interpreter's culture in the reading of any text, which can never be reduced to mere decoding, or the mechanical application of interpretive 'methods,' as jurists once held but that P.-A. Côté, for example, has for years shown to be only an appearance. These 'methods are made up of contradictory directives not organized into a hierarchy and whose relative weight varies depending on the circumstances.'[33] This reinforces the *constituting* character of the *context*, of the *circumstances*, for the comprehension of any text, of cases for the living meaning of the law.

This way of thinking about the mutually constituting collaboration of the Subject and the Object in the *act of cognition* – conceived therefore as hybrid – makes it possible to understand epistemological propositions that are incoherent in the framework of a science synonymous with ontological truth, neutrality, and pure observation. For example, Popper offered the following: 'there is no such thing as an unprejudiced observation. All observation is an activity with an aim (to find, or to check, some regularity which is *at least* vaguely conjectured); an activity guided by problems, and by the context of expectations (the "horizon of expectations" [...]). There is no such thing as passive experience [...] All this led me to the view that conjecture or hypothesis must come before observation or perception: we have inborn expectations.'[34] It is a long way from the purely descriptive science of a scientist external to the studied phenomenon, for he collaborates in it. Reference should therefore be made to B. Latour, who presents interpretation or *exegesis* as the *matrix common* to hard sciences and social sciences.[35]

2.3. *Nature in Law: When the Precautionary Principle Sheds Light on the Change of Paradigm in Hard Sciences*

A great many legal theorists are still reluctant to recognize the *intrinsic* collaboration of the interpreter and the text, the motive being notably that the judge would thereby seem to wield exorbitant power. Yet law *as far as it is applied* corroborates the creative power of the judge. This power is framed, however, often strictly so, thus eluding the arbitrary while leaving a role for subjectivity. This framing results notably from procedures that, for instance, limit the *relevant* facts, and from law which is *adequate to* a certain acceptable conception of what is just.[36]

We can understand that nature forces us to make the problem of commensurability explicit through the fact that by polluting nature, we pollute ourselves and we know it. 'Co-belonging' now represents a shared destiny, namely, the highest form of *relation*. Interdependence becomes explicitly *constitutive* of the poles, which places us in a *relational* philosophy, that is, a new paradigm.

By admitting that law is relational[37] and a relation between people (even if it is about things), when we speak of 'law of the environmental milieu' we admit *in this specific perspective* that the Earth *as our habitat* cannot do without humans. In environmental law, theirs is a *reciprocal* relationship, without being *synallagmatic*. It is a fundamentally *asymetrical* relationship, both in existence (Earth without humans but not the contrary) and in responsibility (exclusively of humans). The production of world-objects[38] has made this interdependence indisputable, just as the measuring instrument makes the *equipped* observer and the *provoked* nature interdependent. Most remarkable perhaps is how law apprehended the 'object' nature. First by means of *principles* (of polluter/payer, of prevention, of precaution, etc.) whose characteristic is to make sense only by, and in, the cases that gradually enrich their practical scope by following a bottom-up logic.

This pragmatic vision (based on *pragmata*) that places the *'jurisdictio'* ('saying the law') at the centre of the legal process is enhanced by the *precautionary* principle since it *requires* to act in a context of *uncertainty* that it expressly assumed with its canonical definition at the World Summit in Rio: 'Where there are threats of serious or irreversible damage, lack of full scientific certainty shall not be used as a reason for postponing cost-effective measures to prevent environmental degradation.'

The legal standard thus adopted in the 'framework' of the *precautionary principle* is hardly worth more than a hypothesis *from an epistemological perspective*, submitted to trial and error and generally allows for its own revision, in a manner *analogous*[39] to a 'falsification.' The Object here is explicitly structured by the choice of the Subject, within certain limits set by the *purpose* that the legislator (and then the judge) has established for himself. *Finalized* thinking depends upon a 'horizon of expectations' that is itself built around a certain *acceptability* emerging from a balance of multiple heterogeneous causes: technical and economic feasibility, public health, taxation, etc.

Acceptability even becomes a determining factor in a context of uncertainty, since ontology, the 'very nature of things,' becomes problematic. It is thus up to the Subject to set the relevance but not according to his 'goodwill,' as in 'in-finite' will, but according to a point of view shared by peers and still limited by a certain residual unavailability of the Object. As such, acceptability seems quite *subjective* (decision of Subjects) but not *arbitrary*, since the Object offers its own resistance. This 'communitarization' of the Object even becomes universal in environmental law – not sufficiently respected, granted – in as much as the environmental problem is not structured in any way by borders. Furthermore, this 'communitarization' distances *subjectivity* from *arbi-*

trariness and places *intersubjectivity* as near as possible to the 'objectivity' that is aimed and indeed is always to be constructed.

In this form, law is close to the hypothetical approach of sciences to the point that Popper can present them as being part of the jurist's emblematic figure of the *jurisdictio* informed by acceptability: the common-law *procedure* of the jury. He makes an analogy between the 'basic statement' of sciences and the 'statement about a factual occurrence' by claiming that 'their acceptance is part of the application of a theoretical system; and it is only this application which makes any further application of the theoretical system possible.'[40] In both cases, there is choice in the form of *protocols* or determined *procedures*, of *admissible* arguments, of *relevance*, of acceptance by peers, and therefore of controlled, institutionalized interpretation yet never perfectly univocal: 'most theories can be interpreted in more than one way,'[41] which jurists, namely litigators and doctrinal writers, know and practice so well, which does not mean that the rule or norm is stripped of its authority in the classic sense of *auctoritas* (as opposed to power, force or *potestas*), namely the respect that stems from the recognition of a higher competence, of superior knowledge or know-how, in which one's trust is placed for this reason.

Authority (*auctoritas*) no doubt conflicts with the *tabula rasa*, which could exist only rhetorically because of the extent to which diachrony penetrates synchrony, the past penetrates the present, as we have seen with the jurist and *stare decisis* or the rule of precedent (i.e., which 'precedes' diachronically to govern synchroncially). Popper expresses it for the scientist who 'engaged in a piece of research, [...] can go at once to the heart of the matter: to the heart, that is of an organized structure. For a structure of scientific doctrines is already in existence; and with it, a generally accepted problem-situation.'[42] The convergence of these two cultures is literally edifying in this instance, to the point of opening up thinking to *epistemodicy*,[43] the common and often conflictual history of law and science. If the 'confusion' (transcendental relation) Subject-Object, which has been made so clear in environmental law, is typical in the humanities, then by henceforth placing *choice* or *pertinence*, and as such *judgment*, at the heart of its approach, contemporary scientific culture could reconnect with its own foundations: 'at the base of epistemology, a normative discipline, must lie a set of values, a code of ethics.'[44] And if ethics should be embodied in the *judgment* by peers, the fibre of philosophy of law would not be foreign to scientists.

In fact, in Antiquity, a time when law essentially revolved around '*prudence*' (ancestor of 'precaution'), the core concepts of legal *dialogue* ('dia-logos': dia – between; logos – word or reason, hence a *relation*) were appropriated by scientists. The *causa*, in the sense of legal case, led to both 'thing' and 'causality,' and to the idea of 'evidence,' and even to the idea of *reason* itself. Indeed Cicero used reason as a justification for an action considered to be criminal. Thus an 'argumentative' twist, which, in the Middle Ages, allowed 'reason' (*ratio*) to mean 'dispute, discussion.' Then Cartesian and modern 'reason' predominantly characterized sciences, which were submitted to demonstration and termed as 'hard' because they are precisely 'rational.' And demonstration, or logic, itself comes from *logos*, one genuine sense of which is *judicial affair*, a ground or foundation for a lawsuit.

As a final point, let us remember that the word 'science,' etymologically speaking, is only secondarily linked to 'knowledge' or 'understanding,' since the Latin *scire* meant to slice, to split, and subsequently to decide, to decree! In numerous languages, the equivalent of 'science' originally meant to learn, to teach, in other words a process, a *relation* (!), which, just like law, is intrinsically linked to praxis, to practical philosophy.

NOTES

1 The very difficult obstacle of expressing my ideas in English would not have been overcome without the extraordinary cleverness and culture of Iwan Chan and Rémi Samson from Ottawa. I remain exclusively responsible for any ambiguous passages.

2 R. Dworkin, *Law's Empire* (Cambridge, MA: Harvard University Press, 1986).

3 The history of science turns out to be enlightening in that it condemns the pure vision of the 'scientist' (i.e., shielded from any societal or religious influence). We need only mention Isaac Newton, the great scientist, father of the universal law of gravity, founder of the Royal Society and ... obsessive alchemist, which is precisely what gave him the audacity to extend to the entire universe a phenomenon (summed up in the mythical incident of the apple) observed locally – in an alchemical vision of the world, all the elements of the universe correspond to each other and if one discovers a *true* law of matter, then it must govern the entire universe. Descartes, on the contrary, for fear of lapsing into alchemy in par-

ticular, refused the notion of force and launched into explanations based on vorteces, which kept him from making a number of discoveries that were nevertheless commensurable with his work. This shows that science itself turns out to be a mixture of reason and irrationality (for instance, the very long time it took for the Arabic zero to make its way into medieval mathematics), of purity of research and funding requirements (Da Vinci sold his 'engineering' talents, particularly for war machinery, to various noblemen). In short, culture is ever present in science, as the works of Bruno Latour have demonstrated in philosophy and sociology of sciences, for example.

4 G. Minois, *Galilée* (Paris: Presses universitaires de France, 2000), 7.

5 J. Lenoble and F. Ost, *Droit, mythe et raison: Essai sur la dérive mytho-logique de la rationalité juridique* (Brussels: Publications des Facultés universitaires Saint-Louis, 1980), 120. My translation.

6 M. Van Hoecke, *Law as Communication* (Portland, OR: Hart Publishing, 2002), 8.

7 Univocal means having a single meaning, exhibiting one unique and clear meaning, not giving rise to interpretation but being objectively self-revealing to anyone who uses reason to observe reality or to read the sign or the text declared to be univocal.

8 Monological, as in strictly 'mono-logical': constructed from a *single logos*, a *single* type of logic, thought, or discourse.

9 Following the *Discourse on Method*, trans. F.E. Sutcliffe (Harmondsworth: Penguin Books, 1968), 41]: 'never to accept anything as true that I did not know to be evidently so [...], and to include in my judgements nothing more than what presented itself so clearly and so distinctly to my mind that I might have no occasion to place it in doubt.'

10 'Simple' things are those regarding which 'the cognition of which is so clear and so distinct that they cannot be analysed by the mind into other more distinctively known. Such are figure, extension, motion, etc.; all others we conceive to be in some way compounded out of these.' R. Descartes, 'Rules for the Direction of the Mind,' rule XII, in *The Philosophical Works of Descartes*, trans. E.S. Haldane and G.R.T. Ross (Cambridge: Cambridge University Press, 1967), 40–1. The analytical conception of the world – 'the whole is but the sum of its parts' – is explicit here. Incidentally, it is correlated with its mechanicism.

11 In other words, hold together, articulate intellectually, and not only juxtapose i.e., pose one next to the other while leaving unexplained the relation between the juxtaposed elements; e.g., for the jurist, the links between *form* and *substance*, between *procedural* and *substantive law*.

12 In the philosophical sense of 'contingent,' which could have been other than what it is, without a change in the essence of the thing of which it is said to be an accident; it therefore adds itself to that thing, and characterizes it, but not in its principles or essential features – for instance, having white or black skin, a pug or aquiline nose, or a piercing, all the while remaining human.

13 The Greek word for 'thing,' namely, 'pragma, pragmata,' is truly edifying in as much as it underlines a 'pragmatic' conception of reality as a matter of fact, in other words a *concrete* and *inductive* (bottom-up) vision: thought starts from exisiting things, pragmata, in order subsequently to go back to generalities (the *genus* as opposed to the *species*) and principles using comparison and abstraction. Here, the idea or concept (of such things) *results* from pragmata and is not given a priori, namely, outside of and before any concrete experience. This inductive approach characterizes *realist* philosophies in contrast to idealist philosophies.

14 Yet isn't the distinctive feature of law the achievement of justice in a concrete case, in a given specific situation? The application of the law then becomes as important as the creation of the law.

15 With the classic confusion surrounding 'form': *morphē* (appearance, external form) and *eidos* (essence, idea). The second meaning of form should be emphasized here, despite the logic of the example.

16 Concepts – more precisely 'universals' – do not exist; they are but words, names (*nomen* in Latin, hence the term 'nominalism').

17 In brief, 'infinite' – 'in-finite' – i.e., without 'end,' without 'natural goal' or 'natural aim.' See below.

18 Sole, universal, and eternal Reason, identical for everyone, became the leitmotif of the Enlightenment, a claim that was made possible notably by a priori philosophies, namely, a knowledge whose *principles* are not induced from experience or from induction, but are innate or the exclusive property of a *transcendental* Subject (as in Kant, for instance) and hence disembodied.

19 F. Ost, *La nature hors la loi: L'écologie à l'épreuve du droit* (Paris: La Découverte, 1995/2003), 52.

20 W. Molesworth, ed., *The English Works of Thomas Hobbes* (London: John Bohn, 1840), vol. 4, 129.

21 This is where the epistemological roots of human rights and the rule of law can be found, both aimed at rebalancing the pans of the scale.

22 This is still evidenced today, for example, in that branch of linguistics inspired by Noam Chomsky's avowedly Cartesian epistemology. See ch. 5 in this volume, R. Samson, 'Language and Law as Objects of Scientific Study.'

23 That is to say the forms law should take on in order to force itself as legal rules as opposed to material sources, namely, the set of facts, needs, expectations, and ideas that have led to the adoption of a norm.

24 Even today, resistance to the recognition of such creative power is still very strong. The current American controversy surrounding 'strict constructionism' and 'original intent' in constitutional cases exemplifies this quite clearly.

25 Except for committing a paralogism by *postulating* what constitutes the expected result of the search, namely, the medium (interface) between the *res cogitans* or thinking substance and the *res extensa* or extended substance, like divine ideas, innate ideas, a priori forms of understanding, and other a priori synthetic judgments.

26 M. Serres, *The Natural Contract*, trans. E. MacArthur and W. Paulson (Ann Arbor: University of Michigan Press, 1995), 15.

27 *Ibid.*, 38.

28 E. Klein, *Sous les atomes les particules* (Paris: Flammarion, 1993), 8. My translation.

29 *Ibid.*, 142.

30 J. Barnes, ed., *The Complete Works of Aristotle: The Revised Oxford Translation* (Princeton, NJ: Princeton University Press, 1984).

31 A. Papaux, *Essai philosophique sur la qualification juridique : De la subsomption à l'abduction* (Paris/Brussels/Zurich: LGDJ/Bruylant/Schulthess, 2003).

32 How, for instance, do you explain to the non-jurist that their dog is legal terms merely 'a movable' or that 'fish' in the legal terms of some French laws of fish farming also include crustaceans and frogs? Or yet that under the unacknowledged birth regime in French law (*'accouchement sous X'*) a child can be found to have no legal mother even though doctors and the authorities know full well who she is?

33 P.-A. Côté, notably 'Fonction législative et fonction interprétative : conceptions théoriques de leurs rapports,' in *Interprétation et droit*, under the direction of P. Amselek (Brussels: Bruylant, 1995), 189ff. My translation.

34 K.R. Popper, *Unended Quest: An Intellectual Autobiography* (London: Routledge, 1992), 51–2.

35 In *La fabrique du droit* (Paris: La Découverte, 2002), 235ff.

36 K. Llewellyn, in *The Common Law Tradition* (Boston: Little, Brown & Co., 1960), has also shown how the institutional character of the judicial function serves as a steadying factor in the reckonability of judicial decisions.

37 The presence of the other is indispensable to law exemplified by Robinson Crusoe stranded alone on his island and for whom enjoying fundamental freedoms has hardly any meaning: freedom of expression?, of assembly? of association? right to a healthy environment? right to privacy?

38 M. Serres, *supra* note 26.

39 And not *identical*, since the status of exception, for example, is not the same as in hard sciences, although these are not unfamiliar with ad hoc hypotheses, such as epicyle, ether, phlogistics, etc.

40 K.R. Popper, *The Logic of Scientific Discovery* (New York: Science Editions, 1961), 109–11.

41 Popper, *supra* note 34 at 29. The same is true for 'Schrödinger's cat' in quantum mechanics, *idem*, ch. 34.

42 Popper, *supra* note 40 at 13.

43 'The history of the sciences often merges with that of the pronouncements of courts – or of authorities, scientific or otherwise ... The knowledge recognized as scientific ensues from this "epistemodicy"; I mean by this new word all relations of science and law, reason and judgment.' (Serres, *supra* note 38 at 22).

44 J. Monod, 'Préface,' in K.R. Popper, *La logique de la découverte scientifique* (Paris: Payot Ed., 1990), 5. My translation.

5 Language and Law as Objects of Scientific Study

RÉMI SAMSON*

It is certain that words are the traces or impressions of reason.

Francis Bacon, *Advancement of Learning*

Then it is not for every man, Hermogenes, to give names, but for him who may be called the name-maker; and he, it appears, is the lawgiver, who is of all the artisans among men the rarest.

Plato, *Cratylus*

Introduction

Interdisciplinarity in law and linguistics represents a fascinating and worthwhile project, but it is a recent endeavour that is difficult to foster.[1] Good reasons for engaging in such scholarship include the fact that 'new perspectives provided by one side can introduce wonderful new questions, and often satisfying answers, for the other that would not have otherwise emerged,'[2] while forcing both sides to re-examine acknowledged and unconscious assumptions.[3] Further, the fields of semantics and pragmatics are viewed as being in a position to help jurists 'in disambiguating and otherwise making determinate problematic legal texts.'[4] Yet collaboration is still relatively limited, perhaps because both law and linguistics view themselves as self-contained disciplines, or perhaps because of a lack of faith in the possibility of experts from each field 'actually managing to combine to say something [...] illuminating.'[5]

I would venture to say, however, that much could be learned by practitioners in both areas if these subjects were approached from a vantage point that serves to bridge the gap between their respective ivory towers. For the purposes of this essay, the insights of epistemology will serve as an instrument to help bring about such a rapprochement. The value of epistemological enquiry has been recognized in linguistics; J. Kristeva voiced early on the need for 'the elaboration of an epistemology of linguistics that has yet to be done.'[6] The task has already begun in the field of legal theory, be it in continental Europe[7] or in the United Kingdom.[8] The insistence on the importance of epistemology for law and linguistics is constantly being reaffirmed.[9]

Before going further, some terminological clarifications are in order. In the course of this essay, I will not ordinarily refer to 'epistemology' in the usual Anglo-American fashion to denote the study of human cognition,[10] but will instead use epistemology to mean the critical study of scientific principles, hypotheses and results in order to determine their (non-psychological) origin, their value, and their scope.[11] In short, I view epistemology here as a study of the 'paradigms' of a particular discipline at a particular point in time. In any event, both meanings are not airtight and tend to raise certain metaphysical questions that have long been viewed as not 'to the taste of everyone.'[12]

A word, also, on paradigms. The practice of any hard science is usually based on a particular unspecified world view guaranteed by little more than faith.[13] 'Paradigms' are what Thomas Kuhn calls those sets of beliefs, those sets of 'accepted examples of actual scientific practice ... [that] provide models from which spring particular coherent traditions of scientific research.'[14]

It is undeniable that the formal approach to linguistic study developed by Noam Chomsky during the 1950s and onwards, avowedly Cartesian in inspiration, remains, even today, one of the most influential schools of thought in the area of linguistics, at least in North America. It was very early on recognized as a scientific paradigm.[15]

In legal theory, the Anglo-Saxon tradition of legal positivism, now criticized by much of academia, is still very much alive in the official practice of law. Its continued dominance is most apparent in the centrality a doctrine such as the rule of law plays in contemporary legal systems of common-law heritage and, notably, in constitutional theory. H.L.A. Hart's contribution to legal theory, also viewed as a paradigm,[16] has been particularly influential.

From my perspective as a practising lawyer, a student of linguistics, and a teacher of legal philosophy, it has become apparent that Hart's legal positivism and Chomsky's approach to linguistics share a specific world view that interdisciplinarity can best uncover. By shedding light on some basic tenets of those two paradigms and underscoring the similarities between their epistemological presuppositions, it will be possible to show how both disciplines treat their respective subjects, that is language and law, as static objects to be studied scientifically.

This 'scientific method' is akin to that of the modern natural sciences and serves a very useful heuristic purpose. Its epistemological legacy is traceable, in particular, to the figure of René Descartes. It is not, however, devoid of serious shortcomings; these are being slowly revealed, notably, by developments in contemporary natural sciences and in cognitive psychology.

In the first two parts of this essay, I attempt to flesh out some of the basic tenets of Chomsky's project of generative grammar and the Cartesian influences that underlie it. In the third part, I use basic concepts of Hart's positivism to highlight shared epistemological presuppositions and their metaphysical implications. In the fourth part, I underscore some of the challenges that have been levelled against these two analogous systems of belief by rising schools of criticism.

I believe that epistemological interdisciplinarity is useful for two main purposes. It helps to reveal many underlying assumptions of scientific and legal traditions, such as their paradigmatic nature. It also points to the kind – or quality – of knowledge required, perhaps ironically, to properly conduct one's reason to seek truth in science and assess daily practice with a healthy dose of critical thinking.

1. Philosophical Roots

The work of René Descartes is one of the explicit foundations of Chomsky's theories. In this essay, I contend that it also constitutes one of the philosophical roots of legal positivism and, by extension, of much of current legal practice.

Descartes' scientific project was universal in ambition. He aimed to develop a scientific method that, if observed accurately, would lead to 'a knowledge which takes in all things.'[17] According to him, 'the end of study should be to direct the mind towards the enunciation of sound and correct judgments on all matters that come before it.'[18] The senses are not to be relied on during the search for truth because 'bodies themselves are perceived not from thence that they would be touched or seen, but rather from thence only that they were to be understood, [therefore] nothing can be perceived by me more easily or more evidently than my mind.'[19]

The *Discourse on the Method of Properly Conducting One's Reason and of Seeking the Truth in the Sciences*, published in 1637, lays down the fundamental methodological precepts that are to ensure the correctness of human cognition. The cogito, in conjunction with the presupposed existence of God, is the origin[20] of all true knowledge: 'from this it follows that the natural enlightenment or the faculty of knowing given to us by God, can never attain any object which is not true.'[21] Once this first foundational truth is secured, reason must be exercised in conformity with four general rules if it is to find truth.

First, 'never to accept anything as true that I did not know to be evidently so: that is to say, carefully to avoid precipitancy and prejudice, and to include in my judgements nothing more than what presented itself so clearly and so distinctly to my mind that I might have no occasion to place it in doubt.'[22] Jurists will recall how often judges rely on the 'obvious' or 'clear' or 'evident' nature of a set of facts or of the law to explain their decisions, much to the dissatisfaction of the losing party, for which the facts and the law are not so clear and distinct.

Second, I must 'divide each of the difficulties that I was examining into as many parts as might be possible and necessary in order best to solve it.'[23] Here linguists will recognize their own methodology of parsing sentences into constituents (for syntacticians) or arriving at a compositional account of the meaning of sentences (for formal semanticists).[24]

Third, thought must be conducted in an orderly fashion, starting from simple objects and moving on to more complicated ones, 'and even supposing some order among those objects which do not precede each other naturally.'[25] Thus, the primacy of structure, irrespective of objects, is assured. In a positivist account of law as well as in a Chomskyan approach to linguistics, the *rules* must always exist *before* the actual languages or laws.

The system is closed, fourthly, by ensuring exhaustivity through review such 'that I would be sure to have omitted nothing.'[26] In the following section, I will point to Chomsky's concept of 'universal grammar' and Hart's concept of 'rule of recognition' as evidence of this fourth methodological precept.

Descartes' approach is reminiscent of the ancient objectivist paradigm according to which the whole of reality is composed of entities, properties, and relations between them, thus presupposing 'a unique, correct, complete structure'[27] that exists irrespective of any human knowledge or understanding. Under this 'metaphysic of univocity,'[28] categories serve to group entities that share the same essential properties, which are, in turn, necessary and sufficient to define the categories. Categories thus defined correspond objectively to the kinds of things that exist in the world, and the objective existence of those categories 'provides logical relations that hold objectively in the world.'[29] True knowledge, then, is guaranteed by the presupposition that the mind mirrors nature perfectly:

> In objectivist cognition, the mind can achieve real knowledge of the external world only if it can represent (that is, *re-present*, make present again) what is really in the world; true knowledge must not be in any way an artifact of the nature of the thinking beings. Hence, the concern in the objectivist tradition with cognitive *representation* of external reality. The position is not that mental representations must resemble the external world. It is only that they must be able to correspond directly to them in a systematic way. Mental representations must thus be 'semantically evaluable' – capable of being true or false, of referring correctly or failing to refer correctly.[30]

This is validated by Descartes' discussion of 'innate ideas': 'the sense organs do not bring us anything which is like the idea which arises in us at their stimulus, and so this idea must have been in us before.'[31] For him, however, language was excluded from a universe composed of objective things and innate ideas, since it constituted a source of error for the proper conduct of reason.[32] In any event, it would only be a matter of time before this 'mind as a mirror of nature' world view would develop into that of 'language as a mirror of the mind,' therefore establishing a relation of identity between language, thought, and reality.[33]

The work of the linguists of Port-Royal, in the seventeenth century, avowedly Cartesian in inspiration, was the first since the Middle Ages to put forth the idea that languages follow the laws of the mind, which are valid for all of humanity.[34] The Solitaires sought to specify the laws that permitted the construction of well-formed propositions. This 'innovation' served as inspiration for the development of Chomsky's theories.[35] Chomsky, however, rejected Cartesian dualism between body and mind, since Newton had already exorcised the machine, leaving the ghost intact.[36] The 'language of the brain organ'[37] was therefore viewed by Chomsky as an emergent property of the brain,[38] the laws of which linguists should somehow discover and describe.

2. The Objectification of Language

Linguistics views itself as a science akin to the natural sciences. What guarantees this status, at least formally, is its adherence to the 'scientific method.' In this context, the Chomskyan approach also pays homage to the rationalist tradition that views language as a 'mirror of the mind,'[39] and presupposes an 'objectivist'[40] world view. As J. Kristeva has noted, it is ironic that Cartesian philosophy, which perceived language to be a source of error, would go on to serve as a foundation for the study of that very object.[41]

Linguistics as an autonomous scientific discipline is a fairly recent phenomenon.[42] As J. Kristeva has remarked: 'Language at some point was made the privileged object of thought, science, and philosophy. The full import of this gesture has not yet been determined.'[43] The significance of the work of the nineteenth-century Swiss linguist Ferdinand de Saussure, who established the autonomy of the field, is not to be underestimated. The 'fundamental tenet' of his *Cours de linguistique générale* was precisely that 'synchronic aspects of language – such as its principles of sound patterning and word formation – as well as diachronic can be studied productively as an autonomous entity.'[44] The last sentence of his *Cours* reads as follows: 'the true and unique object of linguistics is language studied in and for itself.'[45] The structuralist enterprise sought to describe the *langue* by identifying the linguistic universals that make the rules of the system hold together. *Langue* is understood as a set of impressions – or miniature identical dictionaries – mapped on the brain of every individual. The concept of *langue* is opposed to that of *parole*, the sum of people's utterances. Linguistic change, instead of being explained by historical or socio-political reasons, results from the nature of the elements of the *langue* and the structural relations among them.[46]

Chomsky's work flows from this structuralist tradition. Although his contribution to linguistics has been characterized as a 'revolution,' Chomsky never challenged the idea of the grammar of a language as an autonomous structural system. From *Syntactic Structures*[47] onward, however, the study of language would cease to be constrained by empirical evidence,[48] and the very goal of linguistic theory would morph into that of explaining the 'limits within which all languages function,'[49] or rather, what language *is*, its nature, or essence. Key to the approach is the use of abstract theories to 'discover basic truths about the world.'[50] As F. Newmeyer puts it, 'autonomous linguistics seems to bridge the natural sciences and the human sciences, to combine thoroughly human subject matter with a precision and depth matched only in the hard sciences.'[51]

Chomsky views language as 'a natural object, a component of the human mind, physically represented in the brain and part of the biological endowment of the species.'[52] Three basic questions arise from this new approach to the study of language as object: 1) What constitutes knowledge of language? 2) How is language acquired? 3) How is linguistic knowledge put to use?[53]

Chomsky focuses linguistics on the study of the 'language faculty,' unique to human beings, and which can be studied 'more or less as we study some complex bodily organ.'[54] He explains that this faculty

> serves the two basic functions of rationalist theory: it provides a sensory system for the preliminary analysis of linguistic data, and a schematism that determines, quite narrowly, a certain class of grammars. Each grammar is a theory of a particular language, specifying formal and semantic properties of an infinite array of sentences. These sentences, each with its particular structure, constitute the language generated by the grammar. The languages so generated are those that can be 'learned' in the normal way. The language faculty, given appropriate stimulation, will construct a grammar; the person knows the language generated by the constructed grammar. This knowledge can then be used to understand what is heard and to produce discourse as an expression of thought within the constraints of the internalized principles, in a manner appropriate to situations as these are conceived by other mental faculties, free of stimulus control.[55]

It is important to understand the significance, for linguistic theory, of what is entailed by Chomsky's rule-based model of human cognition. According to this view, it is the language faculty, an essential property of human beings, that is the origin of all true knowledge of any language. The initial state of the language faculty represents the innate 'universal grammar,' shared by all human beings, 'a component of the mind/brain, part of the fixed biological endowment.'[56] As its name suggests, universal grammar comprises a set of rules or principles that make all else possible. Through sensory experience, the principles of universal grammar become parametrized and result in particular grammars that, in turn, generate a particular language of the world.[57]

Thus language, according to this framework, is viewed as 'a particular generative procedure that assigns to every possible expression a representation of its form and its meaning, insofar as these are determined by the language faculty.'[58] To have internalized the rules of a particular grammar, then, is to *know* a language. Chomsky hopes that 'by studying language we may discover abstract principles that are universal by biological necessity and not mere historical accident, that derive from mental characteristics of the species.'[59] The task of linguistics, then, should be to offer an objective description of *linguistic competence*, that is, the initial state of the language faculty.

Chomskyan linguistics deals with the issue of relating the structure of the mind to the outside world as follows. The correspondence between the words of a particular language and reality is left to the field of semantics, which is shielded from the study of the structure of the language faculty. Thus, grammar is deemed 'autonomous and independent of meaning.'[60] 'Knowledge' of a language is elicited from the innate cognitive system through stimulation by the senses, or, to use Descartes' words, 'the idea which arises in us at the senses' stimulus.'[61] In effect, such 'knowledge' is nothing more than a set of conditions that make it possible for a competent speaker to judge the grammaticality of a sentence (from a syntactic point of view) or the truth of a sentence (from a semantic point of view). Knowledge of a language is knowledge of its objective truth conditions. As will be shown shortly, the critics were quick to point to problems raised by this 'meaning-less' cognitive structure that is universal grammar.

3. Hart's Legal Positivism

In a manner similar to Chomskyan linguistics, the schools of legal theory suggestively called *legal positivism* have generally embraced a rationalist conception of their object of study, namely law. In *The Concept of Law*, H.L.A. Hart's preoccupation is to show what the law *is* by isolating and characterizing elements that elucidate three main issues: 1) Whether law is more than mere orders backed by threats; 2) How legal obligation differs from moral obligation; and 3) What the nature of rules is and to what extent law is an affair of rules. Hart's account purports to be descriptive. He believes that 'truths about certain important aspects of law' can be 'clearly presented, and their importance rightly assessed.' He states that his theory 'is morally neutral and has no justificatory aims: it does not seek to justify or commend on moral or other grounds the forms and structures' it contains.[62]

Hart portrays law as a self-regulated system distinct from morality. The idea of 'rule' is, self-evidently (i.e., clearly and distinctly), the starting point of the analysis, and holds legal systems together. According to Hart, a legal system can best be described as a system that results from the union of primary and secondary rules. Primary rules impose duties in that they require human beings to act or to refrain from acting in a certain way (e.g., 'thou shalt not kill'). Secondary rules are power-conferring rules. They 'provide that human beings may by doing or saying certain things introduce new rules of the primary type, extinguish or modify old ones, or in various ways determine their incidence or control their operations.'[63]

It seems that the metaphor of a 'generative grammar' could perhaps have been useful to describe such a system.[64] The secondary rules include rules of change, which empower 'an individual or body of persons to introduce new primary rules for the conduct of the life of the group, or of some class within it, and to eliminate old rules.'[65] Rules of adjudication, on the other hand, identify the individuals who are to adjudicate disputes and also define the appropriate procedures to follow. The rule that closes the system is a *rule of recognition*, which specifies which particular features a rule must have to qualify as a rule. As is the case with Chomskyan linguistics and Cartesian metaphysics, structure exists here irrespective of objects: whatever the particular laws may be, the particular categories of rules and the relations that hold among them exist. Finally, in order for a particular legal system (a particular grammar?) to exist in a given society, it is a sufficient and necessary condition that the rule of recognition and the other secondary rules be recognized and accepted as binding by the officials responsible for creating, modifying, interpreting, applying and enforcing the primary rules of obligation.

Hart accepts the traditional positivist doctrine of the separation of law and morality. What law *is* does not depend on what law *ought to be* in a given society. Therefore, it is possible to make theoretical enquiries 'to group and consider together as "law" all rules which are valid by the formal tests of a system of primary and secondary rules, even though some of them offend against a society's own morality.'[66]

In a sense, by postulating the separation of law and morality, Hart ensures that legal systems will be viewed as being composed of discrete objects of scientific investigation.

Hart recognizes that legal rules have an *open texture*. For him, however, the difficulties in determining the tenor and meaning of legal propositions does not affect the existence of those propositions. This flows from human beings' 'intentions that a certain type of behavior be regulated by rules':[67] rules come first, meanings second.

According to Hart, 'the general words we use ... must have some standard instance in which no doubts are felt about [the rule's] application.' Accordingly, 'even if there are borderlines, there must first be lines.' When a case falls within the 'core of settled meaning' of the legal term, the judge simply subsumes the situation under the rule and draws the appropriate conclusions. Where there exists 'a penumbra of debatable cases in which words are neither obviously applicable nor obviously ruled out,' judges called upon to apply the law should appeal to the aims, the social policies and purposes contained within the law: 'the social policies which guide the judges' choice are in a sense there for them to discover; the judges are only "drawing out" of the rule what, if it is properly understood, is "latent" within it.'[68]

One is very much tempted to see here evidence of objectivism as defined above. Yet Hart explicitly rejects this.[69] In a very influential lecture,[70] he explains that legal words cannot be defined on a one-to-one correspondence with reality, since their use presupposes the existence of a legal system composed of valid legal rules. Also, legal concepts are necessarily general in nature and are destined to apply to various factual situations. Finally, the status of a legal statement may vary according to context. What is therefore required is that we 'characterise adequately the distinctive manner in which expressions ... are used in a legal system.'[71] Hart thus shifts the focus from the set of entities referred to by legal concepts to the set of conditions under which legal statements are true, or 'applicable.'[72]

4. Criticisms

In the fields of linguistics and legal theory, criticisms of two types abound. Some are internal to the proposed theory. They have, for instance, prompted Chomsky to revise his initial theories by proposing, successively, his theory of 'principles and parameters,'[73] and his recent Minimalist Program.[74] Hart's postscript to *The Concept of Law* results from the same phenomenon. Criticisms of the second type, however, question the epistemological presuppositions of the established theories, and it is to a deeper understanding of those types of criticisms that interdisciplinary study leads.

Epistemological criticisms have been present in the field of legal theory since its very beginnings.[75] One of the more questionable aspects of Hart's theory is his account of judicial interpretation coupled with his apparent rejection of objectivism. Recall that law, according to Hart, is defined so as to be independent from cognitive capacity. Whatever the meaning of legal propositions may be, there are always, already, propositions of a legal nature. But what makes these propositions legal, and how do we know? According to Hart, the rule of recognition would serve this purpose. But then, what is the nature of the rule of recognition and who determines *its* meaning? This has lead one commentator to state that with respect to Hart's theory, those 'categories which are presented as analytical ultimately reveal themselves as references to presumed social facts.'[76] Unfortunately, Hart's analytical approach has systematically privileged conceptual speculation to the detriment of actual sociological inquiry into 'the actual conditions ... under which interpretive agreement about the meaning of legal rules becomes possible or becomes problematic.'[77]

In the field of linguistics, an analogous issue is tackled by proponents of an approach usually termed 'functionalist.' Although the positions of those accepting the label are often diverse, functionalists tend to view the form of language as being significantly tied to its function of, notably, communication. In other words, 'any so-called competence grammar is really a performance grammar in disguise, a grammar that has already assumed the knowledge ... from which its mechanisms are supposedly abstracted.'[78] On a functionalist account, any airtight separation between form and function is deemed inadequate to account for the complexity of a phenomenon such as language.[79] To them, Chomsky's approach seems suspiciously ahistorical and universalist, censoring what historical scholarship has shown as being the truly signifying character of language, and refusing to acknowledge the inputs of history and tradition that form and inform any purportedly objective description.[80]

Realizing that objective meanings never exist in practice but only in theory, linguists working in the field of 'cognitive linguistics,' for instance, have followed developments in cognitive psychology and have rejected a view of semantics as being concerned with objective truth conditions.[81] Since language form is viewed as intrinsically tied to its signifying function, the study of grammatical rules must be extended to the effective use of language. The nature of the 'faculty of language' ceases to be a set of static rules and becomes a dynamic reality.[82] Thus the question of who determines the meaning of the rules that form part of the language faculty – an inevitable conundrum for generative linguists – loses all relevance for cognitive linguists. The meaning of utterances, instead of being 'generated' by the language faculty, is rather influenced by the interaction of idealized cognitive models[83] that are not meant to correspond exactly and objectively to the world, but that certainly reflect the assumptions of 'interpretive communities.'[84]

The developments of cognitive psychology are being gradually introduced into the study of law from an interdisciplinary perspective. A recent study by R. Chen and J. Hanson shows particularly well the psychological and social origins of the cognitive biases to which judicial decision makers are inevitably subject.[85] The authors show that deciding a case does not merely involve selecting the applicable law, interpreting its meaning (if unclear), and 'applying' it to the 'facts' of the case. Much, much more is at play in decision making than what finds its way into the text of the judgment.

Yet jurists often fall into this trap of objectivism, since they are 'always tempted to believe that the quality of a legal concept can be measured very exactly by its capacity to express reality.'[86] According to a prevailing view among jurists, 'the ultimate goal of law should indeed be to embrace, as exactly as possible, all the forms of facts and their solution. This means that there are the world of facts (equated with reality) and the world of law, i.e., what has been worked at by reason in order to organize that reality. A perfect society would be one that rejected any misfit between reality and its legal organization; in other words one that could always juridically reflect any social novelty, immediately representable by the notion of facts.'[87]

The inextricable links between language, meaning, and cognition can be further illustrated through one of the main metaphors of law: that of judicial interpretation seen as the search for the 'intention of the legislator.' According to settled, official legal doctrine, a legal rule that is clear must not be interpreted: *claris non fit interpretatio*. In case of ambiguity, however, the judge must attempt to discover the true meaning of the rule as it was intended by the legislator at the time of its enactment.[88] This is done by relying on rules of interpretation. As

P.-A. Côté explains: 'The official doctrine also reveals a concern with legal certainty: the predetermination of the meaning and the passivity of the interpreter, in particular the judge, ensure stability in legal relations. Respect for the meaning intended by the author enables the citizen to organize his affairs based on an "objective meaning" of the rules expressed in the enactment, free of the risk of encountering the unexpected. Not only is the official doctrine the guarantor of legal certainty: it also ensures legal stability, by affirming the unchangeability of the enactment's meaning at the time of its adoption, failing any subsequent legislative intervention.'[89]

The view of language as a mirror of the mind clearly underlies such an objectivist approach. The role of the jurist is seen as one involving the determination of an object impervious to doubt and of unquestionable pedigree that 're-presents' reality perfectly. The use of rules of interpretation licences, in a way, the judge's interpretation in what Hart would call the hard, or penumbral, cases. Thus, from the equivalent of Descartes' point of origin, the legislator, flows the whole of legal knowledge.[90]

This view of the judicial power as the mere 'mouth of the law' serves both as a foundation and a justification for the 'static ideology of interpretation.'[91] As one theorist has noted, however, 'there is a very important sense in which the idea that democracy entails "a government of laws and not of men" is complete and utter fantasy and nonsense.' The idea of the rule of law 'incorrectly imagines that "laws" and "humans" reside in two utterly different logical spaces—that THE LAW represents a realm in which musty documents from the past push or can push people in the present like so many levers on a complicated machine, and that humans, who are fated always to live their lives in the present, are or can be miserable slaves of the documents that their ancestors deposited in the past.'[92]

In the legal context, concepts such as the 'intention of the legislator' and the 'separation of powers,' viewed as mirrors of reality, raise fundamental political and ethical questions. The myth of the rule of law becomes an origin story 'designed to authorize or confer authority on preconceived political solutions.' These myths are 'a contentious and political means by which western society organizes and represents its experience – both real and imagined,' thereby 'allowing us both to explore our fundamental questions and problems and to assign meaning to our human existence.' Furthermore, 'to delineate beginnings is to set the course for what is to follow; it is to carve out an identity for those who see their experience reflected in myth.' The upshot is that attention is diverted from the conflictual mess that is politics to simplistic 'questions to which there might never be satisfactory answers.'[93]

Philosophers opposed to positivistic – we could say objectivist – conceptions of law recognize that knowledge of the law and practice of the law are mutually constitutive: 'there is no pause or gap in time—no stasis of time between the past and the present—that could ever be filled by THE LAW *before* it gets received and applied in just the way that it is received and applied. Therefore humans must always make their appearance in time before the Law can appear, and never the other way around.'[94] An objectivist approach to legal language is perceived to flatten and confine in absolutes the complexity of meaning that inheres in any given problem,[95] and obscure the traditionality that pervades the practice of law.[96] As any good jurist understands, it is not enough to learn the rules of a system to know a legal system. One must also understand how the rules are put together, how they are interpreted within the community.[97] Could the same not be said of such a uniquely human phenomenon as language?

Cognitive linguists such as G. Lakoff are well aware of the high stakes of the debate they raise. They are putting into question an ancient world view that presupposes a fit between thought, language and reality. Should such a view be deemed deficient, generative grammar as a linguistic theory risks becoming irrelevant. It should come as no surprise, then, that those aspects of legal positivism most closely associated with objectivism also stand much to lose should the world view on which they rest be exposed and judged unacceptable.

Conclusion

Paul Feyerabend has remarked that 'all methodologies, even the most obvious ones, have their limits. The best way to show this is to demonstrate the limits and even the irrationality of some rules which [one] is likely to regard as basic.'[98] I believe that this is fruitfully achieved from an interdisciplinary standpoint. Our brief foray into the realm of comparative epistemology will perhaps have shown that this type of enquiry lays down the groundwork for an exchange and 'requires that both disciplines accept the implicit challenge to reconsider the prejudices that help to shape their disciplinary boundaries and to reconstruct their understanding of legitimate modes and purposes of inquiry.'[99]

In addition, the epistemological insights gleaned through comparison between disciplines help us escape the naivety of objective descriptivism,[100] and show the extent of the role scientific discourse is called to play in the construction of its object of study. We can begin to feel the extent to which a single, ancient world view permeates the study of language and the practice and theory of law. It has certainly been a key instrument in the establishment of linguistics as a science, and lies at the very core of the idea of the Modern State. These are no small feats and are surely worthy of study, for through this very idea of objective form and structure is exercised great power.

Acknowledging this state of affairs and the interests at stake raises a host of difficult but fascinating questions. For instance, just what is it that formalist models fail to capture of reality? Why do they tend to enjoy so much prominence today in so many disciplines? Is the refusal of those who believe in them to reconsider their basic presuppositions a reflection of the natural tendency of human-kind to let well-settled beliefs go unquestioned? If so, this would not speak very highly of human nature:

> What is the implication of believing that there is an underlying rational truth, a rational godhead? Well, since we have never come up with such a truth, in spite of having tried over the centuries, what we are left with is the ultimate meaning of ideology. That is, we insist upon treating speculation as a statement of the absolute. Note: the term here is speculation, not uncertainty. This is not imagination, which flourishes through the maintenance of uncertainty. This is logical speculation as certainty; and therefore speculation as a decision-making mechanism. This is not imagination seized by intuition to produce action. Instead, we are to leap from the delusion of certainty to instrumental action; from deluding ourselves about what we know to action. Neither thought nor argument has a role here.
>
> This is false reason or reason as irrationality. What is speculation masquerading as certainty? 'I think therefore I am.'[101]

Fortunately, there are the critics who attempt to convince others of the proverbial emperor's state of undress. Thomas Kuhn wrote that when a profession 'can no longer evade anomalies that subvert the existing tradition of scientific practice – then begin the extraordinary investigations that lead the profession at last to a new set of commitments, a new basis for the practice of science.' These 'extraordinary episodes in which that shift of professional commitments occurs'[102] are signs of scientific revolutions that gradually result from social, technical and cultural conditions.[103] At the level of underlying assumptions, in law as well as in the other social sciences, revolutions are rare and usually limited in scope.[104] Perhaps functionalist approaches to linguistics, along with the various schools or movements of critical analysis of law, are indications of a need – and a will – to adopt new paradigms in those disciplines?[105] Comparing the two certainly helps to point out the theoretical inconsistencies, call into question interpretive assumptions, and perhaps hasten change.

NOTES

* I am indebted to Diana Majury and Logan Atkinson for their trust and support, and to Iwan Chan, Archibald McDonald, Alain Papaux, and Timothy Wilson for their helpful suggestions and penetrating insight.

1 J.N. Levi, 'Introduction: "What is Meaning in a Legal Text?" A First Dialogue for Law and Linguistics' 1995 73 Wash.U.L.Q. 771, 772 ff.

2 *Ibid.*, 782.

3 D.R. Klinck, *The Word of the Law* (Ottawa, Carleton University Press, 1992), 2.

4 The editors of the *Washington University Law Quarterly*, 1995 73 Wash.U.L.Q. 769, 770 (Editors' forward). See also C.D. Cunningham, J.N. Levi, G.M. Green, and J.P. Kaplan, 'Plain Meaning and Hard Cases' 1994 103 Yale L.J. 1561; P. Barbaud, 'Les mots en cause ou la sémantique dans les jugements de cour,' in *Language and Law: Proceedings of the First Conference of the International Institute of Comparative Linguistic Law*, ed. P. Pupier and J. Woerling (Montreal: Wilson and Lafleur, 1989), 551.

5 Law and Linguistics Conference, 1995 73 Wash.U.L.Q. 785, 969 (comments by Kent Greenawalt, professor, Columbia Law School).

6 J. Kristeva, *Language the Unknown* (New York: Columbia University Press, 1989), 147.

7 C. Atias, *Épistémologie juridique* (Paris, Dalloz, 2002).

8 G. Samuel, *Epistemology and Method in Law* (Burlington, VT: Ashgate, 2003).

9 M. Saint-Hilaire, 'Pour un développement de l'épistémologie juridique au Canada ... comme ailleurs,' 2004 30 Man. L.J. 463; G. Lakoff, 'Philosophical Implications,' in *Women, Fire, and Dangerous Things. What Cate-*

gories Reveal About the Mind (Chicago: University of Chicago Press, 1987), 155ff.

10 A. Lalande, 'gnoséologie,' in *Vocabulaire technique et critique de la philosophie*, 5th ed. (Paris: Quadrige, PUF, 1999). See also H. Barreau, *L'épistémologie*, 4th ed. (Paris: Que sais-je, PUF, 1998).

11 A. Lalande, 'épistémologie,' in *Vocabulaire technique et critique de la philosophie*.

12 R. Descartes, *Discourse on Method*, trans. F.E. Sutcliffe (Harmondsworth, UK: Penguin Books, 1968), 53.

13 T. Kuhn, *The Structure of Scientific Revolutions*, 2nd ed. (Chicago: University of Chicago Press, 1970), 4; K. Popper, *The Logic of Scientific Discovery* (New York: Science Editions, 1961), 30–2.

14 T. Kuhn, *ibid.* at 10.

15 J. Thorne, 'Review of P. Postal, Constituant Structure,' *Journal of Linguistics* 1 (1965): 74.

16 R. Dworkin, 'Hard Cases' (1975) 88 Harv.L.Rev. 1057, 1057.

17 R. Descartes, *Rules for the Direction of the Mind*, rule IV, in *The Philosophical Works of Descartes*, trans. E.S. Haldane and G.R.T. Ross (Cambridge: Cambridge University Press, 1967), 9.

18 *Ibid.*, rule I.

19 R. Descartes, *Meditations on First Philosophy*, ed. and trans. G. Heffernan, (Notre Dame: University of Notre-Dame Press, 1990), 117. See also H.M. Bracken, 'Rationalism and Dualism in Descartes,' ch. 1 in *Mind and Language: Essays on Descartes and Chomsky* (Dordrecht: Foris Publications, 1984), 1ff.

20 A. Papaux, *Essai philosophique sur la qualification juridique: de la subsomption à l'abduction; l'exemple du droit international privé* (Zurich: Schulthess, 2002), 49–50. See also C. Atias, *Philosophie du droit*, 2nd ed. (Paris: PUF, 2004), 35–6.

21 R. Descartes, *Principles of Philosophy*, trans. V.R. Miller and R.P. Miller (Dordrecht: D. Reidel, 1983), 15.

22 R. Descartes, *Discourse on Method*, *supra* note 12 at 41.

23 *Ibid.*

24 See, for example, B.H. Partee, A. ter Meulen, and R.E. Wall, *Mathematical Methods in Linguistics* (Dordrecht: Kluwer, 1990).

25 R. Descartes, *Discourse on Method*, *supra* note 12 at 41.

26 *Ibid.*

27 G. Lakoff, *Women, Fire, and Dangerous Things*, *supra* note 9 at 159.

28 A. Papaux, *Essai philosophique sur la qualification juridique*, *supra* note 20, pp. 37ff.

29 Suppose we consider the set of all the animals that exist in the world. The individual members of the set would correspond to the objective category 'animals.' Human beings, since they can be distinguished from other animals by the essential property that is 'reason,' form part of the subcategory 'rational animals.' These categories and the logical structure between them exist even without human knowledge. See also Lakoff, *Women, Fire, and Dangerous Things, supra* note 9 at 162.
30 Lakoff, *Women, Fire, and Dangerous Things, supra* note 9 at 163.
31 R. Descartes, *Letter to Mersenne, 22 July 1641*, in *Descartes' Philosophical Letters*, ed. and trans. A. Kenny (Oxford: Clarendon Press, 1970), 108.
32 R. Descartes, *Principles of Philosophy, supra* note 21, part I, principle 74, pp. 34–5.
33 U. Eco, *Le signe* (Paris: Le livre de poche, 1992), 198.
34 *Ibid.*, 199.
35 *Ibid.*, 199 and 201. See also N. Chomsky, *On Nature and Language* (Cambridge: Cambridge University Press, 2002), 1 (editors' introduction); J. Kristeva, *Language the Unknown, supra* note 6 at 147.
36 N. Chomsky, 'Perspectives on Language and Mind,' in *On Nature and Language, ibid.* at 53.
37 *Ibid.*, 57.
38 *Ibid.*, 55.
39 N. Chomsky, *Reflections on Language* (New York: Pantheon Books, 1975), 4.
40 This discussion follows Lakoff, *Women, Fire, and Dangerous Things, supra* note 9 at 157ff.
41 J. Kristeva, *Language the Unknown, supra* note 6 at 160.
42 F. Newmeyer, *The Politics of Linguistics* (Chicago: University of Chicago Press, 1986).
43 Kristeva, *Language the Unknown, supra* note 6 at 3.
44 Newmeyer, *The Politics of Linguistics, supra* note 42 at 27.
45 F. de Saussure, *Course in General Linguistics* (London: Peter Owen, 1959), 232.
46 J. Kristeva, *Language the Unknown, supra* note 6 at 218. See also E. Benveniste, 'Tendances récentes de la linguistique générale,' *Journal de psychologie normale et pathologique* (1954) 130–45.
47 N. Chomsky, *Syntactic Structures*, Janua Linguarum Series Minor 4 (The Hague: Mouton, 1957).
48 Until the 1940s, empiricism was key to the development of linguistics in the United States. Leonard Bloomfield represented a main influence in this respect. See Newmeyer, *The Politics of Linguistics, supra* note 42 at 47.

49 *Ibid.*, 67.

50 N. Chomsky, 'Reply to Lycan,' in *Chomsky and His Critics*, ed. L.M. Anthony and N. Hornstein (Cambridge: Blackwell, 2003), 255. See also N. Chomsky, 'Linguistics and Adjacent Fields: A Personal View,' in *The Chomskyan Turn*, ed. A. Kasher (Cambridge: Blackwell, 1991), 13.

51 Newmeyer, *The Politics of Linguistics*, *supra* note 42 at 7.

52 Chomsky, *On Nature and Language*, *supra* note 35 at 1 (editors' introduction).

53 Chomsky, 'Linguistics and Adjacent Fields: A Personal View,' *supra* note 50 at 6. See also Chomsky, *Knowledge of Language: Its Nature, Origin, and Use* (New York: Praeger, 1986), 3; Chomsky, 'Language and Problems of Knowledge: The Managua Lectures,' Current Studies in Linguistics 16 (Cambridge, MA: MIT Press, 1988), 3.

54 Chomsky, *Reflections on Language*, *supra* note 39 at 10, 13.

55 *Ibid.*, 12–13.

56 Chomsky, 'Linguistics and Adjacent Fields: A Personal View,' *supra* note 50 at 9.

57 These particular grammars are very different from what is commonly understood as grammatical rules. The former must account for all utterances by native speakers within the limits of what is permitted by Universal Grammar. Particular grammars are sets of rules that enable the production of an infinite variety of sentences of a language. Conversely, 'ordinary' grammatical rules purport to prescribe how native speakers should speak or write. In other words, while ordinary grammars specify the ways that sentences *should* be put together, linguists' grammars specify how sentences *can* be put together.

58 Chomsky, 'Linguistics and Adjacent Fields: A Personal View,' *supra* note 50 at 8.

59 Chomsky, *Reflections on Language*, *supra* note 39 at 4.

60 Chomsky, *Syntactic Structures*, *supra* note 47 at 17. Semantic considerations, however, are not wholly without interest, but any *necessary and constitutive* role for the construction of grammar is excluded. See Chomsky, *Aspects of the Theory of Syntax* (Cambridge, MA: MIT Press, 1965), 226.

61 Chomsky, *Reflections on Language*, *supra* note 39 at 6–7; Descartes, *supra* note 31.

62 H.L.A. Hart, *The Concept of Law*, 2nd ed. (Oxford: Oxford University Press, 1994), 100, 240. For his descriptive enterprise, Hart adopts the point of view of an uncommitted observer in a position to make normative statements about the legal system that do not entail personal normative commitment to the system. See, on this 'hermeneutic' point of view;

J. Raz, *The Concept of a Legal System: An Introduction to the Theory of Legal System*, 2nd ed. (Oxford: Oxford University Press, 1980), 236; D.N. MacCormick, *H.L.A. Hart* (London: Edward Arnold, 1981), 38; H.L.A. Hart, *Essays on Bentham: Studies in Jurisprudence and Political Theory* (Oxford: Oxford University Press, 1982), 153–5; H.L.A. Hart, *Essays in Jurisprudence and Philosophy* (Oxford: Oxford University Press, 1983), 14.

63 H.L.A. Hart, *The Concept of Law*, *ibid.* at 81.

64 It is tempting to link the generative character of both linguistic and legal positivistic systems with the notion of autopoiesis; see, e.g., N. Luhmann, *Essays on Self-Reference*(New York: Columbia University Press, 1990); G. Teubner, *Law as an Autopoietic System* (Oxford: Blackwell Publishers, 1993).

65 H.L.A. Hart, *The Concept of Law*, *supra* note 62 at 95.

66 *Ibid.*, 209; see also H.L A. Hart, 'Positivism and the Separation of Law and Morals,' 71 (1958) Harv.L.Rev. 593.

67 Hart, 'Positivism and the Separation of Law and Morals,' *ibid.*, 607.

68 *Ibid.*, 607, 612, and 614.

69 H.L.A. Hart, 'Jhering's Heaven of Concepts and Modern Analytical Jurisprudence' (1970), reprinted in: *Essays in Jurisprudence and Philosophy*, *supra* note 62 at 271, 274.

70 H.L.A. Hart, 'Definition and Theory in Jurisprudence' (1953), reprinted in: Hart, *Essays in Jurisprudence and Philosophy*, *supra* note 62.

71 *Ibid.*, 42.

72 In a famous debate, L. Fuller criticizes Hart's appeal to the 'pointer theory of meaning,' a theory, he contends, that 'ignores or minimizes the effect on the meaning of words of the speaker's purpose and the structure of language.' See L. Fuller, 'Positivism and Fidelity to Law – A Reply to Professor Hart' (1958) 71 Harv.L.Rev. 630, 668–9.

73 N. Chomsky, *Lectures on Government and Binding*, Studies in Generative Grammar 9 (Dordrecht: Foris, 1981).

74 N. Chomsky, *The Minimalist Program* (Cambridge, MA: MIT Press, 1995).

75 In the theories of the American Realists of the 1930s and 1940s, for instance, and within the various theses of the critical legal studies movement.

76 R. Cotterrell, *The Politics of Jurisprudence* (Philadelphia: University of Pensylvania Press, 1989), 105–6.

77 *Ibid.*, 106.

78 S. Fish, *Is There a Text in This Class? The Authority of Interpretive Communities* (Cambridge, MA: Harvard University Press, 1980), 247.

79 F. Newmeyer, *Language Form and Language Function* (Cambridge, MA:

MIT Press, 2000), 18; M. Noonan, 'Non-Structuralist Syntax,' in *Functionalism and Formalism in Linguistics*, vol. 1, ed. M. Darnell et al. (Amsterdam: John Benjamins, 1999), 12; Lakoff, *Women, Fire, and Dangerous Things*, *supra* note 9 at 585.

80 J. Kristeva, *Language the Unknown*, *supra* note 6 at 231, 244–5.

81 See P.F. Campos, 'This is not a sentence' (1995) 73 Wash.U.L.Q. 971; also Law and Linguistics Conference, *supra* note 5 at 838 (comments by G. Green).

82 M. Durie, 'The Temporal Mediation of Structure and Function' in *Functionalism and Formalism in Linguistics*, vol. 1, ed. M. Darnell et al. (Amsterdam: John Benjamins, 1999), 417. For a fascinating view of grammar as an emergent and fluid reality, see P.J. Hopper, 'Emergent grammar and the Apriori Grammar Postulate,' in *Linguistics in Context: Connecting Observation and Understanding*, ed. Deborah Tannen (Norwood, NJ: Ablex, 1985), 117–34, 132.

83 Lakoff, *Women, Fire, and Dangerous Things*, *supra* note 9 at 68ff.

84 On the notion of interpretative communities, see Fish, *Is There a Text in This Class? supra* note 78.

85 R. Chen and J. Hanson, 'Categorically Biased: The Influence of Knowledge Structures on Law and Legal Theory,' 1989 77 Calif.L.Rev. 1103.

86 P. Nerhot, 'The Law and Its Reality,' in *Law, Interpretation and Reality*, ed. Nerhot (Dordrecht: Kluwer Academic Publishers, 1990), 52.

87 *Ibid.*, 53; references omitted.

88 In the context of Canadian law, however, interpretation in constitutional law is usually deemed to be governed by different, more dynamic rules, but rules nonetheless. See P.-A. Côté, *The Interpretation of Statutes in Canada*, 3rd ed. (Scarborough: Carswell, 2000), 11.

89 *Ibid.*, 9.

90 C. Atias, *Philosophie du droit*, *supra* note 20 at 38–40.

91 J. Wroblewski, 'Interprétation juridique,' in *Dictionnaire encyclopédique de théorie et de sociologie du droit*, 2nd ed., A.-J. Arnaud (dir.) (Paris: L.G.D.J., 1993), 316.

92 L.E. Wolcher, 'What is the Rule of Law? Perspectives from Central Europe and the American Academy,' 2003 78 Wash.L.Rev. 515, 517.

93 J.H. Wright, *Origin Stories in Political Thought: Discourses on Gender, Power, and Citizenship* (Toronto: University of Toronto Press, 2004), 7, 8 and 10.

94 Wolcher, 'What Is the Rule of Law?' *supra* note 92 at 518.

95 P.J. Williams, *The Alchemy of Race and Rights; Diary of a Law Professor* (Cambridge, MA: Harvard University Press, 1991), 6

96 M. Krygier, 'Law as Tradition,' 1987 5 *Law and Philosophy* 237, 256.

97 A. Watson, *The Making of the Civil Law* (Cambridge, MA: Harvard University Press, 1981), 14.
98 P. Feyerabend, *Against Method* (London: Verso, 1979), 32. To this end, comparative disciplinary histories might prove indispensible. See, for example, J. Habermas, 'What Is Universal Pragmatics?' in *Communication and the Evolution of Society*, trans. Thomas McCarthy, 1–68 (Boston: Beacon Press, 1979).
99 F.J. Mootz III, 'Desperately Seeking Science' 1995 73 Wash.U.L.Q. 1009, 1010.
100 Kristeva, *Language the Unknown*, *supra* note 6 at 237.
101 J.R. Saul, *On Equilibrium* (Toronto: Penguin Canada, 2001), 290.
102 Kuhn, *The Structure of Scientific Revolutions*, *supra* note 13 at 6.
103 H. Barreau, *L'épistémologie*, 4th ed. (Paris: Presses universitaires de France, 1998), 15.
104 Krygier, 'Law as Tradition,' *supra* note 96 at 248.
105 Mootz III, 'Desperately Seeking Science,' *supra* note 99 at 1021.

PART TWO

Dissent

6 I Beg to Differ: Interdisciplinary Questions about Law, Language, and Dissent

MARIE-CLAIRE BELLEAU AND REBECCA JOHNSON

The lawyer and judge live constantly at the edge of language, the edge of meaning, where the world can be, must be, imagined anew; to do this well is an enormous achievement; to do it badly, a disaster of real importance, not only for the lawyer or judge but for the social world of which they are a part, including the particular people whose lives they affect.

James Boyd White[1]

Introduction

Stability. Change. Each is necessary, each is feared, and law is deeply implicated in both. Modern law, Fitzpatrick reminds us, is stretched between the demands of stable determination and responsive change.[2] There is a constant risk that the demand for equal application of law can blind law to the demands of particular justice, just as there is an equivalent risk that attention to the particular can threaten to undermine the stability of law itself. Each time a new dispute comes before the court, a judge is required to ask whether this case is like others before it, whether it differs, and in what ways. Each story, as well as its outcome, must be articulated through language, with its nuance, promise, and instability. And so it is that the judge lives, as White suggests in the epigraph above, at the edge of language, at the edge of meaning, constantly charged with the tasks of both maintaining stability and of imagining anew.

In this paper, we consider the linking of law and language in the space of the judicial opinion. We are particularly interested in those insights about law and language that can be gained by focusing attention on the space of judicial dissent. In section 1, we offer some introductory remarks about language and the operations of force and persuasion in judicial decision making, turning our attention in section 2 to the specific practice of judicial dissent. In section 3, we describe a category of dissenting practices that implicate what one might call a 'noetic' space of judgment, and consider how the resources of language might operate in this space. Finally, in section 4, we examine the deployment of language in majority and dissenting opinions, using *Mossop v. Canada* as an example. We suggest that there is much to be learned about dissent and judgment from taking an interdisciplinary approach that draws law and the humanities into closer dialogue.

1. Persuasion and Force in the Space of Judgment

> The power exerted by a legal regime consists less in the force that it can bring to bear against violators of its rules than in its capacity to persuade people that the world described in its images and categories is the only attainable world in which a sane person would want to live.
>
> Robert Gordon[3]

Judges, working in that space on the edge of meaning, are called upon not merely to settle the claims of particular litigants, but also to participate in the stabilization and/or reimagination of the world in which we live. Judgment always involves more than the resolution of a workplace dispute, the granting of joint custody, the sentencing of an accused to a term of imprisonment, the declaration that a category of business transactions is exempt from taxation, or an assessment of the damages to be paid by one neighbour to another. The judge must not only pronounce an outcome, but must also provide an explanation in language – must offer *reasons*.

In his or her reasons, the judge sketches out the dimensions of the legal and social worlds, articulates the social and legal standards against which behaviour will be measured. The judicial opinion tells us which harms are legally cognizable, and which are not; establishes codes of conduct, and zones of protection; decides which relationships will be fostered, and which denied legal recognition. These reasons give substance to a host of presumptions, maps, and blueprints about the world and its operations, about what it is to be an individual, about how individuals relate to each other and to the state.[4] Critical theorists, asked about the significance of judicial texts, might make the observation that this process is ideological at its core, and that judicial opinions are but another form of political discourse.[5]

Certainly, judicial discourse draws on the same resources of language used in other forms of political discourse that urge us to understand the world and its occupants in certain ways. Judges (like politicians, teachers, artists, and scientists) necessarily rely upon 'culturally shaped processes of categorizing, storytelling and persuasion in going about their business.'[6] What language can lead us to 'know' about the world is a matter of some consequence, as knowledge is deeply implicated in power. Certainly, there are parallels in the construction of knowledge through judicial decision writing and in the construction of knowledge in the humanities, the arts, and the sciences. In all these forms of discourse, language plays a crucial role.

In producing a set of reasons, the judge uses these resources not simply to tell the reader 'what will be,' but also to *convince* the reader that the result is just, or inevitable, or necessary. As Robert Gordon so eloquently put it, a significant part of law's power lies in its capacity to persuade its readers that 'the world described in its images and categories is the only attainable world in which a sane person would want to live.'[7] The task of the judge is thus not simply to imagine the world anew, but also to share that imagination through language in a manner that draws readers to make common cause with the reasons, to willingly govern themselves in accordance with the dictates of the world there described. Law is most efficacious when it has the consent of the governed. Judges seek to persuade.

And yet, it is worth attending to Fried's reminder that, in the world of political discourses, the judicial opinion is unique: it is an *authoritative* explanation.[8] Supported by a majority of the court, a judicial opinion 'is not just power disciplined by reason; it is also reason disciplined by power.'[9] The language of law is backed up by the threat of force.[10] A judge does not merely describe the world that is, or indeed, a world that would be desirable. A judge has the power and ability to make that world real. Even those who are not persuaded – who do not believe in the images and categories described in judicial decisions – will be made subject to them; they are required to live as if those images and categories are real. Judicial opinions, in their pronouncements of social and legal knowledge, play a very real part in the maintenance (and disruption) of systems of power, with the accompanying race, gender, class, corporate, colonial, or imperializing inflections.

Up to this point, we have been speaking as if the judicial voice were 'singular,' but often it is not. Judges are not always of the same mind about the questions raised by the cases before them. Judges can and do disagree about the shape of the world as it exists, and about the ways that the world should be legally ordered. In struggles over meaning, judges, like the rest of us, sometimes find themselves in the space of dissent.

2. Judging in the Space of Dissent

'With the greatest respect, I cannot agree...'
'With respect, I must dissent in part...'
'I am unable to concur...'
'I must dissent from the judgment herein...'
'I must dissent to the judgment of the majority.'[11]

'Dissent' is the written (published) expression of judicial disagreement, in a context where an appellate court is not unanimous in its judgment. Where agreement breaks down, a case can produce multiple opinions: a majority opinion, plus one or more additional opinions expressing either 'dissent' or 'concurrence.' Narrowly defined, a 'dissenting opinion' is one in which the author disagrees with the result reached by the majority, and thus writes a set of reasons explaining the different reasoning and results. The 'concurring opinion' is a bit more nuanced. Though the word 'concur' means 'to agree,' a concurrence is a form of judicial disagreement. The judge who writes concurring reasons arrives at the same result as the majority, but finds it necessary to distance him- or herself from the majority's reasoning, or indeed, to provide a completely different rationale for the result. Agreeing with the result, but disagreeing with the reasoning, the concurrence straddles the division between majority and dissent. It can be counted with the majority when it comes to 'result,' but it can instead be counted as a dissent when it comes to 'reasoning.' In a context where the central issue is the shape of the 'reasons' given by a judge, the concurrence is best theorized as a form of dissent.

The published dissenting judicial opinion is not a feature of all legal regimes.[12] Neither has it been an unchanging feature where it has operated. The forms and manners and magnitude of judicial dissent have varied across time and location, with judges feeling, at various historical junctures, more or less pressure to speak with a unified voice.[13] Certainly, both in North America and abroad, there has been a history of debate about the value of judicial dissent: does it improve the system, or undermine the legitimacy and authority of a court?

Those who defend the tradition of dissent have drawn attention to at least three of its functions.[14] First, dissent is said to safeguard the integrity of the judicial institution. The possibility of dissent preserves and strengthens the tradition of judicial independence, fostering collegiality and enhancing coherence.[15] Because opinions can be expressed in dissent, the majority does not need to water down its view, or compromise on important principles in the interest of getting votes. A dissent forces the majority to more sharply justify their opinion and account for the implications of their decision, enhancing the coherence of the resulting opinions. Second, dissent sustains a robust ongoing legal dialogue across multiple constituencies. Dissenters may be speaking to their colleagues, but they may have different (or additional) audiences in mind: the parties themselves, future litigants, academics and other courts, legislatures, the public at large, and students of law. This dialogue is one that occurs across time, drawing connections both with the past and the future. Third, people emphasize dissent's 'prophetic' function. The dissent may provide a source of guidance for the resolution of similar issues in the future, may sow seeds of innovation which sometimes 'take root in the spirit of the law.'[16]

Like a majority opinion, a dissenting opinion seeks to persuade the reader to understand the world in a specific way. However, the dissenting opinion does not wield law's Solomonic sword of power.[17] A judicial opinion has the force of law (the ability to make its vision of law operational in the world) only where its author speaks for the majority of judges on the court. A dissenting opinion is, from this perspective, simply 'not law.' Some have gone as far as to suggest that a dissent is less an exercise of power than akin to a work of scholarship.[18] But this view provides an insufficient account of the authority that judicial dissent possesses, both for the majority judges who must respond to the dissenting text, and for the audiences that read the words of both.

The fact that the substance of the dissenting opinion is produced by a judge is a matter of some significance. Words of dissent are words uttered by a judge acting in the capacity of judge; those words remain enrobed with the authority of judicial office. This makes a dissenting opinion significantly different from other attempts to persuade or convince. A dissenter has the ability to force the majority to respond, to answer, to explain, to shift, or to accommodate. The words of a dissenting opinion are a direct challenge, and the majority may feel required to enter into dialogue. And even where a majority does not respond directly, the very fact of the dissent often means that the majority reasons must be written differently than they would have been in the absence of a dissent.

Indeed, dissents themselves often become part of the 'canon' of law.[19] Some dissents, with time, successfully bring about change in the law. A court may explicitly revisit a problem, expressly overturning the law and adopting what had formerly been a dissenting view.[20] But dissent may also bring about change in a more direct fashion. A dissent may fail to persuade the majority of the court, but encourage other lawmakers to act, and it may convince those with legislative power to propose changes in line with that suggested in a dissent. In the Canadian context, for example, Parliament introduced a set of legal reforms dealing with the disclosure of sexual assault victim's private records. Those reforms rejected the majority view expressed in *O'Connor,* adopting instead an approach like that which had been articulated by the dissent.[21] Legislators can make real that which is imagined in the space of dissent.

The relational nature of struggles over meaning is foregrounded in cases where judges disagree. In the face of disagreement, judges find themselves forced to attend even more closely to the ways in which they deploy all the persuasive resources of language. Though law self-presents as a world in which the heated passions are subjected to the rigour of cold rationality, legal reasoning has always involved appeals to both 'the rational' and 'the passionate' dimensions of human understanding. As Samuel Pillsbury notes, passion, though always present in law, may be more visible in dissenting than majority texts.[22] Though majority and dissenting opinions may have the same range of rhetorical moves available to them, the dissent, deprived of that element of force or violence provided by the legal authoritativeness of a majority opinion, may need to draw even deeper on the available tools of persuasion.

3. Dissent, Noetic Space, and the Resources of Language

> The most enduring dissents ... seek to sow seeds for future harvest. These are the dissents that soar with passion and ring with rhetoric. These are the dissents that, at their best, straddle the worlds of literature and law.
>
> Justice William J. Brennan Jr[23]

In asking about the role of passion and persuasion in the space of dissent, one should note that dissent takes multiple forms.[24] Certainly, even a cursory scan of a single volume of the Supreme Court Reports leaves one struck by variances in the character, length, form, and seeming significance of different dissenting opinions. Some dissents read like novellas, while others consist of a terse, 'I disagree for the reasons given by the judge below.' Some are 'self-contained,' and can be read on their own with no reference to other opinions. Others are clear responses to majority reasons, and make sense only when being read in conjunction with those other opinions. Some dissents concern disputes over technical issues, while others involve policy choices, characterizations of facts, or conflicting values.

Though one might treat all dissent as equivalent for the purpose of certain statistical measures, there are contexts in which it is useful to distinguish between different kinds of dissent. In this discussion, we are interested in judicial dissents that draw deeply on the persuasive resources of language – those that seem most clearly to 'appeal to the future,' capture 'the brooding spirit,' or 'sow seeds for future harvest.'[25] Such dissents articulate an alternative vision of 'the real,' redescribe the facts, redraw the boundary between the legal and the social, and challenge how we think about law itself. We find it useful to think about such dissenting texts using Amsterdam and Bruner's concept of 'noetic space.'[26]

Noetic space is the term they use to describe the distinctive imaginative space maintained in every culture. It is the space linked to 'a distinctively human mental capacity that compels us to project our imaginations beyond the ordinary, the expectable, the legitimate – and to involve others in our imaginings.'[27] The term 'noetic space,' they note, comes from the Greek 'nous,' which includes not only the deliberations of the rational mind, but also its appetites and affections: its beliefs, desires, feelings, hopes, intentions.[28] Noetic space is a space of the mind, a space that integrates emotions and passions. Amsterdam and Bruner tell us that noetic space is specialized for testing the limits of the possible; as such, it is a pragmatic place that 'must honour the limits of lifelikeness – the limits beyond which [it] cannot go without losing the imaginative engagement of the audience.'[29] Noetic space is, they tell us, the space of literature, stories, and plays. We suggest that this is also an apt description of a body of judicial dissent. For judicial dissent is not simply a record of the judicial imaginary. Noetic dissent attempts to involve the legal reader in its imagination. This dissenting imagination does not only sketch out fantasy space, or utopic strivings. It is a purposefully pragmatic space. It attempts to persuade the reader that this alternative is within reach. The dissenter is less interested in documenting alternatives than in bringing the reader onboard. Successful interventions in noetic space say not simply 'things could be different,' but also encourage their listeners to (using the words of *Star Trek: The Next Generation*'s Jean-Luc Picard) 'Make it so.'

Successful work in the noetic draws deeply on the tools of persuasion, attempting to convince its listeners at both the rational and the visceral levels. When interrogating a noetic text for emotion, one should press past a narrow understanding of what the language of 'emotion' looks like, and of the ways emotion can be made textually manifest.[30] It is not just a matter of attending to expressive language, or of focusing on 'hot' emotions like anger or outrage. One can also attend to 'colder' emotional states (like disgust or indifference); scrutinize less overtly expressive uses of language, including the structure of judgments, and textual silences;[31] understand something of the tonality of the texts produced in majority and dissenting space; explore the ways that the text weaves together reason and emotion; look closely at the intersection of law and language; consider multiple avenues of enquiry and methodological approaches.

In their work *Minding the Law*, Amsterdam and Bruner discuss some of the approaches one can take to judicial texts, approaches that help focus attention on the concrete processes of categorizing, storytelling, and persuasion that shape the resulting texts. They suggest watching for the kinds of categories and categorizing moves used. Categories, Amsterdam and Bruner remind us, are made in the mind, rather than found in the world; they are both 'indispensable instruments' and 'inevitable beguilers.'[32] Three of the most visible categories are 'natural theoretical,' 'human narrative,' and 'supernatural religious.'[33] Where the category of 'natural theoretical' is operating, authority comes from the ability to verify. Just as in the natural sciences, the production or existence of knowledge requires that evidence can be seen, witnessed, verified, or confirmed against some objective, abstract, or independent standard.[34] In the category of 'human narrative,' authority comes from verisimilitude: what matters most is the appearance of truth – the extent to which evidence before one conforms with what one expects in a society's stock stories.[35] For example, in the context of a woman charged with murdering her spouse, to what extent do her actions comport with dominant stories about 'battered wives' or 'vengeful and betrayed women'?[36] Where the category of 'supernatural religious' is functioning, authority is dependent on the ability to enlist belief as an act of faith. In this, theological and legal acts of faith are not dissimilar. Cases about 'the sanctity of life' (whether in the context of abortion, assisted suicide, or the patenting of the OncoMouse™) often deploy such acts of faith. But belief as a ground of authority is also visible in the routine sentencing practices of criminal law: one might ask, for example, why, knowing what we know (and don't know) about the relationship between incarceration and recidivism, we continue to use retribution in sentencing.[37]

All categories are put into place through scripts and narratives: stories that provide examples of canonical expectations, and stories that warn us about the threats that confront us when the traditional scripts are thrown off the rails. These stories help us know who the heroes and heroines are, where the threats lie, and what must be done to restore order and balance. In contrasting majority and dissenting judgments, one can often see the struggle to dictate the categories that will transform 'troubles' into 'issues,' and vice versa.[38] Does the dissenter accept the majority's categories, or attempt to shift the narratives, and identify different agents and threats to be avoided? And what rhetorical strategies are used to open up or shut down ways of thinking or understanding?

There are a number of rhetorical devices that judges can use to manage contestability in their opinions. Epistemological techniques can make the facts appear more or less certain. Phrases like 'evidence was presented' or 'nothing before the court indicates' are ways for the court to express epistemological angst or certainty. Ontological techniques of construction allow one to concretize and de-concretize; presuppose the world to be one way, or reify a given set of understandings; structure the possible and even the imaginable. Watch for metaphors of centrality or indispensability. When do courts rely on phrases like 'I am ineluctably led to conclude' or 'the inference is inescapable,' or tell us that the court 'is a prisoner of the case presented to them'?[39] Such techniques allow judges to foreground, conceal, and manage moments of choice.

Watch also for the ways texts make meaning through the deployment of symbols. Are judges evoking prototypes, or attempting to break through typesets? How does a text rely on ideas of 'the ordinary,' 'the normal,' 'the average,' 'the reasonable,' 'the typical'? What does the text tell us about 'the good mother,' 'the ordinary barroom brawl,' 'the average domestic dispute'? How does a text engage with or attempt to disengage coded meanings? Does a text encode new layers of meaning into old words, making those words do a different kind of political work?[40] How does the text draw on language's ability to capture, deploy, and convey passion and emotion? Here, the issue is not just the presence of 'hot' and 'cold' words, but of how texts express the facts, how stories get set up, how characters are (and are not) presented, how the stage is set to foreground an eventual outcome. Attend not only to the 'rich' texts – to those that soar with passion and ring with rhetoric – but also to those that feel flat, because 'flatness' is not necessarily a failure of judicial writing skill. Flatness of characters and of tone can press our affiliations in a variety of directions. By giving (and denying) personality to protagonists, the tonal character of a story can be made to shift. So, too, the moral centre and gravity of a story.

All the above techniques are presumably available to majority and dissenting judges. We are interested here in the ways the techniques are used in practice. Split decisions provide a fertile terrain for examining language, and the deployment of discourses of reason and emotion in law. Because majority and dissent are in dialogue with each other, one needs to attend to the ways in which the language chosen and tools deployed in one judgment are connected to the language chosen and tools deployed in the other.

4. A Case Study: *Mossop v. Canada*

As an example, let us compare three opinions – majority, a dissent, and a concurrence – produced in a single case. The vehicle we will use is *Mossop v. Canada*,[41] an early case in a series of judgments concerning sexual orientation. In this case, Brian Mossop made an unsuccessful argument about the heteronormativity of law's definition of 'the family.' The point of the analysis here is not the legal resolution of the case; rather, it is attention to the tools of persuasion deployed in the three opinions.[42] The legal problem was straightforward: was Brian Mossop entitled to take a day of bereavement leave to attend the funeral of his (same-sex) partner's father? The terms of the collective agreement governing his employment stated that he could have bereavement leave in the event of a death of a family member. The definition of 'family' was fairly broad, including not only legally recognized 'in-laws' but also common-law spouses and their extended family members. However, same-sex couples were excluded from the definition of common-law spouses. In 1993, the Canadian Human Rights Act prohibited discrimination on the basis of a list of grounds: 'family status' was listed, but 'sexual orientation' was not. In denying bereavement leave to Mossop, was the employer discriminating against him on the basis of his 'family status' (prohibited) or on the basis of his 'sexual orientation' (not prohibited)? The majority of the court did not see the denial as based on his family status, and concluded that Mossop was not entitled to bereavement leave. The three judicial texts use quite different categorizing moves, narratives scripts, and rhetorical devices in addressing the problem.

The dissenting text of Madame Justice Claire L'Heureux-Dubé places Brian Mossop inside a narrative of 'family,' setting up the facts in a manner that emphasizes the ordinary dimensions of what are commonly seen as family issues. The opening of her text reads as follows: 'The complainant Mr. Mossop and his male companion Mr. Popert first met in 1974 and lived together from 1976 on in a jointly owned and maintained home. The two men shared day-to-day activities, maintained a sexual relationship, and were known to their friends and families as a homosexual couple. On June 3, 1985, Mr. Mossop attended the funeral of Mr. Popert's father.'[43] This paragraph is notable for its ordinariness. Indeed, it reads very much like the facts in *any* routine family law case involving separation and the division of property. The only difference seems to be that the two parties are both men. Compare that paragraph with the description of the facts in Chief Justice Antonio Lamer's majority reasons: 'In June 1985, the complainant Brian Mossop was employed in Toronto as a translator for the Department of the Secretary of State. On June 3, 1985, Mossop attended the funeral of the father of the man whom Mossop described as his lover. Mossop testified that the two men have known each other since 1974, and have resided together since 1976 in a jointly owned and maintained home. They share the day-to-day developments in their lives and maintain a sexual relationship. Each has made the other the beneficiary of his will. They are known to their friends and families as lovers.'[44] While both paragraphs mention the sexual relationship and the joint ownership of property, this second telling of the facts does so in a way that uses the terminology of sexuality rather than of companionship and family. The text does this by using the term 'lovers' twice in one paragraph. Significantly, one of these uses asserts that those most close to the men know them not as 'a couple' (the language used in the dissenting text), but as 'lovers.' Where a relationship is spoken of using the language of family or couple, the sexual dimension of the relationship is set in an authorized context, implying reciprocal obligations, responsibilities, and permanence. The term 'lover,' on the other hand, carries connotations of that which is unauthorized, illicit, or forbidden. It suggests elements of promiscuity, infidelity, and transience. In the terms used in formulation of the facts, Justice Lamer presses us away from legitimated narratives of 'family' and towards a narrative of individualized (with an edge of taboo) 'sexuality' – something perhaps to be tolerated, but not something to be confused with family.

There is a second set of moves visible in the above two articulations of the 'facts': rhetorical moves that make the facts appear more or less certain, that open up and close down the range of interpretive possibilities.[45] Note that the dissenting text provides a highly concrete description of the men. Consider the use of verbs in an indicative mode: the men 'met,' 'lived together,' 'shared,' 'maintained,' 'were known as.' In the majority formulation of the facts (one that will deny Brian Mossop's claim), things are not quite as solid. We are *not* told that Popert and Mossop *are* lovers. Rather, we are told that Popert is 'described as his lover.' Also, we are told that Mossop 'testified' that the two men had an intertwined life. Though the effect is subtle, this formulation inserts a bit of distance between the parties and the readers. Some rhetorical formulations suggest solidity, stability, reliability, and credibility. Words like 'described,' 'testified,' 'might,' 'alleged,' and other qualifying verbs introduce elements of uncertainty. The majority, using words like 'testified' and 'described as,' trigger the legal reader to ask questions about credibility. Such formulations, if not downgrading the credibility of any particular witness, nonetheless serve to introduce elements of uncertainty, reminding the reader that tales told are not always full descriptions of reality. Such approaches serve to de-emphasize the importance of any given account of the facts, drawing allegiances away from individual parties and towards (more abstract) legal principles, which are presented as being more reliable.

The concurring reasons of Mr Justice Gérard La Forest make another categorizing move altogether. Here, there is no description of the facts, and the male parties go nearly unnamed. A description of the men seems unimportant, since the opinion focuses on the jurisdictional dimensions of the legal problem: first, the standard judges should use before interfering with the decisions of administrative tribunals; and second, discerning the legislative intent behind the prohibition against 'family status' discrimination. Justice La Forest's reasons are built primarily on a narrative concerning the appropriate division of powers between judicial, administrative, and legislative functions. The 'threat' in this story is that judges might wrongly overstep the boundaries of their authority, either by failing to adequately police the behaviour of administrative tribunals, or by engaging in activist reinterpretation of language that does not accord with parliamentary will. The threat is of a court usurping legislative power.

With this different narrative foregrounded, Justice La Forest separates the 'human terms' from the 'legal terms' involved in the story. He disclaims judicial responsibility for the discrimination suffered by any particular party, placing that burden rather on the shoulders of Parliament. At the same time, the categorical and rhetorical moves that have been made affirm the placement of same-sex relationships outside the protective scope of 'family.' Consider this passage: 'I recognize, however, that particularly in recent years the word [family] is loosely used to cover other relationships. The appellant here argues that "family status" should cover a relationship dependent on a same-sex living arrangement. While some may refer to such a relationship as a "family," I do not think it has yet reached that status in the ordinary use of language. Still less was it the case when the statute was enacted. In human terms, it is certainly arguable that bereavement leave should be granted to homosexual couples in a long-term relationship in the same way as it applies to heterosexual couples, but that is an issue for Parliament to address.'[46]

This passage works in complicated ways. First, the language used tends to disembody the case. Mossop is invoked here as 'the appellant,' but only for the purpose of identifying a legal argument. Though made in the name of 'the appellant,' the argument is concretely made through the body of a lawyer. The reader is not forced to grapple with the suffering of the parties before them. Mossop himself doesn't come into view except in the form of an abstract legal argument about statutory interpretation.

Note also that the language used by Justice La Forest to describe this 'abstract' legal argument anticipates the conclusion that family status does not apply. He states that the issue is whether family status 'should cover a relationship dependent on a same-sex living arrangement.' This is neither 'the couple' of Justice L'Heureux-Dubé's reasons nor 'the lovers' of Justice Lamer's. This is a much more vague 'relationship dependent on a same-sex living arrangement.' This terminology carries the air of something loose and unspecified, of uncertain meaning, perhaps vaguely contractual, maybe akin to arrangements between roommates, but certainly not a family. Consider also La Forest's comment that 'the word [family] is loosely used to cover other relationships.' The word 'loosely' does some important work here, helping to establish a boundary between 'real families' and 'other relationships.' The phrase 'loosely used' deprives these 'other relationships' of the dignity accorded to those having a legitimate claim to the imprimatur of the term 'family.' 'Such a relationship,' to use his language, is distinguishable from the real, is perhaps more akin to an approximation, a mock-up, or facsimile (perhaps even a forgery or a fake).

In invoking 'ordinary use of language' to counterpose 'family' and 'other relationships,' Justice La Forest also positions the implied reader (an ordinary user of language) as someone who is not familiar with or living in groupings, close and extended, where one knows of or has homosexual relationships. By invoking the 'human terms' as he does, by suggesting that bereavement leave should perhaps 'be granted to homosexual couples in a long-term relationship,' he also allows himself and the implied reader to position themselves as open-minded, free from prejudicial bias, while simultaneously denying Mossop's claim for equal treatment. Responsibility for the loss rests neither with the Court nor with the implied reader, but with Parliament.

In *Mossop*, the judges divided on strong ideological grounds. However, we do not believe that the language moves used in the case 'belong' to one side or the other, and would emphasize that neither dissent nor 'passion' is the exclusive provenance of 'progressive' or 'conservative' forces. Certainly, the shifts in the sexual orientation cases make this clear.[47] In the ten years following *Mossop*, the Court heard a number of sexual orientation cases. In them, one can see judicial opinions once expressed in dissent shifting to the majority and vice versa. One can also see that, with each new case, the forms of argument and the tools deployed shift back and forth, as the judges grapple with the different moves deemed necessary to persuade readers from within either majority or dissenting space.

For example, two years after *Mossop,* in a 5–4 split in *Egan and Nesbitt,* the majority again declined to grant benefits to same-sex partners.[48] Five of the nine judges concluded that the same-sex male partners had suffered discrimination through being denied access to pension plan benefits. The men, nonetheless, were unsuccessful, because one of those five judges believed that the denial of equality could be (at least temporarily) justified on the basis that Canadians were just getting used to acknowledging same-sex discrimination. Thus, five of the nine judges saw discrimination, but only four of the nine judges found the discrimination to be unjustified. Justice La Forest again wrote an opinion, one holding the day on the result, but in dissent on the question of discrimination. It is worth attending to the language he uses as he moves from majority to dissenting space.

In *Mossop,* Justice La Forest stepped lightly around the question of discrimination, focusing instead on legislative intent and ordinary meaning. In *Egan,* La Forest finds himself in dissent, against a majority who declare the restriction of benefits to opposite-sex couples to be discriminatory. Heteronormativity is no longer to be taken for granted, but must be justified. Justice La Forest takes up this challenge, saying: 'Marriage has from time immemorial been firmly grounded in our legal tradition, one that is itself a reflection of long-standing philosophical and religious traditions. But its ultimate *raison d'être* transcends all of these and is firmly anchored in the biological and social realities that heterosexual couples have the unique ability to procreate, that most children are the product of these relationships, and that they are generally cared for and nurtured by those who live in that relationship. In this sense, marriage is by nature heterosexual. It would be possible to legally define marriage to include homosexual couples, but this would not change the biological and social realities that underlie the traditional marriage.'[49] In this passage, note that categories play an important role. Justice La Forest here draws on both the 'natural/theoretical' and the 'supernatural/religious' in his assertions that marriage is grounded both in a religious and biological higher reality. Recall also that in *Mossop* he suggested that Parliament was responsible for distinguishing between same- and opposite-sex couples. He also implied that 'human terms' might favour the extent of benefits across the sexual orientation divide. Here, however, note his statement that a change to legal definitions cannot alter a deeper reality. The persuasive move here appears to be directed at encouraging the reader to believe and accept something about the necessary heterosexual essence of marriage (if not family). It was not, however, necessary to articulate this vision of the natural/religious grounding of heterosexuality until its givenness was called into question. Here, Justice La Forest is making a passionate categorical argument in what has begun to become noetic space.

Indeed, by 2004, the Supreme Court was unanimous in upholding the constitutionality of the government's legislation making same-sex marriage a legal reality in Canada.[50] What was once articulated in noetic space had become a legal reality. The legal questions raised in the various cases along the path to that conclusion are not identical, and one should attend to those differences. But the cases offer a valuable site for exploring the kinds of shifts in language that one can see as majorities attempt to justify the state of the law that they produce, and as dissenters attempt to persuade readers, other judges, legislators, and the public that things can and should be otherwise. As various positions move from majority to dissent and back again, the cases make it possible to closely explore the deployment of language in majority and noetic space.

5. Conclusion

> The statutes and conventions and authorities and orthodoxies of a culture are always in a dialectical relationship with contrarian myths, dissenting fictions, and (most important of all) the restless powers of the human imagination ... the dialectic between the canonical and imagined is not only inherent in human culture, but gives culture is dynamism and, in some unfathomable way, its unpredictability – its freedom.
>
> Anthony Amsterdam and Jerome Bruner[51]

The pull between the demands of stability and change is one constant in the life of law. Judges are called upon not only to specify the current balance, but also to persuade us that the balance is good, right, and necessary. The space of dissent plays an important role in maintaining a generative relationship between the canonical and the imagined. Noetic dissent is more than a mere failed majority, and what happens in that space is a matter of some significance. There are good reasons to extend the focus of legal enquiry beyond the substance of a dissent to include the language in which it is crafted. How is language practice implicated in the ability of some dissents to so powerfully occupy noetic space? Are there ways of asking about language and noetic space that might help us think in more complicated and nuanced ways about the processes of judging, and of the persuasive calls made by judges to different audiences? Might attention to language use in noetic space help us better grapple with some puzzles about dissent raised by empirical work on the Supreme Court?[52]

It seems clear enough that attempts to grapple with the power of law – in its authoritative and dissenting forms – require close attention to and understanding of the power of language. There are many puzzles to consider. What do dissenting judicial texts desire (or require) of us as readers? What questions do they ask? In what directions do they point? What courses of action do they suggest? How do they focus our attention in some places and not in others? How do judges use language to shore up or revolutionize specific understandings of legal concepts like 'the family,' 'the corporation,' or 'consent?' How do judges set up the facts, describe the context, and elaborate the consequences? How do they characterize the parties, identify agents, describe the threats to be avoided, the choices to be confronted, and the prizes to be won? How do they articulate and disarticulate 'reality,' rending visible the voices and values that are muted or absent in the opposing reasons? And then, do judges do all this differently when writing in dissent than when writing for the majority? These are pressing questions to be explored, questions whose answers may be found at the intersection of law and language.

NOTES

1 James Boyd White, *The Edge of Meaning* (Chicago: University of Chicago Press, 2001) at 223.

2 Peter Fitzpatrick, *Modernism and the Grounds of Law* (Cambridge: Cambridge University Press, 2001) at 71.

3 Robert Gordon, 'Critical Legal Histories' (1984) 36 Stan.L.R. 57 at 109.

4 For a more thorough exploration of the persuasive task of the judge, and operation of maps and blueprints about the world in judicial discourse around sexual assault, see Rebecca Johnson, 'The Persuasive Cartogra-

pher: Sexual Assault and Legal Discourse in *R v. Ewanchuk*' in *Social Context and Social Location in the Sociology of Law*, ed. Gayle MacDonald (Peterborough, ON: Broadview Press, 2001), 247.

5 See, for example, David Kairys, ed., *The Politics of Law: A Progressive Critique* (New York: Pantheon, 1982); Ngaire Naffine, *Law and the Sexes: Explorations in Feminist Jurisprudence* (Sydney: Allen and Unwin, 1990).

6 Anthony G. Amsterdam and Jerome Bruner, *Minding the Law: How Courts Rely on Storytelling, and How Their Stories Change the Ways We Understand the Law – and Ourselves* (Cambridge, MA: Harvard University Press, 2000), 7.

7 Robert Gordon, 'Critical Legal Histories,' *supra* note 3.

8 Charles Fried, 'Scholars and Judges: Reason and Power' (2000) 23:3 Harv.J.L.&Pub.Pol. 807 at 828.

9 *Ibid.*

10 Robert M. Cover, 'Violence and the Word' (1986) 95 Yale L.J. 1601.

11 Justice Iacobucci, *Little Sisters Book and Art Emporium v. Canada*, [2000] 2 S.C.R. 1120; Justice L'Heureux-Dubé, *Harrison v. University of British Columbia*, [1990] 3 S.C.R. 451; Justice Kerwin, *Crighton v. Roman*, [1960] S.C.R. 858; Justice Idington, *Case Threshing Machine Co. v. Mitten* (1919) 59 S.C.R. 118; Justice Henry, *Brassard v. Langevin* (1877) 1 S.C.R. 145.

12 See Wanda Mastor, *Les opinions séparées des juges constitutionnels* (Aix-en-Provence: Presses universitaires d'Aix-Marseille, 2005).

13 Robert Post, 'The Supreme Court Opinion as Institutional Practice: Dissent, Legal Scholarship, and Decision Making in the Taft Court' (2001) 85 Minn.L.R. 1267; Meredith Kolsky, 'Justice William Johnson and the History of the Supreme Court Dissent' (1995) 83 Georgetown L.J. 2069.

14 For a fuller discussion of the functions of and justifications for dissent, see Marie-Claire Belleau and Rebecca Johnson. 'La dissidence judiciaire : Réflexions préliminaires sur les émotions, la raison et les passions du droit/Judicial Dissent: Early Reflections on Emotion, Reason and Passion in Law' in *Claire L'Heureux-Dubé à la Cour Suprême du Canada, 1987–2002*, ed. Marie-Claire Belleau & François Lacasse (Québec: Wilson and Lafleur, 2004) 699, particularly 704–9. Some recent judicial ruminations on dissent are captured in Kermit V. Lipez, 'Some Reflections on Dissenting' (2005) 57:2 Maine L.R. 313.

15 For some interesting observations on the darker (gendered) side of 'collegiality,' see the comments of Bertha Wilson in Ellen Anderson, *Judging Bertha Wilson: Law as Large as Life* (Toronto: University of Toronto Press and Osgoode Society for Canadian Legal History, 2001) at 152–5, and 415 (notes 11 and 12).

16 Claire L'Heureux-Dubé , 'The Dissenting Opinion: Voice of the Future?' (2000) 38 Osgoode Hall L.J. 495–517, at para 47.

17 For two interesting works at the border of law and humanities that explore the law's deployment of the biblical account of King Solomon's judgment, see Marie Ashe, 'Abortion of Narrative: A Reading of the Judgment of Solomon' (1991) 4 Yale J.L.& Feminism 81; and Ann Althouse, 'Beyond King Solomon's Harlots: Women in Evidence' (1992) 65 South.Calif.L.R. 1265.

18 Charles Fried, 'Scholars and Judges: Reason and Power' (2000) 23:3 Harv.J.L.&Pub.Pol. 807 at 827.

19 Anita S. Krishnakumar, 'On the Evolution of the Canonical Dissent' (2000) 52 Rutgers L.R. 181–217. Richard A. Primus, 'Canon, Anti-Canon, and Judicial Dissent' (1998) 48 Duke L.J. 243–303.

20 So, for example, the famous dissent in *Plessey v. Ferguson*, 163 U.S. 537 (1896) would move to the centre in *Brown v. Board of Education*, 347 U.S. 483 (1954). Note that a dissent may be adopted expressly, or in a quiet fashion. For example, in the 1995 equality trilogy cases (*Egan v Canada*, [1995] 2 S.C.R. 513; *Miron v. Trudel*, [1995] 2 S.C.R. 418; and *Thibaudeau v. Canada*, [1995] 2 S.C.R. 627) Justice L'Heuruex-Dubé articulated a new approach to equality problems. At the time, the other judges on the court made no comment on her approach. That is, in the context of the judges mutually referring to each other's reasons in the trilogy of equality cases, for the purposes of expressing both agreement and disagreement, the other judges said *nothing* of the test being proposed by Justice L'Heureux-Dubé. They did not adopt her test, nor did they reject it. The silence was deafening. However, by the time *Law v. Canada*, [1999] 1 S.C.R. 497 was decided in 1999, the test was incorporated by the unanimous court. Perhaps a strategy of silence may be deployed where an idea is sufficiently new that judges simply need time and space to think.

21 Compare the dissent of Justice L'Heureux-Dubé in *R. v. O'Connor*, [1995] 4 S.C.R. 411 on this point, with what is now s. 278.1 to 278.9 of the *Criminal Code of Canada.*

22 Samuel H. Pillsbury, 'Harlan, Holmes, and the Passions of Justice' in *The Passions of Law*, ed. Susan Bandes (New York: New York University Press, 2001), 330.

23 William J. Brennan, 'In Defense of Dissents' (1999) 50 Hastings L.J. 671–82 at 675.

24 Scholars have proposed various typologies of dissent. For example, see Bonnie Androkovich-Ferries, 'Judicial Disagreement Behaviour on the Supreme Court of Canada,' (master's thesis, University of Lethbridge,

2004) at 106, she identifies five types of dissenting texts: 'Decision in Waiting (DIW),' 'Failed Accommodation,' 'Repetitive,' 'Creative,' 'Perfunctory.' In her typology, the 'DIW' is often self-contained, written as if it were a majority opinion, often failing to position itself, or even acknowledge the majority reasons. 'Failed accommodation' bear the marks of a disagreement (with majority or even other dissenters) that could not be resolved. 'Repetitive' is a ditto category, in the form of either 'I agree with the judge below' or 'I am sticking by what I said in an earlier case.' 'Creative' are those that address specific flaws in the majority, and supply new reasons on that point. These are generally short, and deal only with the specific source of disagreement. She uses 'Perfunctory' for cases where there is little or no reasoning given, and it is difficult to guess at why the judge is distancing themself from the majority. See also Christine Joseph, 'All But One: Solo Dissents on the Modern Supreme Court of Canada' (2006), 44 Osgoode Hall L.J. 501; and Wanda Mastor, *supra* note 12.

25 Brennan, *supra* note 23.

26 Amsterdam and Bruner, *supra* note 6.

27 *Ibid.* at 235.

28 *Ibid.* at 237.

29 *Ibid.*

30 Pillsbury, *supra* note 22, nicely documents the presence of emotion in texts by Justice Harlan (one of the first of the 'great dissenters') and Holmes, widely thought of as the dispassionate Boston Brahmin. However, see Morton J. Horwitz, *The Transformation of American Law 1870–1960: The Crisis of Legal Orthodoxy* (New York: Oxford University Press, 1992), 142–3 for a discussion of the influence of Holmes's passion for Lady Castleton on his text 'The Path of the Law,' a piece of work Horwitz describes as 'an astonishing intellectual leap.' Horwitz concludes: 'Now one must ask whether and to what extent it was the discovery of some deep – and previously unfulfilled – love that produced in Holmes what Freud called an 'oceanic' feeling, inducing him to transcend the prior categories of his thought.'

31 Marie-Claire Belleau and Rebecca Johnson, 'Faces of Judicial Anger: Answering the Call,' in *Les sept péchés capitaux et le droit privé*, ed. Myriam Jézéquel and Nicholas Kasirer (Montréal: Éditions Thémis, 2007), 13.

32 Amsterdam and Bruner, *supra* note 6 at 19.

33 *Ibid.* at 31–2.

34 There is, certainly, an extensive literature grappling with 'objectivity' in this category, and with the ways that the supposed 'objective witness' is

actually implicated in the production of knowledge itself. See, for example, Donna J. Haraway, *Modest_Witness@Second_Millennium.FemaleMan©_Meets_OncoMouse™* (New York: Routledge, 1997).

35 Indeed, in their own work with judgment, Bennett and Feldman found that jurors' assessments of credibility were most strongly based on the extent to which the story given by a witness comported with a range of acceptable social stories about behaviour. See W. Lance Bennett and Martha S. Feldman, *Reconstructing Reality in the Courtroom: Justice and Judgment in American Culture* (New Brunswick, NJ: Rutgers University Press, 1981).

36 For an exploration of the pull of such narratives, see Orit Kamir, *Framed: Women in Law and Film: How Law on Screen Constructs Gender, Dignity and Honor* (Durham, NC: Duke University Press, 2006).

37 For an example of the Court's attempt to distinguish retribution from revenge, see *C.A.M.*, [1996] 1 S.C.R. 500.

38 As C. Wright Mills noted, problems concern only the parties before them, but issues concern society as a whole. While judges are concerned also with the parties before them, in appellate courts, one can attend to the ways in which the construction of the case can shift attention away from a resolution that might be best for the parties (and their problems) towards 'larger issues.' C. Wright Mills, *The Sociological Imagination* (New York: Oxford University Press, 1959), 8.

39 For a more extended discussion of the judicial deployment of the language of constraint, see Rebecca Johnson, 'The Limits of Judicial Power: The Court as Constrained,' chap. 5 in *Taxing Choices: The Intersection of Class, Gender, Parenthood, and the Law* (Vancouver: UBC Press, 2002).

40 In the context of government rather than judicial rhetoric, the late Marlee Kline provided a powerful and helpful exploration of the rhetorical devices at play where that the language of 'the left' was picked up by 'the right' and made to do quite different work. See Marlee Kline, 'Blue Meanies in Alberta: Tory Tactics and the Privatization of Child Welfare' in *Challenging the Public/Private Divide*, ed. Susan B. Boyd (Toronto: University of Toronto Press, 1997), 330.

41 *Mossop v. Canada*, [1993] 1 S.C.R. 554.

42 For a more extended discussion of the different textual strategies used in the different opinions, see Rebecca Johnson, '*Leaving Normal*: Constructing the Family at the Movies and in Law,' in *New Perspectives on Deviance: The Construction of Deviance in Everyday Life*, ed. Lori G. Beaman (Scarborough, ON: Prentice-Hall, 2000), 163.

43 *Mossop*, *supra* note 41 at para. 49.

44 *Ibid.* at para 1.

45 See Amsterdam and Bruner, *supra* note 6, chap. 6, 'On Rhetorics' [III.B: 'Epistemological Construction Techniques'].

46 *Supra* note 41 at para. 46.

47 For an overview of the cases, see Robert Wintemute, 'Sexual Orientation and the Charter: The Achievement of Formal Legal Equality (1985–2005) and its Limits' (2004) 49:4 [2004] McGill L.J. 1145.

48 *Egan v. Canada*, [1995] 2 S.C.R. 513.

49 *Ibid.* at 536.

50 *Reference re Same-Sex Marriage*, [2004] 3 S.C.R. 698.

51 Amsterdam and Bruner, *supra* note 6.

52 Peter McCormick's empirical studies of the Canadian Supreme Court, supra, reveal that the first three women appointed to the Supreme Court dissented with greater frequency than their male colleagues. They did not, however, show a pattern of dissenting together, being as likely to disagree with their female as with their male colleagues. What they share seems to have been less any particular vision of law than the fact of dissent itself. Indeed, they showed significantly heightened tendencies not merely to vote in dissent, but to *write* in dissent. See Peter McCormick, *Supreme at Last: The Evolution of the Supreme Court of Canada* (Toronto: James Lorimer & Company Ltd., 2000). For a discussion of the gendered puzzles posed by the phenomenon of dissent, see Marie-Claire Belleau and Rebecca Johnson, 'Les femmes juges feront-elles véritablement une différence? Réflexions sur les décisions des femmes juges à la Cour suprême du Canada' (2005) 17 Can.J.Women & L. 27.

7 Imagining Sedition: Law and the Emerging Public Sphere in Upper Canada, c. 1798–1828

BARRY WRIGHT*

Trials for political offences dominated every major episode of dissent in Upper Canada (present-day Ontario), from the first substantial manifestation of organized political opposition in 1804–8 to the aftermath of rebellion and invasions of 1837–8, and suggest the broader prominence of legal struggles in pre-Confederation British North American politics. While politics and conflict over abuses of authority extended to the more routine business of the criminal courts and civil proceedings, trials for sedition, treason, and related offences were the primary legal engagements between governments and their opponents.[1] This chapter revisits my earlier work on sedition prosecutions in the colony, broadening the analysis from a legal and political focus to further examine the broader social meanings of the proceedings. It does so by taking a closer look at the press, the production and consumption of political expression, and the development of popular political engagement and public opinion, informed by the work of Jürgen Habermas on the public sphere, British literary scholars such as John Barrell on the republic of letters and English political trials, and Jeffrey McNairn on deliberative democracy in Upper Canada.[2]

Barrell's use of the term 'imaginary' and 'imagining' in his examination of late eighteenth-century treason cases is particularly apposite in the context of early nineteenth-century sedition prosecutions in Upper Canada. Those who dominated government 'imagined' criticism of the state as intention to foster disaffection and revolution. While such alarmism seems irrational from a modern perspective, the first generation of political leadership in the colony was dominated by loyalist refugees who had experienced opposition as a prelude to revolution. The potential for the advocates of change, fuelled by a growing independent press, to generate social and political instability was further underscored by the French Revolution and the Irish Rebellion. After the War of 1812 such counter-revolutionary attitudes were increasingly overlaid by fears of American expansionism and Jacksonian popular democracy. Malleable sedition laws were a vehicle for the imaginary, aimed at making these official views authoritative. These laws legitimated the imagined connection between criticism and revolutionary effect and operationalized a repressive response. The proceedings examined in this chapter were designed to characterize criticism and opposition as real rather than perceived threats to the security of the existing order, to marginalize opposition voices and silence their means of expression. For reformers who exploited the counter-hegemonic potential in the law and its administration, the disentangling of official alarmism from privileged self-interest was at the crux of struggles against these proceedings. Formal claims around the rule of law and the British constitution provided a means to effectively contest the repression and a powerful opportunity to debunk the imaginary as a reflection of privileged self-interest.

The sheer number of sedition trials makes it impossible to dismiss them as exceptional. About fifty prosecutions for various forms of seditious expression are indicated in the records up to the early 1830s in a population that grew from approximately 50,000 in the early 1790s to about 160,000 in 1825 and then more than doubled over the following decade.[3] Added to this remarkable figure are related summary deportations under the Sedition Act and punitive parliamentary privilege proceedings for contempt brought against opposition members and outsiders.[4] Practices were comparatively more repressive than in Britain or the United States during this period, the frequency of prosecutions per capita exceeding even that of Pitt's government during the French revolutionary fears in the 1790s and the spate of cases taken late in the second decade of the nineteenth century to deal with the crisis of English urban unrest.[5]

Beyond the impressive numbers, what can be said about the relative importance of the cases? The most significant and heavily punished cases took place at roughly ten-year intervals, corresponding to the apex of official concern about an emergent organized opposition, in particular where such opposition was accompanied by an active independent press, a key vehicle for developing broader public engagement with political issues. The period 1804 to 1808 saw the rise of the province's first opposition party and the prosecution of Joseph Willcocks, editor of the province's first independent newspaper associated with an organized opposition, for seditious libel in the courts and for contempt by parliamentary privilege.[6] In this phase the government's objective of silencing or at least marginalizing opposition was largely met. A decade later, Robert Gourlay faced two unsuccessful seditious libel prosecutions and was deported under the provincial Sedition Act, while his editor, Bartemus Ferguson, was convicted of seditious libel and his newspaper shut down.[7] Instead of silencing opposition the Gourlay affair opened a decade where the means of expressing opposition proliferated with numerous new independent newspapers and widening readership. The issue was no longer whether there would be popular political engagement, but rather the terms of this engagement, and how far law could discipline public debate. This was tested out in a series of indictments for seditious libel against newspaper editors that culminated in the conviction of Francis Collins in 1828.[8] After this period, the government became reluctant to attack the press directly through legal measures. Juries could not be relied upon to comply, acquittals powerfully vindicated opposition and discredited government, and the Sedition Act, used to banish Robert Gourlay from the province when other measures failed, was repealed when petitioned to the British government.

These particular cases demonstrate the discursive prominence of British constitutional and rule of law claims in defence strategies that were increasingly effective in convincing juries and generating broader public support. They also mark distinct phases in the development of organized political opposition and the province's public sphere. Indeed, the struggles around these cases arguably contributed to transformations in the way the public sphere was regarded by the participants. Although the War of 1812 reinforced the marginalization of opposition after Willcocks, Gourlay's dramatic acquittals for seditious libel underscored that legal measures were far from a certain means of repression. Indeed, in the 1820s it was found that the emerging public sphere could no longer be suppressed. Notwithstanding Gourlay's eventual banishment and Collins's later conviction for seditious libel, the government had condemned itself by arbitrary measures, and was compelled to shift from outright rejection of the validity of public opinion and critical political expression to reluctant acceptance of its inevitability. This continued to be qualified by continuing fears of the potential of engaged public debate to undermine governmental authority through distortion and abuse. For the engaged public, the only legitimate legal limits on political expression became deliberate falsehoods or advocacy of violence. As we shall see, a combination of pressure from 'below,' in the form of increasingly engaged public opinion expressed through the jury, and from 'above,' in the form of liberal imperial intervention, effectively curbed the utility of sedition prosecutions.

1. Historiographical and Theoretical Considerations

As Allan Greer and Jeffrey McNairn have recently suggested, the colonial outpost of Upper Canada was not as isolated from the currents of the Enlightenment and the 'age of revolution' as many historians have tended to assume.[9] Recent scholarship has deepened insights into its social, cultural, and intellectual history and reinvigorated study of its political and institutional history. We see, for instance, that responsible government and the restructuring of the colonial state following the crisis of the Rebellion of 1837–8 involved more than liberal imperial paternalism or the leadership of local reform moderates, empowered after the crisis had discredited the forces of radicalism and reaction. The existence of an active public sphere of engaged participatory democracy by the 1840s and 50s, and its supporting constitutional structures and legitimating ideology, were also the product of the previous four decades of local conflict. McNairn's book demonstrates how Upper Canadians became increasingly active participants in an emerging deliberative democracy in the pre-rebellion period. He details their independent engagement with political issues through voluntary associations and the independent press, drawing upon a rich repertoire of language and arguments derived from British constitutional practices. We also see that the courts, in addition to the legislature, were a key political stage where these developments played out.

Our particular interest here is the courts as a site of struggle, how uses of the law to control political expression, and contestation of these uses, illustrate an important dimension in Upper Canadian legal, political, social, and cultural history. Prosecutions of opposition leaders and editors powerfully evoked British constitutional and rule of law claims. The role and conduct of crown law officers, judges, and juries reflected the fundamental political tensions between executive domination and popular accountability. Abuses of prosecutorial power, the compromising of judicial independence, and attempts to manipulate jury verdicts highlighted colonial departures from British advances since the late-seventeenth-century constitutional compromises. The cases examined here reflect the contested colonial constitution, the contestability of law, and mark out distinct phases in the development of political expression, from government control and privileged confining of political debate to reluctant acceptance of the inevitability of oppositional expression, where the general public, rather than the privileged elite, was entitled to judge the merits of political debate and public policy.[10]

My previous analysis of these cases focused on the ideology of the rule of law and British constitutionalism and its tensions with discretionary executive authority, drawing upon the work of E.P. Thompson on the eighteenth-century English criminal courts.[11] Thompson highlights the complexities of legal expressions of power, while avoiding class reductionist portrayals of law as simply an instrument of repression and economic ordering. He identifies the paradox that the formal claims associated with the rule of law limit the repressive potential of law and indeed create possibilities to contest it. The legitimacy of a legal response is diminished by blatant manipulation because of popular expectations based on formal constitutional and rule of law claims: 'For what we have observed is something more than the law as a pliant medium to be twisted this way and that by whichever interests already possess effective power ... Over and above its pliant, instrumental functions it existed in its own right, as ideology ... If the law is evidently partial and unjust, then it will mask nothing, legitimize nothing, contribute nothing to any class's hegemony. The essential precondition for the effectiveness of law, in its function as ideology, is that it shall display an independence from gross manipulation and shall seem to be just.'[12]

The Upper Canadian cases are rich illustrations of what I have described elsewhere as contested legality. Prosecutorial policies and executive influences over the judiciary and other elements of the administration of justice certainly tilted the courts in favour of government interests, but obvious manipulation was self-defeating, leading to loss of credibility rather than enhancing the legitimacy of the government's position. Opposition figures exploited wide awareness of constitutional and rule of law claims in sophisticated and effective ways. Such claims figured prominently in oppositional discursive strategies and were given the 'spin' of libertarian understandings of the eighteenth-century British constitution. They were increasingly effective in contesting government measures. Acquittals or prosecutorial failures not only reinforced the image of the rule of law but also embarrassed governments and promoted the reform cause.

While Thompson's notion of the ideology of the rule of law helps to make sense of the complexity and rich texture of legal repression and its contestation, it is speculative in terms of the wider social meanings of these conflicts. While the discursive prominence of these legal and constitutional claims is evident in the records, there is a tendency to assume popular awareness of formal claims and how they are contradicted by official actions. What further insight can we gain into popular engagement with the legal struggles and the opposition cause? The work of Jürgen Habermas on the public sphere is useful in this respect. Effective defence use of constitutional and rule of law claims resonates with developments in public opinion that are fuelled by a growing independent press and 'republic of letters,' the very targets of much of the repression. The jury plays a pivotal role here, not only as the primary audience for defence arguments given its power over the verdict, but also as a reflection of broader public opinion.

The development of the public sphere can be understood as emerging popular political literacy, or more precisely, increasing popular engagement with politics and public policy through processes of deliberative democracy outside state institutional politics. It is manifested in civil society, at a distance from established institutional processes, where citizens organize themselves to access information, express and assemble views, and formulate public opinion through open argument and participatory deliberation (which differs from the modern concept of public opinion based on polls that give equal weight to every view). As Ely puts it: 'In a nutshell, the public sphere ... mediates between society and the state, in which the public organizes itself as the bearer of public opinion. Historically its growth occurred in the later eighteenth century with the widening of political participation and the crystallizing of citizenship ideals.'[13] Habermas focused on the emergence of a bourgeois public sphere in late-eighteenth- and early-nineteenth-century western Europe and encounters with revolutionary movements that extended it. His sweeping, rather Whiggish historical generalizations and conclusions have been criticized by historians and critical theorists, although his concept has been elaborated to deal with class fractions, gender, and ethnicity, and extended to other contexts.[14] (Marxists point to his uncritical celebration of a public sphere defined by the needs and interests of bourgeois civil society, while postmodernists question his concepts of abstract rationality, rational communication, and discursive exchanges).[15] Michael Warner's thoughtful critique is that the 'public' is a largely imagined reference point with no empirical existence outside its rhetorical expression and the mediating contexts in which it is produced. Despite such concerns, the concept of the public sphere opens up promising avenues for further research, pursued by Warner himself on colonial America and the early U.S. republic, and by British literary scholars who have focused on how it is manifested in print in the emerging 'republic of letters.' Such political expression increasingly reflects awareness of an abstract audience of an indefinite number of others and claims of public disposition. Any person could offer an opinion about public issues and submit that opinion to the test of public debate, free of interested or privileged constraint.[16] Our particular concern here is how such developments were responded to by governments, assuming the dimensions of a security threat to be managed and disciplined by legal means.

By the latter half of the eighteenth century British subjects increasingly exploited opportunities to gather and exercise their reason in public outside established legislative institutions. This political participation not only took the form of newspapers, pamphlets, literature, and petitions but also associational and public meetings. By the 1770s newspapers and magazines in Britain were offering reports of legislative debates and commentary, a development that eventually found notable expression in William Cobbett's *Weekly Political Register*, *Parliamentary Debates* (eventually sold to T.C. Hansard), and a new authoritative series of *English State Trials* (eventually sold to T.B Howell). As Cobbett put it: 'The utility of reading consists in the imparting knowledge to those who read; knowledge dispels ignorance. Reading, therefore, naturally tends to enlighten mankind. As mankind becomes enlightened, they become less exposed to the arts of those who would enslave them.'[17] Governments attempt to deny the possibility of enlightened debate outside established institutional processes, seeing a radical, possibly revolutionary agenda behind the stirring of public opinion, and Cobbett goes on to highlight the role of sedition laws in government attempts to constrain public knowledge in contradiction with constitutional claims of a free press:

> Let us see, then, what is the real state of this press; this vaunted press, which ... represented as being FREE ... In the first place, a man is liable, if he write, or print, or publish any thing, which the Attorney-General (an

> officer appointed by the Crown and removable at pleasure) chooses to prosecute him for ... and to be punished in a manner much more severe than a greater part of the persons convicted of felony ... On the other hand, the Attorney-General may, if he chooses, drop the prosecution [by means of the ex officio information] ... at whatever time he may please to drop it. After having charged a writer with a crime, he may keep the charge suspended over his head for months or years; and then, without even the leave of the Court, and without assigning any reason at all, he may withdraw the charge, and relieve the poor creature and his family from their fears. This is the state of the law. And, under such circumstances, is it to be expected, that the press will convey, freely convey truths to the people? For, you will be particular in bearing in mind, that the truth of any writing, so far from being a justification of the author, is not permitted to be pleaded in his defence. To utter truth, therefore, respecting the measures of the government, the administration of the laws ... may, in the eyes of the law, be a greatly criminal act.[18]

We shall be turning to these laws and their administration in Upper Canada shortly, but before this, some further examination of the work of British literary scholars on the emerging public sphere is warranted. Focusing on late eighteenth- and early nineteenth-century Britain, they have extended concerns about the text – internal matters of the form and expression – to broader external questions about literary production and the conditions of its consumption. This has led to explorations of the text and readers, the social, cultural, and political factors that mediated the reading public, and renewed historical examination of coffee houses, newspapers and pamphlets, the postal service, and public readings as well as related matters such as publishing, literacy, schooling, and the relationship between the enlightened men of letters and the 'marginalia.'[19] They have also revisited government attempts to silence or marginalize these developments by legal means, manifested most dramatically by the political or state trials of the 1790s, part of Prime Minister Pitt's crackdown on political activists and associated publishers and writers in the wake of the French Revolution. John Barrell's recent work shows how the common-law and premodern legislative concepts, which had been under increasingly critical intellectual scrutiny by utilitarian reformers such as Jeremy Bentham, were demolished by the 1794 treason trials. The proceedings became a battle over the meaning of words, with the discourses ranging from Burke's imagining of revolutionary potential and accompanying excesses, to republican imagining of the sovereign's irrelevance. The medieval statute of treasons, requiring proof of acts that compassed the King's death, was administered in the modern context of King George's declining moral authority and the constitutional crisis of the Regency, as well as the procedural advances arising out of the libertarian 1696 Treason Act that were fully exploited by defence counsel. The acquittals helped to articulate a new language of public authority, although in the short term government turned to temporary emergency legislation that attempted to modernize liability for treason (including revolutionary conspiracies against abstracted state authority).[20] The related seditious libel prosecutions in the first three decades of the nineteenth century have been examined in detail by Kevin Gilmartin, and raised similarly contested issues of meaning and effect.[21]

The emergence of the public sphere in Britain was highly contested, reflecting both disciplinary and emancipatory experiences. Paul Keen's recent anthology reproduces a telling extract from the autobiography of Francis Place, the son of a journeyman baker who became an active member of the London Corresponding Society: 'My Landlord, the Cabinet Maker was a member of the London Corresponding Society, and at his request I also became a member. This was in the month of June 1794. On the 12 of May Thomas Hardy the Secretary was seized by order of the Government on a pretended charge of High Treason, and about the same time ten others on the same charge.' Place goes on to reflect his self-improvement during a quarter-century anniversary celebration of Hardy's acquittal:

> The moral effects of the Society were considerable. It induced men to read books, instead of wasting their time in public houses, it taught them to respect themselves, and to desire to educate their children. It elevated them in their own opinions. It taught them the great moral lesson 'to bear and forebear.' The discussions in the divisions, in the Sunday evenings readings, and in the small debating meetings, opened to them views which they had never before taken. They were compelled by these discussions to find reasons for their opinions, and to tolerate others. It gave a new stimulus to an immense number of men who had been but in too many instances incapable of any but the grossest pursuits.[22]

In distant Upper Canada we see equally intense (although slightly later) emancipatory experiences accompanied by disciplinary reaction.

Published commentary by Guy Pollock, a local blacksmith, resonates nicely with that of his contemporaries Cobbett and Place: '... examine for yourselves, read fully and think freely; for there is a great difference between a taught and an acquired belief, and since the mind of man imbibes falsehood as readily as truth, let me admonish you never to place implicit confidence in any man, however commanding his talents may be, for authority is not proof, and assertions are not arguments.'[23] As McNairn points out Pollock was in fact a nom de plume for Dr Robert Douglas Hamilton, a scientific researcher, essayist, and founder of a local library, but his advocacy clearly attacked the presumption that superior social standing and connections entitled the privileged to define the community's interests and deny the general reading public the right to use reason to judge public policy and the existing political order. A flourishing opposition press, 'republic of letters,' and public sphere emerged in Upper Canada by the 1820s, but it was in the face of determined government attempts to suppress these developments. As McNairn puts it, the belief that politics could be widely understood, or that '[t]he idea that authoritative decisions about the common good could and should be generated by critical discussion among the private persons outside the control of traditional authorities or the most privileged, was revolutionary.'[24] When Robert Gourlay noted in 1818 that 'it has been the cant of time immemorial to make mystery of the art of Government,' a government supporter responded, 'here sir, you have passed the Rubicon ... Here is the renewal of the old cry of Revolutionary France, Egalité ... [an] appeal to the ignorant.'[25]

2. The Social, Constitutional, and Legal Terrain in Upper Canada

The sedition proceedings examined in this chapter were flashpoints in political conflict rooted in related economic, social, and cultural divisions that writ large existed between farmers and a ruling alliance, or, more precisely, a loose network of regional elites consisting of officials, lawyers, and merchants bound together by the authority of, and privileged access to, the provincial government. The loyalist and conservative core of this governing alliance became known as the 'Family Compact' by the 1820s. The Compact's power derived from the monopoly of government offices and patronage, facilitated by the executive-dominated structure of colonial government and the government's lack of accountability to the elected Assembly.[26] Not only did farmers face economic policies that favoured mercantile interests, many were neither United Empire Loyalists nor British (until the waves of poor immigrants from Britain and Ireland in the 1830s) but American immigrants lured by cheap land who faced increasing discrimination after the War of 1812.[27] Educated, reform-inclined recent arrivals from Britain and Ireland were prominent as leaders of political opposition. The relation between early opposition and the broader public is unclear before the war, but studies of popular literacy, libraries, education, and voluntary associations, combined with evidence of township meetings and signatures on petitions, suggest increasing popular engagement with public issues after that time.[28] Wide evidence of Upper Canada's emerging public sphere is found most notably in McNairn's recent book on the development of public opinion and deliberative democracy. His research on voluntary associations, public meeting places, and the press provides a comprehensive picture of the sites that fostered popular engagement with political and public issues and the development of critically reflective public opinion.

Voluntary associations such as mechanics' institutes, agricultural societies, literary and scientific societies, and Masons as well as religious and temperance organizations grew from the late 1790s. They operated separately from local political meetings, petitioning, and elections to the legislative assembly, although constitutional societies and political unions provided links to these overtly political processes. These associations transmitted information and knowledge but in many cases also heard different views and debated public issues, with elaborate rules and procedures for their discussion.[29]

McNairn's chapter on the press and its readers looks at the founding of the official *Gazette* in 1793, the initial struggles to establish an independent and opposition press from 1798 to 1808 (the Tiffany's *Constellation* to Willcocks's *Guardian*), and the phenomenal growth in newspapers in the 1820's.[30] The official *Gazette* offered an abstracted description of legislative proceedings, vice-regal speeches, proclamations, and statutes but reproduced little in the way of legislative debates until the 1820s. In contrast, independent newspapers offered more comprehensive renditions of legislative debates accompanied by political commentary. As for readers, provincial literacy rates exceeded those in Britain, approaching 80 per cent by 1840.[31] Leading newspapers had agents in various communities, and postmasters forwarded subscriptions in other locations, with the postal records suggesting a readership rate double that of comparable English towns and counties.[32] Community reading sites that made newspapers even more accessible included public reading rooms and libraries (often founded by mechanics' institutes from the 1820s and largely converted to public libraries by the end of the nineteenth century), newsrooms operated by newspaper editors, and inns, hotels, and taverns.[33] These were largely unregulated public places where many Upper Canadians regularly congregated and exchanged information.

The press played a key role in the development of informed provincial public opinion and was a vital aspect of the emerging public sphere. It is hardly surprising that this powerful means of expressing and spreading oppositional views outside the privileged confines of the legislature would provoke a range of attempts to silence it, most notably the seditious libel prosecutions examined here, but also parliamentary privilege proceedings for contempt (the punishment of Joseph Willcocks, James Durand and William Lyon Mackenzie's repeated expulsions), the suspension of lucrative government printing contracts (Gideon Tiffany, Charles Fothergill), and 'rough justice' handed out by government supporters (the destruction of Mackenzie's press in 1826). The development of engaged public opinion receptive to criticism of government helps to explain why the press came to figure prominently in the security concerns of government, this very development ultimately also helped to curb the repressive law through popular awareness of constitutional and rule of law claims and the key role played by the jury, itself a measure of public opinion.

At the core of Upper Canada's laws were formally received English laws as they stood on 17 September 1792 (when the provincial legislature first met). The colonial legislature and courts could supplement or amend this core of received law, although local legislation was subject to review and possible disallowance by the British government and decisions could be reviewed by the Judicial Committee of the Privy Council after 1833. English laws enacted after the reception date did not apply, unless adopted expressly or passed as imperial legislation. As we shall see, this was thought to be the case with Fox's Libel Act, a reforming clarification of the scope of the jury's verdict in seditious libel trials, when the matter was raised during the Gourlay affair.[34]

Upper Canada was said to be blessed, as the province's first lieutenant governor John Graves Simcoe put it, with a constitution that was 'the very image and transcript of that of Great Britain.' However, this 'image and transcript' was given a decidedly counter-revolutionary spin in practice in reaction to perceived errors in the American colonies and in the wake of the French Revolution. It was nonetheless seized upon by opposition when governments appeared to contradict contemporary British constitutional practices. Libertarian understandings of the British constitution figured prominently and were widely deployed in oppositional discourse and in appeals for broader public support.

Such discourse was readily evoked in the colonial circumstances of executive-dominated government (the essence of the political struggle for responsible government).[35] Heavy reliance on criminal prosecutions to maintain authority and fend off challenges was supported by the colonial organization of the administration of justice. Unlike Britain, where after 1701 judicial tenure depended on good behaviour determined by Parliament rather than royal pleasure, colonial judges could be removed at the instigation of the executive council, as we shall see here in the case of Judges Thorpe and Willis. Most judges were compliant and at the centre of colonial political culture, routinely giving extra-judicial opinions, while the chief justice served as an executive councillor and speaker of the appointed Legislative Council – potential partisan roles that went beyond acceptable conventions in Britain by the nineteenth century. Colonial governments also tightly controlled criminal prosecutions through the law officers of the Crown. There was wide resort to the controversial prosecutorial prerogatives, regarded in England as surviving Star Chamber remnants, that included ex officio informations (which provided procedural advantages such as by-passing grand jury review required for regular indictments, easy change of trial venues, hanging threats of prosecution to induce compliant behaviour, and enhanced powers to pack compliant juries), and the nolle prosequi (enabling the Crown to terminate potentially embarrassing private prosecutions).[36] Finally, justices of the peace, sheriffs, and other local court officials were appointed and tightly controlled by the Executive Council. Sheriffs, for instance, managed jury selection, enhancing government influence on the composition of juries. Despite the available techniques of jury packing, the jury remained beyond the government's control in significant respects, an uncertain element in the administration of criminal law, and one that evoked particularly rich constitutional claims as the 'palladium of liberty.' The jury played a key role in the cases examined here and can be seen as a vehicle for the public sphere in the administration of justice, a deliberative body that served as a barometer of the public opinion.

The colonial administration of law therefore evoked richly contested elements of the British constitution, many of which were resolved by the late-seventeenth-century compromises or battled for over the course of the eighteenth century. The discourse of the constitution, the rule of law, and British justice were readily triggered by both the perception and the reality of colonial executive power. Reformers who battled in the courts and legislatures readily evoked this language to point out how government practices contradicted these claims. Such language powerfully discredited government, legitimated the opposition cause, and proved to be of great utility in contesting government repression.

As much as Upper Canada's government claimed the province enjoyed the 'very image and transcript,' it also adhered to Burke's view of the potential revolutionary dangers of unregulated popular public debate and the 'republic of letters.' Received English criminal laws, and local legislative elaborations, provided powerful means to address these dangers.

The common-law offence of seditious libel was prosecuted for publications that criticized the state on the basis that they promoted discontent and disaffection, although there was no need to prove the accused caused a breach of peace or incited public disturbance. It derived from the misdemeanour of sedition, expressed criticism of the Crown, government, or officials punishable by fines, imprisonment, and the pillory. Prosecutions could be taken with relative ease, unlike treason, which required proof of overt acts against the state and entailed substantial evidentiary and procedural protections for the accused after 1696. Advances such as the Treason Act, 1696, the Habeas Corpus Act, 1679, and the more general constitutional compromises between Parliament and the Crown in that period were accompanied by the convention of 'no prior restraint.' The demise of print licences and government monopoly over printing ended the possibilities of prior control or censorship. Seditious libel was developed to fill the gap, becoming the most important form of the offence as reformers fought governments over the reach of post-publication sanctions.

The courts established the main elements of the common-law offence of seditious libel, distinct from the criminal libel of defamation and the parliamentary privilege offence of contempt, by the second quarter of the eighteenth century.[37] These included extending the minimal proof requirements and judicial control over the most contentious questions. General verdicts were prohibited and the issues to be decided by the jury were narrowed to the fact of publication and innuendo as suggested by the Crown.[38] As reformers pushed towards the modern concept of freedom of the press there were increasing conflicts between juries and judges, particularly those cases defended by the barrister Thomas Erskine, who urged juries to resist instructions from the bench and use their verdicts as a measure of public opinion towards oppressive laws and prosecutions.[39] These seditious libel cases were therefore not only at the centre of political struggles for freedom of the press and political expression, but also related legal issues about the Crown's burden of proof, judicial independence, and freedom of the jury's verdict.

The 1792 Libel Act of opposition leader Charles James Fox marked a reform victory, by vindicating the right of juries to deliver a general verdict on all the factual issues, including intent and seditious inferences.[40] However, the advance was met by a generation-long reaction as seditious libel prosecuted by ex officio informations became an instrument of 'Pitt's Terror' in the 1790s and was again used as a response to urban rioting in the period 1816–20, along with the passage of the temporary Six Acts in 1819.[41] The limited utility of the sedition laws became increasingly apparent by the 1820s. Fears of jury acquittals and the new effectiveness of alternative offences relating to breaches of the peace as a result of the development of professional policing saw the demise of seditious libel in Britain, a development that was reinforced by the passage of Lord Campbell's Libel Act of 1843, which realized the long-standing reform aim of permitting the defence of truth in libel cases.[42]

While the 1792 and 1843 legislative advances reduced the repressive utility of seditious libel, perhaps the most important check was the increasing threat of jury acquittals, which reflected developing wider currents in public opinion. As James Fitzjames Stephen put it, the sedition offences were premised on the view that rulers are social superiors, and that it is wrong to criticize them, regardless of whether the criticism is true or not. These developments reflected increasing recognition of the legitimacy of modern, Lockean-type constitutional premises of popular sovereignty where rulers and their governments are agents of the people, exercising delegated authority. Government could not demand deference, it had to earn it; criticism was therefore a right, and liability should be limited to false allegations.[43] As we will see, the experience of these British struggles informed colonial resistance in the face of seditious libel prosecutions. For instance, when Robert Gourlay and his supporters erroneously thought in 1818 that the province did not benefit from Fox's Libel Act, they resurrected Erskine's arguments about the scope of the jury's verdict.[44]

Colonial governments were determined to fully exploit the repressive potential of the received sedition laws, supplementing them by local legislation that extended the reach of the sedition laws. The Sedition Act in effect from 1804 to 1829 was unprecedented in reach.[45] British concerns about French revolutionary intrigues in British North America, the uncertain loyalty of the francophone majority in Quebec, and the large border shared with the United States resulted in imperial encouragement of temporary enemy aliens legislation in 1797.[46] Similar pretexts existed for the permanent 1804 legislation, but it was also very much the product of specifically local political concerns, passed just as the province's first organized political opposition party took shape to present a concerted challenge to government.[47] There were some similarities to Pitt's 1793 temporary emergency legislation and measures controversially introduced by the Federalist government in the United States in 1798 and overturned shortly after.[48]

Upper Canada's Sedition Act authorized the indefinite detention and deportation of all aliens and British subjects not permanently resident in the province six months before proceedings were initiated, or who had not taken a provincial oath of allegiance. Such persons could be brought before a summary hearing to answer allegations causing disaffection. Refusal to comply with a hearing's order to leave the province constituted an offence for which the accused could be held without bail until trial at the Crown's discretion. Upon conviction the accused could be deported immediately or after a term of imprisonment, with further refusal to leave or return constituting an offence punishable by death. The legislation was used during the War of 1812 to deport more than four hundred recent American immigrants from the province,[49] but as we shall see, the most prominent target was the Scottish reformer Robert Gourlay, who prompted yet further legislation. The Seditious Meetings Act, 1818 was designed to suppress the political meetings outside established legislative processes and popular associations aimed at organizing petitions to the Crown or the British Government.[50] The latter act was repealed in 1820, but as we shall see, Gourlay's questioning of the constitutionality of the measure was the pretext for the Sedition Act proceedings against him, which sparked a protracted legislative struggle to repeal the 1804 act.

3. Case Illustrations: A Selective Account

The archival records for Upper Canada indicate more than fifty sedition and seditious libel prosecutions by the Crown.[51] Further measures included Sedition Act proceedings, parliamentary privilege proceedings for contempt that resulted in imprisonment, and more informal kinds of repression, notably the rough justice that resulted in the destruction of William Lyon Mackenzie's press. The three cases examined in detail here – Joseph Willcocks (1804–8), Robert Gourlay (1818–19), and Francis Collins (1826–8) – represent the apex of government concerns about the related dangers of active organized political opposition, an independent press, and broader popular engagement with political issues. The three cases represent distinct phases, from effective government control over political expression, to the intense contestation of this control, to the effective curbing of repressive control over political expression in the wake of the Collins case. By the 1830s the Sedition Act had been repealed, contempt proceedings confined to expulsions from the legislature, and the government became unwilling to test sedition prosecutions with juries. There was a shift away from repressive attempts to manage political expression and curb the province's emerging public sphere, reflecting a transformation from privileged control over politics and public policy to recognition of the legitimacy of popular engagement with these matters. The legal repression of imagined sedition gave way to a more modern and rational approach to matters of political expression. While governments remained concerned about the undermining of authority through distortion and abuse, they reluctantly recognized the inevitability of popular engagement with public issues and the formation of public opinion and criticism. The only legitimate limits on political expression for the engaged public became deliberate falsehoods or advocacy of violence.

a) Early Opposition: Willcocks

The *Upper Canada Gazette* was established in 1793 and published under licence from the following year by Gideon and Sylvester Tiffany until Gideon's conviction for blasphemy in 1797. The brothers attempted to establish an independent newspaper for the purpose, Chief Justice Elmsley warned, of disseminating political knowledge, and their efforts were frustrated by intimidation and financial difficulties.[52] Official concerns deepened in the period 1804–8 with the rise of the province's first organized political opposition movement and the founding of the *Upper Canadian Guardian and Freeman's Journal* as its mouthpiece.[53] The Sedition Act was passed just before this opposition emerged as a party in the Assembly, led initially by barrister and former United Irishman William Weekes, who won a by-election victory the same year. The opposition was supported by rural interests and moderate Irish Whig reformers, who had migrated to the province after the 1798 Irish Rebellion, articulating a critique that drew parallels between the Irish and Canadian conditions of colonial rule and incomplete implementation of the British constitution.

Weekes was killed in a duel and his more prominent supporters were removed from the scene by Lieutenant Governor Francis Gore.[54] Robert Thorpe, who soon after appointment to the Court of King's Bench encouraged the expression of local grievances in his grand jury charges and advised opposition members from the bar of the House, was removed by the Executive Council.[55] He and another Irish Whig, the recently dismissed sheriff of the Home District, Joseph Willcocks, established the *Guardian* in July 1807. Willcocks was editor while Thorpe was a frequent contributor, and the newspaper voiced concerns that the *Gazette* suppressed, urging readers to speak out in defence of their rights and judge government, and criticizing official 'courtiers' who assumed the exclusive right to decide public measures. Gore described the newspaper as a revolutionary Jacobin plot concocted by United Irishmen, and when Thorpe left for Britain to contest his removal, Willcocks assumed leadership of the party, announcing he would seek a seat in the Assembly.[56]

A complex array of legal and legislative measures followed, opened by an indictment against Willocks for seditious libel authorized by Gore in November 1807, but jury concerns led to conversion of the prosecution to an ex officio information and his eventual conviction by another procedure altogether. Willcocks pleaded not guilty before the King's Bench in January and was given notice that he would face trial at the next assizes in Niagara.[57] He then won a Niagara area by-election, and once in the Assembly moved that members should have full access to records of house debates, deepening government fears since he also continued as editor.[58] The libel indictment was withdrawn and substitute by an ex officio information enabling the Attorney General to change the trial venue to York and select a special jury.[59] The government's ability to pack a jury was then frustrated when Judge William Dummer Powell of the King's Bench accepted Willcocks's request to change the venue back to Niagara, where the newspaper was based.[60] The government then decided on an alternative form of repression, sounding out the Assembly members to see if a majority could be mustered to support parliamentary privilege proceedings for contempt, and Willocks was convicted of that, sentenced by the House to imprisonment in the district jail for the duration of session.

Willcocks attempted to contest these proceedings on the basis that an information had already been filed in the courts for the libel in question, placing him in a situation of double jeopardy (he was later acquitted on charges of seditious libel when the case came up before the court at Niagara).[61] The use of privilege in this manner was questionable. Freedom of speech in the House itself was privileged and precluded sedition prosecutions or libel actions in the courts. While the British contempt cases of Wilkes (1763) and Burdett (1811) suggested that members could be prosecuted for comments made outside the House, Parliament was not entitled to interfere with the regular course of justice in the courts on a matter that was still before the courts. And while Parliament had the power to expel members on separate matters of contempt, punishment that included imprisonment also interfered with the jurisdiction of the criminal courts.[62] As Robert Gourlay, commenting on the case a decade later, declared: 'What would Mr. Fox [sponsor of the 1791 Constitutional Act that created Upper Canada as well as the Libel Act] have said to all of this? – Certainly had he moved at all in the matter, it would have been worthy of him to have gone out to Upper Canada, purposely to kick the dirty fellows of Assembly into Lake Ontario.'[63]

Willcocks was to face two more charges of seditious libel, and a reform pamphlet by John Mills Jackson nearly gave rise to similar contempt proceedings against a person who was not a member of the legislature. The government had largely succeeded in marginalizing opposition voices. Its position appeared to be vindicated by Willcocks's disloyalty during the War of 1812, decisively curbing the resurgence of the opposition apparent in the first few months of the war.[64] Nonetheless, as McNairn puts it, these early experiences marked the opening of provincial contention over government control of political debate and its wider publication.[65] The repressive controls over the emerging public sphere would be shaken during the Gourlay affair and begin to break down in its wake.

b) Resurgent Opposition: Gourlay

Political opposition regrouped after the War of 1812 around grievances such as compensation for war losses, land grants, and discriminatory measures associated with the 'alien question.'[66] The election of late 1816 and the Assembly sessions that followed reflected new divisions. Contempt proceedings were taken against member James Durand and government contemplated suspensions of habeas corpus, while opposition calls for a general committee on the state of the province led to the premature proroguing of sessions in 1817 and 1818.[67] Robert Gourlay arrived in Upper Canada in the midst of this political turmoil, with a background in radical politics in Scotland and more recent radical activity in London in association with Cobbett and Hunt.[68] His proposed statistical account of the province soon caused government concerns when he called for township meetings to collect local grievances in his first 'Address to the Resident Landholders of Upper Canada.'[69] Gourlay's second address, published in the *Niagara Spectator*, openly denounced the government and supported Assembly calls for a general committee.[70] The second abrupt ending of session led Gourlay to declare in a published third address that '[p]arliament is broken up and the Constitution is in danger' and to propose that township meetings elect delegates to a constitutional convention in York designed to send popular grievances direct to Britain.[71] The *Niagara Spectator* was joined by other independent newspapers in Kingston and York, and the legislative sessions of 1817 and 1818 renewed interest in fuller reporting on the legislative debates.[72] Political commentary was also generated in response to Gourlay's meetings, petition and proposed convention, establishing what McNairn describes as 'mutually reinforcing relationships among newspapers, public meetings and petition that came to dominate later reform politics.'[73]

Gourlay, as primary agitator, was placed under close surveillance as the government pondered a response.[74] Attorney General John Beverley Robinson expressed caution, concerned about jurors as well as giving opposition a powerful platform for yet further popular mobilization through legal proceedings: 'It requires undoubtedly to be well considered in cases of this kind how far it may be expedient to commence prosecutions, for however unquestionable the law may be, the improper lenity, or worse conduct of Jurors frequently screens the offender from punishment. This gives importance to what otherwise might perhaps have sunk into contempt, and the acquitted libeller is immediately elevated into a Champion for liberty and against imaginary oppression.'[75] Robinson advised that a seditious libel prosecution by indictment was the best legal option if necessary and that the suppression of popular conventions required new legislation.[76] Gourlay's encounters with the law were to fall into two broad stages, reflecting the full range of sedition laws and their administration in the province. The first involved two prosecutions by indictment for sedition. The second entailed resort to exceptional legislative responses and special procedures: the direct suppression of Gourlay's 'constitutional meetings' with the passage of the Seditious Meetings Act, extrajudicial opinion on the applicability of the 1804 Sedition Act to Gourlay and his subsequent deportation under it, and a prosecution for seditious libel by ex officio information against Gourlay's close ally, Bartimus Ferguson, editor of the *Niagara Spectator*.

Robinson's fears of public opinion, the jury, and creating a platform for the reform cause proved to be well founded. Gourlay was arrested in June 1818 on separate charges against the man described by newly arrived Lieutenant Governor Sir Peregrine Maitland as 'half-Cobbett, and half-Hunt;' one to be tried at the Midland assize in Kingston and the other at the Johnstown assize in Brockville.[77] The indictments were withheld from Gourlay when he requested them, obliging him to prepare a defence based on his arrest warrants, which simply stated 'false, wicked and seditious libel styled Principles and Proceedings of Inhabitants of the District of Niagara and Petition to the Prince Regent,' and his defence was further compromised when he found out at the last moment that the Midland assize was scheduled weeks earlier than usual.

The trial held at Kingston on 15 August was prosecuted by acting solicitor general Henry Boulton before Judge William Campbell.[78] Boulton identified Gourlay's authorship of the libel, compared him to the vilified Joseph Willcocks, and argued that the constitutional meetings promoted by the libel would overturn the constitution. He attempted to steer the jury away from considering seditious intent and effect; If Gourlay was responsible for the publication in question the jurors must find him guilty.[79] Gourlay, defended himself assisted by former Massachusetts attorney general Barnabas Bidwell, pointing out the procedural irregularities around his case,[80] the constitutional right of all British subjects to petition without the threat of criminal charges,[81] and the fact that he was an accessory rather than a principal to the libel in question.[82] Drawing from Erskine's famous defences, he noted that the prosecution must prove intent, while the Solicitor General had simply entered evidence of publication and declared seditious innuendo, and this opened a number of points on freedom of the jury's verdict[83] as well as Fox's Libel Act (erroneously thought not to apply in the province),[84] declaring that '[t]o leave this to the dictum of the bench would be a dangerous sacrifice of liberty.'[85]

The jury returned a verdict of not guilty, but victory celebrations were short-lived as it became clear that Gourlay still faced trial in Brockville at the Johnstown District assizes at the end of August.[86] He requested a discharge on the grounds that he had already been acquitted, but his request was rejected when the Crown indicated that it was proceeding on passages from his Third Address, which was not submitted as evidence in Kingston. A similar defence resulted in a second acquittal.[87]

These embarrassing acquittals prompted the government to turn from the common law to legislation. The Seditious Meetings Act, described earlier, was passed in late October and addressed the lacuna around the prohibition of tumultuous meetings and petitioning noted by Robinson.[88] Gourlay's 'Gagg'd, by Jingo' response published in the *Niagara Spectator* provided the pretext for Sedition Act proceedings.[89] The 1804 legislation was submitted to the court of King's Bench for an extra-judicial opinion on its applicability to Gourlay,[90] and in November the King's Bench responded positively, resolving every ambiguity in favour of the government.[91] As Chief Justice Powell later observed, '[The Act] subjects the Earl [of] Bathurst if he should pay a visit to this Province and his Looks should offend Isaac Sweezy [Swayze, who informed against Gourlay] to be ordered out of the Province by the enlightened Magistrate, and if that disobedience which constitutes the offence is found by a jury, to be banished, under penalty of Death.'[92] 'Gagg'd by Jingo' also had consequences for the editor, Ferguson, who was arrested with his assistant, Benjamin Pawling, on an ex officio information for seditious libel.[93] By this procedure the Crown could proceed at its discretion, leaving a 'hanging threat' that Robinson made, declaring that the subsequent conduct of the newspaper would determine the matter.

Gourlay was arrested and brought before a summary hearing where the commissioners, armed with the extra-judicial opinion, dismissed his claim that the act did not apply to British subjects.[94] He was questioned about his connections with Cobbett, Hunt, the Spa Fields riots, and visits to Ireland and the United States, and failed to convince them that his words and conduct were not intended to promote disaffection despite his recent acquittals. Refusing its order to leave the province as a seditious alien, Gourlay was placed in indefinite detention at the beginning of January.[95] A petition for habeas corpus was denied,[96] but his writing for the *Niagara Spectator* continued until June, when he was ordered into solitary confinement.[97] Gourlay's contributions also had consequences for Ferguson; supported by resolutions in the Assembly, Robinson proceeded on his 'hanging threat.'[98]

The Niagara assizes began on 16 August, with the Chief Justice's compliance well ascertained.[99] The juries appear to have been carefully packed, in Ferguson's case by virtue of the ex officio procedure,[100] and Gourlay's extended confinement left him incapable of challenging the sheriff's selection.[101] Although Ferguson received what was reported as an able defence, he was quickly found guilty at his trial in August.[102] As was possible with the ex officio procedure, sentencing was postponed beyond the end of the assizes to the next term of the court of King's Bench in early November. The sentence would be determined by the legal outcome of Gourlay's trial the next day and its political fallout.[103]

At Gourlay's trial Robinson needed only to prove a lawful order to leave the province and Gourlay's disobedience of it.[104] He did not have to establish the existence of sedition, nor was the jury entitled to enquire into it, and he simply examined the commissioners to establish regularity of the hearing under the terms of the act.[105] Gourlay insisted on defending himself, but as a result of his confinement he became confused about the charge, and thinking it seditious libel, rambled on about his previous acquittals, a display the *Kingston Chronicle* described as 'idle and absurd to the extreme.'[106] A guilty verdict was predictably returned and Gourlay was directed to leave the province within twenty-four hours or face death. Gourlay returned to Britain via the United States and began a campaign of vindication that obsessed him for the rest of his life.[107]

At Ferguson's 'sentence hearing' in November Robinson opposed any leniency, stressing Ferguson's ample warning from the Crown the previous year, his encouragement of the imprisoned Gourlay's continued sedition, and the disaffection generated by the dangerous engine of the press under irresponsible editors. Ferguson received a harsh sentence of imprisonment, the pillory, and fines that proved ruinous for his newspaper.[108] At the lieutenant governor's suggestion, the seditious meetings legislation was repealed at the next legislative session in early 1820 and Ferguson's petition pleading for remission of the remainder of his sentence passed narrowly in the legislature, although a motion to repeal the 1804 Sedition Act was defeated, initiating a series of attempts to repeal it through the 1820s.[109]

c) Established Opposition: Collins

The examples of Gourlay and Ferguson did little to deter the growing opposition movement, fuelled by further discriminatory measures against 'aliens' and reformers, including attempts to preclude them from sitting as elected members of the Assembly based on spurious disqualifications and criminal proceedings.[110] As opposition mounted William Lyon Mackenzie described the eroding deference to the government and shift in public opinion in positive terms in the founding issue of the *Colonial Advocate*, reflecting on 'the difference between passive obedience and non resistance, to a tyrannical government, as compared with free discussion of the public measures.'[111]

As noted earlier, independent newspapers grew apace in the 1820s and government concerns extended even to the official *Gazette*, which tried to compete in accounts of parliamentary debates and political reporting. Richard Horne, the editor of the *Gazette* who had hired Francis Collins to report on debates, faced privilege proceedings and was summoned to the bar of the House and reprimanded in February 1821. His successor, Charles Fothergill, also came under close scrutiny as the office of King's Printer remained tightly controlled.[112] Parliamentary privilege proceedings were also taken against Hugh Thomson, editor of the *Upper Canada Herald*.[113] Three independent newspaper editors became a particular concern for their political commentary: Hugh Thompson of the *Herald*, William Lyon Mackenzie of the *Colonial Advocate*, and Francis Collins of the *Freeman*. Parliamentary privilege proceedings for contempt were taken against Thompson. The dumping of Mackenzie's press into Lake Ontario by young Tory hooligans, many of whom were law students, along with other incidents of 'rough justice' unprosecuted by the Crown (suggesting official complicity with violence against selected reform targets) gave rise to a Legislative Assembly enquiry into the administration of justice and public prosecutions.[114] It heard testimony from recently arrived King's Bench justice John Walpole Willis, who made much of colonial departures from English practices, questioned their constitutionality, and repeated these charges at the assizes. A related series of articles by Collins revealed yet more about government legal abuses and linked the law officers of the Crown to unprosecuted criminal acts.[115]

Attorney General Robinson again expressed caution, the Gourlay affair reinforcing the dangers of creating a powerful platform for the reform cause: 'Within a few Years Two Newspapers have been established in this Town, under the Conduct of Men [Collins and Mackenzie] of much less responsible Stations in Society than the editors of Public Journals commonly are ... I always regretted the Tendency which such Publications might have in misleading the Opinions of People ... and perhaps a Sense of this ought to have induced me, for the sake of the Province, to attempt to put them down by Law ... [but] I feared to call the Papers into Notoriety, and to protract their Existence, by the political Excitements which Prosecutions for Libel usually occasion.'[116] The growing controversy surrounding the attorney general's partisan conduct compounded matters and explains his reluctance to resort to the expedient of an ex officio information, although he was willing to conduct prosecutions by regular indictment upon the lieutenant governor's request or any individuals libelled. As the Home District assize opened on 7 April 1821, the grand jury returned a true bill on an indictment against Collins and another against Mackenzie.[117] Robinson's caution did not, however, extend to anticipating Willis's presence. Just before the trials commenced, Willis permitted Collins to voice concerns about the Attorney General and to lay private charges for alleged acts by government supporters.[118] A furious Robinson withdrew the Collins case to the next assize in October, declaring that subsequent press conduct would determine whether the Collins or Mackenzie cases would proceed.

In the summer the Executive Council recommended Willis's removal and suspended him on the pretext of his challenge to the constitutionality of the King's Bench.[119] A third seditious libel indictment was issued in Kingston when Hugh Thompson of the *Herald* wrote, 'This high handed measure plainly shows that judges who hold their appointments during pleasure may not give an opinion contrary to the will of the Executive, without running the risk of being dismissed.'[120] The Mackenzie and Thompson indictments were dropped, but Robinson proceeded against Collins when the autumn assize opened on 13 October. Collins tried to postpone the case, pointing out that he had not been formally arraigned in the confusion of the spring assize. When this was confirmed, Robinson demanded and won an impossibly high security for Collins's good behaviour, and he opted for immediate trial to avoid imprisonment.[121] The jury acquitted but the Attorney General brought new charges on different evidence—Collins's recently published remarks on Robinson and Judge Hagerman during the trial itself.[122]

The Crown's third attempt against Collins came up on 25 October before Mr Justice Sherwood (whose son and brother-in-law faced Collins's criminal charges at the spring assizes). Collins's counsel, John Rolph, attempted to argue a defence of truth, claiming that the Attorney General had indeed stated a falsehood in court, and moved for an immediate acquittal because Robinson refused to read the alleged libels to the jury.[123] Robinson and Judge Sherwood tried steer the jury clear of these matters, but the jurors struggled with their verdict. While deliberating, Sherwood left the bench to be replaced by Hagerman (who was allegedly libelled). The jury gave a verdict of guilty on the libel against the Attorney General only, which Hagerman rejected, instructing them to give a general verdict, including the libel on him.[124] The jury eventually complied and Sherwood returned to sentence Collins to a year's imprisonment and crippling fines, a sentence which British law officers later declared twice as severe as comparable English cases.[125]

Reformers won an unprecedented number of seats in the 1828 elections. The Assembly petitioned Collins's sentence, Willis's removal, the upper house's repeated refusal to accept jury reform and Sedition Act repeal bills passed by majorities, and a number of other concerns about the local administration of justice. These matters were considered by a special British parliamentary committee, the first of a series of committees on the Canadas in the 1830s. The most immediate result was remission of Collins's sentence and imperial intervention to uphold the eighth majority bill to repeal the Sedition Act in 1829.[126]

Collins marked the demise of seditious libel prosecutions against the press in Upper Canada, although the battles continued in Nova Scotia with Howe in 1835. (Prosecutions for sedition receded outside situations of wartime emergencies, although the lack of definition of seditious intent in the Canadian Criminal Code led to a resurrection of prosecutions against labour leaders in the wake of the Winnipeg general strike of 1919 and the Cape Breton steelworkers and coal miners strike of 1922, and even attempts to use the offence in support of the hegemony of church and state in Quebec in the 1950s.)[127] With the Crown's exercise of prosecutorial authority and other administration of justice matters under such intense public scrutiny, the ex officio prerogative was no longer a feasible option and there was even less confidence in securing compliant regular juries. The government had failed to marginalize oppositional criticism. On the contrary, repressive proceedings attracted greater notoriety, confirming Robinson's worst fears. It seemed that the law could no longer be resorted to in order to discipline the public sphere, and that prosecuting opposition leaders and expression served only to put government under increasingly critical scrutiny from both the provincial public and the imperial government.

The shift away from seditious libel in Britain after the early 1820s is mirrored in Upper Canada from the 1830s, including similar local legislative debates over the truth defence, and eventual adoption of Lord Campbell's 1843 Libel Act.[128] Another seditious libel prosecution against Mackenzie was contemplated by the Crown law officers in March 1832, but the Executive Council, concerned about a jury trial and the notoriety such a case would attract, deemed it politically inexpedient.[129] Instead, Mackenzie was repeatedly expelled from the Assembly from 1831 to 1834 in an attempt to prevent him from sitting as an elected member, but such privilege proceedings were no longer taken directly against the press.[130] Even private actions for defamatory libel against the press had become questionable, if they were perceived as a front for government interests, as suggested by the 1834 acquittal of George Gurnett, editor of the *Courier*. For the province's engaged public, the only legitimate legal limits on political expression became deliberate falsehoods or advocacy of violence.

4. Conclusions

The repressive legal control of political expression in Upper Canada failed to curb an emerging local public sphere. The popular right to access independent information about government and to freely discuss and criticize government had been struggled for and achieved by the 1830s, supported by increasingly critical imperial scrutiny of recalcitrant local elites. As McNairn puts it, 'The most privileged could no longer claim a monopoly on the norms and information required by public deliberation. They could no longer monopolize the right to judge. Government by gentlemen had been replaced by government by public opinion.'[131] Moreover, the acceptable standards for political expression were to be set by informed public opinion, not by the executive, the government, the Crown prosecutor, the courts, or even the legislature itself, a development that Robinson, who became Chief Justice, and other more astute government leaders were obliged to accept. As the editor of the *Guardian* expressed it, 'public opinion is the true supporter of the press – and public opinion is the proper and only effectual corrector of its licentiousness.'[132]

These developments would not have been possible without the contestable potential of the law, and the cases examined here are rich illustrations of Thompson's suggestions about the rule of law. Popular expectations based on formal legal and constitutional claims limited the ability of the government to manipulate proceedings, or to do so at the risk of broad negative approbation, and provided opportunities for contesting the repression. Such claims figured prominently in the perceptions and strategies of defence counsel, in opposition appeals for broader popular support, and had an effect on jurors, who arguably reflected broader currents in public opinion. Government fears of jury acquittals dictated the course of the Willcocks prosecution, and were apparent in the Gourlay and Collins affairs, as explicitly recognized by Attorney General John Beverley Robinson. As we have seen, constitutional and rule of law claims were readily evoked by matters such as the colonial organization of prosecutorial authority (a key subtext of the Collins affair in the aftermath of the failure to prosecute government supporters after the destruction of Mackenzie's press but also raised by resort to the controversial ex officio prerogative in Willcocks and Ferguson) and the issue of judicial independence (the extra-judicial opinion on the applicability of the Sedition Act to Gourlay, which reflected the central role of judges in colonial political cultures and the rapid removal of troublesome judges such as Thorpe and Willis). Executive influence on the administration of justice extended to the jury, the palladium of liberty for late-seventeenth- and eighteenth-century Whig constitutionalists and celebrated as such in Gourlay's trials for seditious libel, manifested in controversies over jury selection addressed in a series of jury reform bills initiated by Willcocks that paralleled attempts to repeal the Sedition Act.[133] These frustrated bills, along with Assembly enquiries into the administration of justice, demonstrate the close relationship between legal struggles and legislative struggles for responsible government. The bypassing of the jury in the Sedition Act proceedings against Gourlay and the packed jury in Ferguson secured convictions, but they were widely perceived to the government's discredit. The government had won that battle, and the later one against Collins, but lost the war in terms of public opinion.

While the cases examined here highlight the validity of Thompson's assertions about the rule of law, Habermas's work on the emerging public sphere helps to clarify the connections between the opposition targets of prosecution and broader public opinion. The development of challenges to privileged control over politics and public policy associated with the independent press, and the growing popular engagement with these matters, deepened government anxieties and resulted in the legal responses examined here. In the longer term, the underlying imaginary behind the offence of sedition, one that equated critical political expression with the disloyalty or revolutionary undermining of authority, was decisively undermined. The cases examined here were markers in the development of the province's public sphere. Willcocks reflected the outright rejection of the validity of public opinion as manifested in oppositional political expression, and although Gourlay and Collins were ultimately punished, the 1820s saw a decisive shift to reluctant acceptance of its inevitability. Dissenting political expression could no longer be convincingly imagined as sedition and potentially revolutionary, although there was certainly continuing concern about forms of expression that undermined governmental authority. Again, for the increasingly engaged public, the only legitimate legal limits on political expression became deliberate falsehoods or advocacy of violence. The law, as is usually the case, belatedly followed, but despite legislative advances, the 1892 Canadian Criminal Code retained sedition's repressive malleability by leaving the definition of intent to the common law.

There are two key elements of this narrative that warrant further examination. First, as suggested above, the jury plays an important role in these cases, not only in the obvious way of deciding outcomes through its verdict, but also as a sort of barometer of the public sphere within the administration of justice. It reflects informed popular opinion, and its own deliberative processes mirror those outside institutional processes. This suggests that the jury is an important site for further research on the public sphere. Second, it should be recognized that restraints on sedition prosecutions after 1828 came from 'above' as well as 'below.' The local reform struggle was greatly assisted by imperial intervention as Upper Canada's governments came under increasingly critical scrutiny from the British government, beginning with the 1828 Canada Committee and continuing with the liberal Whig ascendancy in the 1830s. Just as the struggle for responsible cabinet government reflected a mixture of local and external factors, so too did the struggles around the provincial administration of justice. In reacting against the traditional narratives that emphasize matters such as Lord

Durham's Report and imperial policy reform in the wake of the 1837–8 rebellions and border raids crisis, there is a danger of a parochial over-romanticizing of local struggles and neglect of context. The political and bureaucratic pressures of imperial reconfiguration deserve critical reassessment. Events in the Canadas took place within a larger imperial network of similar struggles in other British colonial settings that warrant further comparative work.

The cases examined here suggest the importance of the law and its administration in the regulation of public forms of expression and the complexities of the relationship between law and politics. It also suggests the limits of the rationality of law, how it can be employed as a vehicle for the imaginary, for emancipatory as well as repressive objectives. While the offence of sedition articulated and activated the official perception that equated criticism with revolution or disloyalty, it is also significant that counter-perceptions that portrayed this as privileged self-interest and aspired to broader engagement with public affairs could be effective in challenging the administration of such repressive laws.

NOTES

* The author wishes to thank Bruce Curtis and Jeffrey McNairn for their comments on an earlier version of this chapter.

1 See Wright, 'Sedition in Upper Canada: Contested Legality,' 29 (1992): *Labour/Le Travail*, 7, and chapters 12, 14 and 15 in F. Murray Greenwood and Wright, eds., *Canadian State Trials*, vol. 1, *Law Politics and Security Measures, 1608–1837* (Toronto: University of Toronto Press, 1996). The treason proceedings during the War of 1812 and in the wake of the 1837–8 rebellion and invasions are examined in detail in P. Romney and Wright, 'State Trials and Security Proceedings During the War of 1812,' in *Canadian State Trials 1*, 376, and in several essays in part 1 of *Canadian State Trials*, vol. 2, *Rebellion and Invasion in the Canadas, 1837–9* (Toronto: University of Toronto Press, 2002). On politics in the routine business of the criminal courts and civil proceedings see, for example, P. Romney, 'From Constitutionalism to Legalism: Trial by Jury, Responsible Government, and the Rule of Law in Canadian Political Culture' (1989) 7, 133 *Law and History Review*.

2 Jürgen Habermas, *The Structural Transformation of the Public Sphere: An Inquiry into a Category of Bourgeois Society*, trans. Thomas Burger (Cam-

bridge: MIT Press, 1989), C. Calhoun ed., *Habermas and the Public Sphere* (Cambridge, MA: MIT Press, 1992); John Barrell, *Imagining the King's Death: Figurative Treason, Fantasies of Regicide, 1793–1796* (Oxford: Oxford University Press, 2000) and 'Imaginary Treason, Imaginary Law: The State Trials of 1794,' in *The Birth of Pandora and the Division of Knowledge* (Philadelphia: University of Pennsylvania Press, 1992), 119; Paul Keen, *The Crisis of Literature in the 1790s: Print Culture and the Public Sphere* (Cambridge: Cambridge University Press, 1999); Kevin Gilmartin, *Print Politics: The Press and Radical Opposition in Early Nineteenth-Century England* (Cambridge: Cambridge University Press, 1996); Jeffrey L. McNairn, *The Capacity to Judge: Public Opinion and Deliberative Democracy in Upper Canada, 1791–1854* (Toronto: University of Toronto Press, 2000).

3 See *infra* note 51. Population figures are derived from plate 10 (B.S. Osborne) in J.C. Robert and D.A. Sutherland, eds., *Historical Atlas of Canada*, Vol. 2, gen. ed. R.L. Gentilcore and G.J. Matthews (Toronto: University of Toronto Press, 1993).

4 For Sedition Act deportations, see also Romney and Wright, note 1 above, and Wright, 'Migration, Radicalism, and State Security: Legislative Initiatives in the Canadas and the United States c.1794–1804,' *Studies in American Political Development* 16 (2002): 48. On privilege proceedings for contempt, see Greenwood and Wright, 'Parliamentary Privilege and the Repression of Dissent in the Canadas,' *Canadian State Trials 1*, 409

5 See C. Emsley, 'An Aspect of Pitt's Terror: Prosecutions for Sedition During the 1790's,' *Social History* 6 (1981): 155–75; F.K Prochaska, 'English State Trials in the 1790s: A Case Study,' *Journal of British Studies* 17 (1973): 63 82. See also Michael Lobban, 'From Seditious Libel to Unlawful Assembly: Peterloo and the Changing face of Political Crime c.1770–1820,' (1990) *Oxford Journal of Legal Studies* 10, 305. See also text at note 42 below.

6 See Greenwood and Wright, 'Parliamentary Privilege,' *supra* note 4, and text below.

7 See Wright, 'The Gourlay Affair: Seditious Libel and the Sedition Act in Upper Canada, 1818–19,' *Canadian State Trials 1*, 487, and text below.

8 See Paul Romney, 'Upper Canada in the 1820s: Criminal Prosecution and the Case of Francis Collins,' *Canadian State Trials 1*, 505, and text below.

9 Allan Greer, '1837–38: Rebellion Reconsidered,' *Canadian Historical Review* 76 (1995): 1 at 6–13 and 'Rebels and Prisoners: The Canadian Insurrections of 1837–38,' *Acadiensis* 14 (1984): 137 at 145; McNairn, *The Capacity to Judge*, *supra* note 2 at 9 and 19. On the province's parochial or particular political culture see, for instance, Frank Underhill, 'Some Reflections

on the Liberal Tradition in Canada,' in *In Search of Canadian Liberalism* (Toronto: Macmillan 1960), 12; S.F. Wise, *God's Peculiar Peoples: Essays on Political Culture in Nineteenth Century Canada*, ed. B. McKillop and P. Romney (Ottawa: Carleton University Press, 1993).

10 McNairn, *supra* note 2 at 13, 16

11 See, e.g., E.P. Thompson, *Whigs and Hunters: The Origins of the Black Act* (Harmondsworth, UK: Penguin, 1977) and 'The Moral Economy of the English Crowd,' *Past and Present* 50 (1971): 76–136; D. Hay et al., *Albion's Fatal Tree: Crime and Society in Eighteenth-Century England* (New York: Pantheon Books, 1975).

12 Thompson, *Whigs and Hunters*, 462–3.

13 Geoff Eley, 'Nations, Publics, and Political Cultures: Placing Habermas in the Nineteenth Century,' in Calhoun, *Habermas and the Public Sphere*, 290.

14 See, e.g., his suggestion that by the time of the British Reform Act, 1832 public political reporting was widely accepted and the British reading public 'were no longer treated as people whom, like strangers, one could exclude from [Parliament's] deliberations.' Habermas, *Structural Transformation*, *supra* note 2 at 60.

15 See, e.g., essays in Calhoun, *supra* note 2.

16 Michael Warner, 'The Mass Public and the Mass Subject,' in Calhoun, *Habermas and the Public Sphere*, 379–82. See also Warner, *The Letters of the Republic: Publication and the Public Sphere in Eighteenth-Century America* (Cambridge, MA: Harvard University Press, 1990).

17 William Cobbett, *Political Register*, 11 December 1813, quoted in Paul Keen, *Revolutions in Romantic Literature: An Anthology of Print Culture, 1780–1832* (Toronto: Broadview Press, 2004), 25–6.

18 *Ibid.*

19 See, e.g., Jon P. Klancher, *The Making of English Reading Audiences, 1790–1832* (Madison: University of Wisconsin Press, 1987); Alan Richardson, *Literature, Education, and Romanticism: Reading as Social Practice, 1780–1832* (Cambridge: Cambridge University Press, 1994); Keen, *The Crisis of Literature in the 1790s*, *supra* note 2.

20 Barrell, 'Imaginary Treason, Imaginary Law,' in *Imagining the King's Death*, *supra* note 2.

21 Gilmartin, *Print Politics*, *supra* note 2.

22 *The Autobiography of Francis Place* (1824), reproduced in Keen, *Revolutions*, *supra* note 17 at 70, 77.

23 Guy Pollock (Robert Douglas Hamilton), *Upper Canada Courier*, 22 March 1832, reproduced in McNairn, *supra* note 2 at 3–4

24 McNairn, *ibid.*, 6

25 John Simpson quoted in McNairn, *ibid.*, 58

26 See, e.g., R.E. Saunders, 'What Was the Family Compact?' *Ontario History* 49 (1957): 165–78; S.F. Wise, 'Upper Canada and the Conservative Tradition,' in *Profiles of a Province*, ed. E.G. Firth (Toronto: Ontario Historical Society 1967), 20–33; Jane Errington, *The Lion, the Eagle and Upper Canada: A Developing Colonial Ideology* (McGill-Queen's University Press, 1987); David Mills, *The Idea of Loyalty in Upper Canada, 1784–1850* (Kingston and Montreal: McGill-Queen's University Press, 1988).

27 See P. Romney, 'Reinventing Upper Canada: American Immigrants, Upper Canadian History, English Law and the Alien Question,'in *Patterns of the Past: Interpreting Ontario's History*, ed. in R. Hall, W. Westfall, and L. Sefton Macdowell (Toronto: Dundurn, 1988), 78–107.

28 Literacy rates in the province before the 1840s are uncertain, although Graff's work on mid-century Kingston, Hamilton, and London suggests that literacy ran from 70 per cent to over 90 per cent, see H. Graff, *The Literacy Myth: Literacy and Social Structure in the Nineteenth-Century City* (New York 1979), 59. Grafff's work has been much debated; see also B. Curtis, 'Littery Merritt: Useful Knowledge and the Organization of Township Libraries in Canada West 1840–60, *Ontario History* 78 (1986): 265; C. Benn, 'The Upper Canada Press,1773–1815,' *Ontario History* 70 (1978): 91; S.E. Houston and A. Prentice, *Schooling and Scholars in Nineteenth-Century Ontario* (Toronto: University of Toronto Press, 1991). J.H Wadland and M. Hobbs, *Historical Atlas of Canada 2*, plate 51.

29 McNairn, *supra* note 2 at 63–107. York/Toronto had twenty voluntary associations in a population of 9254 in 1833–4 (p. 67)

30 By 1819 newspapers had been published in six towns and by 1829 ten communities boasted of at least one newspaper. Between 1830 and 1839 seventy-three newspapers were published in the province. McNairn ibid., 121

31 *Ibid.*, 116–33. See also *supra* note 28.

32 *Ibid.*, 126–8

33 *Ibid.*, 144–8

34 Fox's Act was in fact proclaimed before the reception date and was part of the province's law (see note 44 below). There had been uncertainty over Upper Canada's reception date, whether it was the 1774 Quebec Act or the Constitutional Act of 1791 (which divided Quebec into the two Canadas) because Upper Canada's first chief justice, William Osgoode, did not think legislation necessary to expressly adopt English criminal law. Confusion over the corpus of English law led to legislation in 1800 that specified the 1792 date (40 Geo. III, c.1).

35 The colonial administration of justice was elaborated in the 1794 Judicature Act. See R.L. Fraser, 'All the privileges which Englishmen possess: Order, Rights and Constitutionalism in Upper Canada,' in *Provincial Justice: Upper Canadian Legal Portraits*, ed. R.L. Fraser (Toronto: Osgoode Society, 1992), xxi–xcii; F.H. Armstrong, *Handbook of Upper Canadian Chronology* (Toronto: Dundurn Press, 1985).

36 See P. Romney, *Mr. Attorney: The Attorney General for Ontario in Court, Cabinet and Legislature, 1791–1899* (Toronto: University of Toronto Press, 1986), W.R. Riddell, 'The Information Ex Officio in Upper Canada' (1921) *Canadian Law Times* 41, 5–12, 87–96. Romney notes that statutory rewards were regarded by crown laws officers as a perquisite of office. Other explanations involve the persistence of local practices after the Quebec Act, 1774 and the small bar. English sedition cases were effectively conducted the Crown, usually by lawyers retained as agents in the provinces, the law officers personally in London.

37 See generally, J.F. Stephen, *A History of Criminal Law*, vol. 2 (London 1883), 298–300, Thomas Andrew Green, *Verdict According to Conscience: Perspectives on the English Criminal Trial Jury 1200–1800* (Chicago: University of Chicago Press, 1985), 319; P. Hamburger, 'The Development of the Law of Seditious Libel and Control of the Press' (1985) *Stanford Law Review* 37, 661; and on the Canadian scene, Greenwood and Wright, 'Introduction: State Trials, the Rule of Law, and Executive Powers in Early Canada' and 'Parliamentary Privilege' in *Canadian State Trials 1*, 27–31, 409. Defamatory libel is directed at an individual allegedly held up to contempt or ridicule, pursued by way of a civil court action or private prosecution. Seditious libel is directed at the state, where the authority of its policies or representatives is allegedly undermined, and proceedings were invariably taken by law officers of the Crown or other agents retained by the state. Sedition is also conceptually related to the offence of contempt against the privileges of Parliament, an offence that could be heard against members resulting in expulsion and even imprisonment, as well as reprimand of non-elected public officials called to the bar of the house. Reflecting its early role as a high court, Parliament retained powers to protect its effective functioning as well as its position and dignity. Privilege therefore not only protected members' freedom of speech but could be used in quite the opposite way to restrict expression or criticism of the state by majorities sympathetic to governing executives or challenged by political deliberations outside the legislative sphere. See, e.g., the expulsions of John Wilkes, 1769–74, and the imprisonment of Francis Burdett in 1810.

38 Hamburger, 'Development,' *supra* note 37 at 738, 742, 761; Green, 'Verdict,' *supra* note 37 at 321.

39 *In Dean of St. Asaph* (1783–4) serves as a good illustration. The jury urged by Erskine declared that the accused parliamentary reformer was 'Guilty of publishing *only*.' On application for a new trial, Chief Justice Lord Mansfield condemned the notion of juries usurping the judicial function by deciding matters of law through general verdicts. Howell, ed., *State Trials*, vol. 27 (1816), 847, 950, 1033–40.

40 32 Geo.III c.60 sought to correct errors, doubts and ambiguities that had developed in the common law by reiterating that in any criminal libel case judges were entitled to instruct on law, but the jury could 'give a general Verdict of Guilty or Not Guilty ... and shall not be required ... to find the Defendant or Defendants Guilty merely ... of the Publication ... and of the Sense ascribed.'

41 See E.P. Thompson, *The Making of the English Working Class* (Harmondsworth, UK, Penguin, 1984), 135; Emsley, 'An Aspect of Pitt's "Terror,"' note 5 above; Prochaska, 'English State Trials in the 1790s,' 63, *supra* note 5.

42 *Lord Campbell's Act*, 6&7 Vic.96. On the shift away from seditious libel in the 1820s see Lobban, 'From Seditious Libel to Unlawful Assembly,' *supra* note 5. Lobban notes 103 prosecutions between 1789 and 1810 with peaks of 16 in 1817 and 33 in 1819 followed by a shift, clearly established by the time of the Chartists, to threats to public order by assembly rather than punishment of expressions of words and ideas.

43 Stephen, *supra* note 37 at 299

44 'This act [Fox's Libel Act] was passed the year after the constitution was given to this Province. The right of juries, therefore, is here, still, only an arbitrary right. It might be well, therefore, to have it made absolute by provincial statute.' See 'Address to the Jury, at the Kingston Assizes, in the Case of the *R. v. Robert Gourlay* Kingston, August 20, 1818,' repr. in Greenwood and Wright, *Canadian State Trials 1*, *supra* note 1, 697 at 700. Fox's Act was proclaimed 15 June 1792, three months before the province's reception date so was in fact part of the province's received laws. The issue came up again in 1828 when the judges instructions to the jury was questioned in the Collins case. The Crown conceded the applicability of Fox's Act and John Beverley Robinson later confirmed this explicitly as did his successor as attorney general in assembly debates over libel law reform in December 1831 (see testimony to the Select Committee on the Petition of Francis Collins, *Journals, House of*

Assembly [1829] Appendix, Report on Collins' Case; Sherwood to Colborne, 26 March 1829, PRO (Public Record Office) CO 42 vol. 388, 134–41).

45 'An Act for the better securing of this Province against all Seditious Attempts or Designs to disturb the Tranquility thereof' (1804) 44 Geo.III c.1 (U.C.), reproduced in Greenwood and Wright, *Canadian State Trials 1*, 661–4.

46 Enemy Aliens Act (1797) 37 Geo III c.1 (U.C.). See NAC (National Archives of Canada), 'Political State of Upper Canada in 1806,' *Report of the Canadian Archives, 1892* (Ottawa 1893), xivii, lii, 383; see also F.M. Greenwood, *Legacies of Fear: Law, Politics in Quebec in the Era of the French Revolution* (Toronto: University of Toronto Press, 1993).

47 Introduced in the Legislative Council and passed immediately before the opposition became well organized in the Assembly, the Sedition Act was extended from visiting foreign 'enemy' subjects to include recently arrived British subjects. Concern about alliances with foreign intrigues encouraging insurrection was extended to include a broad range of opposition activity. All but two members of the Assembly supported the law as a permanent rather than temporary measure. *Journals*, February-March 1804, House of Assembly and Legislative Council, reproduced in AO (Archives of Ontario), *Sixth Report of the Archives for the Province of Ontario* (Toronto, 1911). William Weekes vigorously attacked the measure in his election broadside following its passage as an infringement on the ancient English liberties and an example of the need for vigilant legislators to check executive and judicial abuses. See G.H. Paterson, 'William Weekes,' *Dictionary of Canadian Biography*, vol. V, 844–5. See also W.R. Riddell, 'Mr. Justice Thorpe: Leader of the First Opposition in Upper Canada' (1920) *Canadian Law Times* 40, 912

48 Pitt's measure extended prerogative powers to indefinitely detain or deport enemy aliens to all foreigners as well as British subjects who resided in or invested in France since 1789. See (1793) 33 Geo.III c.27; (1794) 34 Geo.III c.54. Lower Canada passed similar temporary legislation in 1794 (34 Geo.III c.5), which was renewed in modified form until 1797, combining the immediate British legislative precedents on registration, deportation, and internment but widening the ambit of prohibited activity from treason to sedition (see also Greenwood, *Legacies of Fear*, *supra* note 46). The 1798 Federalist legislation was part of a package to clarify federal powers to regulate the acquisition of U.S. citizenship and deportation powers, to punish false statements against the government by aliens and residents and. extended detention and deportation powers to alien 'friends' and made it an offence, punishable by up to two years

imprisonment for citizens who 'defamed' the U.S. government. This latter provision was was repealed by Jefferson in 1800, not because it violated the First Amendment, but because it intruded on state jurisdiction over criminal law. See B. Wright, 'Migration, Radicalism and State Security,' *supra* note 4.

49 See Romney and Wright, 'State Trials and Security Proceedings During the War of 1812,' in *Canadian State Trials 1*, *supra* note 1 at 380–2.

50 'An Act to Prevent Certain Meetings in the Province of Upper Canada,' 58 Geo.III c. 11. Based on Pitt's temporary 'seditious meetings' act 36 Geo.III c.8 (1796), it addressed a lacuna in the sedition laws by prohibiting participation in oppositional associations and it anticipated the similar temporary British Six Acts, passed the following year but the latter also restricted the use of ex officio informations as a political concession. Although the Upper Canada act was passed as a permanent law it was repealed after Gourlay had been deported, a political concession that was not extended to the Sedition Act, although the former's restrictions on petitioning might well have led to British government's disallowance in any event.

51 See AO RG 22 series 134, 'Court of King's Bench Assize Minutebook,' series 134. This is the main technical record of Crown prosecutions before the Court of King's Bench, but reference to other King's Bench series (series 125 Termbook [York], series 136 Minutebook transcribed and 138 Criminal Filings) and associated records for the War of 1812 (e.g., RG 22 series 143) reveal at least a dozen more cases than the thirty-four indicated in my 1992 *Labour/Le Travail* article. (The revised count includes findings of no true bills and withdrawn indictments but excludes private libel prosecutions and blasphemy cases and scattered private complaints of sedition indicated brought to the government's attention by informations made to local justices of the peace and grand juries but not pursued by the Crown, indicated in the Quarter Session Records RG 22, series 14 and 31.) Roughly half the sedition prosecutions resulted in not guilty verdicts or were withdrawn after the accused was bound over. With the exception of a handful of cases during the War of 1812 (see Romney and Wright, *Canadian State Trials 1*, *supra* note 1 at 386), the most heavily punished cases include Willcocks (whose case was transformed into parliamentary privilege proceedings for contempt), Gourlay (whose acquittals led to banishment under the Sedition Act), Ferguson, Mackenzie (withdrawn), and Collins.

52 See Douglas G. Lochhead, 'Tiffany, Silvester,' *Dictionary of Canadian Biography*, vol. V, 814; also W. Colgate, 'Louis Roy: First Printer in Upper

Canada,' *Ontario History* 43, (1951): 123–42; W.S. Wallace, 'The First Journalists in Upper Canada,' *Canadian Historical Review* 26, (1945): 372–81. Gideon Tiffany's conviction in April 1797 resulted in a sentence of one month's imprisonment, substantial fines, and loss of the lucrative appointment as King's Printer (see AO RG 22, Series 134, Court of King's Bench Assize Minutebook). Tiffanies were warned that they risked prosecutions for seditious libel when they established independent papers, the *Canadian Constellation* in 1800 and the *Niagara Herald* in 1801, but financial difficulties silenced them instead.

53 See W.R. Riddell, 'Mr. Justice Thorpe,' 907–24; H. Guest, 'Upper Canada's First Political Party,' *Ontario History* 54 (1962), 275–96; G. Patterson, 'Whiggery, Nationality and the Upper Canadian Reform Tradition,' *Canadian Historical Review* 56 (1975), 25–44; NAC, 'Political State of Upper Canada in 1806,' *Report, 1892;* Archives of Ontario (AO), *Sixth and Eighth Reports* (Toronto, 1911, 1912).

54 See NAC, 'Political State of Upper Canada' 67; Guest, 'First Political Party,' 284; and S.R. Mealing, 'Gore, Francis,' *Dictionary of Canadian Biography*, vol. 8, 336. Gore had been involved in the Irish repression and pursued all avenues to undermine the opposition including secret surveillance and paid informers. See, e.g., Gore to Watson York, 4 October 1807, NAC, 'Political State,' 113.

55 As Gore put it, Thorpe had encouraged 'strictures on the government from every description of persons, however incompetent they might be to form any correct opinion upon the subject, or however foreign such a subject might be.' Gore to Windham, 13 March 1807; see also jury addresses Home District 29 March 1806 and 5 April 1806; Western District 4 and 6 September 1806; London District 17 September 1806; Niagara, 6 October 1806; Home District 30 October 1806 in NAC 'Political State,' 48–65. For Thorpe's removal from the bench and Gore's justifications to the British government see Report of the Executive Council York, 4 July 1807, Castlereagh to Gore, 19 June 1807, Gore to Castlereagh, York, 14 November 1807, Gore to Watson, York, 4 October 1807 in NAC, '1892 Report,' 80, 82, 87, 114; Gore to Cooke, York, 14 January 1808, NAC State Papers, Upper Canada Q Series, 311, 2.

56 According to Gore's sources 'the Jacobin paper' was sponsored by exiled United Irishman Thomas Addis Emmet and Monsieur Genet from France (see Gore to Castlereagh, York, 21 August 1807, NAC, 'Political State,' 81–6).

57 See RG 22 series 125/127 AO Court of Kings Bench Termbook, 14 November 1807, 4 January 1808. See also Riddell, 'Information Ex Officio,' *supra* note 36 at 91–2.

58 McNairn, *supra* note 2 at 157.

59 AO RG 22 series 127 King's Bench Termbook, 16 February 1808, and Riddell, *supra* note 36 at 91–9.

60 AO RG 22 series 134 King's Bench Assize Minutebook.

61 Willcocks wrote, 'There were two or three glaring contradictions in the evidence of those gentlemen [Crown witnesses], that would in a court of justice have destroyed the veracity of the whole; but in a court of parliament was considered as nothing ... I never saw a prosecution conducted with more evident disadvantage to the defendant ... I implored the House to have witnesses sworn, but this benefit was denied me as were the advantages of representation. I had but one clear day's notice of trial; and when it did commence, I was not permitted to put a single question to a witness that was at all likely to make him contradict or invalidate his testimony.' See 'Address to the Electors [Willcocks's constituents] from the Home District Gaol, March 6, 1808,' *Upper Canada Guardian*, 6 February and 18 March 1808, reproduced in Gourlay, *Statistical Account of Upper Canada*, vol. 2, *supra* note 36 at 655–9.

62 See Greenwood and Wright, 'Parliamentary Privilege,' *Canadian State Trials 1*, *supra* note 36 at 423.

63 Gourlay was also referring to proceedings against James Durand in 1817. See *supra* note 61 at 650–1.

64 Willcocks was able to resurrect his paper and his parliamentary career, and although threatened again with sedition charges in late 1809, he went on to lead an opposition that controlled close to half the votes in 1812. He initiated what became a series of bills to reform the jury, and with the outset of war he led the Assembly's intransigence on proposed emergency measures despite facing yet another sedition indictment. Willcocks later fled to the United States and was killed during the war.

65 McNairn, *supra* note 2 at 158–60.

66 On the series of discriminatory measures against non-loyalist American immigrants, see P. Romney, 'Reinventing,' *supra* note 27, and *Mr. Attorney*, note 36. After the war executive orders were issued to limit American immigration and to make an oath of allegiance to the Crown a prerequisite to holding land. Magistrates were directed to refuse to administer the oath of allegiance to all Americans, to make all American residents register, and to use the Sedition Act to deport any Americans deemed a security threat. See *Journals*, House of Assembly 1816; NAC RG 1 E1, Minutes of the Executive Council, York, 7 October 1815; Report, Gore to Bathurst, York, 17 October 1815.

67 See *Journals*, House of Assembly, 1817, 1818. The policy on aliens angered

Niagara speculators on the land market. See also A. Dunham, *Political Unrest in Upper Canada, 1815–1836* (repr, Toronto: McClelland and Stewart, 1963), 49.

68 See Wright, 'The Gourlay Affair,' *Canadian State Trials 1, supra* note 7 at 487, and more generally Lois Darroch Milani, *Robert Gourlay, Gadfly: Forerunner of the Rebellion in Upper Canada 1837* (Toronto: Ampersand Press, 1971); W.R. Riddell, 'Robert (Fleming) Gourlay, As Shown by his own Records,' *Ontario History* 14 (1916): 5–133; E.A. Cruikshank, 'The Government of Upper Canada and Robert Gourlay,' *Ontario History* 33 (1936): 65–169; S.F. Wise, 'Gourlay, Robert Fleming,' *Dictionary of Canadian Biography 9*, 330–6. Notable among the prolific Gourlay's publications: *Statistical Account of Upper Canada,* 2 Vols. (London: 1822, repr. New York: East Ardsley, 1966); *The Banished Briton and Neptunian* (Boston, 1843).

69 *Upper Canada Gazette*, 30 October 1817. On Gourlay's falling out with leading officials see Riddell, 'Gourlay,' *supra* note 68 at 16; Strachan to Harvey, 22 June 1818, repr. in J.L.H. Henderson, ed., *John Strachan: Documents and Opinions* (Toronto: McClelland and Stewart 1969), 67.

70 *Niagara Spectator*, 5 and 12 February 1818.

71 *Niagara Spectator*, 2 April 1818 (repr. in Cruikshank, 'Government,' *supra* note 67 at 134–8).

72 McNairn, *supra* note 2 at 154–5, 160–1.

73 *Ibid.*, 183

74 Robinson arranged close surveillance and interception of Gourlay's mail. See Smith to Bathurst, York, 18 April, 1818, repr. in Cruikshank, 'Government,' *supra* note 68 at 139–41, also Strachan to Harvey, 22 June 1818, repr. in Henderson, *Strachan, supra* note 68 at 68; Gourlay, *Chronicles of Canada* (St Catharines, 1842).

75 Robinson added, 'No time more than the present ever afforded stronger evidence of this truth in the experience of the Mother Country.' Robinson to Jarvis, York, 13 June 1818, reproduced in Cruikshank, 'Government,' *supra* note 68 at 145–6.

76 Robinson wrote, 'The only Law I know of, under which these meetings ... might be suppressed is the British Act against tumultuous petitions. It has indeed been asserted that this act is virtually repealed by the Bill of Rights [1689] ... nothing certainly would give more consequence and popularity to Mr. Gourlay's wild measures than to attempt to suppress these meetings by any harsh construction of Law ... But as there can be no doubt that Mr. Gourlay's publications are gross libels on the administration of the Government, I apprised Your Honour of my intention of adopting the only course sanctioned clearly by the Law ...' Robinson to

Smith, 29 June 1818; repr. in Cruikshank, 'Government,' *supra* note 68 at 150–2. In a further letter Robinson solicited opinion from the Court of King's Bench on prohibiting the meetings. See Robinson to Smith, 4 July 1818; Powell to Smith, 7 July 1818 (repr. in Cruikshank, 'Government,' *supra* note 68 at 153–4).

77 See Maitland to Bathurst, 19 August 1818, reproduced in Cruikshank, 'Government,' 156–7; Gourlay, *Statistical Account*, vol. 2, 665; Riddell, 'Gourlay,' *supra* note 68 at 28–9.

78 It is unclear why Boulton rather than Robinson prosecuted as the former's appointment was only confirmed in 1819 and he was under a cloud from his recent involvement in the Jarvis duelling death. The clerk's entry on AO RG 22 Series 134 (vol. 5, p. 22) reads 'The minutes of Proceedings for the Eastern, Johnstown and Midland Districts were taken away from the Crown Office by Henry John Boulton Esquire, Solicitor General, *personally*, and never returned, although often asked for, for want of which, they are not recorded.' Fortunately, a record of the Kingston trial survives in the form of the pamphlet published by the *Kingston Gazette* reproduced in Greenwood and Wright, *Canadian State Trials 1*.

79 Address to Jury, 4.

80 Address to Jury, 19–20, 6, 21. The rescheduling may have be an attempt to prevent his return to the province since Gourlay was expected to be in New York and contempt of court finding could prevent his return to the province.

81 Address to Jury, 13–16.

82 Address to Jury, 5.

83 Address to Jury, 20.

84 Address to Jury, 21.

85 Address to Jury, 21

86 *Kingston Gazette*, 18 August 1818; Address to Jury, 22.

87 The assize court records for Johnstown assizes are also missing but unfortunately, unlike Kingston, there is no outside report. The Crown had evident difficulty with the wording of the indictment and the Johnstown evidence was complicated by Gourlay's action against the government informant Fraser for assault. This along with the *autrefois acquit* gave rise to government concerns about an action for malicious prosecution. See Riddell, 'Gourlay,' *supra* note 68 at 28–9.

88 See *supra* note 50. After Maitland offered concessions on economic matters, the Assembly apologized for its previous lack of cooperation and Robinson brought forward the legislation he had drafted with the

assistance of the judges. See Debates, House of Assembly, 21, 22, 23, and 31 October (repr. in Gourlay, *Chronicles of Canada*, 30–4); also, Robinson to Hillier, 18 November 1818, in Cruikshank, 'Government,' *supra* note 68 at 165.

89 See also Gourlay, 'Recapitulation and Conclusion, Concerning the Convention and Gagging Law,' *Chronicles of Canada*, No. 1, 38–40. (Ingersoll, C.W. [Ont.]: Chronicle)

90 The Judges were actively assisted by the Attorney General. For Robinson's report on the Sedition Act and its application to Gourlay, see NAC CO 42 vol. 368, 153–9, 161–7. The soliciting of judicial opinion before trial had been a means of manipulating the bench in politically sensitive cases in Britain before the eighteenth century but extra-judicial opinions were seen to compromise judicial independence by the noneteenth century. See Greenwood, *Legacies of Fear*, *supra* note 46 at 32–4.

91 Report of the Judges to Sir Peregrine Maitland 10 November 1818, NAC RG1 E3, Executive Council Submissions. Gourlay had resided in the province for more than six months but he left several times without leaving a permanent residence.

92 Powell to Gore, 18 January 1819 quoted in Riddell, 'Gourlay,' *supra* note 68 at 41.

93 Swayze to Hillier, Niagara, 16 December 1818, repr. in Cruikshank, 'Government,' *supra* note 68 at 165. See also Gourlay, *Banished Briton and Neptunian*, no. 16, 163; no. 22, 263; *Statistical Account*, General Introduction, lxviii; vol. 2, 498; *supra* note 68.

94 See 'Order to Commit Robert Gourlay, 4 Jan., 1819,' NA, 'Documents Relating to the Constitutional History of Canada, 1819–28,' vol. 1 (Ottawa, 1914), 14.

95 See 'Order to Commit' in Const.Docs, *ibid.*, 14–15. See also Gourlay, *Banished Briton and Neptunian*, no. 16, 165; Cruikshank, 'Government,' 97; Milani, *Gadfly*, *supra* note 68 at 187–8.

96 See petition of 13 January in Gourlay, *Statistical Account*, 'General Introduction,' xl. On 20 January Powell endorsed the writ and ordered Gourlay delivered to his chambers in York, where Gourlay demanded an immediate hearing before the King's Bench. Powell left to consult with the Attorney General, and returned declaring that the act allowed neither a hearing or bail. See Gourlay, *The Banished Briton and Neptunian*, 189; Gourlay, *Statistical Account*, 'General Introduction,' x, xli–xliii.

97 Milani, *Gadfly*, *supra* note 68, describes Gourlay's ordeal in detail.

98 The information was triggered by a libel in the June 28 issue. See *Journals*, House of Assembly, 5 July 1818, 173; NAC RG 5 B3 vol. 21. (His co-

accused Pawling died shortly after the initial arrests in December.) As a result of the ex officio procedure, Ferguson's pre-trial proceedings were limited to his exceptional appearance before the full bench of King's Bench in York (the prerogative by-passed the grand jury). He was remanded for trial at the next assizes in Niagara. See Riddell, 'Gourlay,' 51; Riddell, 'The Information Ex Officio in Upper Canada,' *supra* note 36 at 93–4; *Niagara Spectator* 29 July, 1819; Gourlay, *The Banished Briton and Neptunian* no. 34, *supra* note 68 at 476.

99 Powell's private reservations about the Sedition Act were belied by his public actions; the extra-judicial opinion and consultation with the Attorney General on Gourlay's application for habeas corpus. As for the mode of prosecuting Ferguson, Powell privately noted, 'what is laughable in this is that the Gov't. in Compliance having ordered the Att. to prosecute, is now condemned, by themselves for the mode adopted by that officer, by Information instead of Indictment.' (Powell to Gore, 11 July 1819 in Riddell, *The Life of William Dummer Powell* (Lansing, 1924) 119. See also Milani, *Gadfly, supra* note 68 at 202, 208–9; Riddell, 'Gourlay,' *supra* note 68 at 53.

100 See Gourlay, *The Banished Briton and Neptunian*, no. 34, *supra* note 68 at 477.

101 Gourlay later claimed the sheriff's selection resulted in a notoriously packed jury – see Gourlay, *Statistical Account* 'General Introduction,' *supra* note 68 at xv-note; *Statistical Account*, vol. II, 342. See also Milani, *Gadfly, supra* note 68 at 200–1.

102 R.L. Fraser, 'Ferguson, Bartemus,' *Dictionary of Canadian Biography*, vol. 6, 247.

103 See Milani, *Gadfly, supra* note 68 at 199; Dickson to Hillier, Niagara, 23 August 1819, in Cruikshank, 'Government,' *supra* note 68 at 172. The Crown may have had reservations about Powell's willingess to impose a heavy sentence on his own, given his private reservations about the measures.

104 See Riddell, 'Gourlay,' *supra* note 68 at 52. Gourlay's indictment can be found in AO RG 22 Series 138, 'Criminal Filings,' Box 1.

105 See Milani, *Gadfly, supra* note 68 at 203; P. Brode, *Sir John Beverley Robinson: Bone and Sinew of the Compact* (Toronto: University of Toronto Press, 1984), 56–7.

106 Reproduced in Gourlay, *Statistical Account* 'General Introduction,' ccclvi. He argued differences of opinion with Cobbett and Hunt, asserted the illegality of his imprisonment, and later admitted he was temporarily incapable of reason. Gourlay, *Statistical Account*, General Introduction, xiv–xv; *Statistical Account*, vol. 1, ccciv.

107 After Gourlay's return to Britain he was imprisoned for horsewhipping Lord Brougham in the lobby of Westminster after the future Lord Chancellor failed to press a petition concerning his treatment in Upper Canada. Gourlay continually petitioned Canadian legislatures for redress until the 1860s. After the findings of the legislative committee in 1841 the government offered a pardon but no compensation. In 1856 a free pardon was granted along with a small pension. He left the province in 1858 and died in Edinburgh in 1862.

108 AO RG 22 series 125, 'King's Bench Term Book'; Riddell, 'Gourlay,' *supra* note 68 at 51; Riddell, 'Information Ex Officio,' 94–5. The sentence included a fine of 50 pounds, imprisonment for a year and a half, and the pillory for one hour daily during the first month of the sentence. Once his term of imprisonment was over, Ferguson would have to secure his release with 500 pounds in personal sureties and two further sureties of 250 pounds each for his good behaviour over a term of seven years. The pillory and half the term of imprisonment were commuted by Powell upon Maitland's instructions (Powell to Maitland, 17 November 1819 NAC RG5 A1, *Upper Canada Sundries* vol. 44, 21683-86).

109 60 Geo.III c.4; *Journals*, House of Assembly, 21 February 1820. See also Maitland to Bathurst, 7 March 1820, in Cruikshank, 'Government,' *supra* note 68 at 174.

110 On the byzantine legislative attempts led by Robinson to disenfranchise Americans, and related attempts to exclude Barnabas Bidwell and Marshall Spring Bidwell from sitting as elected members as well as a prosecution for perjury, with an eye to expelling Robert Randal. See Romney, *Mr. Attorney*, *supra* note 36. See also NAC, 'Constitutional Documents, 1818–28'; NAC RG 1 1186.

111 McNairn, *supra* note 2 at 184–6.

112 Horne was succeeded by Fothergill in 1822, who subsequently lost the position once he became involved in opposition politics.

113 See *Journals*, House of Assembly, 1823; H.P. Gundy, 'Thomson, Hugh Christopher,' in *Dictionary of Canadian Biography*, vol. 7, 773.

114 See Romney, *supra* notes 8 and 36. The reform-dominated Committee used the expropriated Niagara hotelier William Forsyth's petition as the basis for a more sweeping examination of the accumulated instances of partisan administration of justice and, in particular, the exercise of public prosecutions. See *Journals, House of Assembly*, 1828, Appendix, 'Report of the Select Committee.'

115 See PRO CO 42 vol. 386, 'Papers Relating to the Removal of the Honourable John Walpole Willis from the Office of One of His Majesty's

Judges of the Court of King's Bench of Upper Canada' (Printed by the British House of Commons, 1829), 37–47, 216–20; R. Hett, 'Judge Willis and the Court of King's Bench in Upper Canada,' *Ontario History* 65 (1973): 19–30.

116 Robinson to Maitland, 10 May 1828, repr. in 'Papers,' *ibid.*, 24–5.

117 Robinson to Maitland, *ibid.*, 28–9. See also PRO CO 42, vol. 388, 154–7 (Robinson's Report on the events surrounding the Collins Indictment). The grand jury found a bill for a libel based on Mackenzie's 'scandalous comments' about them in the *Colonial Advocate*, 10 April 1828.

118 Robinson missed the beginning of the session and Willis allowed Collins to take his allegations before the grand jury just as the Attorney General arrived. Willis reminded him of his duty to prosecute the known offenders and Robinson replied that he was not a 'thief-taker' and that he was answerable to the government, not the bench. The grand jury returned true bills against Boulton and Small for Rideout's death in 1817 and against the pro-government rioters who destroyed Mackenzie's press in 1826, although the cases failed. Collins and Mackenzie were unable to have their indictments withdrawn as Robinson successfully held the charges over to the autumn assize. See Robinson to Maitland 10 and 20 May 1828, and Willis to Maitland, Spring assizes 1828, repr. in 'Papers,' *supra* note 115 at 16–23, 33, 211. *Canadian Freeman* 17 April, *Upper Canada Observer* 5 May, *Canadian Freeman* 8 May.

119 Willis's objection called into question the validity of years of King's Bench decisions involving less than a full bench, and as Maitland reported to London, would cause 'great public excitement.' When King's Bench reconvened on 16 June, and Willis announced he would not preside until the bench was fully constituted, Maitland and the Executive Council suspended him; see *supra* note 115.

120 *Upper Canada Herald*, 1 July 1828. On constitutional meetings resulting in petitions to Britain in support of Willis, see *Canadian Freeman* 5 June–3 July 1828; Baldwin, Rolph, and Baldwin to Maitland, 23 June 1838; Willis to Stephen, 30 May 1828; Willis to Huskisson, 31 May 1828; Maitland to Huskisson, 6 June 1828, in 'Papers,' *supra* note 115 at 199, 189, 177, 187.

121 See *Canadian Freeman*, 16 and 30 October; NAC RG1 E3, vol. 15, 'Statement of the case of Francis Collins Editor of the Canadian Freeman to be Laid Before His Excellency the Lieutenant Governor.'

122 See NAC RG1 E3, vol. 15 and *Canadian Freeman*, 16 October 1828. Collins drew another charge, writing, 'The Attorney General, with a view of bringing us to trial unprepared, rose and stated a palpable falsehood in Court – namely, that we had been arraigned last assizes. When we con-

tended to the contrary, to the satisfaction of the court, the Attorney, in his native malignancy, took till next day (yesterday) to look up authorities to see if he could force us to trial without the privilege of traverse ... and our old customer Judge Hagerman was in favour of the measure.'

123 See Sherwood to Colborne, 5 December 1828; manuscript report of trial *The King v. Francis Collins*, 25 October 1828, NAC RG1 E3, vol. 15.

124 See NAC, *The King v. Francis Collins, ibid*. The jurors deliberated for more than five hours on the limited evidence that did go to them and their request for a dictionary was refused. See *Canadian Freeman*, 30 October 1828.

125 In responding to petition, recently arrived lieutenant governor Colborne was reluctant to interfere – the constitution supported a 'free and well-conducted press,' but it also bound him not to intervene in the verdict of juries or the opinion of judges. NAC, RG 1 E3, vol. 15, 'Addresses to His Excellency, Sir John Colborne, Lieutenant Governor of Upper Canada,' and 'Reply'; *Journals*, House of Assembly, 1829 Appendix, 'Report of the Select Committee on the Petition of Francis Collins.' The Collins petition was referred by the Colonial Office to the English law officers, who reported that the sentence was grossly out of proportion to comparable English cases and recommended that the sentence be halved. Scarlett and Sugden to Murray, 30 June 1829, PRO C0 42/390/49–50. Collins was released after forty-five weeks.

126 The first repeal bill was brought in the Assembly in June 1819 and from March 1821 repeal bills were passed by majorities in the Assembly to be repeatedly defeated by the upper house. See *Journals*, House of Assembly, 8–17 June 1819; 26 Feb.–8 Mar. 1820; 3 Feb.–8 March 1821; 28 Nov.–4 Dec. 1821; 15–21 Jan. 1823; 17 Nov.–3 Dec. 1823; 10–21 Nov. 1825; 19–27 Dec. 1826 (Legislative Council returned this bill 9 Feb. 1827 with extensive amendments which essentially preserved the Act); 21–23 January and 17 March 1828 (the Assembly declares a constitutional crisis). The bill passed in January 1829 was petitioned directly to the British government. The British Committee on the Government of the Canadas, set up in late 1828, recommended granting the petition, that judges be removed from governing councils (a policy adopted in 1832), and that ways be found to make the Legislative Councils more representative (not resolved until responsible government). Willis ended up on the New South Wales Bench in 1837.

127 On Howe, see Barry Cahill, 'R. v. Howe (1835) for Seditious Libel: A Tale of Twelve Magistrates,' *Canadian State Trials 1*, 522. On the Canadian Criminal Code, 1892 and the 1919 trials, see Desmond H. Brown, 'The

Craftsmanship of Bias: Sedition and the Winnipeg General Strike Trials, 1919' (1984) *Manitoba Law Journal* 14, 1. It was only in 1951 that the Supreme Court of Canada authoritatively adopted a restrictive definition of the residual common law, defining seditious intent as intention to incite violence or create public disorder for the purpose of resisting duly constituted authority (*Boucher v. R.* [1951] 2 D.L.R. 369).

128 See *supra* note 42.

129 Submissions to the Executive Council, Opinion of the Law Officers, 16 March 1832; Executive Council, 17 March, in NAC RG 1 E3, vol. 16.

130 See Greenwood and Wright, 'Parliamentary Privilege,' *Canadian State Trials 1*, *supra* note 1 at 425

131 McNairn, *supra* note 2 at 413.

132 *Christian Guardian*, 7 Dec. 1831, quoted in *ibid.*, 143.

133 See *supra* note 126. In 1811 and 1812, Joseph Willcocks introduced the first of a series of bills to change the jury selection process controlled by the executively appointed sheriff. See also *Journals*, House of Assembly: 16–22 Nov. 1825 (defeated); 8 Dec. 1826–7 Feb. 1827 (passed in House by majority of 15); 18–28 Jan. 1828 (passed in house by majority of 20); 23 Feb.-17 March 1828; 25 March 1828 (passed the Assembly and again defeated by the Legislative Council). Jury reform was only achieved in 1850 (c.55) after responsible cabinet government. See R. Blake Brown, 'The Jury, Politics and the State in British North America: Reforms to the Jury Systems in Nova Scotia and Upper Canada, 1825–68' (PhD thesis, Dalhousie University, 2005) and his study of parallel controversies in Ireland, 'A Delusion, a Mockery and a Snare: Array Challenges and Jury Selection in England and Ireland, 1800–1850,' *Canadian Journal of History* 39 (2004), 2.

PART THREE

Suffering

8 Human Rights Poetry as Ethical Tribunal: Bodies and Bystanders in Margaret Atwood's 'Footnote to the Amnesty Report on Torture'

BRENDA CARR VELLINO*

Law is a language of abbreviation, of limitation, and totalization. Art is a language of infinity, irreducibility of fragments, a language of embodiment, of incarnation ... Because it is by definition a discipline of limits, law distances [trauma]; art brings it closer.

Shoshana Felman, *The Juridical Unconscious*

How selfish soever man [sic] may be supposed to be, there are evidently some principles in his nature, which interest him in the fortunes of others, and render their happiness necessary to him. ... Of this kind is pity or compassion, the emotion we feel for the misery of others, when we either see it or are *made to conceive of it in a very lively manner* ... it is *by imagination only* that we can form any conception of what are [another's] sensations ... It is the *impressions of our own senses only*, not those of his, which our imaginations copy. By the imagination, we place ourselves in his situation.

Adam Smith, *Theory of Moral Sentiment*

With recent attention to human rights education through literature, evidenced by the prominence of studies in trauma and testimonial literatures and the rise of conferences and special issues of journals dedicated to literary human rights, there is a revival of interest in categories of sympathy, compassion, and empathy that may be evoked by literary reading.[1] Contra W.H. Auden's gloomy pronouncement that 'Poetry makes nothing happen,'[2] an affective model of reading suggests that if literature has the capacity to move readers so as to provoke an internal shift, it may also have the capacity to prompt action. Prominent philosophy, law, and literature professors Elaine Scarry, Martha Nussbaum, and

Shoshana Felman have taken this conjunction of reading and affectivity a next step to suggest that literary reading may enable engagement with traumatic suffering due to such violations as torture. Further, responsiveness to another's suffering may be conceived as an important antecedent to legal remedy. Nussbaum argues for the augmenting work of poetic justice to that of juridical justice. Similarly, Felman argues that the trial can be expanded to consider the 'evidence' of embodied trauma, which law typically (but not inevitably) excludes. In contrast, Scarry argues that the 'generous imaginings' produced by literary modes of justice will avail nothing without the implementation of constitutional reform and legal repair.[3] Each of these thinkers in her own way suggests an important relationship between literary and legal modes of justice, which I wish to elaborate and extend. In the following study, I seek to explore the process by which the poetry of human rights witness works towards 'literary justice' in augmentation of 'legal justice.'[4] The process of literary justice may be activated when ethical considerations of correspondences between self and not-self are prompted by vivid, compelling narratives, characters, incidents, imagery, personae, and voices. Literary justice may be one significant outcome of testimonial literature, wherein readers are potentially prompted to shift from bystander apathy to recognition of the connections between their own precarious lives and that of a vulnerable other. Human rights advocacy literature, in particular, enacts a transactional process of stimulating the ethical imagination to the end of awakening privileged Western readers to the possibility of their own complicity, agency, and responsibility.

Human rights witness poetry, then, may contribute to the creation of an ethical precedent for advocacy and legal reform in conjunction with specific projects such as Amnesty International's ongoing anti-torture campaign. Adapting witness poet Carolyn Forché's notion of the writer of witness standing before an 'ethical tribunal,'[5] I wish to suggest that the poem of witness itself becomes a kind of moral court in which not only the implied perpetrator of the human rights violations is put on trial, but also, and in different ways, witnesses of every kind, including the writer and the reader. I conceptualize this tribunal broadly as an alternative to the legal trial; it is perhaps more akin to a truth commission, a specially constituted body of enquiry, in which citizen readers can deliberate together about circumstances requiring new modes or implementations of justice. Much human rights representation works as a first step to prompt the recognition and acknowledgment of specific violations within contexts of national and global practices of 'selective forgetting' or denial. Literary testimony intimately depicts embodied trauma to call for proposals for recourse, remedy, implementation, and monitoring, all of which necessarily involve law.[6] The position of the reader within the ethical tribunal may be conceived like that of a member of the jury, similar to Martha Nussbaum's notion (via Adam Smith) of the 'judicious spectator.' This figure of the reader is one who is awakened to be 'passionate for the well-being of others,' while 'not inserting oneself into the picture one contemplates.'[7] Such a combination of *proximity* compelled by affect and *distance* due to circumstance, time, and geography constructs a productive model of the citizen-reader-juror, who is simultaneously thinking with the heart and the mind. Finally, the 'evidence' that the poet brings forward at this proxy tribunal is not that of the forensic body so critical to human rights criminal trials, but the evidence of the sentient body, which speaks its traumas in ways that may be ruled as inadmissible evidence in court.

I seek to explore the intersection of poetic witness with the promise of international human rights law, the evolving creation of which has long been a necessity for implementing human rights protocols; however, it is also important to recognize that such work is complexly shadowed by law's co-implication in a violent history of punishment and penal institutions. Working with law as an instrument of social remediation requires enduring awareness of law's risks and limits. The proscribed boundaries of legal work, particularly its foreclosure of certain forms of affective testimony, and its vulnerability to being ignored, misapplied, or suspended leaves gaps in what it can do to advance a culture of human rights. Human rights literature may perform as the conscience of law, pointing to its failures and abuses, awakening ethical precedents within readers who contribute to the 'internationalization of conscience,' a global spiral of interconnected local networks of citizens who press for continually renewing and advancing human rights culture.[8] Law, human rights advocacy networks, and literary witness all may be understood to work in overlapping ways to augment, supplement, modify, and nuance the human rights potential of each. Human rights lawyer Naomi Rhoht-Arriaza offers a productive model of intersecting transnational and local NGO, citizen, and legal actors through whom 'ideas and norms [circulate] from one country to another, create joint campaigns and work together to create pressure on recalcitrant governments' through a 'boomerang' or 'spiral' effect.[9] This constellation of mutually reinforcing ideas, norms, and representations may lead to a 'justice cascade' in which 'a confluence of internal and external factors reach a tipping point after which change comes more rapidly and decisively.'[10]

In section 1 of my paper, I discuss the specific tactics by which witness poetry seeks to lay claim to and transform the reader from mere bystander to moral witness; the significance of a bodily rhetoric of human rights at the heart of literary, advocacy, and legal witnessing; the antidote of poetry to the mass-media representations of atrocity; the problem of the bystander in a globalized world of myriad appeals for help; the problem of appropriation when a secondary witness takes up an advocate position; the related problem of universality within human rights advocacy; and debates around the efficacy of witnessing in law and poetry. In section 2, I will closely analyse Margaret Atwood's 'Footnote to the Amnesty Report on Torture' to show her deconstruction of popular representations of torture, which position media consumers as detached spectators; to examine her critique of the complicity of medicine and law with torture; and to explore how this poem subjects bystander apathy to an ethical tribunal through an ordinary-guy protagonist who is complicit with torture and who stands in as a reader proxy.

1

Carolyn Forché asserts that witness poems which 'call on us from the other side of a situation of extremity ... will not permit us diseased *complacency*. They come to us with *claims* that have yet to be filled, as attempts to *mark us* as they themselves have been *marked*.'[11] The legal language of claims implies a claimant who has entitlements and rights that Forché appeals to the reader to recognize. Both claiming and marking convey the agency of the witness and the poem to impress upon the reader's imagination, psyche, and body something of the trace of trauma in such a way that the reader can not remain a merely complacent bystander. Witness poetry makes its claims on the reader in five significant ways: 1) through evocative and intimate imagery of the basic vulnerable body, which becomes a link between the writer, the reader, and the subject of violation; 2) through reader-invoking strategies such as the direct address tactic of the second person pronoun 'you' or through protagonists who are implied reader surrogates; 3) through the moving eloquence of poetry's formal properties, which acquire a subjective depth charge in contrast to the often detached tone of the objective reports, statistics, and case histories central to legal work; 4) through the frequent focus on a single body, person, family, or community, thus making the imaginative encounter more human in scale and potentially more graspable; and 5) through contextual clues which call forth a need in the reader to apprentice more deeply to the historical, political, and social movements and biographical contexts out of which the poem arises. Stanley Cohen notes that Amnesty International appeal letters concentrate attention on individual stories of atrocity for the reasons of securing reader 'sympathy, empathy, and identification' through a process by which one imagines oneself in the position of the person who suffers.[12] A literary representation's capacity to prompt ethical thought experiments is based on its similar ability to secure at least partial identification with characters, protagonists, narrators, and speakers of poems.[13] In addition to offering the opportunity for intimate contemplative encounters with the basic human rights body, poetry of witness often uses its property of concise, condensed, evocative details to imply a larger narrative or historical contextual framework around the poem, which counteracts the fleeting, ahistorical, depthless encounters evoked by a proliferation of media representations. Witness poems perform a human rights pedagogy as their contextual clues prompt readers to work as detectives not only to unravel the mysteries of literary techniques, but also to increase their human rights literacy.[14] Readers thus may be imaginatively compelled to a deeper understanding of the unhinged moral universe of the poem and an acceptance of their potential agency and responsibility for the vulnerable other.

Central to legal, advocacy, and literary human rights culture is a 'bodily rhetoric of human rights' that is deployed to the end of reasserting a humanitarian moral, political, and legal order.[15] Legal narratives produce the forensic 'trial body' and require that it testify to establish causation against those who use the 'politics of atrocity' as a means to secure power.[16] Thomas Lacquer identifies the ways specific dead bodies function to produce 'the sense of substantial fact both in the juridical context of postwar trials and amongst the general public.'[17] Beyond the facticity of the body, Lacquer elsewhere notes that 'the humanitarian narrative [which would include both literary and nonliterary forms] relies on the personal body, not only as a locus of pain but also as the common bond between those who suffer and those who would help.'[18] The witness narratives of Amnesty International and other humanitarian organizations compel the traumatized body to 'speak' in ways that foreground shared sentience and pierce consciousness in order to make bodily pain visible and thus 'bring about the cessation of pain.'[19] Elaine Scarry implies that the translation of a register of pain from one body to another is essential to human rights efficacy. Lacquer suggests one answer to the problem of comprehending large-scale violations such as the Holocaust: 'intense, *almost synecdochic*, attention to the fate of *one body* [Anne Frank's, for instance] ... is a necessary if not sufficient means of comprehending the terror of mass murder.'[20] Twentieth-century poetry that bears witness to the traumatized body in arresting and memorable language makes a particularly poignant contribution to the bodily rhetoric of human rights.

While some human interest stories and advocacy journalism may use a similar rhetoric of the body as exemplified by a powerful witness photograph like Nick Ut's image of napalmed Vietnamese child Kim Phuc, the majority of media representations of atrocity are often sensationalized, and rendered as two-minute sound bites wedged between other news, sports, weather, and advertisements.[21]Stanley Cohen notes that the contemporary bystander is exposed to 'greater variety and intensity of demands in an average media day than the Good Samaritan is exposed to in a lifetime.'[22] Our globalized, mass mediatized, instant messaging world actively discourages the sustained attention required to forge empathic connection and instead produces emotional numbing, tuning out, and compassion fatigue. In a 1979 interview, Margaret Atwood states, 'You can destroy your Amnesty International newsletter without reading it. But that doesn't make it go away. The less you pay attention to it, the more it's going to be there for somebody else.'[23]

In Atwood's human rights poems, her readers are compelled to directly engage the problems of bystander passivity, complicity, or responsibility that arise from their own social locations vis-à-vis that of the protagonists and victims. Stanley Cohen notes that 'bystander' is a tricky term because of its connotation of unresponsiveness in a situation where someone requires help. He, along with other bystander theorists, looks at many reasons for bystander apathy or passivity, some of which are circumstantial, some of which are rationalizations. He urges attention to complexity when thinking through bystander issues in contrast to simple platitudes like 'there are no innocent bystanders' or 'we are all complicit.' I use the terms 'accidental bystander' to suggest someone who unsuspectingly witnesses a situation which they did not anticipate would require their assistance (a passerby, an unwitting observer) and 'complicitous bystander' for someone who chooses for whatever complex reasons to remain detached while witnessing a situation when human conscience would compel assistance. Cohen suggests we all to varying degrees become 'metaphorical bystanders' by virtue of instant access through real-time media representations of atrocity. I use 'moral witness' (some would use 'altruistic bystander' here) to convey the position of someone who responds even from a distance with the intention of providing some form of assistance even if it is indirect. Cohen defines the moral witness as someone who persistently witnesses to what perpetrators deny.[24] Clearly, these distinctions only begin to point to the gradations of possibilities among bystanders and witnesses.

The bodily rhetoric mobilized by human rights poetry may be an effective antidote to the problem of being a mere bystander, from which no one is immune. Readers are summoned by the human rights body to an ethic of altruistic responsibility or what Jewish philosopher Emanuel Levinas identifies as a primary ethical obligation to the vulnerable humanity manifest in the bare face of the other: 'The other becomes my neighbor precisely through the way the face summons me, calls for me, begs for me, and in so doing recalls my responsibility, and calls me into question.'[25] Representations of the vulnerable body can function like the Levinasian face to convey 'the extreme precariousness of the other'[26] within the bodily rhetoric of human rights. Regarding the bare face or basic body of the other in a literary representation may evoke a quality of sustained empathic attention that results in extending the framework of one's moral universe to include 'unknown (and even unlikable) people who are not at all like you.'[27] This may be a key consequence of the claims made upon the reader by witness poems. They seek to subpoena the reader to awaken to her potential as an advocate through a partial translation of the trace of trauma registered on the body. In positioning privileged readers as co-witnesses, they provoke a state of 'empathic unsettlement' that works to disturb the leap to easy generalizations about the human spirit triumphing in adversity,[28] and other modes of denial, dissociation, and psychic numbing.

Inhabiting the position of moral witness by privileged citizens involved in human rights advocacy is fraught with problems of 'dispensing rights from above' on behalf of the 'perennially wronged,' as Gayatri Spivak terms it. Spivak sees the 'righting of wrongs from above' as an 'enabling violation,' yet 'one cannot write off the righting of wrongs. The enablement must be used even as the violence is renegotiated.'[29] Those who seek to represent traumatic events that they did not experience first-hand such as poets like Atwood and who assume the position of 'proxy witness'[30] are thus necessarily contentious figures in the genre of testimonial writing. Literary testimony typically privileges the agency of survivors regaining a voice in the aftermath of traumatic suffering. By 'speaking for' an imagined other, a proxy witness risks redeploying an imbalance of representational and social power in which trauma survivors are reified in a discourse of victimization and paternalism. Witnesses who are not survivors, but who feel a moral obligation to take up a position of human rights advocacy regarding situations of past or ongoing atrocity, are sometimes charged with 'agony envy,' as Frank Davey does Atwood. By this, he means a form of appropriation that results in mobilizing the pain of political trauma to enhance one's own moral status.[31] While such a critique has some validity and needs to be considered on a case-by-case basis, the critique must not be allowed to paralyze the possibility of human rights defence by committed bystanders who undertake the complex position of moral witness. A critical impulse that assumes any writing position from a location other than one's own to be ethically untenable falls into a category I call the 'appropriation fallacy.' While it is important for moral witnesses from privileged backgrounds to work against reinforcing 'hierarchies of power and status,'[32] it is also imperative to recognize how much work needs to be done to increase human rights literacy among citizen-readers who are even talking together *at all* about the responsibilities of their privilege, let alone deconstructing it.

Linda Alcoff, in 'The Problem of Speaking for Others,' proposes useful criteria that may be applied to representations by proxy witness poets: is the writer accountable to her own social locations as constitutive of her analysis, investments, and social power? Is she attentive to the historical and economic ways her situation may be entangled with that of the imagined other? Does she demonstrate awareness of the context of the other and the potential outcomes of her words on the historical contexts and implied persons involved?[33] Similarly, poet Carolyn Forché suggests that even the first-hand witness must submit herself to an 'ethical tribunal, a place which recognizes the claims of difference, the otherness of others, and the specificity of their experience.'[34] Such self-interrogation can result negatively in a collapse into paralyzing guilt or positively in a position of ethical humility in which one is willing to risk getting it wrong in order to take up the position of advocate witness. The speakers of Atwood's advocacy poems frequently probe the complex interconnections between homeplace and 'elsewhere,' which is one tactic by which she acknowledges her bystander complicity in atrocity happening elsewhere. In 'It Is Dangerous to Read Newspapers,' written during the Vietnam War, Atwood's speaker states:

> Each time I hit a key
> on my electric typewriter,
> speaking of peaceful trees
> another village explodes.[35]

In a powerful image of interdependency between Canada and elsewhere, Atwood's speaker suggests that benign Canadian representations of nature are somehow implicated in the bombing of Vietnamese villages. In this case, it is the absence of a proxy witnessing role in her writing, an indictment of bystander passivity, that Atwood considers in terms of complicity and consequences.

When evaluating the complex position of a proxy witness, one must attend to the context in which a writer works. Frank Davey does not contextualize his critique of Atwood's 'agony envy' within her advocacy work as a long-time member of Amnesty International and past president of PEN Canada from 1984–1986, nor does he consider the significant role of transnational human rights NGOs in concentrating world attention on some of the worst cases of political imprisonment, extrajudicial executions, and torture. That he does not suggests a postmodernist impulse to disengage from humanist projects, including human rights discourses, which rely on universalizing principles. Along with reconstructive theorists like Edward Said, I call for a critical humanism that upholds notions of provisionally universal shared agendas for social and legal justice. By a 'provisional universal,' I mean a generalizable notion that is nuanced by attention to the particular complexities of history, context, and body (a notion I adapt from Seyla Benhabib in her 'The Generalized and Concrete Other').[36] Said points the way to such a critical humanism in *Humanism and Democratic Criticism*: 'I ... believe that it is possible to be critical of humanism in the name of humanism and that, schooled in its abuses by the experience of Eurocentrism and empire, one could fashion a different kind of humanism ... attuned to the emergent voices and currents of the present, many of them exilic, extraterritorial, and unhoused.'[37] Amnesty's major anti-torture campaigns have been a response to the call of exiled voices from Chile, Guatemala, El Salvador, Greece, Iran, the United States, and Great Britain, among others, and have galvanized the movement to extend the work established by the Nuremberg trial precedent towards establishment of universal jurisdiction for crimes against humanity that will end impunity cloaked in the alibi of state sovereignty.

In human rights culture, efficacy of tactics is a central problem. Interestingly, both Margaret Atwood and Elaine Scarry emphasize the activist potential of law to implement effective change in contrast to the 'soft' work of literature. Atwood expresses her scepticism about the activist potential of poetry: 'If you want to change the world, you do not choose poetry as the means for accomplishing it ... You can make change a possibility in the imagination, but *[poetry] can't effect change the way law can effect change.*'[38] Similarly, Elaine Scarry concludes her 'The Difficulty of Imagining Other Persons' by saying 'the work accomplished by a structure *of law* cannot be accomplished by a *structure of sentiment*.'[39] I am sympathetic to their pragmatic apprehension about the 'severe limits' of literature's ability to actually 'ensure the diminution of injury to live persons.'[40] Yet Atwood's vision of literature rendering 'change a possibility in the imagination' seems integral to the possibility of legal reform. The incremental reader-by-reader work of the poetic imagination cannot effect change the way law can, but law cannot effect change without the auxiliary representational work, which conveys a glimpse of the bare humanity of the other so as to elicit compassion, empathy, responsibility, and agency. Scarry also makes the link between limited imagination and injury emphatic: 'the human capacity to injure other people is very great precisely because our capacity to imagine other people is very small.'[41] Along with Martha Nussbaum and Paul Ricoeur, she credits fiction, poetry, theatre and film with being central vehicles through which the human capacity to imaginatively extend oneself into the space of the other is catalyzed by the capacity to achieve 'a vividness that approximates perception.'[42] While expanding the human capacity to imagine 'oneself as another' is celebrated as part of literature's historic humanizing function, it must go beyond vicarious displacements such as losing one's self in a novel or film character or temporary responses of 'unanchored good will.'[43] Ego divestment, recognizing the claims of the other on one's self because of her precarious and precious life, is central to the cultural work of witness poetry.

In contrast to privileging the efficacy of law above poetry, critical legal scholars argue, 'we turn to literature to remember precisely what cannot be made available in law.'[44] In *The Juridical Unconscious*, Shoshana Felman contrasts the priorities of the Nuremberg trials, which allowed only documentary evidence, and the Eichmann trial, which heard personal testimonial evidence. What is most interesting about these two trials is that they can be seen as representing a debate between law and poetry.[45] This is illuminated by Hannah Arendt's passionate privileging of the 'objective' documentary evidence of the Nuremberg trials against the 'subjective' testimonial evidence of the Eichmann trials in *Eichmann in Jerusalem*. Shortly after the Holocaust, German philosopher Karl Jaspers instructed Hannah Arendt to resist the temptation to use poetic metaphors to account for the Nazi 'banality of evil'; consequently, Arendt judged the Eichmann trial to have been a failure because one of the witnesses lapsed into poetic speech and eventually collapsed while testifying.[46] The trial judges ruled his testimony inadmissible, at the same time as acknowledging that the enormity of these crimes exceeded the capacity of a trial to represent them: 'Who are we to try to give it adequate expression? This is a task for great writers and poets. Perhaps it is symbolic that even the author himself who went through the hell named Auschwitz, could not stand the ordeal in the witness box and collapsed.'[47] Their commentary suggests that even the judges recognized that poets may accommodate the elusive traces of embodied traumatic experience in ways that legal proceedings, categories, and language cannot. When Camus asserted, 'true artists testify not to law, but to the body,'[48] he was perhaps reminding us that the arts in their capacity for nuance and complexity bring a register of affect and embodiment to contexts of public recognition that critical legal scholars are pushing law to accommodate.[49]

2

My focus in the second half of this chapter is on the proxy poetic witness of Canadian poet, novelist, and essayist Margaret Atwood. For three decades, she has positioned herself as an engaged citizen addressing national, international, environmental, gender, and human rights concerns, not only in her poetry, fiction, lectures, essays, and interviews, but also in her public interventions such as her April 2003 'Letter to America,' published in the *International Herald Tribune*, which took a clear stand against the second war in Iraq.[50] To date, Atwood's justice advocacy poems have been overshadowed by the critical attention paid to her feminist, environmental, and national work. In her human rights poems, Atwood negotiates a complex citizenship location that is at once Canadian and international to take up the position of moral witness. Atwood conveys in her 1981 address to Amnesty International that North America's cherished right to freedom of expression is foremost a privilege that comes with attendant responsibilities to the less privileged: 'We in this country should use our privileged position not as a shelter from the world's realities but as a platform from which to speak. Many are denied their voices; we are not. A voice is a gift; it should be cherished and used, to utter fully human speech if possible.'[51]

The title of Margaret Atwood's 'Footnote to the Amnesty Report on Torture' signals its auxiliary relationship to the 1973 *Amnesty Report*, which was the first major initiative in Amnesty's thirty-year (and counting) advocacy campaign against the 'epidemic' growth of torture as a mechanism of state power.[52] The initial campaign was designed to address the gap between the UN Declaration that prohibited torture and the absence of legally binding obligations that compelled and monitored compliance.[53] The report, like all of Amnesty's public education initiatives, was based on the principle of providing extensive supporting details for claims against offending states from the full interdisciplinary spectrum, reflecting the 'medical, legal, socio-economic, and political dimensions of torture.'[54] It contributed directly to the 1975 ratification of the UN Declaration on the Protection of all Persons from being Subjected to Torture and other Cruel, Inhuman or Degrading Treatment or Punishment and the 1984 UN adoption of the Convention Against Torture and other Cruel, Inhuman or Degrading Treatment or Punishment. Amnesty further urged that the UN appoint an independent High Commissioner for Human Rights and called for an independent 'international court for the trial of crimes under international law' – a vision finally realized in 2003. As a consequence of an activist human rights NGO and civil society culture, high-ranking state and military officials can no longer be assured of immunity from international justice when their responsibility for crimes against humanity is in question.[55] Amnesty's story is exemplary in demonstrating how human rights advocacy leads to legal change and how one context of witnessing sets off a 'justice spiral' of overlapping contexts for witnessing atrocities.

It was in these formative years of the growing international consensus against torture of political prisoners that Atwood published her

1978 poem 'Footnote to the Amnesty Report on Torture.' This poem defamiliarizes expectations for a footnote to provide scholarly references or statistical addenda to the main report; it opens a parenthesis on the main narrative of the *Amnesty Report*, secondary it would seem to the main text. Yet this footnote is reframed as the main textual event, confirmed by its publication in *Two-Headed Poems* and anthologized many times over.[56] Atwood expands the effect of the *Amnesty Report* through alternative documentation that bears the vulnerable body before a jury of readers, whose impulse to turn away in horror, fear, or fatigue is challenged. Her poem opens up insights into the psychology, representation, staging, and far-reaching consequences of torture, as well as foregrounding its historic entanglements with the institutions of law and medicine. This uncannily predates and parallels Elaine Scarry's observations in her phenomenological meditation 'The Structure of Torture' in *The Body in Pain*. Scarry argues there that while the torture victim's body is unmade through the application of pain, essential elements in human society at large are also symbolically wrenched apart through their appropriation. A terrible scene of double unmaking unfolds; key elements of the body's public world are unmade at the precise moment they are co-opted to the end of unmaking the body, dignity, and integrity of the one who is being tortured.[57]

Atwood's poem concentrates attention explicitly on an everyman janitor or complicit bystander who cleans up the bodily aftermath of torture – vomit, teeth, piss, and liquid shit – in a torture chamber that looks remarkably like an ordinary, seedy train station departure lounge. The poem maintains an uncomfortably close-up gaze on the vulnerable body under the duress of torture to foreground the strategies of denial and distancing that are at the crux of compassion fatigue and citizen disengagement. Stanza 3 presents a brutal corporeal catalogue of the aftermath of torture:

every morning the same vomit,
the same shed teeth, the same
piss and liquid shit, the same panic.[58]

This litany of bodily bits, fluids, and fear registers the interior facts of the bodies which have passed each day through an intimate disintegration. Torture turns the body against itself and inside out. The body reflexively pours out vomit, piss, liquid shit – a somatic sign that as the body is unmade, so too is the subject's agency, identity, and world. In this way, the body is rendered complicit in the scene of its own torture. The repetition four times of 'the same' to refer to a commonality of bodily fluids and fear when 'every morning' implies a different set of detainees being interrogated daily emphasizes a basic bodily affect that all humans share as a fundamental starting point for human rights protections and interventions. The vulnerable body here appears as 'the threatened vehicle of human being and dignity.'[59] Individuals or states that employ torture reject the core of human rights ethics – the essential inviolability of individual human dignity grounded in the body.[60] The debate between those who sanction torture and those who abhor it turns upon a bodily rhetoric. While the one makes a spectacle of the vulnerable body to the end of establishing power through fear, the other represents the body's intimate experience of trauma in such a way that bystanders may become proxy witnesses through registering the shock of a body's unmaking in their own body. The stomach may tense, the heart and lung muscles may contract with a sharp intake of breath, the fists may clench, the eyes may burn with unshed tears. Even through the veil of representation, one's body responds to another's body, which stands in for those in the many locations where torture is practised.

In human rights and criminal law, forensic pathologists read the signs marked on recovered bodies, not only to establish evidence against the accused, but also to restore the one who has disappeared to a name, identity, family, and community.[61] The proxy bodies in Atwood's poem cannot restore a precise historical name or context, but the physical immediacy of bodily details allows a reader to grasp the veracity of the violation. Further, they compel the reader to become informed on the countries in which state administered torture galvanized Amnesty's 1970s campaign against it – Greece, Israel in the Occupied Territories, Britain in Northern Ireland, and the U.S.-supported dictatorships in Nicaragua, Chile, and Argentina. Human rights literacy of any one of these historical and in some cases ongoing locations of the 'politics of atrocity' may awaken in readers a commitment to be part of the network of advocates who work in myriad ways to bring state-administrated torture to an end.

While the third person omniscient narrative voice adopted by Atwood's speaker in 'Footnote' and the terse documentary tone initially appear to distance the poem's speaker and the reader from an encounter with torture, this mimics a first level of defence when one is confronted by disturbing information. However, the poem quickly confronts the reader with an extreme close-up of the impact of torture on the part of victims and an immediate bystander who may himself become a victim. The first two stanzas of Atwood's arresting poem begin with the torture chamber, the physical space of a room, the most basic and simple unit of shelter and safety, which the torturer transforms into a weapon – 'barred, sealed, guarded.'[62] The heavily ironic names often used for torture chambers such as 'guest house' call attention to the civilizing impulse of hospitality often associated with human shelter, only 'as a prelude to its annihilation.'[63] Atwood's opening stanzas evoke familiar popular-culture representations of the generic torture chamber, which a contemporary citizen of the mass-mediated world would likely bring to an imagined encounter with the scene of torture:

> The torture chamber is not like anything
> you would have expected.
> No opera sets or sexy chains and
> leather-goods from the glossy
> porno magazines, no thirties horror
> dungeon with gauzy cobwebs; nor is it
> the bare cold-lighted
> chrome space of the future
> we think we fear.[64]

Because most privileged citizens of Western democracies have little experience with situations of atrocity, access comes through layers of multiple mediums that filter, frame, and interpret.[65] Even after 9/11, witnesses and metaphorical bystanders described it as being like a disaster movie. Stripping off the layers of overlaid representational echoes is essential to transforming the reader from a mere bystander to an engaged witness. Atwood also distinguishes here between different kinds of uses of the imagination – escapist and ethical. She deliberately closes the loophole against any presumption that her poem will allow an escape into a parallel universe like a sci-fi, horror, or porn film may do.

Beyond the obvious deconstruction of pop culture with which representations of torture may get entangled, Atwood's poem intersects with Elaine Scarry's critique of actual torture as being staged as a theatre of cruelty: 'It is not accidental that in the torturer's idiom the room in which the brutality occurs was called the "production room" in the Philippines, the "cinema room" in South Vietnam and the "blue lit stage" in Chile: built on these repeated acts of display and having as its purpose the production of a fantastic illusion of power, torture is a grotesque piece of compensatory drama.'[66] Atwood's opening stanza calls attention to the ways in which the room becomes a stage for the sadistic performance of agency on the part of the torturer, a theatrical set which some pop-culture representations of torture chambers may indirectly reinforce. Atwood points out how a media-tutored public may have come to expect such voyeuristic displacements onto the always conveniently elsewhere pornographic and genre film settings. Through four negations of these expected representations, Atwood defamiliarizes the familiar by placing the torture chamber in a seedy British Railways station and confronting the reader (addressed by the intimate second person pronoun, 'you') with an ordinary working-class protagonist – 'a stooped man / who is always cleaning the floor.'[67] This has the effect of uneasily propelling the reader into the frame of the poem, much like a film viewer is interpolated by character identification into the cinematic frame. However, the inescapable familiarity of the protagonist in this poem creates a discomfort zone of all too familiar unfamiliarity.

Rather than a distant space, Atwood suggests that a torture chamber may be an extension of the domestic and public spaces we inhabit daily. The 'scratched green walls,' 'spilled tea,' and crumpled papers all implicate the banal textures of ordinary life. Situating the torture chamber in the British railway station recalls the British security forces' administrative use of detention without trial, brutal 'deep interrogation' tactics of hooding, sense/sleep deprivation or overstimulation and electroshock applied to suspected IRA revolutionaries. These practices were in sharp conflict with the long tradition of British legal rights and protections that Amnesty International (founded in London in 1961 by British lawyer Peter Beneson) built upon. This location for a Canadian reader whose history is imbued with the legacy of British colonialism also implies that a similar contradictory relationship between law and violence needs to be interrogated in Canada. Ultimately, it challenges privileged citizens of Western democracies to rethink assumptions that torture is something remote from them – something that always happens elsewhere.

When the bodies of the tortured are thrown on the 'Consul's lawn' in Atwood's poem, the implication of many states, including Western ones, in the administration of torture is highlighted. As Amnesty's

Torture in the Eighties notes: 'Torture is usually part of the state-controlled machinery to suppress dissent. Concentrated in the torturer's electrode or syringe is the power and responsibility of the state.'[68] The consulate or embassy is a transitional space where the interests of a guest nation are represented in a host nation, a place of diplomatic, economic, cultural, and social exchange. The consulate is also a place where immigration and refugee status may be adjudicated, conferred, or denied. By locating the practice of torture in a consulate, Atwood is pointing to the way that states which perpetrate torture use categories of race, colour, ethnicity, nationality, class, politics, and religion to separate out the 'torturable' from the 'non-torturable,' the non-human from the human, the citizen from the non-citizen, the bearer of rights from the non-entitled.[69] The public display of bodies on the consul lawn also points to the way torture is an open secret, punishable by death if you talk about it, but necessarily positioned as a partly visible spectacle of terror. Its capacity to control dissent through fearful recognition would otherwise be moot.

The second through sixth stanzas of Atwood's poem suggest the ways in which the civilizing institutions of medicine and law (along with their shadow histories as accomplices of torture) are invoked in the torture chamber so as to annihilate the civilized world as we know it. In stanza 2, the torture chamber 'stinks'

> Like a hospital
> of antiseptics and sickness
> and on some days, blood.[70]

This figurative collapse of torture chamber into hospital suggests the way in which torture often doubles as medical experiment and deploys a kind of surgical precision to achieve its goals. Elaine Scarry observes that the torture chamber is sometimes called an operating theatre.[71] Amnesty's *Torture in the Eighties* states: 'It is not uncommon in many countries that a doctor is present to supervise interrogation under torture or available to ensure that the victims can survive to be tortured further.'[72] The 1982 Code of Medical Ethics adopted by the UN General Assembly relevant to the 'Role of Health Personnel, especially Physicians, in the Protection of Prisoners and Detainees against Torture' reveals by what it mandates that medicine has enabled state administration of torture: 'It is a gross contravention of medical ethics, as well as an offence under applicable international instruments, for health personnel ... to engage, actively or passively, in acts which constitute participation in, complicity in, incitement to or attempts to commit torture or other cruel, inhuman or degrading treatment or punishment.'[73] Mutation of a social institution upholding the Hippocratic oath into an instrument of injury results in the simultaneous unmaking of the body and the body's world. It is encouraging to recognize those courageous doctors under brutal regimes who risk their lives rather than be accomplices. Many have provided crucial expert testimony confirming evidence of torture based on a medical examination, as in the case of the Iranian doctor Shahram Azam (now a Canadian political refugee), who testified to the torture-inflicted injuries of Iranian-Canadian photojournalist Zahra Kazemi.

Stanzas 4 and 5 of Atwood's poem focus on how the structure of torture co-opts, inverts, and destroys another major institution of the body's world – the trial. While international criminal law is today seen to be an essential antidote to torture, historically, law was an institution that sanctioned selective application of torture. From the thirteenth to the eighteenth centuries, legalized torture served to 'produce confessions and information for the judicial system.'[74] Clandestine 'trials' in secret detention centres that apply torture tactics to allegedly elicit confession retain the memory of the past sanction of law. Paralleling the international code of medical ethics, the 1979 Code of Conduct for Law Enforcement Officials states, 'no law enforcement official may inflict, instigate or tolerate any act of torture ... and no law enforcement official may invoke superior orders or exceptional circumstances as a justification of torture.'[75] Since 2001, 'war on terror' apologists like Alan Dershowitz have argued precisely that 'exceptional circumstances' may trump international law protecting detainees from torture, resulting in the Abu Ghraib debacle, the ongoing incarceration of prisoners at Guantanamo Bay, Canada's own 'Guantanomo North' in Kingston, Ontario, and regressive legal reform in the U.S. 'Military Commissions Act,' which suspends habeus corpus.[76]

In stanza 5, Atwood offers another grim catalogue of the aftermath of trial by torture – 'warped bodies,' 'torn fingers,' 'ragged tongues'—culminating with 'the bodies of children / burned to make their mothers talk.'[77] It is commonly assumed that the physical and mental infliction of pain is a compliance tool to force a confession. The victims in Atwood's poem are divided into two groups: those who demonstrate courage by not talking and those who talk. In this strange equation, the tortured are put doubly on trial by the torturers and by the public expectation that they will not comply. One trial demands that they talk, the other that they don't. Either way the tortured are forced to become agents in the scene of their own unmaking. 'There is not only among torturers but also among people appalled by acts of torture ... a covert disdain for confession ... The nature of confession is falsified by an idiom built on the word 'betrayal': in confession, one betrays oneself and all those aspects of the world – friend, family, country, cause – that the self is made up of.'[78] Elaine Scarry argues that the question-and-answer structure of the interrogation is less about procuring information by force than about a display of sadistic agency. If the victim of torture talks, the world at large judges the victim through common notions of betrayal, lack of courage, and weakness of character. Such a misreading confers agency on the torturer, whose cruelty is implicitly credited with a motive, while simultaneously judging the victim to have 'failed' the test.

Atwood suggests that ultimately it 'doesn't matter' who talks and who doesn't. The confession is secondary to the display of power. For those who are being tortured, 'confessing' would *seem* to be the way to end the torture; for the janitor protagonist of the poem, not talking would *seem* to keep him and his children safe. However, behind this safety in silence, there is always a shadow of fear:

> The man who cleans the floors
> is glad it isn't him.
> It will be if he ever says
> what he knows.[79]

The janitor tries to exclude sentient knowledge by making his body into a soundproof barrier:

> a wall
> a thick wall, a wall
> soft and without echoes[80]

While he tries to exclude the kind of dangerous knowledge which would put him on the inside of the torture chamber, it appears that a wall of the torture chamber becomes interchangeable with the soft flesh of his body. Elaine Scarry suggests that a room is 'like the body' – 'its walls put boundaries around the self preventing undifferentiated contact with the world' – but here the torture chamber swells to incorporate the janitor through what he takes in through his senses: 'Inside and outside give way and merge with one another.'[81] His senses are permeated by the torture he witnesses only as aftermath: 'The man who works here / is losing his sense of smell,'[82] and yet the smell invades his body through taste. The torture chamber walls become interchangeable with the body of the janitor who smells what he does not want to smell and hears what he does not want to hear. In stanza 6 he literally eats his work. The meal he brings from home

tastes
of old blood and the sawdust
he cleans the floor with.[83]

All day as he sweeps, he thinks of the moment he can go home and open the door to his children 'with their unmarked skin and flawless eyes / running to meet him.'[84] This reference to unmarked children invites a foreboding comparison with the burned bodies of children thrown on the consul's lawn earlier in the poem. Threatened or perpetrated assault on the body of a child as a torture device attacks a central matrix of human relationships and being.

The torture chamber expands again to include the janitor's home. The word 'door' is repeated four times in the last three stanzas to indicate a traumatically disorienting threshold space where the door to the torture chamber and the door to home become coextensive. The door to the janitor's house, like the wall of his body, becomes a permeable boundary that is marked by ambiguity and danger:

he is afraid of the door,
he is afraid, not
of the door, but of the door
opening;[85]

The poem builds through the obsessive focus on the door to a kind of heart-stopping suspense that conveys the pervasive force of fear as the torture chamber expands to incorporate the body's world:

sometimes, no matter
How hard he tries,
his children are not there.[86]

Remaining silent for the state has not protected the janitor's children. While in his own mind, 'he isn't a torturer, he only cleans the floor,'[87] the state ultimately mistrusts his complicity and pronounces him guilty of betraying them by his proximity to the torture chamber.

As the poem builds to an exclusive focus on the janitor and his children, the reader is increasingly identified with this ordinary man who is 'glad to have this job, because//there are few others.'[88] The expansion of the torture chamber to incorporate the janitor's body, home, and children leaves us with the verdict that no one in the end escapes its reach. Imaginative identification with the janitor allows the reader to try on the moral dilemma of the proxy bystander and be subject to the proxy tribunal which the poem enacts. Atwood's janitor becomes a reader surrogate through whom the reader may investigate the ethics of being a 'metaphorical bystander.' The janitor, on the one hand, is a type of the aloof, unconcerned, or disengaged bystander made so famous in the case of the many neighbors who failed to come to the assistance of Kitty Genovese in New York City,[89] but, on the other hand, he becomes a paradigmatic means of exploring and expanding the problem of complicity and proximity. What counts as proximity to a situation in which someone urgently requires help? Questions arise such as whether such violations of bodily integrity are happening in prisons, police stations, or group homes in my town, province, or country or in other countries to which my country turns a blind eye. If they are, what is my responsibility to know? Is it possible to say one didn't know? What is a reader's obligation to assist once knowledge is registered? Stanley Cohen looks at debates around the ethical and more radical legal proposals for a 'duty to know,' in which one has a moral and even legal duty 'to make serious attempts to become and remain informed about distant atrocities (particularly in your country's sphere of influence).'[90] Following from this, does knowledge imply a 'duty to assist,' a kind of ethical or legal extension of the Good Samaritan principle even for proxy witnesses?[91] An overriding question is who is responsible to know and assist – individual citizens, whole communities, governments – and for what kinds of assistance? Variations on the janitor's rationalization that 'he just works here' and he's lucky to have a job are offered by many bystanders who justify their non-intervention and their cooperation with the state's agenda: I was just following orders, just trying to live my life, I didn't want to get involved, I didn't really know, I was afraid of what would happen if ... When readers are compelled to identify with a bystander figure proximate to torture, they are compelled to question their own role as metaphorical bystanders and potentially as moral witnesses.

Central thinkers around humanitarian and human rights advocacy frequently calibrate efficacy of intervention in terms of mobilizing a broad public (e.g., through mass demonstrations, boycotts, or letter-writing campaigns) in order to appeal to governments, corporations, funding bodies, and agencies that may be in a position to actually *do* something. No one can deny that in urgent cases, numbers of actors count. Further, mass media such as television, print, and Internet journalism are often the most immediate means of awakening public conscience in crisis situations. However, Chilean human rights lawyer Naomi Rhot-Arriaza concludes her reflections on the far-reaching consequences of Augusto Pinochet's extradition to Spain from England by noting that the best outcome in Chile was that small groups of people who had never talked together about torture or political exile were now talking, and that therein lies a critical link in the expanding spiral of 'transnational advocacy networks' within which global justice can be moved forward:[92] 'It will be ordinary people, organized into various and ever-changing groups, who will hold states to their promises to respect and ensure basic human rights. And it is ordinary people who again and again and again, until its not necessary anymore, will demand justice of the national and ... transnational kind.'[93]

Margaret Atwood's 'Footnote to the Amnesty Report on Torture' remains current in pressing forward the need for sustained attention to the unclosed cases of torture. In the post-9/11 world of a U.S.-led 'war on terror,' the debates around the potential legality of torture for such imagined scenarios as the 'ticking bomb' informant and the outing of the consequence of tacit state sanction of torture in the pictures from Abu Ghraib remind us that human rights defenders can never rest on provisional gains made. Because there are now many documented instances of counter-terrorism measures trumping human rights, notwithstanding those of Canadian citizens like Maher Arar, the ongoing 'internationalization of conscience' is all the more urgent. The tentacles of the torture chamber extend from Canada to New York City to Syria and back to Canada. The Canadian branch of the International Commission of Jurists, whose mandate is 'to promote the legal protection of human rights throughout the world,' expresses its 'profound alarm' and 'grave concern' over the ways in which 'Human rights ... have been or may be undermined by certain counter-terrorism measures adopted or contemplated, including, *inter alia*, the practices of administrative detention without judicial review; prolonged incommunicado detention; transfer, return, extradition, denial of entry, or expulsion of persons at risk of being subjected to torture in contravention of the principle of asylum; the adoption of loose definitions of "terrorism" ... The removal of safeguards to prevent torture or cruel, inhuman or degrading treatment or punishment and violations of the right to life.'[94]

Testimonial poems and other forms of witness literature must continue to do the pedagogical work of pressing for recognition and acknowledgment of historical and ongoing atrocities to the end of new norms for ethical consensus and unfolding laws, implementation, and monitoring. In so doing, they fulfil the standing imperative of the UN Declaration to keep 'this declaration [and its ethical offspring] constantly in mind' and to strive by 'teaching and education to promote respect for these rights and freedoms.' The work I seek to identify for witness poetry is modest, yet I contend that the practices of anthologization, Web circulation, and teaching ensures that the reading of witness poems will remain an infinitely repeatable ethical encounter for successive generations of readers and students. Poems by the very nature of their compact brevity and complex verbal structures stop time and compel modes of contemplation necessary to ethical imagining. Thomas Lacquer in his keynote address (2006) to the 'Humanitarian Narratives of Inflicted Suffering Conference' foregrounds the ways in which moral regard and aesthetic regard both compel the art of slow looking (2006).[95] Human rights witness poetry such as Atwood's activates moral regard through the strictures of aesthetic regard to summon the reader towards awakening to her potential as an advocate. Writers, artists, critics, and readers are part of the global movement of transnational advocacy that must persist in bringing the vulnerable body again and again before an ethical tribunal of ordinary citizens. Atwood's advocacy poems may be seen as part of a larger Canadian advocacy for consensus on international justice in which crimes against humanity perpetrated by states against their citizens cannot be committed with impunity.

Human rights witness poetry that brings the traumatized body into focus becomes a form of arresting evidence by which the rupture in the social order that a violation constitutes is rendered visible, tangible, and affecting. The witness poet, then, bears the body before an ethical tribunal, a potential jury of readers turned witnesses, who are compelled by the evidence before them towards education, empathy, and, ideally, participation in a community of vigilance, which is essential to the incremental advancement of human rights culture, legal and paralegal alike. Both require a network of awakened citizens for whom the impress of pain marked on the body has already in some measure reached them in such a way that they have been compelled to regard themselves even briefly as interchangeable with the other. The basic body of human rights becomes a means by which the precariousness of all life becomes visible, and thus becomes a primary node of connection across the distances of writers, narrative situations, poetic speakers, and readers. If, as I claim, Atwood's witness poem succeeds in bearing forward the intimate and vulnerable body to trigger somatic recognition in the body of the reader, she answers Camus's call for the twentieth-century writer to witness to the body, not to the law. Witness to the body, focused on shared sentience, pierces consciousness at a level that abstract law may not be able to do. At the same time, it can be hoped that such witness will create pressure for laws that will recover the non-torturable legal person from the evidence of the tortured body.

NOTES

* I wish to thank the Carleton University Department of English Colloquium (fall 2003) participants for their insightful responses to an early version of this paper. I am profoundly grateful to Diana Majury for encouraging me to think more deeply about the relationship between law and witness poetry and for so generously giving of her time and intellect. My thanks is always due to my partner Andre Vellino and my two daughters Karuna and Sarah for the time I borrow from them and for inspiring me to care ever more deeply about a more just future.

1 See 'The Humanities in Human Rights: Critique, language, Politics' *PMLA* 121 (2006): 1515 for the proceedings of 'The Humanities in Human Rights' Conference at CUNY in 2005; see also Kay Schaffer and Sidonie Smith, eds., *Human Rights and Narrated Lives: The Ethics of Recognition* (New York: Palgrave Macmillan, 2004); Elizabeth Goldberg, *Beyond Terror: Gender, Narrative, Human Rights* (Rutgers University Press, 2007); and Joseph Slaughter, *Human Rights Inc.: The World Novel, Narrative Form, & International Law* (New York: Fordham, 2007).

2 W.H. Auden, 'In Memory of W.B. Yeats,' in *20th-Century Poetry and Poetics*, 5th ed., ed. Gary Geddes (Don Mills, ON: Oxford University Press, 2006), 161 at 162.

3 See Martha Nussbaum, *Poetic Justice: The Literary Imagination and Public Life* (Boston: Beacon Press, 1995); Elaine Scarry, 'The Difficulty of Imagining Other Persons,' in *Human Rights in Political Transitions* (New York: Zone Books, 1999), 277, 278, 302; and Shoshana Felman, *The Juridical Unconscious: Trials and Traumas in the Twentieth Century* (Cambridge, MA: Harvard University Press, 2002).

4 Shoshana Felman poses a central question that inspires my study: 'What indeed is literary justice, as opposed to legal justice? How does literature do justice to trauma in a way that law does not, or cannot?' (*ibid.*, 8).

5 Carolyn Forché, ed., 'Introduction' in Against Forgetting: Twentieth-Century Poetry of Witness (New York: W.W. Norton, 1993), 37. I am quoting Forché slightly out of context for she is speaking of poems by participant witnesses and I wish to extend her observations to the situation of the proxy witness poem.

6 See Adrienne Rich's 'Resisting Amnesia: History and Personal Life,' in *Blood, Bread, and Poetry: Selected Prose, 1979–1985* (New York: Norton, 1986), 136–59, on poetry's facilitation of the choice to become consciously historical in contrast to the many forms of 'historical amnesia' around which national narratives are constructed. Stanley Cohen traces a history and psychology of personal and collective denial in response to atrocity, as well as the antidote in social movements that work towards a public culture of acknowledgment in *States of Denial: Knowing about Atrocities and Suffering* (Cambridge, UK: Blackwell Publishers, 2001).

7 Nussbaum, *supra* note 3 at 74–5.

8 This provocative phrase, the 'internationalization of conscience,' is cited from a Canadian IDRC Report, *The Responsibility to Protect*, in Ramesh Thakur's 'Dealing with Guilt Beyond Crime: The Strained Quality of Universal Justice,' in *From Sovereign Impunity to International Accountability: the Search for Justice in a World of States*, ed. Thakur and Peter Malcontent (New York: UN University Press, 2004), 272–92. In Thakur's usage, the internationalizaiton of conscience precedes advances in the internationalization of criminal law, especially universal jurisdiction for crimes against humanity, which may be theoretically prosecuted before the courts of any country. I say theoretically because as Naomi Rhot-Arriaza documents in *The Pinochet Effect: Transnational Justice in the Age of Human Rights* (Philadelphia: University of Pennsylvania Press, 2005), attempts to bring crimes against humanity cases from Guatemala before the Spanish court (and other European courts, now including the International Criminal Court) have met with many impediments.

9 Roht-Arriaza, *ibid.*, 208–11.

10 Lutz and Sikkink, cited in *ibid.*, 210.

11 Forché, *supra* note 5 at 31–2, emphasis added.

12 Cohen, *supra* note 6 at 216–17.

13 I adapt Paul Ricoeur's notion of fiction as an ethical laboratory where one can imaginatively try out ethical possibilities that may lead to the development of 'the ethical imagination.' See Ricouer, *Oneself as Another*, trans. Kathleen Blamer (Chicago: University of Chicago Press, 1992), 164–5.

14 Ervin Staub, 'Transforming the Bystanders: Altruism, Caring, and Social Responsibility,' in *Genocide Watch*, ed. Helen Fein (New Haven, CT: Yale University Press, 1992), 162–81, suggests that human altruism and prosocial behaviour are influenced by mentoring from parents, influential adults, and teachers; as well, exposure to bystander dilemmas and circumstances of people with 'persistent need' through education and discussion are critical to 'increasing helping behavior in emergencies.' See pages 167 and 176–8. For a discussion of how literature teaching may contribute to human rights literacy, see my '"Everything I Know about Human Rights I Learned From Literature": Human Rights Literacy in the Canadian Literature Classroom,' in *Home-Work: Postcolonialism, Pedagogy, and Canadian Literature*, ed. Cynthia Sugars (Ottawa: University of Ottawa Press, 2004), 135–50.

15 Caroline Picart, 'Human Rights and the Body in Law and the Humanities,' http://globetrotter.berkeley.edu/AISUA-syl/picart.html, viewed 19 July 2004; and Michael Humphrey, *The Politics of Atrocity and Reconciliation: From Terror to Trauma* (London: Routledge, 2002), 10. Clearly, Foucault's reading of the bodily rhetoric of state power, especially his analysis of the history of public spectacles of torture and execution of prisoners of the state in *Discipline and Punish: the Birth of the Prison*, 2nd ed., trans. Alan Sheridan (New York: Vintage, 1992), is a central inspiration behind any endeavour to read a bodily rhetoric of human rights that answers to a bodily rhetoric of terror. See Timothy Cloyd, 'Torture, Human Rights, and the Body,' in *Politics and the Human Body: Assault on Dignity*, ed. Jean Bethke Elshtain and Timothy Cloyd (Nashville: Vanderbilt University Press, 1995), 243–257 at 244–8 for a specific application of Foucault to the phenomena of human rights culture which foregrounds its concern for the body as object of punishment.

16 Humphrey, *ibid.*

17 Thomas W. Lacquer, 'The Dead Body and Human Rights,' in *The Body*, ed. Sean T. Sweeney and Ian Hodder (New York: Cambridge University Press, 2002), at 79.

18 Thomas W. Lacquer, 'Bodies, Details, and the Humanitarian Narrative,'

in *The New Cultural History*, ed. Lynn Hunt (Berkeley: University of California Press, 1989), 176–204 at 177.
19 Elaine Scarry, *The Body in Pain: The Making and Unmaking of the World* (New York: Oxford University Press, 1985), 9.
20 Lacquer, *supra* note 17 at 78. Italics added.
21 For explorations of the impact of violence-saturated media and sensationalized representations of atrocity on the human capacity for compassionate engagement, see Susan Sontag, *Regarding the Pain of Others* (New York: Farrar, Straus and Giroux, 2003), Susan D. Moeller, *Compassion Fatigue: How the Media Sell Disease, Famine, War and Death* (New York: Routledge, 1999); and Stanley Cohen, 'Images of Suffering,' in *States of Denial*, *supra* note 6.
22 Cohen, *supra* note 6 at 163.
23 Margaret Atwood with Alan Twigg, 'Interview: Just Looking at Things That are There,' in Earl G. Ingersoll, ed., *Margaret Atwood: Conversations* (Princeton, NJ: Ontario Review Press, 1990), 121–30, at 126.
24 Cohen, *supra* note 6 at 15–17, 68–70, 140–67, and 256.
25 Emmanuel Lévinas, *The Levinas Reader*, ed. Sean Hand (Cambridge, MA: Basil Blackwell, 1989), 83.
26 Emmanuel Lévinas, cited in Judith Butler, 'Precarious Life,' in *Precarious Life: The Powers of Mourning and Violence* (London: Verso, 2004), 128–51 at 134.
27 Cohen, *supra* note 6 at 183 and 216–17.
28 Dominick LaCapra, *Writing History, Writing Trauma* (Baltimore: Johns Hopkins University Press, 2001), 41–2.
29 Gayatri Spivak, 'Righting Wrongs,' in *Human Rights, Human Wrongs*, ed. Nicholas Owen (Oxford: Oxford University Press, 2002), 168–227 at 169.
30 Susan Gubar, 'Poets of Testimony: C.K. Williams and Jacqueline Osherow as Proxy Witnesses of the Shoah,' in *Mapping the Ethical Turn: A Reader in Ethics, Culture, and Literary Theory*, ed. Todd F. Davis and kenneth Womack (Charlottesville: University Press of Virginia, 2001), 165–91 at 168.
31 Frank Davey, 'What's in a Genre: Margaret Atwood's "Notes Towards a Poem,"' in *Inside the Poem: Essays and Poems in Honour of Donald Stephens*, ed. W.H. New (Toronto: Oxford University Press, 1992), 48–54.
32 Nicholas Owen, 'Introduction,' in Owen, *Human Rights, Human Wrongs*, *supra* note 29, 1–25 at 25.
33 Linda Alcoff, 'The Problem of Speaking for Others,' *Cultural Critique* 20 (Winter 1991–2): 5–31.
34 Forché, *supra* note 5 at 37.

35 Margaret Atwood, 'It Is Dangerous to Read Newspapers,' in *The Animals in That Country* (Toronto: Oxford University Press, 1968), 31.
36 Seyla Benhabib, 'The Generalized and the Concrete Other: Gender, Community, and Postmodernism in Contemporary Ethics,' in *Situating the Self* (New York: Routledge, 1992), 148–77.
37 Edward W. Said, *Humanism and Democratic Criticism* (New York: Columbia University Press, 2004), 10–11.
38 Margaret Atwood with Karla Hammond, 'Interview Articulating the Mute' in Ingersoll, ed., *supra* note 23 at 119–120. Italics added.
39 Scarry, *supra* note 3, 277–309, at 302.
40 *Ibid.*, 285.
41 *Ibid.*
42 *Ibid.*, 285–7.
43 *Ibid.*, 278.
44 Austin Sarat and Thomas R. Kearns, 'Writing History and Registering Memory in Legal Decisions and Legal Practices: An Introduction,' in *History, Memory, and the Law*, ed. Austin Sarat and Thomas R. Kearns (Ann Arbor: University of Michigan Press, 1999), 1–24, at 15.
45 Felman, *supra* note 3, 135–50.
46 *Ibid.*, 139–40.
47 *Ibid.*, 155.
48 Cited in Shoshana Felman and Dori Laub, *Testimony: Crises of Witnessing in Literature, Psychoanalysis and History* (New York: Routledge, 1992), 109.
49 Susan A. Bandes, ed, in her 'Introduction' to *The Passions of Law* (New York: New York University Press, 1999), asks 'what accounts for the law's insistence on neutral, emotionless judging?' when other disciplines like neurobiology suggest that 'it is not only impossible but *undesirable* to factor emotion out of the reasoning process' (7).
50 Margaret Atwood, 'A Letter to America,' *International Herald Tribune*, 4 April 2003.
51 Margaret Atwood, 'Amnesty International: An Address,' in *Second Words: Selected Critical Prose* (Toronto: Anansi, 1982), 396.
52 For details of the invaluable NGO contribution to the formation of a transnational justice networks, see Thomas Risse, 'The Power of Norms versus The Norms of Power: Transnational Civil Society and Human Rights,' in *The Third Force: The Rise of Transnational Civil Society*, ed. Ann M. Florini (Tokyo: Japan Center for International Exchange, 2000), 177–209, and Helen Durham, 'We the People: The Position of NGOs in Gathering Evidence and Giving Witness at International Criminal Trials,' in ed. Thakur and Malcontent *supra* note 8, 169–185. Durham writes:

'NGOs are currently the most basic form of popular participation and representation in the modern world. Thus, the relationship between NGOs and international criminal law, philosophically, should be a close one' (170).

53 Jonathon Power, *Amnesty International: The Human Rights Story* (New York: McGraw-Hill, 1981).

54 *Ibid.*

55 For a rich history of Amnesty's successive anti-torture campaigns, see Amnesty International, *Report on Torture* (London: Duckworth, 1973); Amnesty International, *Torture in the Eighties* (Oxford: Roberston, 1984); ed. Duncan Forest *A Glimpse of Hell: Reports on Torture Worldwide* (New York: New York University Press, 1996); and Ann Marie Clark, *Diplomacy of Conscience: Amnesty International and Changing Human Rights Norms* (Princeton, NJ: Princeton University Press, 2001).

56 *Margaret Atwood, 'Footnote to the Amnesty Report on Torture,'* in *Two-Headed Poems* (Toronto: Oxford University Press, 1978), 45–7.

57 Scarry, *supra* note 19 at 45.

58 Atwood, *supra* note 56.

59 Thomas Csordas, 'Introduction,' in *Embodiment and Experience: The Existential Ground of Culture and Self*, ed. Thomas Csordas (Cambridge: Cambridge University Press, 1994), 1–24, at 3–4.

60 Cloyd, *supra* note 15 at 248.

61 Lacquer, *supra* note 17 at 76.

62 Scarry, *supra* note 19 at 38.

63 *Ibid.*, 38–41.

64 Atwood, *supra* note 56.

65 Cohen, *supra* note 6 at 168.

66 Scarry, *supra* note 19 at 28.

67 Atwood, *supra* note 56.

68 Amnesty International, *Torture in the Eighties*, *supra* note 55.

69 Amnesty International, *Report on Torture*, *supra* note 55 at 219–20.

70 Atwood, *supra* note 56.

71 Scarry, *supra* note 19 at 42.

72 *Supra* note 68 at 20.

73 Eric Prokosch, 'Amnesty International's Anti-Torture Campaigns,' in *A Glimpse of Hell*, *supra* note 55.

74 Lacquer, *supra* note 17 at 23.

75 Cited in Prokosch, *supra* note 73 at 28.

76 For a sampling of the 'torture debates' between Alan Dershowitz, Elaine Scarry, and others, see Sanford Levinson, ed., *Torture: A Collection*

(Oxford; Oxford University Press, 2004). See Susan Sontag's 'Regarding the Torture of Others,' for her scathing indictment of the U.S. administration's refusal to take responsibility for their construction of a discourse of the non-citizen and non-human detainee beyond the law whom 'rogue soldiers' took trophy photographs of undergoing forced sexual humiliation at Abu Ghraib: http://southerncrossreview.org/35/sontag, accessed 19 May 2007.

77 Atwood, *supra* note 56.

78 Scarry, *supra* note 19 at 29.

79 Atwood, *supra* note 56.

80 *Ibid.*

81 Scarry, *supra* note 19 at 29.

82 Atwood, *supra* note 56.

83 *Ibid.*

84 *Ibid.*

85 *Ibid.*

86 *Ibid.*

87 *Ibid.*

88 *Ibid.*

89 Leon Shaskolsky Sheleff, *The Bystander* (Lexington, MA: Lexington Books, 1978), 2.

90 Cohen, *supra* note 6 at 271.

91 *Ibid.*, 270.

92 *Supra* note 8 at 209–11.

93 *Ibid.*, 224.

94 www.icjcanada.org, viewed 31 May 2005.

95 Thomas Lacquer, 'Reason, Popular Radicalism, and the Human in Human Rights,' Humanitarian Narratives of Inflicted Suffering Conference, University of Connecticut, 13 Oct. 2006.

9 Who Do We Blame for Blame? Moving beyond the Fiction of Blame in *The Sweet Hereafter*

DIANA MAJURY

Having taught with Russell Banks's novel *The Sweet Hereafter*[1] in a Law and Literature seminar, I became fascinated with the issue of blame and its relationship with law, which is one of the novel's central themes. In this paper, I use *The Sweet Hereafter* as the entry point from which to examine the pre-eminence accorded to blame in social and legal contexts and to explore how the two contexts interact to produce an escalating focus on, and need for, blame.

Through this examination, I see blame operating as a cultural fiction of resolution that appeals to and relies on a fictionalized version of law that in turn re-enforces the cultural fiction of resolution through blame. According to this story, law takes on the role of assigning blame in order to help people to get past the helplessness and arbitrariness that blame is often intended to displace.[2] In this vindication scenario, law is invoked to certify the blame and provide resolution. This legal fiction is then reinscribed as part of the cultural fiction of closure through blame so that we have law and culture mutually augmenting the central significance and cathartic potential of blame. As a result, we create a self-perpetuating cycle of blame without the closure or movement beyond blame that people expect or anticipate or have been led to believe will emanate from or through the invocation of law as the blame enforcer. *The Sweet Hereafter* exposes and critiques this mutually reinforcing process and offers some inklings of alternative ways to move beyond the emptiness of blame. This chapter follows a similar exploratory trajectory, starting by looking at the pervasive cultural context of blame and then at Russell Banks's critical examination of the process of blame and its interconnection with law. In conclusion, I respond to Banks's alternative glimmerings with further related glimmerings derived from a short article by Mari Matsuda in which she echoes what I read as Banks's nudge towards social responsibility and community as more cathartic and more constructive responses to tragedy than blame.[3]

A Culture of Facile Blame

Adapting Peter Brooks's notion of what he describes as our contemporary 'culture of facile confession,'[4] I see the resort to law as the blame enforcer as a reflection and promoter of our contemporary culture of facile blame. In his article 'The Future of Confession,' Brooks presents the culture of facile confession that is promulgated by the myriad of contemporary TV talk shows such as Oprah and Jerry Springer in which ordinary people are paraded out to confess their hidden deeds and secret thoughts in a bid to be seen as an interesting or as a 'real' (in the Reality TV sense of real) person.[5] According to Brooks: 'We have come to inhabit a society where confessional performances are ever more frequent, public, easy, almost banal, where people go on television to confess intimate and shameful things in ways that would have been inconceivable just a generation ago ... [T]he law, like culture at large, appears addicted to confessional speech, it regularly declares it cannot do without confession.'[6] In a culture 'overburdened by confessional speech,' confession has come to be seen as an expected and essential part of the criminal justice process, to be facilitated rather than restrained. The complexities of motive and of context that are key to understanding and interpreting a confession have been vitiated by a society 'hooked on confession.' In this context, the role of law is 'to simplify what we as a culture know about human character and motive in order to get on with its task of adjudicating – of assigning guilt and punishment and getting on with life in a rough and ready way.'[7] Confession is decontextualized and used instrumentally. Similarly, in the context of a society hooked on blame, law is expected to cut through or to sidestep complexity and ignore social context in order to deliver a clear perpetrator for public catharsis and as a means for closure. Blame imposed through law offers a similar process of oversimplification and certainty and a similar promise of facilitating 'getting on with life in a rough and ready way.' Hence we become invested in a culture of facile blame.

Once there is injury or harm, our societal perception is that there must be someone to blame, to hold to account for the injury. Stephen

Carter describes this as 'bilateral individualism,' whereby victimization is seen as 'the result of concrete, individual acts by identifiable transgressors.'[8] Victims and offenders are mutually exclusive but interdependent categories. In order for there to be victims there must be corresponding offenders; the role of law is to identify and punish those offenders, as well as to deter would-be transgressors. This is the central focus of law, and the failure of law occurs when it is unable to prevent, or at least assign blame for, disasters or other wrongs. According to Carter, bilateral individualism provides the false security of knowing that there is a wrongdoer, with the comforting implication that the wrong can be prevented. From the perspective of bilateral individualism, the naming and striking back at perpetrators and the ferreting out of would-be offenders are necessary to protect us against the uncertainty and fearfulness of transgressorless victims, of misfortunes or larger social ills. Bilateral individualism is a driving force in *The Sweet Hereafter*. Like Carter, Banks portrays bilateral individualism as a destructive and illogical force, despite its superficial appeal.

Bilateral individualism is central to the concept of injustice that Judith Shklar explores in her book *The Faces of Injustice*.[9] Shklar interrogates the distinction between misfortune and injustice, a distinction that North American society desperately clings to as protection against the arbitrariness, resignation, and lack of control that inhere in the ascription of misfortune. 'The notion that there is a simple and stable rule to separate the two [injustice and misfortune] is a demand for moral security, which like so many others, cannot be satisfied.'[10] Shklar describes this desire for a clear and definitive rule as leading to a tendency to 'either blame irrationally or accept our fate too easily.'[11] In *The Sweet Hereafter*, it is blame, not acceptance, that is too easily ascribed. And it is an easy blame more than an irrational blame; it is a blame that fosters and is fostered by a culture of facile blame. Blame is invoked as the way to avoid passivity and resignation in the face of disaster. Blame becomes the way to explain in concrete terms that which otherwise would be inexplicable, the way to transform misfortune into injustice. According to Shklar, injustice is perceived as concrete, preventable, the work of some 'ill-intentioned agent, human or supernatural.' Injustice warrants 'indignation and outrage' [blame] directed towards the wrongdoer. Conversely, misfortune begets only resignation. Caused by 'external forces of nature,' misfortune is arbitrary and unpredictable. There is no one to blame or to hold to account; there is no action to be taken.[12]

Shklar is not arguing for the elimination of the distinction between injustice and misfortune, but for a more fulsome and thoughtful analysis of where and why we draw the line between the two:

> [T]he difference between misfortune and injustice will not go away, and there are good public reasons why we should retain it. We need it not only to make sense of our experiences but also to control and restrain the public sources of danger to our safety and security. But we must recognize that the line of separation between injustice and misfortune is a political choice, not a simple rule that can be taken as a given. The question is, thus, not whether to draw a line between them at all, but where to do so in order to enhance responsibility and avoid random retaliation.[13]

In pursuing this question, Shklar ultimately turns towards a more shared sense of responsibility for wrongs that occur. While Shklar would achieve this through an expanded understanding of injustice, *The Sweet Hereafter* suggests an alternate route, through which misfortune would be grieved and accepted and blame abated.

Shklar's argument is that the erroneous 'belief that we can know and draw a stable and rigid distinction between the unjust and the unfortunate ... inclines us to ignore passive injustice [civic failure to stop private and public acts of injustice], the victim's sense of injustice, and ultimately the full, complex, and enduring character of injustice as a social phenomenon.' [14] This leads her to advocate a 'more complete account of the social character of injustice' that would include the victim's version and his or her sense of injustice.[15] The focus of Shklar's analysis is injustice. My focus, in the context of this paper, is on misfortune. This leads me to examine the flip side of Shklar's coin. I argue that the erroneous 'belief that we can know and draw a stable and rigid distinction between the unjust and the unfortunate ... inclines us' to want to opt for the label of injustice in order to legitimate and focus our rage and indignation, and to justify the ascription of blame, rather than to opt for the label of misfortune and the resignation and accompanying sense of helplessness that seem to attach to misfortune.

In the face of this expanded notion of injustice that engulfs misfortune, blame comes easily, almost automatically. The role of law in this scenario is to vindicate the need for blame by assigning blame unequivocally and by holding the perpetrator to account, thereby releasing the victim from the painful thrall of the harming event. The perception of such vindication and release through law reinforces the emphasis on blame as the appropriate, even necessary, response to tragedy. The blame cycle perpetuates itself even though law often does not, even cannot, deliver; frequently it cannot even deliver a perpetrator, and almost never does it deliver the hugely desired closure. And yet the fiction continues and the expectations of law seem to increase rather than diminish. In a culture of facile blame, law and blame are inextricably intertwined, with law playing a major role in the 'faciling' of blame.

Blame in Response to Tragedy

In Popular Culture[16]

An episode of CSI with the title 'Chaos Theory,'[17] provides a classic example of the culture of facile blame at work. A young university student, Paige, goes missing between her dorm room and the taxi she called. Initially there is no body and no evidence, but investigation discloses an 'affair' with a married professor. And thus we have an initial likely candidate for the role of murderer. In the CSI world, one suspect quickly leads to another – in this case, the professor's wife, the long sufferer of her husband's sexual harassment escapades (or, sticking more accurately to the story line as given, his affairs), who fears losing her cad husband to Paige and so confronts Paige ... and perhaps kills her. Or maybe the murderer is the male college student in the same dorm who raped Paige's roommate after slipping her the date rape drug rohypnol.[18] As the list of suspects grows, the body is finally found, in true *CSI* fashion, hideously compacted into grisly body bits in the local dump.

In the end, science is forced to acknowledge accident in a chain of events that led Paige to be searching in the dumpster for her waste basket, which had been catapulted down the garbage chute along with her garbage. Paige, climbing up between the dumpster and the brick wall, in the dark and in the rain, was crushed and fell into the dumpster when a car swerved to miss a van and hit the dumpster, slamming it and Paige into the wall. The car driver, of course, momentarily becomes the fourth murder suspect until science points to the truth: it was just a terrible series of coincidences; it was an accident.[19]

In the culminating scene in this episode Gil Grisson, the lead investigator, has to tell the parents the news that, worse than murder, their daughter's death was an accident. This is a conclusion the parents cannot accept and to which the father responds by vowing to spend whatever it takes to find out who is to blame for his daughter's death. Grisson's colleague, Catherine, explains that the parents were looking for closure. And we are left with Grisson's inappropriatism – 'truth brings closure' – and Catherine's retort – 'not always.' In this episode, we see the prospect of closure as coming, not through knowledge or understanding, but through blame.[20] From this perspective, murder is explainable; there is someone to blame. Murder is a wrong, an injustice. On the other hand, accidents are ... misfortunes, accidental; blame is less easily attributed. One cannot control or prevent a terrible series of coincidences. This makes murder more knowable and more contained and thus, perversely but apparently, easier to live with. The inability to ascribe blame, the absence of someone to hold responsible, leaves uncertainty and vulnerability.

In Daily Life

It seems to me that this *CSI* episode, echoing Judith Shklar's claim that 'passing the blame' is 'America's favorite game,'[21] is on the cultural mark in its depiction of the deep need for certainty and for blame in the face of tragic misfortune. There are any number of examples in our daily lives,[22] but a story covered by the *Globe and Mail* in May 2005 about a tragic accident in Saskatchewan, in which four young people were killed, particularly struck me given that I had just finished teaching with *The Sweet Hereafter* at the time I read the newspaper account.[23] Six young people, aged twelve to fifteen, got in an SUV driven by their fourteen-year-old friend and ended up on the Trans-Canada highway, in the middle of the night, driving eighty kilometres an hour head-on into a semi-tractor trailer. The young driver survived but did not remember what happened, and the RCMP were unable 'to determine the cause of the accident,' as if there was a specific, determinative 'cause' beyond the events and factors I have just described. The decision was made not to lay any charges – not the possibly serious charges of criminal negligence causing death or dangerous driving nor a minor charge like driving without a licence. The parents of three of the dead children (the fourth child killed was the younger brother of the driver) were extremely upset that charges were not laid and the driver held accountable. They wanted the law to step in; they wanted someone charged. Convinced that there were answers to why this tragedy happened, and in the absence of legal action, they alleged a cover-up and made complaints to the justice minister and to the ombudsman. The *Globe* reporter comments: 'Nobody of course will say these are simply grieving parents who are unable to accept their loss and are looking to lay blame to help them get through the tragedy.'[24]

This story portrays the culture of facile blame in operation: grief morphs into blame and blame into legal action, perceived as a means of assuaging the grief. The assumption is that the legal process will somehow provide answers, make comprehensible the incomprehensible, ease the pain, help the victims move on, provide 'closure.' This has become the burden of law, and it seems that the less law is able to meet that burden, the greater the need becomes and the higher the expectations placed on law. Instead of turning away from law and recognizing the hollowness of law in this context, the momentum is towards more law and heavier reliance upon law. [25] No one is willing to say that the emperor has no clothes, that blame and law have no curative powers.

If the blame cycle is to be disrupted, we need to expose the culture of blame as facile and to challenge the assumption that blame heals. This is the story of *The Sweet Hereafter*.

Blame in *The Sweet Hereafter*[26]

The Story

The terrible accident that is at the centre of *The Sweet Hereafter* elicits a reaction similar to that of the parents of the Saskatchewan children killed in the highway accident. However, there are those in *The Sweet Hereafter* who resist blame and in so doing resist law. One of the primary tensions in the novel is between those who believe that there are such things as accidents and those who do not, and thus between those who seek resolution through law and those who eschew the law and its potential for destructiveness.

The Sweet Hereafter is the story of the response of the residents of a small town that saw fourteen of its children killed when their school bus swerved off the highway, crashed through the guard rail, and skidded down an embankment, ending up in a sandpit filled with water.[27] It is a story about pain and loss and guilt and anger and the attempt to redirect, assuage, or get over those feelings by finding someone, preferably a stranger, even better an anonymous corporation with deep insurance-filled pockets, to blame for the incomprehensible tragedy. Lawsuits become the vehicle for focusing that blame and the whole town is engulfed in and divided by a myriad of burgeoning lawsuits.[28] The novel traces the brief history of what turns out to be the pivotal (and blighting) lawsuit.

The story is told by four protagonists, from four different perspectives. The novel starts and ends with Dolores Driscoll, the driver of the bus. Dolores is tortured by the fear that she may be to blame but is actually relieved when, through a deliberate lie, the blame is ultimately placed directly on her. Knowing the lie and accepting the role of scapegoat give Dolores solace and peace. The second storyteller, Billy Ansel, the father of two of the dead children, was driving behind the school bus when it went over and is the only potential external witness to the event. Billy finds no comfort and no meaning in the prospect of blame for what he sees clearly as an accident. He tries to dissuade his friends and neighbours from pursuing the lawsuit that he recognizes will only protract the agony and the uncertainty. The third storyteller is the lawyer Mitchell Stephens, who cultivates and directs the need for blame into a lawsuit even though he knows that the lawsuit he promotes cannot relieve the pain or enable the families to re-establish control. Mitchell sees himself and his clients as motivated not by greed, but by anger, and he sees his role as lawyer as giving voice to that anger. The fourth storyteller is Nichole Burnell, former cheerleader, queen of the high-school harvest ball and president of her high-school class, who was rendered unable to walk as a result of the accident. It is Nichole who deliberately lies in her deposition, so as to place the blame on the driver of the bus and thus nullify the lawsuit brought against the state and the town.

The novel begins with Dolores. She could be testifying in a trial as she describes what happened, but she is simply telling her story: 'A dog – it was a dog I saw for certain. Or thought I saw. It was snowing pretty hard by then, and you can see things in the snow that aren't there, aren't exactly there, but you also can't see some of the things that are there, so that by God when you do see something, you react anyhow, erring on the distaff side, if you get my drift.'[29] Here is the crux of the novel – uncertain certainty or certain uncertainty. It is not possible to know what happened, what 'caused' the accident, who is at fault, or even if there is a fault. Given this, the novel asks, on what side do we err and why? As outsiders, we see things that others cannot see, but we too are not able to see things that are there, and we may see things that are not exactly there. We are in a unique position to assess and determine blame, to judge. But while we may have a fuller picture as readers, it is not necessarily a more accurate picture, and as readers we do not all put together the same picture. Blame becomes more complicated when there is no unitary picture, no single story.

As in a trial, the novel tells a number of different stories, different versions of what happened. As with each of the storytellers, the reader is in the position of having to fit the pieces together, to put to the side the segments that do not seem to fit and to rearrange the others. In *The Sweet Hereafter* there is no legal judgment, no legal resolution; law instead is one of the discordant pieces in the story. Ultimately, we, the readers, pass judgment. Our judgment is not directed towards determining the 'facts' of what actually happened but towards assessing the responses to what happened. And our judgment too is merely a response, not a determination. There are always the loose bits that we see out of the corner of our eye and the bits that seem to belong even though at the same time they seem to conflict. We are left with the uncertainty, the unknowability, and the unfixability that inhere in an accident, that haunt the death of children, that permeate any major loss. It is this uncertainty, and the sense of helplessness that accompanies it, that both trigger and gainsay the desire for blame. One of the items that is up for our judgment is the role of blame that is so clearly a central character in the novel.

Aided by the lawyers who flock to the site, the townspeople engage in a desperate search for a cause, to find someone to blame, someone to sue – the driver of the bus, the state for not keeping the guard rail in good repair, the town highway department for digging a sandpit and then abandoning it full of water, or perhaps the legislators who made mandatory the bus seatbelts that trapped the children in their seats in the back of the bus. These are the questions that trouble the town in the aftermath of the tragedy – who or what caused this accident? Whom can we blame? There is an intense need to assign blame in the hope of eliminating the arbitrariness of accident. Law provides the vehicle through which blame can be crystallized and pursued. Law is seen to offer the alleged comfort that there are no accidents, that there is always someone to blame. This is the mantra of lawyer Mitchell Stephens, the line that he offers to his clients as consolation for their loss.

The novel offers a sympathetic, but critical, picture of the invocation of blame as an easy way to try to avoid the unavoidable, to deal with uncertainty by trying to impose answers. The novel offers a critical, and less sympathetic, picture of law as the vulture that feeds off the need for blame with false promises on which it cannot deliver. According to Billy Ansel, law, like religion, is merely a form of denial.[30]

The Lawyer: The Blame Promoter

Mitchell's immediate response when he reads of the bus tragedy in the morning paper is to reject the characterization of it as an 'accident': 'I knew at once it wasn't an "accident" at all. There are no accidents. I don't even know what the word means, and I never trust anyone who says he does. I knew that somebody somewhere had made a decision to cut a corner in order to save a few pennies.'[31] What is it about an accident that is incomprehensible to Mitchell? What is it that he cannot understand or refuses to acknowledge? Accidents are anathema to Mitchell. The novel portrays him as a man who is alive only when he is in total control, when he is corralling clients and building a case,[32] when he is pursuing blame. From this perspective, blame is seen as a way to try to regain control, but the novel portrays the control provided by blame, and by inference by law, as illusory and empty, and ultimately as destructive.

Before he knows any details about what happened, Mitchell knows who is at fault. He describes it as his mission to rout out the corporate culprits whom he knows must lurk behind the euphemism of accident. He wants to summon the cost-accounting apparitions who would have decided that the lower price of shoddy equipment was worth the risk of a lawsuit. Mitchell perceives his job as making them pay for that decision, making them pay so dearly as to flip the bottom line in future cost-accounting analysis, to make it cheaper to do the job properly than to risk a lawsuit. 'That's the only way you can ensure moral responsibility in this society. Make it cheaper.'[33]

Mitchell is hugely invested in the image of himself as channelling his anger and aggression into socially useful lawsuits against corporate greed or incompetence. He goes to great lengths to persuade us, himself, and his clients that he is not the stereotypical lawyer/ambulance chaser driven by greed. But his actions often belie his words, and he gives us contradictory messages about what motivates him, about what he is doing and why. Mitchell is himself full of contradictions; he is in conflict with himself at many levels. He portrays himself as the ethical voice of righteous anger that will protect the future against corporate cost cutting. But he knowingly crosses the line of ethics, perhaps even morality, a line-crossing that he rationalizes as a legal necessity.[34] He is the agent of revenge and punishment, the one who will 'strip and hang the hide of the sonofabitch responsible.'[35] He will find the one to blame and hold him to account. But, at the same time, Mitchell rejects the portrayal of himself as heroic in this mission. He is 'no Lone Ranger riding into town in my white Mercedes-Benz to save the local sheepherders from the cattle barons in black hats.'[36] He is no do-gooder who burns himself out with tragic cases in order to make himself a better person. But, despite his protestations, he clearly does burn out. He himself invokes the image of total burnout when he talks about the impact the cases have on him once they are over. The spectacular high of building the case inevitably plunges into an equally spectacular low: 'They humiliate me. They make me burn inside with shame. Win or lose, I always come out feeling diminished, like a cinder.'[37] But, in the face of this pathetic picture, he is adamant that he is not a victim or a victim sympathizer. He has no patience or tolerance for victims; victims are losers, and he is no loser. Mitchell sees himself as a winner who relishes the win – 'the real satisfaction, the true motivation, is the carnage and the smoldering aftermath and the trophy heads that get hung up on the den wall. I love it.'[38]

Burnt-out cinder or smouldering firebrand ready to reignite? Mitchell portrays himself as both and he comes across as both. These are the warring sides of Mitchell – he is only truly alive when he is in control and engaged in battle, but ultimately he knows the battle is meaningless and the control illusory and that he will crash and burn as soon as the fight is over. The emptiness haunts him, but to succumb to it, or even fully to acknowledge it, would be weak, would mark him as victim. So he continues in a self-perpetuating cycle of blame and destruction.

Mitchell describes himself as perpetually angry, a mix of conviction and rage. He is 'on a personal vendetta' to reclaim/assuage his guilt for/unleash his anger over his daughter, Zoe, whom he has lost to drug addiction and the streets. While he does not explicitly blame her for his lonely, aimless life punctuated only by the temporary thrill of building a legal case, his flashbacks to her childhood and to his later attempts to rescue her and his sense of helplessness in response to her phone calls demanding money seem laden with blame, both self-blame and blame of his daughter. It is when he gets to focus that blame externally, to mould it and direct it, that he feels in control again. Like

Zoe, he too is addicted, in search of the high that makes him feel confident, alive:

> Nothing else provides me with the rush that I get from cases like this. There is a brilliant hard-edged clarity that comes over me ... an intensity and focus that makes me feel more alive than at any other time.
>
> It's almost like a drug ... The rest of the time, like most people, I muddle lonely through my days and nights feeling unsure, vaguely confused, conflicted, and aimless. Put me onto something like this school bus case, though and zap! all those feelings disappear. Nothing else does it ... Nothing.[39]

Blame, the pursuit of blame, lawsuits – these give focus and direction, meaning, certainty, and control, although short-lived, in a life otherwise troubled by uncertainty (including uncertainty about the meaningfulness of the very lawsuits that he thrives on) and events beyond Mitchell's control. As peddled by Mitchell, blame and law become the vehicles through which the townspeople try to re-establish control, bulwarks against being overwhelmed by uncertainty and randomness. This push to have the event understood as injustice rather than misfortune is the desire for moral security that can never be satisfied that Judith Shklar describes.[40] As with Mitchell himself, the desire is consuming and its insatiability renders it all-consuming, consuming all.

While he talks of corporate wrongdoing, it is ability to pay, not wrongdoing, that is the focus of Mitchell's search for defendants. It is for this reason that he dismisses the bus driver, Dolores, whose 'pockets weren't an inch deep,' as the potential wrongdoer.[41] Also, Dolores is too close, too real, for her to be an acceptable target for blame. She is a well-liked member of the community who has herself suffered greatly as a result of the accident. Dolores is not the one to blame. For the townspeople, blaming her would be like blaming themselves. The parents want someone towards whom they can direct their anger unequivocally and against whom they can exact revenge. Mitchell determines that he will have to establish that Dolores was driving safely within the speed limit; if there is evidence to the contrary he will ignore it or undermine it, even if it means lying, which, ultimately, of course, it does.[42]

In soliciting the parents of the dead children to sue, Mitchell plays upon their desire for revenge and punishment, even though he knows that revenge is unsatisfying and impossible: 'They wanted revenge, which was useless to them of course – they weren't going to get it, but they didn't know that yet.'[43] And he knows that the damage award he is pursuing on their behalf is similarly empty: 'I'm under no delusions – I know that in the end a million-dollar settlement makes no real difference to them, that it probably only serves to sharpen their pain by constricting it with legal language and rewarding it with money, that it complicates the guilt they feel and forces them to question the authenticity of their own suffering.'[44] Nonetheless, he uses the lure of compensation to entice the Walkers, who had been poor and desperate long before their son was killed, into the lawsuit. And to the angry and distraught Ottos, he promises punishment. Even as he peddles blame, he knows that it is incapable of providing any of the things for which it is being invoked. Austin Sarat portrays Mitchell as the sole force behind the lawsuit, coercing susceptible people to participate. He describes Mitchell as cajoling, pleading, misleading, and seducing grieving parents to join the lawsuit, preying on their vulnerabilities and exploiting their pain.[45] I am not quite so willing to ascribe blame solely to the lawyer and the law. I see the parents who sign on to the lawsuit as willing participants, quick to accede to law the roles of vindication, punishment, and compensation that they are seeking. In the cultural context of facile blame, it is 'natural' for the parents of dead children to resort to blame and to turn to law as the legitimater and enforcer of that blame. Mitchell does not create these desires, he simply channels them.

Mitchell is full of contradictions and, despite his protestations to the contrary, full of delusions. The delusions percolate just below the surface of his consciousness, haunting him continuously and erupting periodically. He knows that what he offers his clients – revenge, punishment, compensation – is illusory, and that moral responsibility cannot be imposed by law or through civil lawsuits. The blame that he cultivates and that is nurtured and focused through law is destructive both of the blamer and of the blamed, as well as of the community divided by the blaming.

The Victim: Blame as Lie

Nichole Burnell was the town's sweetheart – smart, attractive, a youth leader, a beloved babysitter. The bus tragedy has relegated her to a wheelchair for the rest of her life.[46] She symbolizes all the potential the town has lost through the tragedy. Alive but permanently 'damaged,'

Nichole is the ideal plaintiff, the perfect 'linchpin of the case,' bound to garner huge sympathy from a jury both for herself and for her parents. Mitchell is gleeful at the prospect.

But, just as the lawsuit is built upon lies and obfuscation, the town's image of Nichole as she existed before the accident is a mirage. The perfect life of the perfect Nichole, 'the all-American teenaged beauty queen,'[47] was a lie. She was being sexually abused by her father. She lived her life ashamed and afraid and lay awake at night thinking up ways to kill herself, the only way she could think of to end the abuse.[48] After the accident, she is angry but she is very much alive; she no longer wants to die. Her father is uncomfortable and afraid of her, hardly able to touch her. Prior to the accident, she had felt complicit in the abuse, 'not knowing for sure what had happened or who was to blame,'[49] but the accident gives her clarity and control. She is no longer afraid of her father; she knows who is responsible. Her life after the accident is much more her own, despite her apparent dependency.

From the beginning, Nichole resists the law and the need for blame in response to the accident. Her immediate reaction when her parents tell her that Mitchell Stephens is her lawyer is to ask 'What do I need a lawyer for?'[50] She is suspicious of the computer Mitchell has purchased for her; she assumes that insurance will cover the costs resulting from her injuries and she does not think suing is right. She was lucky; she survived. Why then would she be suing? Nichole understands that the parents whose children died in the accident might feel driven to sue, but she still does not think it is right.[51] She never wavers from the position that the lawsuit is wrong. To her what happened 'was an accident, that's all. Accidents happen.'[52]

Nichole is sceptical about the law but, interestingly, likes and trusts the lawyer, Mitchell. He treats her like a 'normal person' and he understands her. Mitchell is able to assure her that testifying only requires answering the lawyers' questions truthfully, and Nichole agrees to participate despite her misgivings. She is adamant that she will not lie, even though she recognizes that the lawsuit is not about truth – 'No one was interested in the truth ... Because the truth was that it was an accident, that's all, and no one was to blame.'[53] But, given that she does not actually remember the accident itself, she is comforted by her belief that nothing she says 'could be used to blame anybody for it.'[54]Nonetheless, 'the whole thing' makes her feel 'greedy and dishonest.'[55] Her discomfort is exacerbated by a conversation between her parents and Billy Ansel that she listens in on. Billy has come to try to persuade them to drop the lawsuit and allow the townspeople to mourn properly and get on with their lives. He describes his friends and neighbours as having gone crazy, caught up in lawsuits against each other, turning the town into a 'hateful place to live.' Like Billy, Nichole recognizes the lawsuits as people's attempts to avoid their own pain by turning against others. But avoidance is not possible; instead the pain festers and intensifies, inflamed by blame and the strife that accompanies it. The lawsuits further fuel the flame.

Contemplating the destruction ahead, Nichole realizes that she has the power to stop the lawsuit. She gives her deposition at the courthouse. She truthfully answers the lawyers' questions about her injuries and about her school life and her social life before the accident. Then she describes the events leading up to the accident, apparently remembering more than she had anticipated as she goes along in her testimony. And then she lies. Knowing that to blame Dolores would put an end to the lawsuits, Nichole says that, at the time the bus went off the road, Dolores was going well over the speed limit in a heavy snowfall. Mitchell and her father know that she is lying, but they are unable to intervene or to stop the process. The lie is irrefutable and thus its falseness is irrelevant. Lawyer and father are shocked. Mitchell is perplexed and alarmed as to why she would have lied, reckoning that 'a kid who'd do that to her own father is not normal.' But Nichole knows that her father knows why she lied. Her father knows the truth.[56]

Some commentators read Nichole's lie and her subversion of the lawsuit as a statement of blame, an act of revenge against her father for the incest he perpetrated against her.[57] I read it not as blame but as an act of independence, Nichole standing up for what she believes and asserting her view of the world against the wishes of her father. Her action is totally consistent with the ideas that she expressed all along. She opposed the lawsuit from the beginning. She thought it was wrong, and her belief in its wrongness was affirmed and strengthened by Billy's description of the harm the lawsuit was causing. And, although her parents stood to gain significantly from the lawsuit and would experience financial hardship as a result of its withdrawal, this was not her father's claim; it was Nichole's. She is asserting control over the injury that was done to her, not robbing her father of something that was rightfully his. Nichole's action is about reclaiming herself and her dignity, not about blame. Even though we as onlookers might be invested in blame and want to blame the person who stole her soul and made her fearful, this is not Nichole's path. Her lie is a moment of truth, a moment of reckoning in which her father acknowledges – 'Yes ... We know the truth, Nichole. You and I.'[58]

Nichole worries about the impact of her lie on Dolores, on the one whom she has blamed. Her father corroborates her fear that people will blame Dolores: 'Those that don't know the truth will blame Dolores. People have got to have somebody to blame.'[59] It is in relation to Dolores that Nichole seeks confirmation from her father that he knows the truth. Her insistence on this acknowledgment is intended to displace wrongful blame, not to assert her own blame against her father.

The One Who Is Blamed: Blame as Illusion

With the exception of Dolores, the blame that we see in the novel is directed outwardly, channelled through law towards strangers or anonymous corporations, those whom it feels safe and easy to blame. But this outward blaming seems like a thinly veiled cover for inward blaming, that is, parents' self-blame over the fate of their children whether killed in a bus accident or succumbing to HIV through drug addiction, like Mitchell's daughter. While self-blame might seem to be equally inappropriate and equally destructive, Dolores's relief at accepting the blame, at least when she knows that the blame is premised on a lie, offers a different, more complex perspective on the role and process of blame.

While blame is invoked as the means to impose order and certainty in the face of the intolerable uncertainty of a tragic accident, it is an impossible task. The search for and choice of a target for blame can be fraught with conflicting and confounding emotions and factors that may contradict and undermine the very certainty being sought. Thus the townspeople resist the logical target for blame and, for very different reasons, the lawyer also rejects her as a defendant in the lawsuit. The community's reluctance to blame Dolores, even though as the driver of the bus she is the most obvious focus for their blame, reflects an ambivalence about blame: '[The towns people] felt as profoundly sorry for her as for themselves; but they also could not help blaming her and wanting to cast her out. They would have preferred that she simply disappear from town for a while ... They wanted her to stash her pain and guilt where they didn't have to look at it.'[60] But Dolores refuses to disappear; she attends the funerals of each of the children killed in the accident, where 'she plunk[ed] herself down in the exact center of the town's grief and rage compelling them by her presence at those funerals to define her.'[61] But it is the lawyer, Mitchell, who wants to control the defining, to ensure that Dolores is defined as blameless so that the path to the corporate defendants is unobstructed. He promises Dolores that if she agrees to join the lawsuit, she will be exonerated, she will not have to bear any of the blame. To which she responds with anguish, 'I'm not to blame ... I'm not to blame.'[62] In order to decide whether or not to participate in the lawsuit, Dolores seeks the counsel of her husband, Abbott, who is disabled as the result of a stroke and whose cryptic speech only Dolores can decipher. He advises her against turning to strangers for resolution, that it is only the townspeople who can decide her guilt or innocence. The crime, if there was one, was against them.[63] According to Abbott, 'Blame creates comprehension.'[64] This is not the blame that Mitchell pursues; his blame obscures and distorts rather than clarifies. However, it is not clear to me that the novel depicts the possibility of comprehension through blame unless it is the insights that can come from the introspection of self-blame or the cathartic potential of resisting blame.

The novel ends with a demolition derby, a community event that is the culmination of the county fair. As she does every year, Dolores takes Abbot to the derby. However, unlike past years when neighbours materialized immediately to assist in carrying Abbott up into the grandstand in his wheelchair, no one comes forth to help. Dolores struggles on her own until eventually a drunk Billy Ansel appears at her side and insists on helping. It is from a reluctant Billy that Dolores finds out that Nichole had lied in her deposition, testifying that Dolores had been speeding at the time the bus went off the road. When Billy tells Dolores of Nichole's lie, Dolores seeks confirmation from Billy that he knows the truth. She rejects his apologies and his sympathy but she is comforted by the knowledge that she, Billy, and Nichole know the 'truth,' or at least recognize the lie. Given this comforting affirmation, there is no blame for the lie. Dolores is grateful to Billy for telling her and she is grateful to Nichole for having done it.[65]

Dolores's reaction to the information that the whole town holds her responsible for the accident, for the death of the children, is relief and gratitude. A terrible weight has been lifted from her shoulders, and she feels strong and she feels alone.[66] A survivor of tragedy and the bearer of the burden of blame, she is completely and absolutely alone and she is at peace. She is the willing scapegoat.[67] Dolores's acceptance of blame seems to contradict her earlier anguished denial. In a perverse way, perhaps the acknowledged certainty of the lie counters her own uncertainty about her role in the accident and frees her to accept the blame, knowing that it is premised on a lie.

The demolition derby provides the townspeople with their opportunity to pass judgment on Dolores. Boomer, the car that Dolores had used decades earlier as the first school bus, had been entered in the derby by one of the men Billy Ansel employed at his garage. If the demolition derby can be seen as a modern-day jousting tournament, Boomer is Dolores's knight, her champion wearing her favours into the arena. Boomer carries the weight of the blame attributed to Dolores, and the crowd cheers wildly every time Boomer is hit by another vehicle, any other vehicle. The drivers eventually gang up on Boomer, sacrificing better opportunities in a united attack on the outcast. Sustained applause accompanies what looks like certain defeat for Boomer. But a deft move by Boomer's driver has his opponents colliding and Boomer in an advantageous position. Without hesitation, the crowd shifts allegiance and 'erupts joyously' as Boomer smashes into and eliminates the other contenders to chants of 'Boo-mer! Boo-mer! Boo-mer!'[68] Boomer is victorious; Dolores has been vindicated by her knight. Everyone in the place is happy, except Dolores, who describes herself as 'neither happy nor disappointed' but as 'utterly and permanently separated from the town of Sam Dent and all its people.'[69] But the derby and the resolution it provides are about the town more than about Dolores, and the townspeople have taken her back. They move in to help her take Abbott down the stairs when she gets up to go. The townspeople, who had initially shunned Dolores and cheered as Boomer was pummelled, are unwilling to sustain the animosity against one who is among them, who is one of them. They do not want to be stuck in the mire of blame; like Boomer they are able to work their way out of the corner into which they had backed themselves.

Blame has been assigned and mitigated. The lawsuits have ended. The town is coming back together. Billy Ansel describes Nichole as having done the town and everyone in it, including Dolores, a valuable service,[70] and this is the understanding we are left with. There has been a purgation in which emotions were vented and released. We are left with a sense of catharsis, healing, and reunification. But Dolores, who bears the blame, is forever apart from the community. Her tie to her neighbours, even though they now accept her, has been severed. Her connection is to Nichole Burnell and the dead children. That is where she finds her peace, not through blame but through shared experience. And it is the same for the townspeople: it is shared experience and shared process that gives them closure.[71] Blame has been worked through, and ultimately rejected, within and by the community affected, not by some external process; law has been circumvented; there is peace.

Blame and Law

In *The Sweet Hereafter,* the community regains itself and control over itself through the rejection of law. This issue of control, and lack of control, is a common theme in law and literature. Gretchen Craft, in her article 'The Persistence of Dread in Law and Literature,' discusses the 'mutual preoccupation'of law and literature with the fear induced by uncertainty and lack of control in our lives.[72] She describes the roles of literature and law in addressing this fear as very different, as two separate paths that may veer close to one another but never meet. According to Craft, literature provides the opportunity 'to contemplate the perils of arbitrary fate' while law provides 'the antidote to fate' through explanation and the allocation of fault. [73] 'While literature admits and examines this fear, law restrains it with a showing of illusory control.'[74] Craft discusses both the restraining role of law and the illusory nature of that restraint. From law's perspective, law dissolves ambiguities and provides certainty and clarity. 'But from another perspective, law's certainty appears a construction, imposed on elusive reality in an attempt to create order. Literature reveals what the law denies: there is no defense against the fateful tendencies of the world.'[75]

In *The Sweet Hereafter* these two perspectives do come together; literature exposes law's perception and promotion of itself as false, as damaging. *The Sweet Hereafter* depicts the underlying and omnipresent fear and desperation, the need for certainty and control that give law its power. The novel lays bare the culture of facile blame that fortifies and is fortified by law, and it unmasks the illusory nature of the resolution offered by law. It uncovers the cultural complicity that fashions blame as the placebo that both feeds the fear and invests authority in law as the cure. In *The Sweet Hereafter* one version of law and literature do meet. The novel offers a literary depiction of the issues addressed by Craft in her scholarly article.

But it is not just the critical depiction of law that is interesting in the novel; the interactive relationship between law and culture that the novel reflects, and at the same time potentially shifts, is also of interest. Robert Solomon points out in his article 'Justice and Vengeance' that 'law, like culture, shapes as well as expresses emotions.'[76] According to Solomon, 'one purpose of law is to rationalize and satisfy the most powerful social passions, to make those passions more coherent, more consistent, more articulate, more reasonable, more perspicacious, more subject to scrutiny, more civilized.'[77] This positive view of law is probably the prevailing understanding of law in contemporary western culture, according to which law tames and controls emotions that have the potential to overwhelm and to destroy. *The Sweet Hereafter* exposes this understanding of law as a fiction. With respect to blame – if you can call blame an emotion or a passion[78] – the novel depicts law, or at least the cultural perception of law, as playing almost the opposite role to that described by Solomon. In *The Sweet Hereafter,* the lawyer, Mitchell, portrays law as offering what Solomon describes as its purpose. Mitchell sells the lawsuit as the way to channel the overwhelming grief, anger, and incomprehension that follow the tragic death of one's child into a productive, meaningful process that will provide some sense of resolution and closure. But even Mitchell knows the law cannot deliver on this promise.[79] Instead, we see law fanning the flames of blame, heightening emotions, augmenting irrationality, and dividing the community. Thus the law does shape emotions as Solomon notes but by exacerbating them rather than 'civilizing' them. In *The Sweet Hereafter* we see the attempt to control and contain the emotions through a lawsuit resulting in frenzied finger pointing and blame mongering, causing further harm and injury. The attempt to control and contain emotions through law seems not only illusory but misguided. The emotions do need to be channelled; they do need an outlet, which in *The Sweet Hereafter* is provided by the demolition derby, a community ritual where irrationality and passion are given free rein in a contained setting. The communal cry of pain does not provide answers or resolution for that which is unanswerable and unresolvable, but it does provide some catharsis and allows the people of Sam Dent to come back together and to move on.

As a 'literary narrative of accident,' *The Sweet Hereafter* offers a critical view of the role of blame in law and the role of law in cultural ascriptions of blame. Nan Goodman, in her book *Shifting the Blame: Literature, Law and the Theory of Accidents in Nineteenth-Century America,* juxtaposes a history of literary narratives of accidents through nineteenth-century America with the linear trajectory of tort law through this same time period The literary narratives offer competing, multiple, and varied tales of accidents and of responses to accidents and expose the contingencies of legal history. But there is an interplay between law and literature, as there is between law and culture more generally. Goodman describes 'the modern doctrine of negligence' as having 'altered the story the culture told itself about blame and responsibility.'[80] Prior to the development of the modern doctrine of negligence, strict liability had prevailed in Anglo-American law, pursuant to which liability fell on the individual who caused the accident without any question of the individual's blameworthiness in so doing. Sometimes liability was even premised on status – such as parent or employer – rather than causation. Compensation and causation were largely the focus; blame was not an issue. But universal liability was seen as impeding progress by dampening invention and risk taking. Blame, in conjunction with the constructs of proximate cause and foreseeability, was introduced in the guise of negligence as a means of limiting liability.[81] According to legal historian Morton Horwitz, blame was invoked in order to narrow the legal focus and thus to protect the economic interests of corporations.[82] Meanwhile, society, through its literature and other cultural mediums, picked up and endorsed the concept of blame, finding therein a mechanism to provide certainty and resolution, to transform misfortune into injustice.

If one stopped at the historical moment depicted by Goodman and at Horwitz's version of the story, the lawyer Mitchell in *The Sweet Hereafter* would be a hero. He would be a Lone Ranger-type figure defending the small-town innocents from the inhumanity of corporate greed and indifference – a role that Mitchell simultaneously adopts and rejects, but one that the novel clearly denies him. There are many stirring film and literary depictions of legal heroes holding large corporations accountable for irresponsible cost-cutting measures and indifference to consumer injury.[83] But, just as the Lone Ranger has been exposed as a romantic myth rooted in racism and sexism, *The Sweet Hereafter* exposes the romanticized myth of the tort lawyer as a check on corporate greed. *The Sweet Hereafter* adds complexity and uncertainty to the questions of causation and blame, rejecting easy ascriptions. Mitchell's assumption of corporate wrongdoing is simplistic and unfounded. The lawsuit he is promoting is clearly not adequate to the task of imposing corporate moral responsibility. The novel is agnostic on the question of corporate responsibility. It is not that there was no corporate wrong doing, simply that we do not know. *The Sweet Hereafter* implies that a lawsuit may not be an effective vehicle for making that determination.[84] And the novel depicts the damage done to individuals and communities by those lawsuits and by the corrosive need to blame on which the lawsuits are premised. It is not the story of this novel to offer new ways to impose corporate accountability and morality: the story of this novel is to direct us towards new ways, other than legal blaming, to move through and beyond the grief and pain and helplessness of tragic misfortune.

Since the early days of tort law, blame has gained cultural ascendancy to the point that the contemporary cultural desire seems to be to impose a kind of strict liability in the sense of finding someone to hold responsible and then to attach blame to that person. While the law might still hold to limiting liability to negligence and might still be functioning to protect corporate interests, society is demanding, not necessarily the right to pursue protected corporate purses, but rather simply the legal right to impose blame.

Beyond Blame

The Sweet Hereafter depicts the emptiness and potential destructiveness of blame – destructive of community and of relationships and even of the self, an emptiness and destructiveness that are echoed in the *CSI* 'Chaos Theory' episode and in the tragic Saskatchewan accident. The novel opens up the possibility and the need for rethinking blame and causation. The demolition derby, a community ritual that provides an outlet for grief and anger and an opportunity for reconnection and moving forward, may be the symbol of a more positive response to a community tragedy. I read in this portrayal of a community response superseding a narrow legal response echoes of Mari Matsuda's powerful plea, in her brief commentary 'On Causation.' Matsuda argues that we need to move beyond simplistic notions of blame and individual responsibility to a more broadly collectivist understanding of causation and responsibility that incorporates both individual and social responsibility.[85] She draws her insights into the damaging effects of individualized responsibility from the description of the caustic pain experienced by an Aboriginal World War II veteran who has returned home to his reservation, a pain that seeps into and contaminates his whole community, depicted in Leslie Marmon Silko's novel *Ceremony*. Matsuda argues that a similar process of contamination infects our society through our refusal to take responsibility for the current conditions in which we live. According to Matsuda, 'a narrow understanding of causation, consequence and responsibility is killing us.'[86] The individualistic response of tort law to tragedy after tragedy – from children killing children, to black men being shot by police, to women living in constant fear of rape – compounds rather than alleviates the social harm. Matsuda does not reject assigning individual responsibility where it is warranted, but she is looking for something more fundamental and more responsive to the problem than simply whom to blame. She argues that, in addition to individual responsibility, we need a communal and connected understanding of social responsibility that recognizes that we are part of the society in which these tragedies take place and that we participate in creating the conditions that allow these tragedies to occur.[87] It is not a question of finding an individual (or even corporate) perpetrator to blame, but of taking responsibility and action ourselves.

The Sweet Herafter similarly moves away from the individualistic and narrow construction of blame provided by law to a more community-based, collective response that, as such, offers better hope for healing and [re]integration and thus better hope for our collective futures. Neither Matsuda nor Banks provides concrete suggestions for how to facilitate the shift towards social responsibility and community action, nor what that process might look like, but both poignantly depict the corrosive effects of our current overreliance on narrow legal constructs and offer inklings of the possibilities of more communal, more effective responses to social harms, misfortunes, and tragedies.

NOTES

1 Russell Banks, *The Sweet Hereafter* (New York: Harper Perennial, 1992).
2 In this role, blame becomes the stand-in for the more difficult emotions (e.g., anger, sadness and guilt) that accompany a loss. The focus is thus directed outward rather than inward.
3 Mari Matusuda, 'On Causation' (2000) 100 Col. L.R. 2195.
4 Peter Brooks, 'The Future of Confession' (2005) 1 *Law, Culture and the Humanities* 53.
5 *Ibid*. at 54.
6 *Ibid*. at 70.
7 *Ibid*. at 72.

8 Stephen Carter, 'When Victims Happen to Be Black' (1988) 97 Yale L.J. 420 at 421.
9 Judith Shklar, *The Faces of Injustice* (New Haven, CT: Yale University Press, 1990).
10 *Ibid.* at 2.
11 *Ibid.* at 50.
12 *Ibid.* at 1.
13 *Ibid.* at 5.
14 *Ibid.* at 9, definition of passive injustice at 6.
15 *Ibid.* at 14.
16 *CSI* and its multiple spin-offs, being among the most frequently watched current TV shows, would seem to provide a prime exemplar of popular culture.
17 Chaos theory is about finding the underlying order in apparently disordered, random data (http://www.imho.com/grae/chaos/chaos.html, 15/01/06) The title of the episode implicitly raises what is a theme in the novel *The Sweet Hereafter*: the question of whether there is such a thing as an accident and what we really mean when we describe something as an accident. Blame might be seen as a tool of chaos theory, that is, a means of assigning order in the face of disorder and randomness.
18 I have a mixed response to the seemingly gratuitous insertion of date rape into this plot. While it is important to portray the frequency of date rape and the heinous practice of drugging women in order to rape them, employing date rape as a plot device to augment the pool of murder suspects seems to trivialize it, even though the rape is otherwise taken seriously in the episode.
19 I could not resist giving my somewhat snide plot synopsis. In part I do this in the spirit of the culture of facile confession. I provide these details as a confession that I know all this, not just through the *CSI* web site (http://www.cbs.com/primetime/csi) – an interesting cultural experience in and of itself — but because I sometimes watch *CSI* and saw this episode. I was fascinated when I watched it by the ricocheting concept of blame employed in the face of what turns out to be an accident. And in part I provide all this *CSI* trivia because the show and all its trappings are so facile, so glibly superficial (despite the detail and precision), so scientifically, gruesomely violent, so reflective of current cultural obsessions. The *CSI* shows are part of the backdrop, or the foreground, to the culture of facile blame that I am exploring in this essay.
20 This promise of closure through blame is probably implicit in most if not all *CSI* episodes, perhaps even most police/law TV shows. The notion

becomes explicit in this 'Chaos Theory' episode, where the absence of someone to blame renders closure impossible.

21 Shklar, *supra* note 9 at 55.

22 Evidence of the apparently deep need to blame ranges from minor interpersonal interactions like spilled coffee to stories of lawsuits over falls on icy streets. In making this point, I am not taking a position in the debates over whether or not we actually have increased litigation or are living in an overly litigious time. See Austin Sarat, 'Exploring the Hidden Domains of Civil Justice: "Naming, Blaming and Claiming" in Popular Culture' (2001) 50 DePaul L.R. 425 and his earlier co-authored article, William Felstiner et al., 'The Emergence and Transformation of Disputes: Naming, Blaming and Claiming' (1980–1) 15 Law & Soc. Rev. 631, for a discussion of this question. Sarat argues that '[t]he conviction that we are a distinctively, if not uniquely, litigious society, and the legal profession shares a large share of the blame for this condition' is inaccurate and itself the creation of the media and popular culture ('Exploring the Hidden Domains of Civil Justice' at 428). My comments are directed at the central role that blame and blaming play in contemporary society and so align with Sarat's point about popular culture. But unlike Sarat, I see law, understood as the potential enforcer of blame, as a central element in this culture of facile blame, however misguided that cultural perception of law might be.

23 *Globe and Mail*, 21 May 2005, at A4.

24 *Ibid.*

25 This type of interplay and escalation between law and society, premised on an intransigent fiction relating to the curative potential of law, occurs with respect to a number of different issues. For example, in criminal law, we see a similar pattern in the continuing and intensifying cries for tougher laws and tougher sanctions, despite the strong evidence that tougher laws and tougher sanctions do not work – they do not deter would-be offenders, they do not provide greater protection, they do not rehabilitate those who commit the offences. Nonetheless, the public response, in the face of media-induced perceptions of rising crime rates, tends to be to call for more of the same, rather than to demand a new approach or at least concede to employing less of what has been shown to be ineffective. The two fictions reinforce each other: the fear of increasing crime induces the desire for tougher sanctions, and the failure of tougher sanctions to reduce crime exacerbates the fear, and so the saga continues. For a discussion of this phenomenon, see Dianne Martin, 'Retribution Revisited: A Reconsideration of Feminist Criminal Law Reform

Strategies' (1998) 36 Osgoode Hall L.J. 151. This is a criminal law version of the blame story line that I am exploring in this chapter.

26 There are a number of articles that look at *The Sweet Hereafter* from a 'law and literature' perspective, and blame is a central focus in a number of these. See Paul LeBel, 'Giving Voice to Anger: The Role of the Lawyer in *The Sweet Hereafter*,' Florida State University College of Law, Public Law, and Legal Theory Working Paper No. 76, March 2003, forthcoming in *Screening Justice: The Cinema of Law,* ed. Rennard Strickland and Teree Foster; Tony McAdams, 'Law and Film: Blame and *The Sweet Hereafter*' (1999) 24 Legal Stud. For. 599; James Olchowy, 'Russell Banks' *The Sweet Hereafter*, Legal Storytelling and ADR; Bypassing Court and Bringing the Town Back Together' (2002) 14 Windsor Rev. Legal & Social Issues 115; and Austin Sarat, 'Imagining the Law of the Father: Loss, Dread and Mourning in *The Sweet Hereafter*' (2000) 34 Law and Soc. Rev. 3 and 'Exploring the Hidden Domains of Civil Justice: "Naming, Blaming and Claiming" in Popular Culture,' *supra* note 22. Many of the ideas that I explore in this essay are echoed in these other articles, with different emphases and different directions. I find it interesting that, with the exception of James Olchowy, these authors worked with the film version of *The Sweet Hereafter,* whereas I am working with the novel. I suspect the choice to use the film reflects, among other things, a perception that films are even stronger mediums of popular culture than novels. I have not seen the film and therefore do not know if our differences in interpretation are partly due to differences between the two versions.

27 The story for *The Sweet Hereafter* was apparently drawn from a school bus accident that occurred in a small, poor, Mexican-American community in Texas in 1989. (See Tony McAdams, *ibid.*) Twenty-one of the eighty-one children on the bus were killed when the bus was hit by a soft drink delivery truck that failed to stop at a stop sign. A total of 350 law suits was brought by a wide of array of claimants, including estranged parents, witnesses, rescuers, and bystanders, as well as the driver of the delivery truck, and against a similarly wide array of defendants including not only the delivery company and driver, but the bus manufacturer for installing only a single rear exit, the town for failing to adequately barricade the pit into which the bus was pushed, and lawyers suing lawyers for stealing clients. The town was torn apart and the large monetary settlements that were paid out added to the stress and the conflict. Russell Banks's decision in *The Sweet Hereafter* to stage an accident for which there was no clear cause and for which ascription of blame was accordingly more remote allowed him and us to explore the role of blame

more fully and critically. But the analysis of the novel's story should be capable of translation to other situations where there is more clearly a party at fault and push us to question the attempt to assign blame even where we might think blame is readily apparent and appropriate. As the multitude of lawsuits in the Texas case demonstrates, the tentacles of blame can be far reaching and the resulting damage widespread.

28 The novel focuses on a single lawsuit but, as in the accident on which this novel is based, there are references to numerous lawsuits spinning wildly off the central tragedy. Billy Ansel, in his attempt to dissuade the Burnells from proceeding with their suit, warns: 'This thing is never going to go away ... We got lawyers suing lawyers ... they've even started a law suit against the school board, because they're not happy with the way they decided to use the money that got collected around town last winter ... I heard somebody wants to sue the rescue squad .... Because they supposedly didn't act fast enough. ' *Supra* note 1 at 194–5.

29 *Ibid.* at 1.

30 *Ibid.* at 79. See also 26, 73–4.

31 *Ibid.* at 92. As a believer in 'accidents,' I cannot resist Mitchell's challenge to try to explain what is meant by the word. The web-based dictionary at dictionary.reference.com provided six entries for 'accident.' Suprisingly, to me, two of the entries for 'accident' are from medical dictionaries. The law dictionary entry was surprising only in that it is the single law dictionary entry; however, other entries confirmed the legal significance of accidents by referring to possible legal relief in the face of an accident. The common characteristics in the definitions of 'accident' relate to unforeseeability, unexpectedness, chance, and absence of intent, usually but not always in relation to an event resulting in damage or injury. In addition, an accident is defined either as without apparent cause, fault, or misconduct or as resulting from carelessness, ignorance, unawareness, or a combination of causes. Presumably it is the first half of this definition that Mitchell rejects, the idea that an event that resulted in injury could occur without fault or misconduct. To him, there is always someone at fault, someone to blame. It is interesting in this context that the notion of potential fault has been absorbed into current definitions and understandings of accident, that an accident can be the result of carelessness or lack of awareness. The debate in the novel between Mitchell asserting that there are no accidents and Billy and Nichole asserting the bus accident was just an accident is a debate over blame and the [in]appropriateness of blame (*ibid.* at 181 and 186), but it is not clear whether the debate is over the appropriateness of blaming someone in the absence of fault or

of blaming someone for mere carelessness, ignorance, or unawareness. Judith Shklar's description of the distinction between misfortune as 'caused by the external forces of nature' and injustice as brought about by 'some ill-intentioned agent, human or supernatural' (*supra* note 9 at 1) does not help here as it does not address human agent[s] who may be well intentioned but at the same time careless, ignorant, or unaware, nor does it address the existence of multiple agents with complex and varied motives. Perhaps Billy and Nichole do not accept the distinction or do not see it as meaningful – an accident is just an accident.

Consistent with a footnote that commenced with acknowledging an inability to resist, I cannot resist the further digression of noting the sixth dictionary entry, which references a small town in Maryland called Accident. I am still puzzling over the meaning and intention of such a naming and its impact on the town's 345 residents, made even more intriguing when considered in conjunction with the name of its nearest neighbour, Friendsville.

32 Mitchell describes only one other event in his life as coming close to the high he gets from running a huge legal case. The comparable event was rushing Zoe, his two-year-old daughter, who had been bitten by a black widow spider, to the hospital. His wife drove while he rocked Zoe in his arms, singing to keep her calm and to slow the spread of the poison. In his pocket he clasped his Swiss army knife, blade open, ready to cut Zoe's throat if she stopped breathing. What he felt in the face of his daughter's terrifying condition and her smiling, complete trust was certainty and 'clear headed power.' He was in control: '[A]s in so many of the suits I've undertaken since, it turned out that I did not have to go so far as I was prepared to go. But this is only because I was prepared to go all the way. I was at peace with myself and the world' (*supra* note 1 at 124). But as Zoe grew up, Mitchell lost control of her and was unable to regain it, despite having in his view 'done everything the loving father of a whacked-out drug-addicted child is supposed to do, ' including Rambo-like invasions to drag her out of her filthy apartments and locking her up in varied rehab facilities (at 100). However, in our last view of Zoe, Mitchell has finally regained control and is once again feeling powerful and at peace. Zoe has phoned to tell him that she has tested HIV positive. She needs him now:

> Suddenly I was the man I had been twenty years earlier with the knife hidden in my hand, my child in my lap ...
> 'I love you, Daddy. Oh, God, I'm scared,' she sobbed.

> 'I love you too. I'll be there soon, and I'll take care of you, Zoe. No matter what happens, I'll take care of you.'
> I felt incredibly powerful at that moment, as if I had been waiting for the moment for years. (at 155 and 157)

My reading of this event differs from that of other commentators, who tend to see Mitchell sympathetically as still subject to his daughter's manipulations and struggling to do right by her even when she has so clearly rejected him. See Lebel, *supra* note 26 at 13 and Sarat, 'Imagining the Law of the Father,' *supra* note 26 at 27–9. In my reading of this relationship, Zoe rebelled against her controlling father, a father who felt exhilarated when he held her life in his hands and who seeks to replicate that high of power and control in all aspects of his life, including his relationship with his daughter. When Zoe's rebellion takes her into dangerous territory, her father tries to force her back under his authority, in highly controlling ways. He ultimately regains dominance over her when she is sick and afraid and needs him for more than his money. In the face of her vulnerability, he is once again made to feel powerful and exhilarated.

33 *Supra* note 1 at 91.
34 'Now I had to turn him [Billy Ansel] *off* me, and in such a way that no other lawyer could get to him instead. This wasn't quite ethical, of course; maybe not even moral. Necessary, however – legal triage.' *Ibid.* at 131. Here Mitchell is strategizing to keep Bill Ansel out of any of the lawsuits in order to preserve him as an impartial witness to Dolores's safe driving.
35 *Ibid.* at 97
36 *Ibid.* at 98
37 *Ibid.*
38 *Ibid.* at 91.
39 *Ibid.* at 120–1.
40 *Supra* note 9.
41 *Supra* note 1 at 105
42 *Ibid.* at 128–9; see also 106.
43 *Ibid.* at 105.
44 *Ibid.* at 98.
45 Sarat, 'Exploring the Hidden Domains of Civil Justice,' *supra* note 26.
46 Litigation seeking damages for disability induced by injury necessarily relies on and fosters ablism.
47 *Supra* note 1 at 110.

48 *Ibid.* at 173.
49 *Ibid.* at 180.
50 *Ibid.* at 167.
51 *Ibid.* at 171.
52 *Ibid.* at 181.
53 *Ibid.* at 186.
54 *Ibid.* at 181.
55 *Ibid.* at 187.
56 *Ibid.* at 216.
57 For an example of this view, see Paul LeBel's description of Mitchell Stephens as the 'astonished and clueless incidental victim of Nichole's revenge on her abusive father' (*supra* note 26 at 7).
58 *Supra* note 1 at 219.
59 *Ibid.*
60 *Ibid.* at 143.
61 *Ibid.* at 143–4.
62 *Ibid.* at 146.
63 *Ibid.* at 151
64 *Ibid.* at 150.
65 *Ibid.* at 248.
66 *Ibid.*
67 Judith Shklar notes that self-blame may be preferable to arbitrariness. 'Even blaming oneself is more tolerable than folding up in front of so absurd a life'(*supra* note 9 at 5). 'We often blame ourselves without grounds, simply because an arbitrary and wholly impersonal world seems harder to endure than an unjust one in which some force, at the very least, is in charge of events' (at 54). Perhaps Dolores is able to accept the blame because she comes to know that she is not to blame.
68 *Supra* note 1 at 253.
69 *Ibid.*
70 *Ibid.* at 244.
71 In comments on this chapter, one of the reviewers who assessed this book for publication expressed a very different reading of the derby and of the role Dolores plays in the novel: 'I find the characterization of Dolores in Banks's novel troubling and ambiguous. The collective act of scapegoating is but a symbolic collective act of murderous destruction that, as the essay shows, eschews collective responsibility, and I am wondering to what extent it could be argued that in some respect the law regulates and rationalizes this collective violence. This would explain the ever-renewed expectation and demand that justice be made and the per-

petrators punished.' This comment gave me much pause for thought, rekindling a lurking fear that my personal preference for community self-healing had led me to simplistically read the demolition derby as collective catharsis rather than vicious scapegoating. However, after a thoughtful pause, I remain unconvinced that the derby represents murderous destruction that needs containment through law. Despite my discomfort with the role of catharsis symbolically being assigned to a *demolition* derby and my question as to what would have happened if Boomer had been defeated, I do read the derby as a process that shifts the community from the blame and the scapegoating induced by Nichole's necessary lie, to acceptance and reintegration. It is a summer fair, a community event, and, in the end, Dolores and the community are at peace. In this situation, there are no perpetrators to be punished and collective responsibility is ultimately directed towards the community and each other. In the novel, law does not play the role of justice but is a destructive force that divides and disrupts the community in hugely damaging ways. The fair derby brings them back together.

72 Gretchen Craft, 'The Persistence of Dread in Law and Literature' (1992) 102 Yale L.J. 521.

73 *Ibid.* at 522–3.

74 *Ibid.* at 546.

75 *Ibid.* at 523.

76 Robert Solomon, 'Justice and Vengeance,' in *The Passions of Law*, ed. Susan Bandes (New York: New York University Press, 1999), 123 at 129.

77 *Ibid.* This view of law accords with the role that the reviewer of this chapter saw law needing to play – to contain the murderous destruction reflected in the demolition derby in *The Sweet Hereafter*. *Supra* note 71.

78 If blame is not an emotion, it is certainly very connected to emotions – anger, sadness, and fear among them.

79 Nan Goodman, *Shifting the Blame: Literature, Law and the Theory of Accidents in Nineteenth-Century America* (Princeton: Princeton University Press, 1998).

80 *Ibid.* at 4.

81 *Ibid.* at 4–5.

82 *Ibid.* at 8.

83 For example, *A Civil Action*, directed and written by Steven Zaillian, book by Jonathan Harr (Touchstone Pictures, 1998) and *Erin Brockovich*, directed by Steven Soderbergh, written by Susannah Grant (Jersey Films, 2000).

84 The limitations placed on corporate liability for the injuries and damage

they cause are a major and growing problem in a world dominated by large, multinational corporations. But it is far from clear that the solution to this problem would lie in re-extending liability in actions that tie up both parties in endless legal wranglings and with dubious and, dare I say it, uncertain outcomes. There need to be innovative and effective methods for holding these corporations responsible and accountable that do not rely upon individual, or even class-action, plaintiffs.

85 *Supra* note 3.

86 *Ibid.* at 2197.

87 Judith Butler, in her book *Precarious Life: The Powers of Mourning and Violence* (New York: Verso, 2004), argues for a similar lesson of widespread social responsibility to be learned from the tragic violence of 9/11. Thanks to Dianne George for drawing this interesting connection to Butler's work to my attention.

10 'Our Woe ... Our Great Distress': Law, Literature, and Suffering during the Great Plague of London, 1665

LOGAN ATKINSON

Introduction

The seventeenth century was probably the most tumultuous in English history since the Norman Conquest. Opening with the ascension of the Stuarts, continuing with the constitutional crises of mid-century, shocked by the execution of Charles I and the rule of Oliver Cromwell, apparently stabilized by the Restoration, shaken by the religious uncertainty of the reign of James II and the anticipated succession crisis, and then punctuated by the Glorious Revolution of 1688 – the seventeenth century presented a terrible mixture of confusion, trauma, and bloodshed for the people of England.

As is often the case, it was an unfortunate coincidence of history that with political upheaval came natural crises, too. On many occasions in the years prior to 1665, epidemic disease threatened England's very way of life. Thousands upon thousands of deaths were the result,[1] forcing wholesale adjustments in both commercial and ordinary social life, and deflecting scarce resources away from the basic practices of staying alert and alive in the face of fundamental tensions and uncertainty. The virtually continuous and always unfathomable threat of lethal disease challenged conventional individual and collective strategies of defiance/conformity and survival/surrender, strategies helpful when religious and political allegiances were in issue, but of doubtful efficacy during times of epidemic.

Nevertheless, it was to law, the conventional official response to social and political upheaval, that authorities turned in the attempt to control the spread of disease and the choices of the population during particularly difficult experiences with epidemics. Substantive legal provisions began with the Act of James I in 1603, and then continued with a succession of orders of the Privy Council, local authorities, and justices of the peace, such that by the time Londoners began to recover from the Great Plague in 1666 the English had in place a fairly rigorous regulatory framework for controlling imports and exports, quarantining new arrivals and their goods, isolating and stigmatizing whole families in their homes, and ultimately separating the sick from the well through the establishment of lazarettos.[2]

The wisdom of this regulatory regime was always in doubt. The science of the day was just too uncertain to give any real assurances on the most efficacious legal response, and opinions among medical experts differed dramatically. Some believed that the plague was contagious, transferred directly through person-to-person contact. Others insisted that the plague was infectious, miasmatic, inhabiting the air and impossible to avoid. Belief in one or the other of these explanations had direct application in design of the legal response.

Because of the uncertain value of many legal measures routinely implemented both as prophylaxis and in response to disease, legal authorities suffered a great deal of criticism from intellectuals concerned with the social impact of law. From some quarters came complaints about the abridgment of basic freedoms such as mobility and association. Curtailments in these respects interfered directly with ordinary commercial intercourse, and the argument was that such interference could not be in the public best interest, despite the threat such curtailments were intended to address. From medical professionals we find the debate over miasma and contagion emerging with full force in strident criticism of regulatory initiatives, each side screaming their understanding of the aetiology of plague so as to persuade decisionmakers and the public to a reformed legal framework. From clerics we find equally deep divisions. For some, the plague was divine judgment for earthly transgressions, impossible to resist, uncontrollable, awesome. These opinions scoffed at official attempts to erect instruments of mere temporal control in the path of divine reprobation. For other clerics, a greater sympathy emerged for the struggling enforcement authorities, by which an attempt was made to balance temporal public responsibility and the exigencies of spiritual reconciliation.

Textual evidence of each of these perspectives emerges in speeches, sermons, poems, polemical tracts, pamphlets, treatises – literature that together allows us to experience the social impact of law through voices only occasionally heard in the historical assessment of law and legal process. For the purposes of this chapter, this extralegal textual evidence of law functions in two related ways. First, it stands at times in opposition to, and then at times in congruence with, the dominant political and regulatory discourse of the day. But it is largely independent of that dominant discourse, demonstrating an early example of the emergence of a 'public sphere that functioned in the political realm,' as discussed by Jürgen Habermas.[3] According to Habermas, a public sphere separate from the political sphere that had dominated polemical writing for most of the seventeenth century had to await the 1695 expiration of the Licensing Act of 1662 (and certain early-eighteenth-century developments) before gaining the social space necessary to begin to grow and attract attention.[4] However, in the polemical literature of the Great Plague of 1665, we find a discourse driven by normative frameworks in medicine and theology that did not in turn rely for their promotion on narrow political approbation. This is so, despite the occasional support offered up in these texts for the dominant political approach to the employment of law for prophylactic purposes. In certain of these texts we find authors condemning the methods of lawmakers, criticizing enforcement mechanisms, and generally denouncing the law for its inefficacy. In other texts we find at least cautious support for the efforts of those with supervisory and regulatory responsibility. But in every case it seems that such condemnation or support emanates from a world view informed by considerations that have little or nothing to do with the achievement of the public good as defined in the halls of legal power and uncritically supported through managed debate. In particular, this body of literature functions as a counter-discourse to the dominant regulatory discourse intended to compel individual compliance for the good of the whole. It brings forward the intellectual response to law, sometimes as a counterstroke to the persuasive effect of the dominant discourse, thirty years prior to the defining moment in the emergence of the public sphere identified by Habermas.

In effect, the emergence of the theological and medical discourses about the state's legal response to the Great Plague reflects a continuation of the impulse to propaganda explored so thoroughly by Jason Peacey in his study of the polemics of the mid-seventeenth century.[5] According to Peacey, many motivations functioned to stimulate the production of polemical works, including of course the demands of political patronage. But in addition, men of letters worked to articulate their particular individual positions on the nature of the public good, oftentimes publishing their opinions independently, and regularly assuming a political stance inconsistent with officially sanctioned rhetoric. As Peacey wrote, 'in times of heightened political tension, writers turned [their] selflessness to the advantage of particular groups in society, whether sectional interest groups or political and religious causes.'[6] In other words, writers had causes independent of official causes, and they were sufficient to compel the production of literature that had the potential to undermine prevailing regulatory strategies.

For the purposes of this chapter, there is a second function performed by this collection of literature. The historical coincidence of the dominant regulatory discourse of parliaments and enforcement authorities with the often subversive counter-discourses of theology and medicine allows us to deepen our appreciation for both the general social context in which the law of public health protection was employed, and the inescapable specific context of human suffering raised by the collision of disease and tough law. Our experience of each discursive element informs our experience of the other(s); we examine the historical efficacy of law through lenses coloured by theories of contagion, the lingering subversive appeal of antinomianism, the language of Christian resignation, and an overarching sense of futility. Experienced together, these discourses stimulate a wide range of questions about the social nature of law, largely driven by our problems of interpretation positioned against the political and social uncertainties out of which the discourses emerged.

Yet despite uncertainties respecting the historicity of particular perspectives emerging here, there can be little doubt about the reality of human suffering that, in large part, appears to have motivated the production of this literature. This reality is consistently portrayed, undeniable and fundamental. It is the repository of truth in the investigation of the historical relationship between law and medicine, and law and theology, during this period of epidemic disease. It brings forward 'our woe ... our great distress,'[7] the reality of individual and collective suffering, as the dominant element by which we make connections in our attempt at a more contextualized understanding of law and legal process in history. As represented in the literature to be reviewed in this chapter, suffering captures law. Suffering turns law to its own advantage, co-opting it, reducing law to the level of disease as a participant in generating the miserable conditions of the sick.

In the balance of this chapter, I will investigate the literary representation of law as an appropriated participant in suffering during the

Great Plague of London. As we shall see, while the suffering of plague victims is poignantly presented in the literature, there is nevertheless a palpable tension at work between different interpretations of the significance of law, that is, between the urgency of law on the one hand, and the futility of law on the other. In both cases, however, suffering becomes the only historical certainty as law and disease collide to work out their strange partnership. The understanding of law's participation in suffering revealed through this literature is quite different from the ordinary historical focus on the use of law as a tool of retribution, as an instrument by which suffering is inflicted for socio-political purposes, conventionally in the criminal law.[8] Rather, we find in the literature an early modern attempt to work out the justice of law's engagement with disease, whether through approbation or condemnation of law's involvement. Consistent with the theory of suffering advanced by Joseph Amato,[9] the literature reveals a mid-seventeenth-century cultural representation of suffering that struggles to understand law's participation in, and perhaps exacerbation of, the suffering and sacrifice that ultimately lead to death.

For Amato, pain, suffering, and sacrifice are separate but related phenomena of cultural history. Pain, he suggests, is the province of medicine and magic, while suffering attracts religion and philosophy. Suffering captures the entire being, while pain is merely of the body. In medicine, pain is to be treated, managed, cured; in religion, suffering is to be endured, and then ennobled by reference to its apparent incomprehensibility and occasional connection to the possibility of salvation.[10] But to be consistently represented at particular historical moments, both pain and suffering must be either rationally explained or at least justifiable (and perhaps reducible) by reference to the service of some larger good. In the case of disease-induced pain, scientific rationales satisfy the urge to explanation. In the case of the suffering that overwhelms the sick during particularly devastating visitations of disease, justification comes in the form of either an experience prerequisite to salvation, or in connection with the sacrifice of a particular individual for the sake of the wider community.

The collaboration of law with disease as portrayed in certain of the literature of the Great Plague is disruptive of cultural understandings of suffering and sacrifice. As Amato points out, 'resistant to our attempts to articulate an understanding of suffering is the degree to which certain forms of suffering appear absolutely senseless. They defy not only our calculations and sense of meaning, but negate all purpose and justice themselves.'[11] The injustice of law that separates family members from each other, that stigmatizes the sick, that punishes those who have committed no voluntary or reckless act, ultimately disturbs the rituals of suffering and death on which theological justifications and understandings of suffering and sacrifice are built. The decision as to what counts as suffering is culturally contrived, according to Amato, and suffering is then dissected as noble, or vain, or purposeless.[12] But at the height of the social crisis that was the plague, that dissection was necessarily informed by either the needs of the community, the perceived self-indulgence of the sufferer, or the absence of temporal explanation. At least to the extent that law was ineffective in controlling the spread of disease, or perhaps only minimally successful in that respect, law's contribution to suffering defeated such analysis. It represented a direct human interference with the cultural understanding of suffering and sacrifice on which contemporary rituals were built. As a result, its justice was always in issue.

Representations of Law during the Great Plague[13]

The literature of the Great Plague can conveniently be divided into two groups, the first supportive of or indifferent to the effect of law, and the second critical of the law's enforcement. In both cases, however, the authors' voices are quite distinct from the official voices belonging to those responsible for the design, passage, and enforcement of the law, and that fact makes their record valuable in our attempt to expand on the history of the law that emerges through a review of doctrine. There is little doubt that the voices we hear in listening to this literature are independent of the dominant political voices, primarily because they draw to a large extent on norms prevailing in medicine and theology that are distinct from the requirements of politics and state law. They are motivated by the immediacy of healing or salvation, and not so much by the political exigencies connected to the urgent preservation of community health and commercial viability, even at the expense of individual life and liberty.

Therefore, we see Jason Peacey's arguments on the motivations for the production of counter-discourse in the mid-seventeenth century confirmed in part in this literature. Even in cases where approval of the legal regime is explicit, that approval is informed by considerations of individual sacrifice or salvation, through medical and theological frameworks, elements not ordinarily considered during the urgency of implementing law for the control of epidemic disease. As a result, Peacey's observation that intellectuals regularly advanced perspectives on the nature of the public good independent of dominant political perspectives, oftentimes to advance the causes of the particularly oppressed, is supported here. At the same time, however, these perspectives do not necessarily emerge from contrary views raised to challenge the dominant discourse on political grounds, but rather from apparently apolitical medical and theological world views. Each of the authors brought to their writing an intellectual or professional predisposition, whether the inflexibility of seventeenth-century theology or the emerging professionalism of medicine and the related 'arts.' It was in the service of their particular intellectual affiliation, and their understanding of their relationship to the sufferer, that the authors advanced their arguments for or against the design and implementation of the prevailing law, which, from the perspectives of both theology and medicine, could only have been seen as the feeble human response to a powerful metaphysical or natural force. Despite its weakness in dealing with the plague as either a divinely ordained or incomparable natural phenomenon, the law was found deserving of comment, primarily because its application did result in profound implications for ordinary life.

These observations on the production of discourse and counter-discourse led to a recognition of the diseased body as a site of contestation not simply in the practical world of the application of efficacious regulatory power, but rather in the larger conceptual struggle over both the articulation of the relationship between self and community, and the emergence of specific knowledge bases in the mid-seventeenth century. As Foucault pointed out, 'discourse can be both an instrument and an effect of power, but also a hindrance, a stumbling block, a point of resistance and a starting point for an opposing strategy.'[14] The production of counter-discourse at the height of the Great Plague did not depend on political and legal discourse for anything but motivation, drawing on a range of assumptions and arguments assembled to contradict and ultimately disrupt official dominance. Principally, the motivation at work was entangled with established and widely shared understandings of suffering, and the mandate was to restore power over that knowledge to theological and medical discourses. The arbitrariness of law as an instrument of power was thus exposed.

Among those supportive of the design and implementation of law, we can begin with theologian Richard Kephale, author of *Medela Pesti-*

lentiae.[15] Publishing in dialogic style at the height of the Great Plague, Kephale arranged a series of supposed frequently asked questions about plague, and then offered up his answers and observations. Even in the way Kephale framed certain of the questions, it is evident that he draws on his theological orientation to establish a direct connection between the legitimacy of temporal law and God's intervention in human affairs: 'Quest.: What good orders God hath been pleased to blesse, either for the preventing, or, allaying of the Plague, in the fatal years, 1603, 1609, 1625, 1636, and are fit to bee observed by all good people at this time[?]'[16] There is nothing in Kephale's work to suggest that the 'orders' to which he refers are 'good' and 'are fit to bee observed by all good people at this time' except by virtue of their presumed connection to God's blessing. He mentions nothing about their effectiveness in dealing with the plague, in the question mentioning only that they were designed to prevent or allay the disease. While there was important extant opinion that the law's effectiveness was at minimum suspect, and perhaps even harmful, Kephale seems free to endorse the law simply because of its connection to God, irrespective of impact. He follows the question quoted above with a minute examination and then endorsement of every aspect of the central municipal order of the day.[17] Kephale's response to the question, meanwhile, was framed in the context of historical precedent, appealing to his readers' combined faith in God and tradition to rally support for the law. His prose reads as if he were describing a successful legal intervention of years past, an intervention to be supported both for that apparent success and because of its divine ordination. The success of the historical legal orders, however, is merely implicit in *Medela Pestilentiae*, arising out of the assumptions underlying the very way in which Kephale posed his question. He offered no evidence of *actual* success or failure.

Kephale continued this rhetorical technique later in the book when he considered the advisability of fleeing into the country to escape the disease. Kephale's basic position was that escape from London was acceptable so long as honour and the absence of commitment to others permitted it.[18] But this position ran afoul of the opinions of other contemporary theologians who argued that, because our fates are predetermined by an interventionist God, the question of running away or remaining in London was irrelevant. Flight was neither condemned nor supported, such that many succumbed to temptation and ran, irrespective of consideration for others. To counter this argument, Kephale simply recited the law,[19] an order of James I by which those who preached the counter-argument were to be punished by their ecclesiastical superiors, or, in the case of lay preachers, through imprisonment. For Kephale at least, this historical legal precedent, which, after all, had been 'blessed by God,' was enough to overcome his detractors. It was God's blessing, then, that settled the argument, as that blessing had been captured in temporal law.

Kephale was not alone in looking to the law as authority for the way to behave during the plague. But while Kephale considered law's authority as connected to divine approbation, William Kemp looked at obedience as a component of good citizenship. Kemp provided a very stern response to those who would dare defy the law of quarantine, appealing to their character as English citizens in arguing for compliance. 'But would one think there should be any such in England, that in opposition to the good Orders of the Magistrates, and without any regard to their own safety, or the lives of their Families, their Children, Neighbours, Friends and Acquaintance, and all with whom they have to do or come a-near, should not refrain the conversation of the Sick, and coming into infected places, when they have no necessary occasion, that calls them thereunto.'[20] To behave in opposition to the law is not consistent with being English, according to Kemp, such behaviour representing not just unlawfulness, but disregard for the commitment to family and friends that helps to define good citizenship. Kemp's ridicule of the lawbreaker extended, perhaps with more vehemence, to those who disputed the law's effectiveness simply by arguing from experience. Whereas the law of quarantine was based on the assumption that the plague was contagious, and so spread from person to person, many physicians argued that this assumption was in error, proven to be so by virtue of the fact that many healthy physicians and others working with the sick never actually contracted the disease themselves. For Kemp, such an argument defied all that it meant to be English, and was worthy of nothing but contempt. Those who advance the position '[were] middle-witted persons and diseased in the pate, and [were] as fit for a Pest-House as a mad man is for Bethlem; and the proper way to confute them is not with discourse or reason, but with a Padlock and a Watch-man.'[21]

From the treatises left by Kephale and Kemp, a picture of the law of quarantine starts to emerge that positions commitment to the law alongside commitment to God and country. Arguments supporting challenges to the law were overcome simply by reference to the law's tradition or its divine approbation; threats to the force of law were usurped by appeals to the ideals of family and responsibility. For these authors at least, the effectiveness and sanctions of the law, and its inherent coercive power, seemed to carry little persuasive force.

It is important to note, however, that, especially in the case of Kemp, the endorsement of the legal regime was not tied to the autonomy of the law as an inherently just institution, and therefore deserving of individual submission. Perhaps paradoxically, given his contempt for those who would challenge the foundations of law, Kemp insisted that whatever suffering might result from strict obedience to the law was nothing as compared to the tortures to be experienced by those who would defy God:

> What is a burning Fever to the Flames of Hell Fire? To be shut up for a Moneth in your own Habitation, or a Pest-House, and there to be vexed with the Impertinencies of Nurses, the Directions of Doctors, and Operation of Chirurgeons, for a few dayes, in comparison of being imprisoned and tormented with the Devil and his angels in the Lake of Fire and Brimstone for evermore? Is not the loss of Gods Favour more than the lack of Trade, or separation of Friends? ... Why doth the living man complain that suffereth for his sin? Any thing on this side Hell is mercy.[22]

Despite the vitriolic tone of this excerpt, there is at least tacit acknowledgment that aspects of the law of quarantine led to suffering of a sort among the people. But, perhaps in an appeal to Londoners' 'stiff upper lip,' Kemp reminded his readership that earthly torment, no matter how severe, and no matter that it arose through the application of a harsh law, could not compare to the torment that each of them deserved for their sins. The law, as such, was but part of a merciful judgment.

Kemp's insistence that the grief associated with the law of quarantine was nothing compared to the grief of eternal damnation was echoed by another preacher, Matthew Mead, in his short work *Solomon's Prescription for the Removal of the Pestilence*.[23] Even in historical perspective, this work is stunning in its lack of compassion, perhaps the most insistent ministerial harangue of any of the works reviewed for this chapter. The standard symbols of the combined horror of plague and confinement were belittled by Mead as nothing compared to the actual torment to be suffered for the sins of this world: 'Poor stupid sinner, then thou wast stabbing and destroying thy self, then thou wast seiz'd with the most deadly infection. Then had it been no uncharitableness nor absurdity, to have set a *Lord have Mercy upon me* in Capital Letters, on thy forehead; yea, wise and holy men saw it there in that wickedness that broke out in thy life, and look't upon thee as fitter for a Pesthouse, than converse.'[24] Mead is berating those who would complain about the severity of the law in confining them in their misery, when by the sinful actions through which they contracted the disease that led to their confinement they incurred the sanction of a higher and more awful law. How is it that sinners can complain about the 'uncharitableness' and 'absurdity' of temporal law, when those same sinners voluntarily acted in ways that brought the full force of divine law upon them? For Mead, the sick were architects of their own misfortune, and were themselves absurd to complain: 'Then thou wilt confess, that to be shut up from the society of men, hath nothing of dolefulness in it, compar'd to thy being shut up under the burning wrath of an unreconciled God. Then at length, whether thou wilt or no, thou shalt see sin, and cry out of sin, and acknowledge 'tis thy sin that hath ruin'd thee.[25]

Certainly for Mead, and to a lesser extent for Kemp, the law as represented in municipal orders respecting forced confinement, separation from family, and other aspects of quarantine was irrelevant to the larger questions of the role of sin in bringing forth the plague and the need for reconciliation with God as the path leading to release from the suffering of which everyone complained. They wrote from an assumed higher moral ground than that apparently occupied by their readership, and at that higher level temporal concerns had relevance only to the extent they contributed to or detracted from the possibility of eternal salvation. 'Any thing on this side Hell is mercy,' wrote Kemp, meaning that nothing experienced in this life, including the force of an arguably harsh law of confinement, is worthy of complaint. Rather, even the misery of the plague and the disruptions to ordinary life imposed by the law and its consequences were to be understood as an expression of God's mercy.

The lack of empathy for the sick and confined is astonishing in the work of Matthew Mead, and it is important to note that his polemics, informed by theological assumptions that relate to temporal law only through their insistence on transcendence, appear intended to stimulate a fear in the reader that surpasses the isolation imposed by law and the suffering experienced through sickness. From this perspective, submission to the law is quite irrelevant, and succumbing to the disease is nothing more than being swept along by God's plan. For Mead and the others, it becomes a question of the spiritual legitimacy of suffering and fear, the choice between deserved punishment (represented by the experience of harsh law and the threat of death by plague) meted out by a just God on the one hand, and confession and reconciliation on the other. The coercive potential of law is undermined as a result, the motivation for this rhetorical strategy being the urge to persuade transcendence of the complaints of the mere body.

The relationship between suffering, disease, and law is perhaps more central in works through which authors expressed sympathy for the sick and challenged legal authorities to alleviate that suffering through regulatory reform. Generally speaking, clerics and medical men who contested the wisdom of the law respecting disease control were quite systematic in their description of the law, making it their prime focus in at least sections of works devoted in the main to describing the effects of the disease. This is especially the case in the treatises of Thomas Cock,[26] William Boghurst,[27] and John Gadbury,[28] each of which contained long sections complaining about the inhumanity of the shutting up of houses in particular, and of other aspects of the law as well. Cock and Boghurst were well-known medical men, and Gadbury was an astrologer and 'man of God.'

Two other works with relevance to this section of the chapter, those by Richard Kingston[29] and Thomas Vincent,[30] are not so thorough in their reflections on the law, and I will consider them first. Both Kingston and Vincent were prominent preachers, and the sympathy they expressed for the poor during the time of the epidemic distinguishes them quite clearly from other contemporary clerics.[31] Kingston, for example, provided his readers with a relatively dispassionate and prosaic account of the role of sin in contributing to the severity of the plague, but interspersed throughout the otherwise dry text are short poetic verses, set apart through the use of italics, that describe Kingston's understanding of the terrible suffering experienced by the people. It is in these verses that Kingston mentions the law, referring to certain aspects of London's municipal orders in an attempt to describe the disruption to ordinary life that accompanied the plague:

No Paper then over our Dores were set
With Chambers ready furnish'd to be Let;
But a sad *Lord have mercy upon us*, and

A Bloody *Cross*, as fatal marks did stand
Presaging th' noisome *Pestilence* within,
Was come to take revenge of us for Sin.[32]

Kingston leaves little doubt as to his association of the law of the shutting up of houses with other miserable consequences of the plague. He describes the plight of the people with a tone of resignation, a sadness that, for the most part, escapes many of his contemporaries. For Kingston, law is a contributing factor in that mood, its marks upon infected houses acting as portents of death.

Thomas Vincent's prose is perhaps the most accomplished, in the sense of its technical and aesthetic qualities, of any of the works reviewed for this chapter. As was the case with Kingston, Vincent understood that the suffering of the poor was overwhelming, despite the fact that, in the author's assessment, they brought it on themselves through their sinful behaviour. But Vincent took his description of the impact of the plague to a different plane, concentrating in large measure on the psychological consequences of the disease and the attempts to control it through the law of quarantine. Certainly, at least among those preachers who left written record of their experiences during 1665, Vincent is alone in identifying and sympathizing with the enormous stresses placed on ordinary people as a result of the restrictions suffered under the law, and he seems to have a particular understanding of the changes undergone in citizens' states of mind: 'Now many houses are shut up where the Plague comes, and the inhabitants shut in, lest coming abroad they should spread infection. It was very dismal to behold the Red Crosses, and read in Great Leter LORD HAVE MERCY UPON US on the doors, and Watchmen standing before them with Halberds, and such a solitude about those places, and the people passing by them so gingerly, and with such fearful looks, as if they had been lined with Enemies in ambush, that waited to destroy them.'[33] Here we have a beautifully constructed vision of the impact of the orders of the London Municipal Council, the pall that was cast both within and without an infected house by the markings of the law, the stigma that was attached to the realization that the inmates of the house were confronting together the plague, the law, and all the horrors that accompanied them. The consequences of the law were 'dismal'; they stood for 'solitude'; they provoked fear and thoughts of personal destruction. And here we find the only reference anywhere in the literature to the watchmen carrying arms, the halberd, that particularly dreadful axe and spear combination that must have served the watchmen in gaining access to locked-up houses, in subduing the residents in times of especial distress, and, of course, in self-protection.

Vincent's concern with the psychological impact of the plague and the legal measures that were used to confront the disease permeates his book, a preoccupation that emerges with more or less clarity depending on the author's particular focus. Later in the book, Vincent repeats his claim that the practice of the shutting up of houses evoked fear in the residents, causing many to abandon their homes in advance rather than wait for the compulsion of the law:

> Now most parishes are infected both without and within; yet there are not so many houses shut up by the Plague, as by the owners forsaking of them for fear of it; and though the Inhabitants be so exceedingly decreased by the departure of so many thousands, the number of dying persons encreaseth fearfully ... & the Serjeant Death hath arrested them, and clapt to the doors of the Houses upon them, from whence they have come forth no more, till they have been brought forth to their Graves: We may imagine the hideous thoughts, and horrid perplexity of mind, the tremblings, confusions, and anguish of spirit.[34]

In these lines, Vincent treats the law as the awful companion of the plague, the symbol of death, the instrument of confinement that helped to drive people away from their dwellings by the thousands. It was through the force of the law that the sick and the members of their families were abandoned to their isolation, left to suffer in solitude both the physical ravages of the disease and the mental strain of fear and seclusion. And Vincent, alone among the authors surveyed for this chapter, recognized the disruption that the shutting up of houses imposed on otherwise ordinary relationships, inserting a barrier between the confined and the free: '[W]hen their doors have been shut up and fastned on the outside with an Inscription, *Lord have mercy upon us*, and none suffered to come in but a Nurse, whom they have been more afraid of, than the Plague itself; when Lovers and Friends, and Companions in sin have stood aloof, and not dared to come nigh the door of the House, lest death should issue forth from thence upon them.'[35] Vincent presents a horrible vision of fear and anxiety, a picture of the ways in which the legal measures imposed by the London Municipal Council, in combination with the dread of the plague itself, affected the lives of the common people. But while he is quite unique among preachers in understanding the combined psychological impact of the plague and the law of quarantine, he does return to the standard ministerial refrain, that those who were fortunate enough to escape the horror should count themselves among the blessed, and should take the opportunity to reform their otherwise sinful lives in case they were put to the test again. Yet in this more reflective writing, Vincent does not miss the opportunity to define the suffering of the afflicted by reference to both disease and tough law:

> Think with your selves, you that are alive, and remain escaped; how fearful would the Plague have been, if it had come home to your houses: you were afraid to hear of others houses visited and shut up; what would you have been, if it had entred your doors? You were afraid when others were struck with the disease, what would you have been, if you had been struck your selves? Sinners, what would you have done if the arrow had pierced through your Livers, if under such guilt and wrath you had been smitted? When you had such a plague of sin in yoar hearts, if you should have had the Plague of Pestilence in your bodies; if when you were so rotten and corrupt and defiled inwardly, you should have had boyls, and blanes, and running sores outwardly.[36]

Vincent's rhetorical technique is obvious, combining a sympathetic and graphic account of the horrors of the plague with an admonitory plea to survivors of the epidemic to repent and reform so as to avoid a similar fate. For Vincent, the law was an element of the horror, a collaborator with disease to generate the conditions of suffering, another aspect of the terrible judgment against which his readers might protect themselves through reconciliation with God.

While both Vincent and Kingston understood the plight of those who experienced the law of quarantine first-hand, and expressed considerable sympathy for their predicament, neither writer explicitly recognized that the law, as a contributor to that plight, was actually in the control of legislators and other officials, and, as a result, was not an inevitable consequence of God's judgment, even if it were true that the plague itself was a product of sinful lives. Vincent and Kingston did not weigh into their thoughts the effectiveness of the law in dealing with the disease, but rather chose to concentrate on its impact on other aspects of their readers' lives. This is especially true of Vincent, given his preoccupation with the psychological impact of the plague and quarantine.

Such is not the case, however, with the work of Thomas Cock.[37]His book, *Hygiene, or a Discourse upon Air*, included in its preface (called 'A Peroration to the Right Hounourable the Lord Maior, with the Right Worshipful the Aldermen his Brethren in general; and all the worthy Members of it In Particular') a direct appeal to responsible officials. This was an impassioned plea to reform the law of quarantine and to lobby for the repeal of King James's Act, advanced by a physician who drew upon his experience with the sick to argue for the ineffectiveness of the law as represented in the terms of the various municipal quarantine orders. But despite its tone of urgency, Cock's work appears perfectly logical and rational, an appeal to the officials' sense of the contingencies of history which, when coupled with the unfortunate consequences of the law, made a compelling case for repeal of the legislation.

Cock began by arguing that when King James's Act was first debated in 1603, the choice facing the legislators was between the shutting up of houses on the one hand, and separating the sick from the well on the other.[38] In Cock's argument, King James's Act was passed and promulgated while the memory of the plague of 1603 was still very fresh, such that Parliament decided on the shutting up of houses as the appropriate remedy only reluctantly, and because of the immediacy of the danger. Otherwise, argued Cock, the preferred alternative, separating the sick to isolated locations, would have prevailed in debate. Cock suggested that the error was recognized in later years, even during the then current reign of Charles II, when 'the Lords of his Privie-Council' were appointed as 'a Committee for Inspection, into what was most expedient and proper, for the preventing, spreading and increase of this Plague,'[39] Cock's suggestion being that the ineffectiveness of King James's Act was at least tacitly recognized through the establishment of this committee. But then, as Cock reported, the Lords delegated their responsibility to the College of Physicians, and, in doing so, removed the possibility of corrective legal measures. 'Their Lordships accordingly required the Honorable and Learned Colledge of Physitians to 'Add, alter, and ordain as they should find the present times and occasion to require: But still with this Restriction, *viz. In pursuance of former Presidents in the Reign,'* &c. Or else, surely it would have been thought on as a thing most eligible to have caus'd a Separation of the Well and Sick, (which cannot but be acknowledg'd as necessary as water to quench fire) but yet by such proper aids and helps as might best answer its end and Intention.'[40] The College of Physicians, as a result, was forced to continue with the practice of the shutting up of houses, not because it was the most expedient means of dealing with the plague, but because it was the only method available, given historical and legal precedent.

Cock goes on to advance his argument for abandoning the historical practice and for substituting what he calls a middle ground between shutting up the well with the sick, and letting the infected run free in the streets. This middle ground, he wrote, involves removing the sick to isolation, away from the healthy population. He admitted that the shutting up of houses had many good arguments in its favour (though he failed to suggest what those arguments were), but insisted that the practice contributed just as much to the spread of the disease (and therefore the suffering of the afflicted) as did letting the infected people run free. In Cock's opinion, those who survived the experience in a shut-up house were actually more likely to succumb to the disease later on, due to their weakened condition, and then suggested that the greatest plagues in London's history were those in which the shutting up of houses was employed most insistently. For all these reasons, he argued, a reform of the law was needed.[41]

Cock's sensitivity to the persuasive authority of history continued in his reliance on examples from the reign of Charles I. He cited to the mayor and aldermen evidence from a great plague during that reign[42] in which he suggested that the mortality rate actually declined when people were separated rather than shut up. This was the case, he argued, for both the sick and the well, meaning that the law of quarantine represented in King James's Act and the various orders of London's municipal authority contributed to a high mortality rate for all residents of the city. The reason, according to Cock, was 'imputed to their freedom of Airing, Walking, Recreating, and refreshing of themselves by an honest and free Conversation one with another,' and, instead of the visits of medical personnel encouraging anxiety and symbolizing impending death, 'they had the voluntary, free and frequent Visits of the best and most able Physitians, Chirurgeons, and Apothecaries, little hazard by this means attending their Cures: the dejection, horror, fear, and consternation of their Spirits (great Incendiaries and Promoters of a Pest) were hereby also taken off, and much abated: searchers, Bearers, Nurses, and other licensed Visitors (whose walks are far more perilous then divers that are occluded and shut up) would hereby also become almost void and useless.'[43] Here we find the first clear statement by any of the authors reviewed to this point that the law actually contributed to an increase in the plague, and consequently to an increase in the level of suffering endured by the public at large. It is the first argument we have encountered that suggests that law was not simply the irrelevant tool of the officials, an impotent human construct with little importance in resisting God's judgment, or perhaps the plague's accomplice in spreading misery and consternation. Here we find an assertion that those who are responsible for the law are also responsible for its effects, that the power of the law of quarantine might be harnessed and redirected so as to contribute to a lessening of the plague's horrible consequences. The law, argued Cock, had real social potential, and it was up to those with the requisite authority to ensure that that potential was realized for the benefit of the citizens: 'Hereby also the Publick magistrate may with Courage, Confidence and Security, manage city affairs: Citizens and Tradesmen, safely keep their houses, and follow their imployments: many childing-women, and sucking children, fatherless, helpless, and friendless persons supported and preserved ... The outrages, insolencies, number and neglects of Nurses restrained, prevented, and abated: Thousands of persons lives preserved; poor people cheaper and better provided for and attended; and above all, God better pleased.'[44]

Cock's insistence that the law of quarantine actually contributed to the severity of the disease and the extent of suffering among the people was supported by apothecary William Boghurst in his lengthy work *Loimographia: an Account of the Great Plague in London in the Year 1665.*[45] In various places in this treatise, Boghurst complained that the law of confinement made the experience of the disease much worse for the citizens. In a list of one hundred factors called by Boghurst 'Some other more generall observations proving fatall this plague,' Boghurst cites the shutting up of houses and 'removeing servants and poore people to Pest-houses and to other houses in their sickenesse' as number 59B, arguing that these practices 'killed many' and could only be termed 'preposterous Physick.'[46] As number 81, Boghurst echoed Vincent's concern for the psychological impact of quarantine law, suggesting that weakened spirits contributed to weakened bodies as well: 'One friend growing melancholy for another was one maine cause of [the plague's] goeing through a family, especially when they were shutt up, which bred a sad apprehension and consternation on their spirits, especially being shutt up in dark cellars.'[47]

In a further list of treatments that Boghurst suggested were widely thought to be 'preservative against the plague,' but which Boghurst claimed were largely ineffectual, he included the 'shutting up of houses, warding towns, prohibiting goods and people intermission coming from infected places and noe less ineffectual is the shunning and running away from searchers, warders, dead-carts, shut up houses.'[48] Under the heading of 'Other Things to be Avoided,' Boghurst lists 'shutting up of houses when once it is hot weather, and the disease is grown thick (for it hath been oft enough tried and always found ineffectual).'[49] Boghurst believed that the despondency suffered by those confined to their houses by the law contributed greatly to the intensity of the disease, writing that 'one great cause why this disease sweeps away whole families is because they grow Melancholy and discontented, one friend for another, especially being shut up brings a sad cloud upon their spirits.'[50] And finally, in a direct indictment of those responsible for the law but slow to heed the warnings of Cock and Boghurst of its dangers, Boghurst wrote that 'as soone as any house is infected all the sound people should bee had out of it, and not shut up therein to bee murdered.'[51]

If Boghurst invoked a reference to murder in an attempt to stimulate action towards reform of the law of quarantine, then famous astrologer John Gadbury suggested that the failure to act was unchristian, too. In his work *London's Deliverance Predicted*,[52] Gadbury made direct reference to official inaction, arguing that the restraint of historical precedent, likely the same issue referred to by Cock in which the Privy Council tied the hands of the College of Physicians, made the plague all the worse for the citizens. For Gadbury, the plague 'proves Custome a most terrible Tyrant, in following whereof, the Magistrates shut up people infected in Houses or rooms, to prevent the spreading thereof.'[53] Further, shutting up actually contributed to the spread of the disease, and 'denying [the people] the advantage of the Air, is no small propinquate cause (at least) of the increase of the Contagion.' The magistrates were responsible for 'abridging the customary liberty' of the people, and that, in turn, was directly connected to an increase in the people's fear. At least according to Gadbury, 'the greater their fear, the sooner do they meet the ill they dread.'[54] And, in a direct reference to ancient Jewish law,[55] Gadbury closed his attack on official ineptitude in the following words, holding up the law of quarantine as reprehensible and misguided: 'A custome strangely tyrranous! And I am afraid favors more of a Barbarism then Christianity; and as it is contrary to the Laws of Old, and to Charity, so beyond question it is, and hath been considerably detrimental, and injurious to the lives of very many thousands in this great City!'[56]

Conclusion

From the literature reviewed for this chapter there starts to emerge a picture of law that contrasts with what one might expect to discover from a review of more conventional official sources. The pragmatic considerations of lawmakers are missing in this material. There is nothing of import and export restrictions, controls on the mobility of the citizenry, and the concerns of domestic commercial interests, and very little of the law's utility in actually slowing the progress of the disease. In the comments we have reviewed from a majority of clerics especially, it is quite clear that the effectiveness of the law in addressing these issues was, for the most part at least, an insignificant factor in reflecting on the plight of the sick. Indeed, for some authors the law was actually irrelevant, although unpleasant. One's level of discomfort in this life, generated by the awful combination of plague and invasive regulatory measures, was dwarfed when measured against the ultimate damnation to be experienced unless reconciliation with God was first achieved. Considered as polemical pieces, much of the literature of this sort appears to emerge from considerations that, quite simply, transcend both the concerns of lawmakers and the immediate peril of the victims of disease.

It is the transcendence of earthly concerns that separates this discourse from the mundane concerns of the political sphere. We see here the emergence of a literary public sphere generated through the polemics of clerics motivated by the requirements of reconciliation and salvation, yet revealing nevertheless a disavowal of law that is itself telling. Law's potential as a mechanism of response in a crisis is minimized; law's centrality as a tool of public authority is dismissed. This discourse, then, exists as a counter-discourse, raising the urgency of otherworldly salvation to pre-eminence, and deflecting the focus away from threats to commerce and general community health.

At the same time, however, we discover authors (from both theology and medicine) whose position, while perhaps equally polemical, is much more compassionate. Conventional understandings of suffering, whether as punishment for legal infractions or as the necessary consequence of ill health, are disturbed when law appears to conspire with disease to exacerbate that suffering for no apparent good reason. Victims have done nothing to deserve their position, as is ordinarily necessary in advance of legal sanction. There is no culpability, yet punishment (and suffering) results. Suffering is heightened by the dramatic combination of deadly physical sickness, the psychological trauma of experiencing the symbols of death firsthand, and the force of state authority in delivering 'death's warrant' through well-recognized interventions.

This is an unusual response to law. Standard criticisms of law for occasional injustices and ineffectiveness are barely evident in this material. Instead, we see glimpses of law understood as an active force for suffering without justification, an unsettling realization that disturbed cultural conventions on both suffering and law. Suffering at the hands of the law during the plague was neither purposeful (in the sense of a sacrifice for the sake of public well-being) nor vain (in the sense, perhaps, of an urge to martyrdom). Suffering at the hands of the law raised the deepest frustration, futility, and powerlessness, made even more profound by the constant fear of God's wrath and the realization that law's intervention was the irresistible result of human deliberation. And so intellectuals struck back through a bitter denunciation of law and the instruments of law, of the watchmen and their weapons, of the nurses and other medical personnel whose legally required efforts were seen to torture the sick and deny them their nobility as sufferers.

But then again, all of this might have been accepted by the clerics and physicians whose work we have reviewed for this chapter, had the law been successful in stemming the spread of disease through practices such as the shutting up of houses. But intellectuals dismissed the prevailing regulatory framework as ill-considered and disastrous, citing examples from history both to deny the efficacy of conventional practices and to support their argument for alternatives. From this perspective, the failure of the law made the suffering of victims a waste, sufficient for neither assuring the victim's spiritual salvation nor the survival of the community. Such suffering, then, is futile, sympathetic, and, ultimately, unjustifiable in both theological and medical terms.

NOTES

1 For a tabulation of plague years in fourteen English towns between 1581 and 1666, see Paul Slack, *The Impact of Plague in Tudor and Stuart England* (London: Routledge and Kegan Paul, 1985), 62.

2 The statute was 1 Jac. I c.31, and it remained in force, unamended, beyond 1665. It will be referred to as 'King James's Act' in the balance of

this Chapter. Examples of Privy Council and other orders from the period include 'Orders Conceived and published by the Lord Major and Aldermen of the City of London, concerning the infection of the Plague' (London: 1665) and 'Privy Council Rules and Orders to be observed by all Justices of the Peace, Mayors, Bayliffs, and other officers, for the prevention of the spreading of the infection of the Plague' (London: 1666). King James's Act was the first English statute to address the problem of epidemic disease, but of course authorities had issued hundreds of specific orders to control activities during epidemics prior to 1603. For a review of pre-1603 official action, see F.P. Wilson, *The Plague in Shakespeare's London* (Oxford: Clarendon Press, 1999).

3 Jürgen Habermas, *The Structural Transformation of the Public Sphere: An Inquiry into a Category of Bourgeois Society* (Cambridge, MA: MIT Press, 1989), 57–67.

4 *Ibid.*, 59. See also Mark Rose, *Authors and Owners: The Invention of Copyright* (Cambridge, MA: Harvard University Press, 1992), especially ch. 3, 'Making Copyright,' for a short history of the Licensing Act of 1662 and the attempts to extend it during the 1690s.

5 Jason Peacey, *Politicians and Pamphleteers: Propaganda during the English Civil Wars and Interregnum* (Aldershot, UK: Ashgate, 2004), especially ch. 2, 'Authors and the Propaganda Impulse.' Another interesting and important treatment of the relationship between politics, law, and theological polemics in the seventeenth century is found in Tim Cooper, *Fear and Polemic in Seventeenth-Century England: Richard Baxter and Antinomianism* (Aldershot, UK: Ashgate, 2001).

6 Peacey, *supra* note 5 at 67.

7 Quoted from John Tabor, 'Reflections on the Pestilence,' in his *Seasonable Thoughts in Sad Times* (London: 1667), 18.

8 See, generally, Marvin Henberg, *Retribution: Evil For Evil in Ethics, Law, and Literature* (Philadelphia: Temple University Press, 1990).

9 Joseph A. Amato, *Victims and Values: A History and a Theory of Suffering* (New York: Greenwood Press, 1990).

10 See *ibid.*, 1–42, for a general discussion of these ideas.

11 *Ibid.*, 16.

12 *Ibid.*, 3.

13 For a medical historian's interpretation of much of the literature referred to in the balance of this chapter, see Charles F. Mullett, *The Bubonic Plague and England: An Essay in the History of Preventive Medicine* (Lexington: University of Kentucky Press, 1956), especially ch. 10, 'The Plague of 1665 in Literature.'

14 Michel Foucault, *The History of Sexuality, Volume I: An Introduction*, trans. Robert Hurley (New York: Vintage Books, 1980), 101.
15 Richard Kephale, *Medela Pestilentiae* (London: 1665).
16 *Ibid.*, 8.
17 *Ibid.*, 8–11.
18 *Ibid*, 26–7.
19 *Ibid.*, 35–6.
20 William Kemp, *A Brief Treatise of the Nature, Causes, Signes, Preservation From, and Cure of the Pestilence* (London: 1665).
21 *Ibid.*, 16–17.
22 *Ibid.*, 5.
23 Matthew Mead, *Solomon's Prescription for the Removal of the Pestilence* (London: 1667).
24 *Ibid.*, 6. Emphasis in original.
25 *Ibid.*, 7.
26 Thomas Cock, *Hygiene, or a Discourse upon Air* (London: 1665).
27 William Boghurst, *Loimographia: An Account of the Great Plague of London in the Year 1665* (London: 1894). This volume was first printed privately by the author in 1665.
28 John Gadbury, *London's Deliverance Predicted* (London: 1665).
29 Richard Kingston, *A Spiritual Receipt for Cure of the Plague* (London: 1665).
30 Thomas Vincent, *God's Terrible Voice in the City* (London: 1671). This volume was first printed privately by the author in 1665.
31 See the references to Matthew Mead and William Kemp, *supra* notes 23 and 20, respectively.
32 Kingston, *supra* note 29 at x. Emphasis in original.
33 Vincent, *supra* note 30 at 26.
34 *Ibid.*, 28–9.
35 *Ibid.*, 29. Emphasis in original.
36 *Ibid.*, 133.
37 *Supra* note 26.
38 The pages of Cock's 'Peroration' are unnumbered. His discussion of King James's Act begins at the second unnumbered page.
39 *Ibid.*, third page.
40 *Ibid.*, third and fourth pages. Emphasis in original.
41 *Ibid.*, fifth, sixth, and seventh pages.
42 Cock does not reveal the year to which he refers, but we can speculate that it was 1644, the year in which 'An Order for the Observance and Execution of the Statute made for the Reliefe and Ordering of Persons

infected with the Plague' (Oxford: 1644) was published by 'the Lords and Commissioners of Oxford University and the City of Oxford.'

43 Cock, 'Peroration,' sixth page.

44 *Ibid.*, eighth page.

45 *Supra* note 27.

46 *Ibid.*, 25.

47 *Ibid.*, 27.

48 *Ibid*, 54–5.

49 *Ibid.*, 57.

50 *Ibid.*, 65.

51 *Ibid.*, 99.

52 *Supra* note 28.

53 *Ibid.*, 36.

54 *Ibid.*, 39.

55 See 'Leviticus,' ch. 13, in *The Holy Bible* (the text conformable to that of the edition of 1611 commonly known as the authorized or King James version) (Philadelphia: A.J. Holman Company, 19**), at 132–5.

56 Gadbury, *London's Deliverance Predicted*, *supra* note 28 at 40.

PART FOUR

Transcendence

11 The Strange Gospel and a Common Law: The Reconciling Word to a Fragmented World

M.H. OGILVIE

'I was getting too addicted to speculation. I sometimes felt that if I could hang on just a little longer I would receive some perfect illumination about everything.'

'Why don't you hang on?'

'Because I know that if it did come it would be an illusion – one of the most, oh, splendid. The original *felix culpa* in thought itself.'

'That sounds like despair.'

'The point is, one will never get to the end of it, never get to the bottom of it, never, never. And that never, never, never is what you must take for your hope and shield and your most glorious promise. Everything that we concoct about God is an illusion.'

'But God is not an illusion?'

' "Whosoever he be of you who forsaketh not all that he hath, he cannot be my disciple." '

'I don't believe you've given up theology at all. Theology is magic. Beware.'

'I know.'

'I must go and catch my train to Leeds.'

Iris Murdoch, *Henry and Cato*

I. Prelude

If theology and law have anything in common, surely it is a delight in seemingly endless speculation. Mapping the perfect city, whether heavenly or earthly, inspires debates without end over terrains without signposts, yet seems as eerily similar as Earth and Mars, except not quite the same. The conceptual pieces each discipline moves, chess-like, about also seem familiar, nor did they change over the course of the twentieth century. Intellectual activity at the end of the century occupied the same disturbing zone evoked at the end of the previous century by Nietzsche in 1888 in *The Twilight of the Idols*. But since deconstruction has accustomed us to think sceptically about truth and idols, and beginnings and endings, we seem doomed to drift in intellectual dereliction, apparent nomads for whom directionless wandering is the sum and end of our existence.

Yet, neither theologian nor lawyer act as if mere wandering is the sum of existence. On the contrary, both strive, often mightily, to achieve the perfect city, whether temporal or eschatological. The theologian still distinguishes the temporal as temporary and a necessarily imperfect reflection of the city of God. But the postmodern lawyer denies the existence of another city and dissents from the broad consensus of thought over the past two millennia in the West that the heavenly city of Christian theology should somehow be reflected in the earthly city of human machination. With no transcendent values to guide, the dweller in the immanent city is left to the transient winds of will and power blowing life in the city hither and yon. A few foolhardy theologians and lawyers, however, resist the siren call to dash themselves upon the ultimate meaninglessness of life to reflect upon the possibility that it has a transcendent purpose, no matter how hidden, which also informs its immanent present reality. For such persons, theology has something to say to law. But if God is dead or was only ever a vain delusion of humanity's self-love, then theology has nothing to say to the immanent city about the rules that should regulate its power struggles. Readers inclined to this view need read no further.

On the other hand, serious, thoughtful atheism that ponders the temporal world and searches for the best way to live happily within it deserves attention: it entails suffering a long sadness at the end of each day at the thought of one less. Willing disbelief is bitterly courageous, yet not as bitter as the absence of a friend known long and loved. To know God is to know the infinite suffering his absence would bring. Within every believer is a non-believer. A believer knows atheism as no atheist can.[1] So for as long as there is belief, believers will speculate on how belief and its transcendent source should be brought to bear on life in the temporal city to blot out the sadness of the human condition with the joy of the eternal presence of God.[2]

Recently, a theological school has grown up that takes seriously the insights of twentieth-century deconstruction of the postmodern human condition in order to recover orthodox Christian theology as metanarrative. Members of this group assert that postmodern nihilism is not the end of modernity, but more radically, that at the end of modernity, Christian theology returns differently as the metanarrative that positions all other narratives and discourses. This school has been labelled postmodern Augustinianism and smeared as sophisticated fundamentalism, but its members call it 'radical orthodoxy,'[3] and so we shall call it. Radical orthodoxy's claim that it provides a new way to think about the world has been tested in relation to politics, music, art, and philosophy,[4] but if its claims are indeed of universal application, it should also yield new ways to think about law. The purpose of this paper is to explore whether radical orthodoxy offers new ways to think persuasively about law.

II. How Firm a Foundation

The movement to place humanity at the centre of human concern instead of God is normally traced in the West to certain developments in later medieval theology, whose original goal was to enhance the omnipotence, majesty, and reliable benevolence of God in caring for his creation.[5] But by emphasizing the distance between God and humanity, theologians such as Duns Scotus (c. 1266–1308) facilitated the separation of humanity from God and suggested that the inscrutability of God rendered futile human efforts to know him. The sixteenth-century Reformers responded by restoring Scripture, especially the Gospels' evidence for Jesus Christ as incarnating divine revelation about the nature of God and his will for the world, while Renaissance thinkers, inspired by the recovery of classical writers, rekindled interest in human possibility and scientific exploration of the temporal world. By refocusing on God through a single book interpreted as God's revelation of himself through one person to whom that one book bore testimony, the Reformers sought to repristinate the divine origins of their faith in contrast to the all-too-human corruption of the late medieval Church. In hindsight, they also set that book up for a fall should its contents be doubted in the light of human experience and subsequent scientific discovery.

During the seventeenth and eighteenth centuries, these intellectual trajectories bore predictable fruit: God ceased to be the ultimate focus of human aspiration or even central to temporal existence, and Christian theology no longer provided the sole overarching narrative for human experience. Humanity and human potential to discover and govern the world assumed centre stage. The elevation of human nature and the potential of reasoning humanity to change and improve the world replaced the earlier ideal of the contemplative soul with a restless spirit constantly searching for novelty and so constantly discontented. But by focusing on humanity distanced from God, Enlightenment thinkers also demoted and demeaned humanity. No longer made in the image of God to enjoy communion with him as the pinnacle of creation, humans were reduced to bit players in the human story, here today and gone tomorrow, of no significance and dispensable.

The displacement of God did not displace the desire for truth. René Descartes (1596–1650), for example, strove to find a method of investigation to discover certain truth, influenced by the growth of mathematics in the seventeenth century: if human reason can discover mathematical certainties, then it should be able to discover other scientific certainties. His famous adoption of Augustine's adage, '*Cogito, ergo sum*,'[6] was thought to be the only secure basis for the discovery of the truth about the world. Henceforth the subjective individual would be the source of knowledge about the world and the scientific method the means of achieving that knowledge. Eighteenth-century scientists such as Isaac Newton (1642–1727) regarded their work as illuminating the work of God as the Designer and Sustainer of the world, but in time neither a designer nor a sustainer might be required. Nature and Nature's God might well be parted in human assessment.

With the rise of a human reason capable of discovering scientific truths, both scientists and theologians (often the same person) in the eighteenth century viewed religion as both natural and revealed: natural religion comprised a set of universally applicable truths accessible to human reason, and revealed religion comprised scripture and doctrine derived from scripture in Church tradition. As human reason flourished in the discovery of scientific facts about the world, revealed religion declined in esteem, replaced by scepticism about the ability of human reason to answer ultimate questions no matter how precise and detailed the description of the natural world it achieved.

Scepticism nurtured epistemological problems as to how human reason can know anything. John Locke (1632–1704) responded that the human mind received impressions from the natural world and reformulated these as ideas. But David Hume (1711–76) doubted this explanation because impressions do not explain everyday concepts such as causation that can be described but not unpacked. Hume also asserted that substance (size, colour) is experienced as impression but that actual substances are also difficult to explain. Hume further suggested that even natural religion, which postulated a creator as the first cause, was doubtful if human reason cannot explain causation. But the response from Emmanuel Kant (1724–1804) suggested that knowledge was derived not just from experience but the presence in the mind of formal concepts that allowed for organizing experience, of which two, time and space, were the most important. Without time and space, it is impossible to know the external world.

Kant thought it was possible to know about objects present in human experience (*phenomena*) but not about those beyond experience (*noumena*), thus it was unlikely that humans could argue from phenomena to transcendent concepts such as God or the soul. Rather, knowledge of transcendent concepts is derived from 'practical' reason. As well as being capable of experience, humans are also moral beings as demonstrated by their sense of 'oughtness,' that is, their consciousness that they ought to do or refrain from doing certain things. Kant thought this sense to be fundamentally rational and that humans had a duty, a 'categorical imperative,' to live in accordance with these rational principles. But by asserting that reason could discern moral principles, Kant furthered the gap between God and humanity by elevating the autonomous self to be the centre for thinking about moral principles and by limiting its subject to its own thoughts. Kant assumed that all minds were similar so that it is possible to reason out universal human values across cultures. Kant thought God to be a rational concept as an absolute whose reality is beyond human experience but who can be mediated through the human sense of moral obligation. Kant, the good Lutheran, thought a dynamic relationship with God possible and a source for human knowledge.

Kant's epistemology was challenged early in the nineteenth century by Frederick Schleiermacher (1768–1834), who reconceptualized religion as a feeling of absolute dependence on God that is pre-moral and pre-cognitive, so that it is not primarily about morality or knowledge. For Kant, God was present through the human sense of moral duty, but for Schleiermacher he was present in 'an immediate dynamic relationship that grasps our whole being.'[7] Although originating in the subjective realm of feeling, Schleiermacher asserted that religion could be discussed intellectually in theology and could inform everyday life. Rooted in a dynamic awareness of God, Schleiermacher emphasized the importance of aesthetics in religion. But he also inaugurated modern hermeneutics, that is, the theory of the interpretation of written texts. He thought Scripture to be a creative response to the particular experience and circumstances of the authors, not a set of systematic treatises of revelation. To understand the text, it is necessary to get behind the grammatical meaning to the mind of the author and his underlying psychology. This optimistic view that the author's mind could be recreated was matched by the equally optimistic view that both author and text manifested universal principles that could be abstracted from the text. Schleiermacher is often described, therefore, as the grandfather of liberal theology because of his accommodation of faith with contemporary hermeneutics, although he could also be seen as a progenitor of evangelical theology because of his emphasis on faith as feeling rather than being strictly rational.

With Nietzsche (1844–1900) at the end of the nineteenth century came the major attack on the possibility of truth, whether revealed or scientifically discovered, on the basis that all things and events in the world are unique, therefore universally valid concepts cannot be constructed. Attempts to do so are illusions that disguise the individuality of each fragment in the world. Nietzsche rejected Kant's notion that transcendental categories in all human minds facilitate the construction of the truth about the world. He claimed these were arbitrary fabrications and that 'truth' was simply a function of language. Against nineteenth-century Romantics such as Friedrich Schelling (1775–1854), he regarded artistic expression to be a flight from truth, and so by denying access to reality both rationally and aesthetically, Nietzsche earned his reputation as the philosopher of nihilism: it is impossible to know reality and 'truth' is an error that some require to live.

In place of truth, Nietzsche argued that the world is a continually self-creating work of art: there is no God. Not only has Christianity lost the power it once had in Western society, but all that ever really existed was the primitive instinct for self-preservation captured in the phrase the 'will to power,' that is, the desire to transcend the self by the exercise of personal creative power. Christianity was once such a success story. In place of a value system grounded in God and accessible to human reason, Nietzsche argued that there was nothing underpinning any value system except the will of the person asserting it. 'Truth' is merely an assertion of the asserter and is neither universal nor necessarily rational. Indeed, Nietzsche regarded universal values as dangerous, for example, Christian humility constrains those with great abilities so that the mediocre often flourish instead; in a society where mediocrity prevailed, Nietzsche predicted that the 'last man' would be smug, mediocre, and middle class.

But Nietzsche did not anticipate a last man: rather, he thought that events occurred infinitely without ending or meaning: things eternally return. This was a myth with power to restore meaning to life and to permit humans to become creators of their own lives, inventing the world to suit themselves and using language to describe that world, that is, to create its 'truth.' By constructing the world, language creates truth and interprets it, albeit without the possibility of arriving at a universally agreed correct interpretation. Zarathustra can only speak to himself and has nothing to say to anyone who does not share his perspective.

Martin Heidegger (1889–1976) understood the death of Nietzsche's God as the end of metaphysics, that is, the end of modernity's quest for a foundation, for truth and for God. He asserted that the entire Western intellectual tradition had erred in searching for a Being as something beyond by beginning with things as they appeared here. Instead, humans should work out who they are from within themselves rather than find out by living in the world and without the prospect of a final answer. Humans do not experience the world as object but by being there (Dasein) in the world. Heidegger wished to avoid the dualism of self and the world in favour of a Being together of subject and object. Being is not about presence alone but about past, present, and future, so that Being includes presence and absence. Their connection if any is unclear but Heidegger based his claim that there is no truth out there on it. There is no absolute, autonomous, and certain truth; we can only speak about truth as participants in it. To achieve truth, a new way of thinking is required that appears to be meditative in nature. Art can be one means for the creation of truth but language is more so because of its close connection with thought. By moving within language, which is Being or reality, language will transform us but will leave us with a view from nowhere. This emphasis on self-discovery discounted as impossible any transcendent Being beyond this world but retained the Enlightenment importance of the self as the centre of meaning.

Kant's difference between the phenomenal and the noumenal, which we can only know because things as they are provide in some way the condition for our experience of the world, is overcome by Nietzsche and Heidegger by asserting a human-centred perspective.

There is no transcendence, no world out there, and no essential nature in things here; there is only our perspective. But by asserting that being there can be the basis for Being, Heidegger once more suggested that Being can be considered. His position may not be transcendent but it is holistic; ontological difference exists but metaphysics requires that it be forgotten. But if difference is forgotten, then how to proceed becomes problematical.

Hans-Georg Gadamer (1900–2002) suggested it was possible to overcome the relativism inherent in Heidegger's understanding of Being by arguing that behind different perspectives lies a shared reality, 'a fusion of horizons,' which results from a conversation among different interpretations that fosters a communion and a common language from which meaning emerges, although not necessarily a single meaning. Meaning does not come from out there but from conversations with the world that we necessarily have by being in the world. This refocus to language as a means of understanding the reality of existence was also asserted by Ferdinand de Saussure (1857–1913), who thought language to be an inherently coherent system rather than merely a historical outcome of trends and patterns that can be scientifically deciphered. Language is a social convention, not a reflection of thought or a representation of external facts, truth, or reality. It is arbitrary and cannot be explained; it is just a system of sounds. Language can be thought of as a symphony, a network of relationships of sounds and meanings. Words are not signs of something out there but derive their meanings from their internal relationships with other words and are confirmed through repetition. We come to know the world through the difference of the sounds in language conveying differences of ideas.

Originally based on the study of language, Saussure's ideas became influential as a way to understand human life in general in structuralism as expressed in various scholarly disciplines that completed the subversion of the human self in Western thought. The human self was portrayed as a cultural construction, and persons and texts were thought of as having the meaning the interpreter places on them. As Claude Lévi-Strauss put it: 'I believe the ultimate goal of the human sciences to be not to constitute, but to dissolve man.'[8] While structuralists continued to search for systematic knowledge of the world, their intellectual successors rejected these last vestiges of the Enlightenment as completely irrational.

Thus, Michel Foucault (1926–84) rejected as a starting point the rational autonomous self capable of scientifically accessing the world objectively, as well as notions of universality, in favour of the specific and of infinite variety in the world. Although he thought the self to be socially constructed, he also thought there to be no underlying structures in reality; there was only complexity. There is no neutral, objective, universal truth or knowledge, only a will to knowledge that dictates its own truth. For Foucault, power is the source of knowledge, the practice of power is the basis for knowledge, and knowing is an act of violence. There is no truth, only myths. Foucault attempted to debunk the unifying themes of history, the genealogies, as myths masking the exercise of power in order to show that the story of history is not predestined but merely a series of haphazard events. The past is meaningless and the future will be the same.

While Foucault attacked Enlightenment understandings of the human self, knowledge, and truth, Jacques Derrida (1930–2004) focused on language, 'logocentrism,' as a means to understand the world by doubting whether language can represent the world as it really is. He thought that words, especially written rather than spoken words, have no meaning because there is no 'presence' of being or an essence that we can know. Derrida thought that there is no ultimate basis for thought or language, only a 'myth of presence,' which he called the 'onto-theological tradition' of Western thought. Even if meaning did exist, it would lie beyond human language.

So how does language have meaning? Following Saussure, Derrida argued that words acquire their meanings from their textual locations, not any relationship to corresponding mental concepts. Language is self-referential, that is, its meaning is derived from its relationships to other words, so there can never be a single true meaning. Meanings change over time and context, so that we should *defer* any temptation to give meaning (*différance*). The apparent similarity of meaning and consciousness is dependent on language, so that apart from language there is no meaning and no self separate from language. Human experience of the self is an illusion; there is only a complex web of changing meanings. But Derrida also suggested that such meaning as there is can only be possible because of a trace of a now absent reality of meaning, that is, a word's former connections to other words, so that meaning is derived from the relationship of presence and absence. Meaning is fluid and interpretation is always repetition without reference to external meaning. Derrida proposed nothing in place of his deconstruction of Western logocentrism and the resulting death of any metaphysics of presence.

The intellectual movement in the West to this bleak perspective on life is mirrored in Western legal systems that have abandoned Christian moral theology for the use of state law to administer, manage, and referee the competing claims within Western societies by a state officially assumed to be neutral, secular, and above the social fray. Western legal systems are postmodern in the fullest sense. Their avowed goal is to promote the dignity of individuals by maximizing individual choice, not promote any particular version of the good, that is, godly, life; to focus on the present, not the future, and to forget the past; to avoid truth in favour of the workable compromise, however temporary; and to constrain, by state sanction if necessary, groups or individuals who assert otherwise, even if only by words, not acts. Two examples from Canadian Charter jurisprudence are apposite: decisions of the courts asserting the value of preserving earthly life in medical consent cases over the religious litigants' preference for eternal life should death result from a refusal of medical treatment, without explaining why earthly life is to be privileged;[9] and decisions in which 'marriage' has been deconstructed from its historical meaning of a union of one man and one woman until death for same-sex partnerships today and possibly other arrangements in the future.[10] In medical consent cases, the courts no longer acknowledge the earlier view that life is a gift from God to be given and taken in his own time and by his own rules, while in the marriage cases, the courts no longer acknowledge the earlier view that heterosexual marriage for life is the way of life God has chosen as best for his creation, both views derived from an authoritative scripture.

Christian theology, on the other hand, could only become fully postmodern by abandoning its claims to objective truth about the world, to universality, and to ultimate purpose in life, centred on the revealed eternal Word of God in Jesus Christ and present among us through the Holy Spirit. Christian thinkers can readily agree that reason alone is insufficient for the discovery of universal truth but are obliged to continue to assert that there is such truth, that there is a grand narrative at work in human history, that each individual has transcendent worth, and that the scientific discoveries of human reason are good and play a good role in that story. So, it is now necessary to turn to a brief overview of how Christian thinkers have responded to the movement towards postmodernity in Western thought.

III. What More Can He Say

As a young Reformed pastor in a small Swiss industrial town before World War One, Karl Barth (1886–1968) struggled each Sunday to preach to a working-class congregation on their only day off. The experience of trying to explain why attending church mattered compelled him to read the Bible, not as his theological education had taught him as an objective guide to moral and religious rules, but rather as a book about the Kingdom of God, which he experienced as a 'strange new world' that could only be understood by inhabiting it. Instead of thinking about the world in relation to God, he came to think about God in relation to the world; instead of thinking about God from the perspective of the world, he came to think about the world from the perspective of God as revealed in Scripture.[11] Barth concluded that Descartes' epigram should be reworded: *Cogitor ergo sum* – I am thought about (by God), therefore I am.[12]

Barth reversed the approach of nineteenth-century liberal theology of beginning with the human self as the perspective from which to view the truth about the world. He accepted the infinite qualitative difference between time and eternity but also crucially recovered the assertion that Jesus Christ was the point at which time was touched by eternity. The assertions of faith have their own internal logical coherence and need not be assessed for rationality by reference to external standards. Instead, by reference to a historical event outside the assertions of faith, the event of Christ, the entire web of assertions about faith and truth can be found to be coherent. In Jesus Christ, time and eternity join without merging and the infinite distance of God from humanity encompasses humanity in Christ.[13] In Christ, Barth argues, humanity can come to know about God for the simple reason that God chose to make himself known in this one man. Christ was not a static first Being but a life, that is, an event and an action. By trusting in the reality of God's self-revelation, it is possible to understand reality. For Barth, the life of one person served the same purpose as Being in Western metaphysics.[14] But Christ can actually be known through the stories about him, while Being can only be thought about as an object out there.

Barth further asserted that it is logically necessary that this revelation be understood as a Trinitarian event because God's self-disclosure in Christ involves three moments in one event: Revelation (Christ), Revealer (God), and Revealedness (Holy Spirit).[15] The Christian understanding of God is triune from the outset, and as such, distinctive from other conceptions of transcendent reality. The Trinity is integral to all knowledge about God and reality. In so asserting, Barth was illuminated by an insight from Hegel who thought of God as an Absolute Spirit that was required to differentiate itself in order to know itself. For Barth, this differentiation took place in history thereby wrapping all human history and experience up in it.[16] All understanding of reality must begin with the Trinity self-disclosed in Christ and recounted by Scripture within a believing community.[17] Barth's direct challenge to modernity and postmodernity's scepticism about discovering the truth about life was to restore the historical event of Jesus Christ to the centre of his theology and to enfold the significance of that event into a Trinitarian theology that encompasses past, present, and future. In Christ, humanity can know what God wishes to reveal about himself, and in his continuing body, the Church, that revelation can be passed on until the end of time as the true story about the meaning of the world.

Barth's Christocentric approach to ultimate meaning redirected twentieth-century theology to the texts of that revelation and the community within which they are interpreted. Biblical scholarship over the previous three centuries had largely discredited the simplistic view that Scripture was in some sense directly dictated by God, a view more caricatured by anti-Christian polemicists than ever actually held by the Christian Church over the millennia, although subscribed to by a tiny minority even today.[18] Through historical, archaeological, philological, and other disciplines, scholars thought that by peeling away the myths and traditions of interpretation they would be able to construct the core facts about ancient Jewish and Christian belief and life. However, the facts have eluded reduction to a scientifically provable chronicle of ancient events because the scholarly disciplines themselves have yielded disputed findings without disproving the basic story. Yet, the records of human experience of God contained in Scripture continue to inspire belief and the community of belief no matter how much they have dumbfounded enlightened scholarship. Notwithstanding continuing disagreement among Christians as to the relative authority of Scripture per se, or of tradition, that is, the authoritative interpretation of Scripture as mediated by some ecclesiastical authority, such as a bishop or council, in determining precisely how a text is to be interpreted, there is complete agreement that Scripture remains the source beyond all sources for knowledge about divine revelation and that its meaning can be discerned through its words and their interpretation within the community of believers led by the Holy Spirit, who speaks with authority through the text. It is not the literal words that are authoritative but the message contained in the words spoken by the third person of the Trinity.[19]

The move away from the text of Scripture alone as literally authoritative ended the epistemological crisis that the Reformers' *sola scriptura* had posed for Western thought: rival interpretations founded on individual reason conflicted by Cartesian anxiety had dethroned the text and the rational self but also cleared the way for Scripture to be read in a thoroughly postmodern way. Human reason demystified Scripture so that it could be treated like any other book and tradition that could be dismissed as just another prejudice.[20]

Beginning with Gadamer's position that humans can only view things from here not from out there, suggests that the meaning of Scripture is not objective but something the reader discovers by immersion in dialogue with the text in the context of the reader's own time and community. Stanley Fish (1938–) made the reader subservient to the community or tradition[21] and Alasdair MacIntyre (1929–) agreed that all reasoning is within a community and a product of the tradition of that community.[22] But the rehabilitation of tradition to textualize Scripture in a postmodern manner does not dispose of the problems of authority and of finding definitive meaning within the tradition of the interpreting Christian community. So much contemporary theology revised its focus from the stating of dogmatic principles said to be contained in Scripture to the community within which Scripture operates and its own tradition of interpretation. Learning from Barth that Christian faith does not rest on human reason or self-consciousness to ascertain the truth about reality, but on the person of Jesus Christ as revealed in Scripture, some recent theologians have explored the idea that faith and meaning are best gained and nurtured by commitment to the narrative, or story, of Jesus, and by living that story. It is not supported by any other story or theory out there but becomes a habit of the heart giving meaning and reality to life here.

Of the various contemporary schools of theology,[23] that which is labelled 'postliberal' or the 'Yale school' is most associated with finding meaning within Scripture within the narrative tradition of a community.[24] Hans Frei (1922–88) showed how theologians in the seventeenth and eighteenth centuries, following secular philosophers, started to interpret Christianity from the external perspective of the individual in place of the traditional approach of interpreting the world through the Christian story.[25] He argued that Scripture meant what it said so that the world should be fitted into the story it told about God rather than God into the story of the world. Once the reader is consumed by the text of Scripture, the world can be viewed from the

Scriptural perspective. Frei depicted the Bible as a world with its own linguistic integrity like a literary work, except that we all live in its world, and asserted that theology should begin with the Scriptural story not some general theory about the world.[26]

Although Frei began with the Scriptural narrative about Jesus in the manner of Anselm's *credo ut intelligam* rather than any prior metaphysical theory, the category of narrative itself could be construed as a prior theory. But Frei did not think it necessary to regard narrative as an independent category of which Scripture is an example, nor the distinction as significant, because there is nothing in the content of narrative only specific narratives. For Frei, the narrative about Jesus is Jesus, that is, Jesus is his story; his identity is what he did as the crucified saviour of the world.[27]

The naive idea that assertion of a narrative without hermeneutical apparatus is sufficient to explain the meaning of the world gave way in Frei's later work to the need for some authority to give meaning to the story, and Frei, influenced by his fellow Yale theologian George Lindbeck (1923–), accepted that the authoritative meaning was the Church's version of the *sensus literalis* of the text: the meaning of the text can only be deciphered through the communal reading. Frei thought an authoritative reading necessary to ensure that the story is a true story: the meaning in the text is the truth of the text. The connection between a definitive community reading and the narrative lies in the text itself, which proclaims that the story of Jesus continues in the story of the Church and has not come to an end. Christ is not dead but alive in the Church. Christ has left the past in order to return from the future; he has gone on ahead to await those who follow after. The story is a continuous story to the end of time.[28]

Frei was not concerned with whether the story of Jesus told in Scripture was factually and historically true, rather that the story told the true story of who Jesus was. Critical Biblical scholars who question the accuracy and ridicule the discrepancies in the four Gospels, for example, miss the point that Scripture, like literature, faithfully conveys the identity of Jesus, that is, expresses truth even in fictive form. But this position brings us back to the community that treats the narrative of Scripture as truth and conducts its life in that light. The meaning of Scripture is to be found in the community, which tries to be faithful to it, and because texts are not autonomous but exist only when read, texts and readers are mutually reinforcing. The truth of the text can only be judged within the community that regards them as truth.[29]

Lindbeck's focus was on the community, and he recast the discernment of meaning in cultural and linguistic terms as a result of that focus. For Lindbeck, the Church is a culture with its own language and criteria for judgment. The only way to understand the truth of Christianity is to practise it within the Church and learn to articulate its rules. Scripture is the framework within which the Christian community comes to understand its identity and the world, not by defining a set of biblical propositions but by continuing a tradition of interpretation understood as a community habit of reading Scripture, which is also a means of socializing members into the community. Theology, then, is similar to sociology in that it simply describes the outcome of that process.[30] In Lindbeck's view, the liturgy and the practices of the community come first and shape the religious experience subsequently. For Lindbeck, theology is only intratextual; the world is consumed by the text.[31]

Doctrines are not, for Lindbeck, the fundamental rules governing practice: rather, they are reflections of a more basic grammar, a 'deep grammar,'[32] in the liturgy, symbols and stories that regulate practice. This deep grammar cannot be fully detected or articulated, so the community requires doctrine as second-order propositions necessary for instruction about the deep grammar. Lindbeck states three examples of this deep grammar: there is one God; Jesus was an actual human being; and every possible importance should be ascribed to him that is not inconsistent with the first two propositions.[33] The authority of the creeds is derived from these three principles of monotheism, historical specificity, and Christological maximalism, respectively, which are deeply embedded in Scripture. The unsatisfactory nature of this approach is obvious: inability to articulate the deep grammar of Scripture renders all attempts to formulate doctrine and any doctrinal statements relativistic and unstable. Indeed, the two criticisms normally directed at Lindbeck are that his position is ultimately irrational and sectarian:[34] Christianity cannot be articulated in autonomous, rational propositions and can only ever be practised within a community self-isolated from the world.

Lindbeck largely accepts these criticisms. He suspects that we live in a world in which there can be no universally agreed rational criteria for making Christianity intelligibly acceptable, but he also suggests that we make decisions between world views on reasonable bases and that the reasonableness of religion is tested by time and responses to new situations. Apologetics is necessarily ad hoc, but as long as the faith endures among communities of believers it meets the test of being reasonable. In the end, Lindbeck's position is based on the conviction that religion is a response to a pure gift experienced as a gracious act of God.[35] In his later work,[36] Lindbeck also agreed with the sectarian criticism and argued that Christianity is required by the world to become more sectarian when the world no longer accepts the Scriptural narrative as the story of the world. However, that emphasis should neither preclude community building nor evangelization to the world.[37]

Recent Christian theology could be construed to eerily mirror Western intellectual trends: the impossibility of human reason to decipher meaning and truth, especially ultimate truth or even its existence; the susceptibility of Scripture to critical scholarship so as to doubt the veracity or historical reliability of its literal meaning; doubt that language, in particular the language of Scripture, can convey true meaning; refocus from the world out there to the experience of living in a narrative, albeit the Christian narrative, here so as to discover oneself; an enhanced appreciation of aesthetic experience as a means to discover reality; the importance of living the narrative in a community to the construction of the self, albeit the Christian self; and a reluctance to assert by rational propositions more than is absolutely necessary about the transcendent meaning and significance of that story.

However, Christian theology also rejected other elements of recent Western philosophy: the myth of the complete autonomy of humanity free from any transcendent origin, rule, or purpose; the trivialization of humanity and of human life as ceaseless wandering that is finally meaningless; the exaltation of the will to power and the exercise of power by violence; the complete impossibility of language, thought, and aesthetic experience to give some hint, even if only by analogy, of out there; and the denial of *différance*. The reason for these rejections is, of course, Jesus Christ.

Barth's recentring of Christian theology on the person of Jesus Christ as divine revelation in a human person to whom Scripture provided as reliable a historical record as any other historical record restored the link between God and creation forgotten by generations of thinkers. Once this link between the transcendent and the immanent is made, then the search for meaning and truth is refocused on the life and teaching of God made man and of those who believed in him after his ascension and who carry on his work in the community he left behind. Jesus Christ is said to overcome the difference between Being and humanity. The difficult part is that this belief may only be achieved as a response to a gracious gift not necessarily extended to all, so that it becomes equally difficult to move beyond sectarianism to a vision for all society and enshrined in the laws that regulate society.[38]

IV. When through the Deep Waters

Postmodern theology can be divided into liberal and conservative camps.[39] Liberal postmodern theologians,[40] working independently from philosophers, have largely reached the same outcomes over the past generation: the death of God in history; absence; the end of metaphysics; the focus on creation, not the Church, as the body of Christ; the end of doctrine and the futility of liturgy; the impossibility of text and narrative; and exhilaration in the face of the flux and variety of life. Liberal postmodern theologians celebrate the contingent meaninglessness of existence,[41] and by so doing they could be more properly characterized as nihilists rather than as Christian theologians, or even as postmodern thinkers, because postmodernity celebrates difference without necessarily denying it.[42]

By contrast, conservative postmodern theologians[43] do not use philosophical or social scientific concepts to question theology but use theology to show the fundamentally theological character of postmodern thought. Although postmodernity defers meaning, it does not erase the possibility of experience of the divine. It concedes that desire for the divine is inherent in creation and can only be experienced through difference, distance, and alterity. But conservative postmodern theologians argue that the divine can be met in the narrative of Jesus Christ, in his life while on earth, and in his Body, the Church, after his ascension.[44] Barth was the first twentieth-century theologian to consider the significance of Christ in the light of modernity and in anticipation of postmodernity.[45] Thinkers such as Lindbeck in the Protestant tradition and Henri du Lubac and Hans Ur von Balthazar in the Roman Catholic tradition have also done so, and so does radical orthodoxy.

Although highly abstract and complex, radical orthodoxy has struck a chord outside the self-absorbed world of academic theology to the extent that evangelicals are paying considerable attention to it for three instructive reasons: (i) its claim that the starting point for overcoming the nihilism of the secular world is theology, not philosophy or the social sciences; (ii) its foundation in classical Christianity; and (iii) its return to the incarnation of God in Jesus Christ rather than individual human reason as the starting point for reflection. In that, although radical orthodoxy employs the best postmodern thinking, its purpose is to challenge it and reclaim the world within a Christian theological framework so as to advance the destruction of the nihilistic trajectory of modernity and postmodernity.[46]

'Once, there was no secular ... The secular as a domain had to be ... imagined,'[47] John Milbank began in *Theology and Social Theory: Beyond Secular Reason*,[48] the book that launched the radical orthodoxy project. Notwithstanding the dense and inelegant prose[49] and the propensity to use postmodern jargon, the book is said to be an orthodox Christian assault on modernity and postmodernity by hoisting secularism on its own petard. Radical orthodoxy has been accused of difficulty of interpretation, controversial and wrong-headed reinterpretations of past thinkers, gaps in its scholarship, bad writing, impractical abstractedness, heresy, and more,[50] but it has commanded the attention of academic theologians and the Christian community internationally for the past decade and a half, and the scholarly output of those who identify with its position, although heterogeneous, has been considerable and promises to grow given their youth.[51] Although radical orthodoxy has covered numerous topics in theology, the present focus is on its core challenge to modernity and postmodernity as set out above, and then on its specific application to politics. Radical orthodoxy has not considered its application to law per se, but it seems easy to extrapolate from its political speculation what might be said about law.[52]

Milbank welcomes postmodernity for several reasons: its rejection of the idea that human reason can arrive at the truth; its embrace of the idea that truth can only be found in the context of a story or narrative; and the end of the metanarrative of the triumph of human reason of the past four centuries.[53] He argues that this clears the way for the return of a theological metanarrative, not because it is provable by reason, but for two other reasons: (i) Christianity has always been internally postmodern because it asserts creation ex nihilo and a reality in constant flux between nothing and infinity without fixed essences and composed only of relational differences and ceaseless alterations just like nihilism; but (ii) unlike the violence and difference of nihilism, the Christian narrative is about peace and harmony, the only other option in postmodernity; Christianity pursues a universal vision where people can 'remain in their many different cities, languages and cultures, yet still belong to the one eternal city ruled by

Christ, in whom all humanity was fulfilled.'[54] Christ brings peace to the world by being the reconciliation between God and humanity and by reconciling God and humanity. Milbank argues that nihilism may seem to assume no transcendental foundations but that it actually assumes something similar, that is, ontological violence. This ontological violence, which assumes the contingency of truth upon language, functions like a condition for the possibility of knowledge that is metaphysical in nature. Milbank argues that Christianity can outnarrate this attempt to overcome metaphysics by its ontology of peaceableness, which modernity and postmodernity cannot recognize because they assume violence as a condition for meaning. Once this foundation for meaning is overcome, theological language can be viewed as representing reality as much as any other philosophical language.[55]

The key to overcoming the violence of nihilism is adopting 'participation' as the central theological framework of radical orthodoxy. Adapted from Neoplatonism and early Christianity, Milbank's focus is less on the Neoplatonic hierarchies of being and Being, and more on the way in which the world is treated as a differentiated realm of beings and events knit together for a harmonious order and a common purpose. Difference is unimportant because by virtue of an underlying harmonious order a person or meaning can be what it is and at the same time depend on that from which it came and to which it is going. By virtue of participation, there can be no space or reserve independent of God as nihilism would suggest, that is, no ontological violence. Participation affirms a theory of meaning based on peaceful harmony.[56]

Although Milbank would deny this insight as derived from Barth,[57] with Barth he sees Jesus Christ as the link between the infinite and the finite, although expressed in the language of postmodernity. Christ fills the space between the infinite and the finite so there can be no conflict or ontological violence, rather the ontological priority of peaceableness.[58] As God and man, there can be nothing outside Christ: 'Jesus' names God's gift of himself in creation and redemption and because Jesus is God, not a copy of God, there can be no postmodern difference. The hypostatic union within the doctrine of the Trinity overcomes the need for a metaphysics of presence, so there is no need either for nihilism's strategy to overcome presence with deferral or nihilism's requirement of ontological violence to explain reality.[59] If radical orthodoxy overcomes metaphysics, then the repressed theological premises of secularism can be revealed and replaced by theology and by God. Radical orthodoxy further asserts that once metaphysics is overcome, the distinction between reason and revelation and nature and faith is meaningful.[60]

If radical orthodoxy has overcome metaphysics, then it must also adequately address the consequences of the metaphysical conclusions of modern and postmodern thinking beginning with the focus on language as the source of knowledge and Derrida's 'there is nothing outside the text' scepticism. In contrast to those who assert that while there may be some transcendental reality, language cannot mediate it, radical orthodoxy takes the more radical position that language participates in God's eternity. The liturgy, in particular, is a place where language and the experience of God are inseparable, so it is impossible to know the actual limits of language.[61] Radical orthodoxy assumes language to be of human rather than divine origin: to think otherwise is both to doubt the mediation of Christ in creation and to think first of ourselves from which to think about God. The key again is participation and analogy.

Philosophers have assumed a distinction between beings and what is common to any class of beings, that is, the 'is' that they have in common; the former can be determined but the latter is indeterminate. Radical orthodoxy returns to Aquinas's use of analogy to overcome philosophy's ontotheological difference: God's essence is God's existence, but in humans, essence and existence are distinct so that through their essential nature they can participate in God by analogy. We do not know much about essence by abstracting from existence, yet by virtue of our existence, particularly our capacity to desire, we can be attracted to the essence of the divine. Radical orthodoxy agrees with Augustine that knowledge is rooted in desire. The experience of desire leads us to experience our own being in relation to God's being, although we can only know about God's essence by analogy. Christ is the typology for this: we can see his human nature but can only know about his divine nature because it is manifested in the unique narrative of his life as a divine person. His essence can be perceived from his bodily presence.[62]

Radical orthodoxy assumes with Augustine that all knowledge is bodily, that is, subjective knowledge is mediated through a desire (which is not sexual) for bodies – social, political, or individual – as well as for God. This desire does not arise from a lack in humanity but from the fullness of God indwelling Christ's glorified body. After his ascension, the Church becomes his body in time and space to mediate that knowledge, most especially in the Eucharist, which assimilates partakers into God's body. Thus the Church and not the state is the true political body; the state is merely a simulacrum and an example of the ontological violence of secularized human existence. Participation in the Church produces a theological understanding of reality through which all other knowledge should be mediated, thus theology is the basis for all knowledge, not as an object but as a gift. Founded in orthodox theology about God as a gift of himself in Jesus Christ, the hypostatic union within the Trinity and the Church as his body in time and space, radical orthodoxy is also radical in its insistence on that gift to give integrity and meaning to the world. By participation in the gift, a comprehensive view of the world is once more possible.[63]

When Milbank turns to the specifics of participation, the role of Scripture, the Church, and Jesus as depicted in the Gospels becomes vague.[64] His engagement with Scripture is always abstract and never specific. The stories in the Gospels and their central character are treated as allegories about God requiring human effort and creativity to decipher. They are never simply the best recollections available, if not completely accurate, about Jesus' life and teaching.[65] Milbank does not treat the Gospels as realistic but rather presents Jesus as a cipher for his own theological intentions. For Milbank, the Gospels are the story of the founding of a new community, the Church, but even here he does not think of the Church as an institution with its own discipline and language but as a process.[66] His highly abstract and speculative interpretation of Christ is mirrored in his view of his body, the Church. There is no saviour in the text; members of the Church can construct their own saviour through their own individual interpretative practice.[67] An ecclesial process of unending exegetical openness means that the Church produces its own saviour. Jesus' saving work was not on the cross to atone for the sins of humankind but to found a practice, so that that practice must be God himself.[68] Jesus is the beginning of the practice and its end as well. The practice is repeated by every follower, so the story of Jesus is every follower's story and their end is his end.[69] Milbank does not emphasize the identity of Jesus as the mediator of salvation as orthodox creedal Christianity suggests.

Theology worth that name should explain all creation, that is, must be universal in its application; if God created the world in his own image, then his goal is to bring the world, including humanity, into conformity with his divine character. So from Milbank's understanding of the Church as the body of Christ, the Church must be a model for the human community, and the human community must be read through that model.[70] This has significance for the interpretation of the world and for other scholarly disciplines that also offer explanations of reality: in short, if they do not conform to the Christian model, they are wrong. Milbank is particularly scathing about the social sciences, which he regards as Christian heresies.[71] In *Theology and Social Theory*, he shows how the social sciences, especially sociology, diverge from Christian truth although they still retain a generic relation to it. However, he also agrees that there is no rational means for preferring Christianity over secular reason; it must simply be accepted. Conversely, Christianity should not accommodate secular reason because this weakens faith and practice. This position of Milbank has earned him the description as a 'despairing, postmodern fundamentalist of paradoxical sophistication.'[72]

Before turning to how radical orthodoxy has followed these insights through into political theory, it is convenient at this juncture to review some of the chief criticisms of its theological foundations because the failings posited of the theology are likely to be reflected in the political expressions of the theology. Critiques of radical orthodoxy are legion,[73] but the serious criticisms are few in number and frequently reiterated.[74]

Radical orthodoxy wishes to restore theology to centre stage after 'the death of God.' But the theology it propounds is hardly traditional notwithstanding its assertions of orthodoxy and a return to Christian roots. It treats Scripture, the Church, the creeds, and historical ecclesial practice as troublesome trivia with which it need not be overly concerned. It is difficult to fit radical orthodoxy into any theological tradition although it borrows from many. It is difficult to discern what Church it is writing for. Its main proponents self-identify as Anglo-Catholics with strong Roman Catholic leanings and self-consciously disassociate themselves from the Reformed theology at the roots of Anglicanism, but they never identify a Church for which they are writing and seem to operate entirely within the world of academic theology.[75] This is strange in light of their emphasis on Christianity as a practice and process within a particular community conceptualized as Christ's body. Even if their understanding of the worldwide Church is also postmodern in its acceptance of a great variety of communities, common sense would suggest that some institutional homogeneity and discipline is required to ensure integrity of practice and process.

Equally strange is the virtual disappearance of the Jesus of the

Gospels from radical orthodox theology. This eerily resembles the accounts of Jesus at the origins of modern theology, which also discounted the human Jesus of Scripture: for Kant, Jesus was an archetype for moral righteousness, and after him the human Jesus was either often absent from theology or treated as a historical person about whom we have few independently verifiable historical facts. Once Jesus' humanity and atoning work receded from Western thought, the violence characteristic of modern and postmodern thought poured in. By turning Jesus into a concept, radical orthodoxy falls into the same trap as the theologies it seeks to overcome and deprives Christian communities of a practical model for human living – a strange move given radical orthodoxy's emphasis on Jesus' followers repeating his life.[76]

These criticisms point, however, to the most profound criticism of all: that radical orthodoxy is just another narrative that proclaims Christianity as the metanarrative, or alternatively, offers itself as a metanarrative, although one that does not necessarily tell the Christian story in a traditional way.[77] If radical orthodoxy is to overcome postmodern nihilism, it needs some knockout argument that it cannot give; instead, meaning continues to be deferred. Nihilism attempts to live without a narrative but in doing so it necessarily overcomes nihilism so that narrative comes back in. Radical orthodoxy does the same thing: it claims a metanarrative but fails to posit one that positions all others. Its narrative, too, is illusory and impossible in the end. Metanarratives seem to be concurrently both unavoidable and impossible. Yet all attempts at metanarrative tend towards theology because humanity is persistently haunted by 'otherness' and theology has the longest and richest history of attempting to do what it admits to being impossible: capturing the God who is identified with otherness. Even secular thinkers cannot avoid the lure of theology to the other out there. Theology has a rich tradition of moral reflection, in contrast to nihilism, which has quickly collapsed into individual debauchery and collective totalitarianism, both of which make theology's return attractive as a means for resisting society's cultural dissolution. So it is possible to agree with radical orthodoxy that at the end of postmodernity the return of theology is unavoidable, if impossible, in the final analysis. What postmodernity has been deferring is the return of humanity's persistent search for the meaning of life.

Augustine and Aquinas agreed that reason is not a sufficient basis for knowing the other: God becomes revelation through faith, and faith is only gained by revelation.[78] If Barth was right that Jesus Christ was God's gift to us as the revelation of who God is, then radical orthodoxy is just another brilliant, if exceedingly complex, failure of human reason employing the best thought of its generation to capture a God who cannot be contained by human reason but who can be experienced by living the life of Jesus in the community that is his body in time and space, as Lindbeck argues. Theories are not the glue holding the world together; the body of Christ is.

Notwithstanding the unpersuasiveness of radical orthodoxy's attempts to use Christian theology to overcome secular nihilism, its contributions to the clarification of the juncture at which Western thought finds itself are considerable. Its consideration of their implications for life in the city, that is, politics and law, is equally problematical as well as illuminating.

V. Thy Troubles to Bless

Radical orthodoxy proclaims that it is a new way of doing theology by reconceptualizing the Christian metanarrative from which to position all other human endeavours, including the arts, music, philosophy, and personal and political life,[79] and radical orthodox theologians have begun to think through its implications for politics, the state, and society. This part of the project is in its early stages and necessarily incomplete but some elements are becoming clear, beginning with the assertion that politics also took a wrong turn in the later Middle Ages when the state became secularized.

Catherine Pickstock traces the separation of the sovereign state from an organic Christian order to Duns Scotus's notion of the supremacy of the human will detached from desire for the good, a synthesis which medieval theology had ambiguously held together. Once the human will is detached from teleological goals, it is free to shape the immanent realm as it thinks best. Paradoxically, while Scotus privileged the will over reason as the part of humanity that is closest to God, once God is also viewed as far off, the will is left on its own to do the best it can in the circumstances. The social realm can now be shaped by the human will; it need not aspire to imitate any other community, no matter how ideal, and the basic source to shape the social realm becomes the sovereign will of the individual possessed of the greatest sanctioning power in any community. The movement from feudalism to nation state ruled by a sovereign prince towards the end of the Middle Ages is the political corollary of the rise of the sovereign will in late medieval theology.

Temporal power posited in the human will becomes conceivable as secular authority established its own aura of 'sacredness' to rival that of the Church, which had dominated Christendom before its fragmentation into nation states. Pickstock characterizes this move as one from a liturgical ordering of society towards a teleological goal, to an organization based on will and power divorced from love. She suggests this can be seen in such social changes in late medieval society as the decline of the lay fraternities and craft guilds where social integration and alliances were important for economic well-being and in the decline of the extended family as a community as godparents disappeared from baptism (the entry into that community) and as marriage came to be seen less as an alliance of families and more as a consensual agreement of two independent parties. Peace in society was no longer ensured by communal practices, derived from the community of the Church in the common cup of the Eucharist, but enforced by a sovereign using law to regulate what was permissible, including regulating the Church, which was coming to be seen as a servant of the state but where certain religious propositions could be maintained privately so as not to complicate state practices.[80]

For radical orthodoxy, the separation of a secular realm into a nation state ruled by a secular sovereign with its own goals constitutes a major challenge for the metanarrative that there can be no secular realm because there can be nothing outside God in whom all participate. The question of how this could have happened in a 'Christian' society is answered by Milbank's suggestion that this originated theologically once Scotus and Occam postulated that the relationship between God and humanity was a covenantal relationship derived from God's *potentia ordinata* rather that his *potentia absoluta*, thereby abandoning participation in Being as the central motif of theology, a model for human relations as contractual in nature was provided. The contract is no longer with God but between humans in the political order.[81] Milbank further suggests that the model for the earliest states was also in the late medieval Church, which itself adopted the covenantal model as shown in the conciliar movement to reduce the power of the papacy, the adoption of canon law to regulate ecclesiastical affairs, notions of sole sovereignty posited in the pope, the use of contract and property for internal organization, and the creation of a top-heavy bureaucracy. In short, the Church failed to be the Church by preserving the rule of the Gospel and accordingly failed to persuade society that the Gospel was the appropriate rule for social life.[82]

Milbank asserts that to restore the Christian metanarrative as the true story of the role of the state, it is necessary to recover the account of history given by Augustine in *De civitate dei*.[83] Augustine contrasted two cities, *civitas dei*, a city of peace, and *civitas terrena*, the city of man, marked by denial of God and love of self, a city of violence. The city of God is the site of salvation initiated by Jesus Christ when God reached down to liberate humanity from the violence of the secular realm and founded a different kind of community providing genuine peace not through subordination of rivals but through reconciliation.[84] *Civitas dei* begins its pilgrimage to God on earth in the Church conceptualized as a household or as a community existing within larger political communities, but with the distinctive feature that its 'direction of desire'[85] is to God. It is the only true society because it is completely conformed to this desire by an absolute consensus and in entire harmony.[86] It provides a 'unique and distinctive structural logic for human society.'[87] The reunification of humanity, in Augustine's vision, depends on recovery of the true citizenship of humanity in the city of God and of the understanding that all are journeying to their true home in heaven. Thus the Church, which unites heaven and earth, is the true politics.[88]

Through his analysis of Augustine, Milbank argues that true political theory begins with the Church so that it is impossible to conceive of any political structures like a state outside the Church. (It is unclear here whether Milbank is referring to the institutional Church or the invisible city of God on pilgrimage through this world.) Any structures outside the Church exist in a realm of sin, that is, where coercive force and self-assertion are engaged for their own sake. Unlike Aquinas, Augustine does not concede the political realm to be a permanent natural sphere, as this would imply the division of the sacred (with God) and the secular (without God). In Milbank's view, this division is not only theologically wrong but bad for the Church, because a separate Church that understands itself to have a sphere of influence will tend to mimic political sovereignty and create a bureaucracy to manage its sphere.[89] Milbank prefers that the bonds between Church and state be 'extremely hazy'[90] so as to control both. His vision is that of the earliest Christian communities: like Jesus, they did not seek to gain power or to overthrow power but created alternative communities of peace and charity,[91] thereby 'interrupting' the operations of the Roman Empire.[92]

The notion that the evolution of the state in the West is a false move is further explored by William Cavanaugh, who attempts to return the state to radical orthodoxy's Christian metanarrative. The normative liberal version of early modern European history is that the rise of the neutral state was an outcome of the religious wars following the Reformation, which were only resolved once a neutral stronger power seized control and secularized public discourse, thereby privatizing religious disagreements and religion generally. But Cavanaugh reverses this version to argue that the wars of religion were actually the outcome of the rise of the modern state, using religion, to aggrandize secular authority over the decaying remnants of the medieval ecclesial order. The privatization of religion was necessary for the state to secure sovereignty over its subjects. The modern state was not the peacemaker among religions but rather used violence to achieve control over religion and society.[93]

The rise of the state predated the Reformation, as did theories of the state. Marsilius of Padua (c. 1275–1342) argued that secular powers should have sole use of coercive force and that, by its nature, coercion was secular; the Church was, at most, a moral not a geopolitical authority. The doctrine of Martin Luther (1483–1547) of the two kingdoms contemplated that coercive power was bestowed by God on the state to maintain civil peace among sinners and that the Church's authority was over the proper preaching of the Word and administration of the sacraments. Concurrently, in all the early modern states of Western Europe, secular princes were embroiled in disputes with the papacy over property, taxation, law, and jurisdiction, and the religious wars were actually started when Charles V sacked Rome in 1527, not Wittenberg. His subsequent attacks on the Lutheran states were to consolidate his authority as Holy Roman Emperor, and Protestant state resistance was more about resistance to the expansion of his authority over largely independent states than about correct doctrine. The sixteenth-century compromise, *cuius regio, eius religio*, recognized the dominance of secular princes over religion within their states. Cavanaugh notes that secular historians of the sixteenth and seventeenth centuries commonly agree that religious issues were among the many that fuelled these wars, but that in the process, religion *qua* religion came to be thought of as a set of personal beliefs separate from a required public loyalty to the state. The rise of the state required the privatization of religion. The religious wars were instigated by princes and nobles, not pastors and parsons.[94]

By the seventeenth century, state theorists such as Thomas Hobbes (1588–1679) thought of religion as a service to the sovereign: both states and religion are responsible for human fear and ignorance, but since the civil sovereign is best equipped to ensure peace, both should be ruled by one absolute civil sovereign so as to foreclose civil unrest. Hobbes's Christian prince is pastor, prophet, peacemaker, and policeman; his subjects may think what they wish provided they are silent in public. The church is the state, so that there are as many churches as there are civil states and no one church universal. Each subject in the state depends not on any horizontal ties to others but only on the sovereign: the Body of Christ is atomized into the body of the state.[95] Once Christians acknowledge the state as lord, it is a matter of indifference whether there is one religion or many, thus religious diversity, or toleration, becomes possible. For John Locke (1632–1704), toleration is a tool by which the state divides and conquers the Church once it is accepted that the state grants and protects religion as a private matter.[96] Thus, in Cavanaugh's view doctrinal conflicts of the sixteenth and seventeenth centuries permitted the state to advance secular goals. Once religion is a private matter, the Body of Christ is not a rival to the body of the state. Not surprisingly, Locke excluded Roman Catholicism from toleration because it considered the Church to be a transnational body.[97] Milbank would see this evolution as flowing from the theological movement in the later Middle Ages, from a theology of participation to a theology of will: God commands obedience from individual wills to his law rather than assuming all humanity into the Trinity to participate in him. The loss of participation is a loss of the teleological ends of human life and the abandonment of individuals to the state of nature in which Hobbes found them.[98]

In succeeding centuries, Christian theology has accepted the saving powers of the state in place of those of the Church, seeing the state as an agent for peace and human unity and accepting the laws of the state as necessary to ensure these ends, even when these laws may not reflect Christian understandings. But radical orthodoxy would assert this to be a false unity and peace fundamentally at odds with the Christian metanarrative.[99] Cavanaugh argues that the rise of the state is predicated on the fragmentation of society into individuals who are freed from ties of family, property, guilds, fraternities and Church in order to be directly subject to the state. Participation in God in the community that is his Body on earth is regarded as a threat to the state, which has no other goal than to perpetuate itself, by violence if necessary. Cavanaugh regards this body as a false copy of the Body of Christ, a 'simulacrum,'[100] and posits the necessity for the Eucharist to be at the heart of the only true body that leads to salvation.[101]

Cavanaugh, along with numerous others, also considers the rise of capitalism to be associated with the rise of the nation state by virtue of direct state support for business, state-sanctioned monetary and taxation systems, and a centralized legal system that contractualized relationships based on land, goods, and labour. The individual was freed from bonds of kinship and community in order to relate to individuals through contract.[102] Radical orthodoxy therefore sees capitalism as another false step destroying the true universal community which is the Church. Radical orthodoxy prefers socialism as the economic mechanism for ordering society, notwithstanding its association with the rise of the monolithic secular state.

Milbank calls capitalism a 'Christian heresy'[103] for several reasons: (i) it celebrates the will separately from any account of the true or the good; (ii) it occupies a secular space; and (iii) it represents a loss of the doctrine of the Trinity through which the world is created for participation with God in favour of the secular political value of contract.[104] A contractual economy assumes exchange based on the will rather than on giving as a gift that gives expecting return, not in the sense of an exchange of equivalent value, but as a gift that can never be alienated and whose givenness always returns. The human economy should repeat the divine economy where God gives himself and infinitely returns, where giving involves shared benefit.[105] Stephen Long, Milbank's most prolific interpreter on economic matters, admits the difficulty of understanding what Milbank is saying here,[106] but he suggests that the general idea is that only socialism can repeat God's giving from his infinite plenitude.[107] Quite how this works in the real economic world in which new economic value must be continually created in order not to run out, that is, is essentially finite in nature unless continually created, is a mystery in Milbank's version of the economic realm.[108]

Nevertheless, Long praises Milbank for reminding us that economic issues depend on the theological end served by exchange: Christian virtue requires that exchange assumes reciprocal relations among persons based on the gift of their labour, which cannot be sacrificed or alienated as in contractual relationships but rather should extend our being as participants in the lives of those who receive the gift.[109] Long also praises Milbank's 'socialism by grace'[110] as reminding us that economic exchange occurs within the definitive social practice for divine and human exchange, the Eucharist, defined as God's self-gift to humans, which ought to be repeated in all human exchanges including economic exchange.[111]

While Milbank advocates that Christians should strive to 'abolish capitalism,'[112] radical orthodoxy remains profoundly ambiguous about how to engage in political and economic life other than by asserting that engagement must be on radical orthodoxy's terms of retheologizing both so as to direct them to their proper teleological end. Milbank suggests that the example of Jesus and the early Christians of refusal to seize power or to overthrow existing structures in favour of creating alternative spaces for Christian practice should be a permanent feature of the Church's life in time and space because intrinsic to the logic of the Gospel.[113] Milbank does not seem to preclude engagement, indeed thinks it necessary, yet another radical orthodox theologian, Daniel Bell, rejects both the nation state and capitalism in favour of reclaiming 'base Christian communities' as social, economic, and political units within any larger civil society.

In an extended essay drawing on liberation theology and its base community experiences in Latin America, Bell argues that forgiveness, reconciliation, and peace, rather than justice and the violence and conflict it necessarily entails, are the antidotes to the state and capitalism, and uses the examples of poor Christian communities in Latin America who have resisted these by refusing to cease suffering like the crucified Christ in extending forgiveness to systems that had caused suffering.[114]

Although he does not personally self-identify with radical orthodoxy,[115] Rowan Williams clearly captures its position when he suggests that while the Church is first of all a community devoted to a distinctive communal life to which individuals can freely commit themselves, it should concurrently be engaged in a dialogue with the world, in a 'long revolution,' not in sectarian separation nor in advancing theocracy. Both assume an end of dialogue and history, and reflect a misunderstanding of the Christian hope for God's kingdom by attempting to fuse divine and earthly sovereignty.[116]

Nevertheless, dialogue requires that both sides have a position to advance, and it is far from clear that radical orthodoxy has advanced any Christian moral teaching on how Christian communities and individuals should live, not even that found in Scripture as traditionally interpreted by the Church over the past two millennia. Interestingly, radical orthodox theologies have hovered around one of the most disputed issues in both Church and society today, that is, homosexual relationships, without resolution, a particularly difficult outcome for the Church because the fundamental issue is the authority and interpretation of Scripture. Milbank,[117] Ward,[118] and Loughlin[119] appear to adopt a positive perspective without expressing approval, while others adopt the extreme opposite of regarding celibacy for all as the price for admission into the peaceful community of the Church.[120]

No radical orthodox theologian has expressly considered its significance for law, but radical orthodoxy's attitudes to the state and capitalism are likely predictive: since law is a creation of the state, whether by legislatures or courts, its specific rules should also reflect the radical orthodox metanarrative of participation. But radical orthodoxy's failure to articulate more precisely how economic relationships of exchange or how personal relationships of affection do this leaves little clue as to how law could do so.

VI. Thy Dross to Consume and Thy Gold to Refine

Comparisons of law and theology can only be worthwhile for those who fit into one or more of the following three categories: believers; non-believers with sufficient open-mindedness to consider comparative approaches to be potentially worthwhile if for purely secular purposes; and non-believers seeking arguments to debunk theological premises for law. Comparisons of law and theology would be considered worthless by those who fit into the following two categories: believers who think the project impossible, or who are committed either to pluralism or sectarianism or both concurrently; and non-believers who see no comparative value in such a project nor any need for arguments to debunk theological premises. Of these five categories, only those in the first two will likely have read this far, and they deserve reward for their patience.

As stated earlier, the choice of radical orthodoxy as the contemporary theological school through which to compare law and theology was predicated upon its status as the group that has taken modern and postmodern thought most seriously for Christianity in the present generation. Unlike some other theologians, they have not given in entirely to nihilism nor have they sought refuge by reciting old formulae in sectarian enclaves. If they fail to persuade, then the value of comparative perspectives is doubtful or at best confirms that while faith may be its own solution, it resolves no earthly debates, especially for those without faith, including crafting the best way to live as a civil community. Law-making and laws remain contested grounds, because there can be no social consensus on what laws should contain.

The outcome of five centuries of speculation can be succinctly summarized. Once late-medieval theology emphasized the inscrutability and distance of God from humanity, human reason was left as the starting point, in place of revelation, for discovery of the nature, reality, and purpose of life. But how can human reason know anything with certainty? While scientifically proven facts about the natural world can be ascertained and manipulated to improve and enrich the physical quality of human life, transcendent concepts, if existing in some virtual reality, seemed impossible to prove by the exercise of human reason. Most philosophers assumed that these existed in some sense because they help to explain how humans know about the world and relate to others. Whether they exist in our minds or out there and are accessible to human reason was debatable.

The other historical source of knowledge about reality and the truth of human existence, Scripture, proved no match for human reason. The text came to be considered so historically unreliable in a narrow factual sense and susceptible to sufficient differences in interpretation as to be inscrutable. It was no longer the transparent revelation of God, although it continued to be a source for a religious sensibility. Once neither human reason nor revelation could be trusted as sources for truth, the existence of truth was doubted as an independent or transcendent concept, and was seen as a function of the will to power of the strongest in any society. There is no truth or reality out there, rather, the world is endlessly self-creating so that humans can become creators of their own lives, using language to describe what is 'true' for them. Self-discovery is the source for truth and being here, participating in the world, is the only way to discover reality, except that it probably cannot be discovered. The language that we use to express our experience of being here ultimately fails to capture reality either because there is no reality to capture or because language cannot do so. Language acquires meaning only from the internal relationships of words to other words, and meanings change over time. Thus, meaning is continually deferred and any meaning asserted today can only be by power and violence and not because it corresponds to some definitive external meaning.

Christian theology responded to the death of transcendent meaning, of God, in history by attempting to restore a link between the immanent and the transcendent by recovery of the centrality of Jesus Christ to the meaning of the world. Since the source of knowledge about Jesus is Scripture,[121] the meaning of the text becomes the key to human understanding of the meaning of the world. But the text is not susceptible to indisputable meaning, so Christian theology in the course of the twentieth century placed increased emphasis on the community within which the text was interpreted. The meaning of the text was the meaning accepted by the community and learned by living the life of Jesus in his body, the Church. However, discernment of the authoritative meaning remained difficult without community acceptance of a single authority to do so, with the result that precise doctrinal statements have lost considerable ascendency in favour of aesthetic experience as the key to the 'deep grammar' of meaning. With this loss has also come the loss of community confidence in the specific rules for Christian life as set out in Scripture.[122] Admission that rational explication may not be possible is compensated by the assertion that so long as the Church endures, Christianity must, in some sense, constitute a rational response to the meaning of the world.

While the response of Christian theology to postmodernity adopted many of the features of postmodern thinking, especially finding meaning by being there in the community and by doubting that it is possible to articulate final meaning in this life, it still required certain leaps of faith at the outset: accepting Jesus Christ as the divine revelation, as God and man; accepting Scripture as the authoritative text; and accepting the requirement to live in the Christian community to learn the deep grammar of reality. It meant accepting the impossibility of explaining why the Christian metanarrative outnarrates all other stories about the world.

Radical orthodoxy attempts to do so by postulating that harmonious peace is the fundamental story about the world, effected by Jesus Christ, who humanizes the transcendent and the immanent. By filling the space between God and man, there can be nothing outside God, and through the body of Christ in time and space, the Church, all participate in God and in his harmonious peace. Jesus Christ overcomes metaphysics. Humanity can know the truth about the world because language, although of human origin, can participate in God by analogy, and most especially in the Eucharist, where language and the experience of God are inseparable.[123] By virtue of the fullness of God filling humanity, human desire is drawn to God and knowledge of God. The Church, as God's body, is the place where that knowledge is received as a gift through participation in the practices of Jesus Christ in the community. Everything outside the Church is false, and only when subsumed once more within the Church, within the body of

Christ, will harmonious peace be restored as the true story about the world in place of the false story of nihilism and violence.

If this characterization of radical orthodoxy is correct, then it is doubtful that it has overcome postmodernity and the problems Christian theology has experienced in the past century or so in overcoming the nihilism of contemporary thought. Radical orthodoxy also requires leaps of faith in relation to the nature of Jesus Christ; the narrative it tells about whom he is; its interpretation of the Church as his body in time and space; the role and meaning of Scripture, especially when it figures so little in its account of the truth about the world. Radical orthodoxy is as reliant on that text as any other Christian theology, yet it drinks deeply from postmodern scepticism about the possibility of an authoritative interpretation. Milbank even suspects that radical orthodoxy offers no knock-down argument, and radical orthodoxy's arms-length relationship with the Scriptural specifics of Christian faith suggests profound ambiguity about how compelling the practices of the earliest Christian communities should be two millennia later. Why radical orthodoxy's narrative is *the* metanarrative remains to be shown.

VII. (Legal) Postlude

What comparative lessons are here for the legal reader? Throughout, it has been assumed that law, in some sense, strives to codify the best rules for both individual lives and for life in society, and should, therefore, be attuned to all serious suggestions. For at least fifteen hundred years in the West, this has meant legal principles broadly mirroring Christian teaching about right and wrong conduct. But once the Christian world view started to lose its hold on the Western mind and imagination, it also lost its hold on Western legal systems. Any Christian theology that seeks to regain influence in public life and law must provide compelling reasons for its assertion that Christianity is the true story about the world and the best way to live. Yet, this analysis suggests, Christian theology has not been able to overcome the nihilism and fragmentation in Western thought and life, both public and private, that can only be refereed by an ostensibly neutral state committed to pluralism if civil strife is to be avoided.

Whether comparisons of law and theology focus on substance, that is, the 'truth,' or procedure, that is, methods for doing the discipline, the result is the same. Neither can find their respective ways to the truth about the world except by leaps of faith, nor escape being mired in texts of human origin and subject to differences of human interpretation reflecting the communities in which those texts are being interpreted. Even radical orthodoxy, which has taken postmodernity most seriously, has been captured by it and rendered incapable of delivering the definitive response. Reason contrives to fall short, yet revelation persists in disturbing us. For those who believe, who believe they have received the gift of the peace of God, in Christ, the temporal realm and the rules, the laws by which societies order their affairs, will continue to be alien when not in conformity with their understanding of what the Gospel requires. For those who do not believe, Christianity will continue to be, as it was for Nietzsche, another ideology that has lost its will to power and its power over the Western mind. The clash of ideologies will continue and civil law will continue to strive to find the fleeting compromise, constantly negotiable, required for civil peace. Speculation will be endless. Yet, 'When I have finished writing, when I am a hundred and ten, all I will have done will have been to attempt a portrait of God. Of the God. Of what escapes us and makes us wonder. Of what we do not know but feel. Of what makes us live.'[124]

NOTES

Epigraph is from Iris Murdoch, *Henry & Cato* (London: Triad/Panther Books, 1977) at 350–1.

1 Bruno Forte, *The Essence of Christianity* (Grand Rapids, MI: Eerdmans, 2003) at 65–6; 74–6.

2 On the yearning of contemporary pagan cultural theorists for Christianity, see Paul J. Griffiths, 'Christ and Critical Theory,' *First Things* 145 (August/September 2004): 46–55.

3 This name was confirmed by the publication in 1999 of a collection of essays: John Milbank, Catherine Pickstock, and Graham Ward, eds., *Radical Orthodoxy. A New Theology* (London: Routledge, 1999).

4 *Ibid.*, for various essays together with the texts cited below.

5 This section is written as historical background and makes no claim to originality. In writing it, the following sources have been extensively used: Philippa Berry and Andrew Wernick, eds., *Shadow of Spirit. Postmodernism and Religion* (London: Routledge, 1992); Conor Cunningham, *Geneology of Nihilism* (London: Routledge, 2002); David F. Ford, *The Modern Theologians*, 2nd ed. (Oxford: Blackwell, 1997); Stanley J. Grenz, *A*

Primer on Postmodernism (Grand Rapids, MI: Eerdmans, 1996); Stanley J. Grenz and John R. Franke, *Beyond Foundationalism: Shaping Theology in a Postmodern Context* (Louisville, KY: Westminster John Knox Press, 2001); Lawrence Paul Hemming, *Heidegger's Atheism: The Refusal of a Theological Voice* (Notre Dame, IN: University of Notre Dame Press, 2002); Graham Ward, ed., *The Postmodern God: A Theological Reader* (Oxford: Blackwell, 1997); and Kevin J. Vanhoozer, ed., *The Cambridge Companion to Postmodern Theology* (Cambridge: Cambridge University Press, 2003). I have largely followed the narrative in Grenz's *Primer* and selected those aspects which portray the movement from modernity to postmodernity from a Christian perspective. I have also omitted the citations from the original texts to save space; these can be found in the texts cited.

6 Augustine's position was the opposite of Descartes's position: to think is to realize one's ignorance of the world, not to build up knowledge of the world fully accessible to the reason. For an extended discussion of these contrasting positions, see John M. Rist, *Augustine* (Cambridge: Cambridge University Press, 1994) at 85–91.

7 Ford, *supra* note 5 at 8.

8 *The Savage Mind* (Chicago: University of Chicago Press, 1966) at 247, cited in Grenz, *supra* note 5 at 119.

9 *B.(R.) v. Children's Aid Society of Metropolitan Toronto* (1995) 122 D.L.R. (4th) 1 (S.C.C.); *H.(B.) v. Alberta (Director of Child Welfare)* [2002] 7 W.W.R. 616 (Alta. Q.B.); [2002] 7 W.W.R. 664 (Alta. C.A.); leave to appeal refused (2002) 295 N.R. 198n (S.C.C.). See also: *Rodriguez v. A.G.B.C.*, [1993] 3 S.C.R. 519.

10 *Egale Canada Inc v. Canada (Attorney General)* (2003) 225 D.L.R. (4th) 472 (B.C.C.A.); *Halpern v. Canada (Attorney General)* (2003) 225 D.L.R. (4th) 529 (Ont. C.A.).

11 This experience is recounted by Robert W. Jensen, 'Karl Barth,' in Ford, *supra* note 5 at 21–2.

12 Cited by Charles Marsh, 'Dietrich Bonhoeffer,' in Ford, *supra* note 5 at 41.

13 Jensen, *supra* note 11 at 28–30.

14 *Ibid.* at 31.

15 Grenz and Franke, *supra* note 5 at 188–90.

16 For the nature of Barth's Christology, see George Hunsinger, *Disruptive Grace: Studies in the Theology of Karl Barth* (Grand Rapids, MI: Eerdmans, 2000) at 131–47.

17 The importance of Barth for narrative theology is shown by Gerard Loughlin, *Telling God's Story: Bible, Church and Narrative Theology* (Cambridge: Cambridge University Press, 1996) at 33–4. Barth's status as a

postmodern thinker is explored in Graham Ward, *Barth, Derrida and the Language of Theology* (Cambridge: Cambridge University Press, 1995), which argues that Barth's doctrine of analogy is a theological reading of Derrida's economy of *différance*.

18 See, for example, Brevard S. Childs, *Biblical Theology in Crisis* (Philadelphia: Westminster Press, 1970); Hans Frei, *The Eclipse of Biblical Narrative: A Study in Eighteenth and Nineteenth Century Hermeneutics* (New Haven, CT: Yale University Press, 1974); David H. Kelsey, *The Uses of Scripture in Recent Theology* (Philadelphia: Fortress Press, 1975); Francis Watson, *Text, Church and World: Biblical Interpretation in Theological Perspective* (Edinburgh: T. and T. Clark, 1994); Roy A. Harrisville and Walter Sundberg, *The Bible in Modern Culture: Theology and Historical-Critical Method from Spinoza to Käsemann* (Grand Rapids, MI: Eerdmans, 1995); Wesley A. Kort, *Take, Read: Scripture, Textuality, and Cultural Practice* (University Park, PA: Pennsylvania State University Press, 1996).

19 Grenz and Franke, *supra* note 5 at 69.

20 Kevin J. Vanhoozer, 'Scripture and Tradition,' in Vanhoozer, *supra* note 5 at 151–2.

21 *Is There a Text in this Class? The Authority of Interpretative Communities* (Cambridge, MA: Harvard University Press, 1980).

22 *Whose Justice? Which Rationality?* (Notre Dame, IN: University of Notre Dame Press, 1989). For an extended discussion of MacIntyre from a radical orthodox perspective, see Tracy Rowland, *Culture and the Thomist Tradition* (London: Routledge, 2003).

23 For these, see Ford, *supra* note 5, and Vanhoozer, *supra* note 5. See also Graham Ward, ed., *The Postmodern God. A Theological Reader* (Oxford: Blackwell, 1988).

24 For the Yale school, see William C. Placher, 'Postliberal Theology,' in Ford, *supra* note 5 at ch. 18; George Hunsinger, 'Postliberal Theology,' in Vanhoozer, *supra* note 5 at ch. 3; and Loughlin, *supra* note 17.

25 *Supra* note 18. For the paragraphs that follow, I am especially indebted to Loughlin, *supra* note 17.

26 Loughlin, *ibid.*, at 33–5, 67–8.

27 *Ibid.* at 68–70.

28 *Ibid.* at 75–76.

29 *Ibid.* at 153–8.

30 Vanhoozer, *supra* note 20 at 160–1.

31 Loughlin, *supra* note 17 at 39–42. For a comparison of Barth and Lindbeck on scripture and truth, see Hunsinger, *supra* note 16 at 305–18.

32 *Ibid.* at 48.

33 *Ibid.* at 48–9.
34 *Ibid.* at 90–6, 158–61. For the sectarian point, see Rowan Williams, *On Christian Theology* (Oxford: Blackwell, 2000) at 35–43.
35 Loughlin, *supra* note 17 at 96.
36 *The Church in a Postliberal Age* (Grand Rapids, MI: Eerdmans, 2002) at 91–105, 144–65.
37 *Ibid.*
38 For the contributions the Evangelicals can bring to postliberalism in relation to the movement from narrative to doctrine, see Hunsinger, *supra* note 16 at 338–60.
39 Graham Ward, 'Postmodern Theology,' in Ford, *supra*, note 5 at 586. See also Gavin Hyman, *The Predicament of Postmodern Theology: Radical Orthodoxy or Nihilist Textualism?* (Louisville, KY: Westminster John Knox Press, 2001).
40 For example, Thomas Altizer, Don Cupitt, David Ray Griffin, Mark C. Taylor, and Paul Tillich.
41 Ward, *supra* note 39 at 592.
42 *Ibid.*
43 For example, Karl Barth, Michel de Certeau, Hans Frei, George Lindbeck, Jean-Luc Marion, and John Milbank.
44 Ward, *supra* note 39 at 598.
45 Barth is sometimes labelled the 'only major' postmodern theologian as a result. See Jensen, *supra* note 11 at 22.
46 Robert E. Webber, *The Younger Evangelicals: Facing the Challenges of the New World* (Grand Rapids, MI: Baker Books, 2002) at 72–3.
47 *Infra* note 48 at 9.
48 (Oxford: Blackwell, 1990).
49 So dense and jargon-filled is Milbank's writing, that it is a standard starting observation of all analyses of it to comment on how difficult it is to understand.
50 Some of the most scathing critiques include Richard H. Roberts, 'Transcendental Sociology? A Critique of John Milbank's Theology and Social Theory: Behind Secular Reason,' *Scottish Journal of Theology* 46 (1993): 527–35; Gareth Jones, 'On Not Seeing the Joke,' *Times Literary Supplement* (2 April 1999), 12; Colin Gunton, Editorial, *International Journal of Systematic Theology* 1 (1999): 217; Steven Shakespeare, 'The New Romantics: A Critique of Radical Orthodoxy,' *Theology* 103 (2000): 163–77; Anthony Kenny, 'Aquinas and the Appearance of Bread,' *Times Literary Supplement* (5 October 2001), 14; Hyman, *supra* note 39; R.R. Reno, 'The Radical Orthodoxy Project,' *First Things* 100 (February 2000): 37–44, reprinted in

In the Ruins of the Church, Sustaining Faith in an Age of Diminished Christianity (Grand Rapids, MI: Brazos Press, 2002), ch. 4. Sympathetic critiques include Kieran Flanagan, ed., *New Blackfriars* (1992) 73; Lawrence Paul Hemming, ed., *Radical Orthodoxy? A Catholic Enquiry* (Aldershot, UK: Ashgate, 2000); Thomas Venard, 'Radical Orthodoxy: Une Première Impression,' fs22 *Revue Thomistein* 10 (2001): 409–44.

51 The major texts are as follows: Milbank, *supra* note 48; Milbank, *The Word Made Strange: Theology, Language, Culture* (Oxford: Blackwell, 1997); Catherine Pickstock, *After Writing: On the Liturgical Consummation of Philosophy* (Oxford: Blackwell, 1998); Milbank, Pickstock, and Graham Ward, eds., *Radical Orthodoxy: A New Theology* (London: Routledge, 1999); D. Stephen Long, *Divine Economy* (London: Routledge, 2000); Milbank and Pickstock, *Truth in Aquinas* (London: Routledge, 2001); Graham Ward, *Cities of God* (London: Routledge, 2000); Daniel M. Bell, *Liberation Theology after the God of History* (London: Routledge, 2001); Cunningham, *supra* note 5; James K.A. Smith, *Speech and Theology* (London: Routledge, 2002); Rowland, *supra* note 22; Milbank, *Being Reconciled. Ontology and Pardon* (London: Routledge, 2003); Michael Hanley, *Augustine and Modernity* (London: Routledge, 2003). In addition, there has been a prolific production of articles, many published in either *Modern Theology* fs22 or *New Blackfriars*.

52 *Infra* section 5.

53 Hyman, *supra* note 39 at 27–8.

54 Milbank, 'Postmodern Critical Augustinianism: A Short *Summa* in Forty-Two Responses to Unasked Questions,' *Modern Theology* 7 (1993): 225–37, repr. in Ward, *supra* note 5 at 267–8.

55 D. Stephen Long, 'Radical Orthodoxy,' in Vanhoozer, *supra* note 5 at 130.

56 Milbank, Pickstock, and Ward, *supra* note 51 at 3–4. See also Reno, *supra* note 50 at 39.

57 Milbank takes pains to distinguish Barth for reasons that may have more to do with his self-conscious Anglo-Catholicism and its longstanding attempts to eradicate Reformed theological influences from Anglicanism. This is evident in his contribution to Milbank, Pickstock, and Ward, *supra* note 51 at ch. 1, and his preference for von Balthazar, which is ironic, since von Balthazar was a close friend of Barth and credited Barth for many of his own theological insights; see John Riches and Ben Quash, 'Hans Ur von Balthazar,' in Ford, *supra* note 5 at ch. 8, and Lucy Gardner, David Moss, Ben Quash, and Graham Ward, *Balthazar at the End of Modernity* (Edinburgh: T. and T. Clark, 1999). Radical orthodoxy's attempts to distance itself from Barth has not foreclosed some theologians from

labelling them as 'flashy neo-Barthians': Gavin D'Costa, 'Seeking After Theological Vision,' *Reviews in Religion and Theology* 6 (1999): 354–9 at 355.

58 Long, *supra* note 55 at 132; Milbank, *The Word Made Strange*, supra note 51 at 150.

59 Long, *ibid.* at 133. Milbank, 'The Name of Jesus: Incarnation, Atonement, Ecclesiology,' *Modern Theology* (1991): 311–33 at 315–17.

60 Long, *ibid.* at 134; Milbank, Pickstock, Ward, *supra* note 51 at 6, 23.

61 *Ibid.* at 135–6. For an extended meditation on liturgy in radical orthodoxy, see Pickstock, *supra* note 51.

62 Long, *supra* note 55 at 139–43; Milbank, *The Word Made Strange*, *supra* note 51 at ch. 2.

63 Long, *ibid.* at 143–4.

64 Reno, *supra* note 50 at 40–1.

65 Reno, *ibid.* at 40; Loughlin, *supra* note 17 at 76, note 57. Milbank, *supra* note 59.

66 Reno, *supra* note 50 at 40; Loughlin, *supra* note 17 at 214–15; Milbank, *supra* note 59 at 317.

67 Reno, *ibid.* at 40.

68 Reno, *ibid.*; Loughlin, *supra* note 17 at 214.

69 *Ibid.*

70 Grenz and Franke, *supra* note 5 at 227–8.

71 Richard H. Roberts, 'Theology and the Social Sciences,' in Ford, *supra* note 5 at 709–11; Roberts, *supra*, note 50, for a defence of the social sciences.

72 *Ibid.* at 711.

73 *Supra* note 50.

74 I will not deal with the problems of basic comprehension, the heterogeneous nature of the group, and the group's attitudes to Reformed theology, all of which are much commented on and problematical. See especially a critique of radical orthodoxy's misunderstanding of Barth's theological breakthrough: James Harvey, 'Conclusion: Continuing the Conversation,' in Hemming, *supra* note 50 at 155–8.

75 Most are also lay persons, although ones who have satisfied the academic criteria for ordination.

76 Reno, *supra* note 51 at 41–2.

77 Hyman, *supra* note 39 is an extended analysis of this failing.

78 Hyman, *ibid.* at 146.

79 Milbank, Pickstock, and Ward, *supra* note 51.

80 Pickstock, *supra* note 51 at 135–58.

81 Milbank, *supra* note 48 at 14–15.

82 *Ibid.* at 16–17.
83 *P.L.* XLI (c. 430 A.D.).
84 *Supra* note 48 at 389–92.
85 *Ibid.* at 400.
86 *Ibid.* at 402.
87 *Ibid.* at 406.
88 William T. Cavanaugh, 'The City. Beyond Secular Parodies,' in Milbank, Pickstock, and Ward, *supra* note 51 at 185.
89 *Supra* note 48 at 408.
90 *Ibid.*
91 *Ibid.* at 116.
92 *Ibid.* at 406.
93 '"A Fire Strong Enough to Consume the House": The Wars of Religion and the Rise of the State,' *Modern Theology* 11 (1995): 397–420 at 398.
94 *Ibid.* at 398–403.
95 *Ibid.* at 405–6.
96 *Ibid.* at 407.
97 *Supra* note 51 at 190.
98 *Ibid.* at 186.
99 *Supra* note 51 at 190.
100 *Ibid.* at 182.
101 *Ibid.* at 194–8.
102 *Ibid.* at 192.
103 D. Stephen Long, *Divine Economy: Theology and the Market* (London: Routledge, 2000) at 242; John Milbank, 'The Body by Love Possessed,' *Modern Theology* 3 (1986): at 61.
104 *Ibid.* at 258–9. John Milbank, *supra* note 48 at 14–15; 'Socialism of the Gift, Socialism by Grace,' *New Blackfriars* 77 (1996): at 545; 'Can A Gift Be Given?' *Modern Theology* 11 (1995): 119–61 at 136.
105 *Ibid.* at 259–60.
106 *Ibid.* at 260.
107 *Ibid.* at 260.
108 Recently, Richard John Neuhaus has declared John Milbank's 'radical posturing' to be 'vacuous': 'The Public Square,' *First Things* 148 (December, 2004): 76.
109 *Supra* note 103 at 268.
110 *Supra* note 104. Also slightly revised in *Being Reconciled: Ontology and Pardon* (London: Routledge, 2003), ch. 9.
111 Long, *supra* note 103 at 268.
112 *Ibid.* at 260.

113 D. Stephen Long, *The Goodness of God* (Grand Rapids, MI: Brazos Press, 2001) at 229.

114 Bell, *supra* note 51.

115 Although John Milbank and several other radical orthodox theologians were doctoral students of Williams at Cambridge, Williams remains theologically elusive.

116 Williams, *supra* note 35 at 33–7, 39–43, 233–4, 284–9.

117 'The Gospel of Affinity,' in *The Strange New Word of the Gospel: Re-evangelizing in the Postmodern World*, ed. Carl E. Braaten and Robert W. Jensen (Grand Rapids, MI: Eerdmans, 2002) at ch. 1. Repr. in *Being Reconciled, supra* note 110 at ch. 10, and Miroslav Wolf and William Katerberg, eds., *The Future of Hope: Christian Tradition amid Modernity and Postmodernity* (Grand Rapids, MI: Eerdmans, 2004) at ch. 8.

118 Graham Ward, *Cities of God, supra* note 51 at ch. 7.

119 Gerald Loughlin, 'Erotics. God's Sex,' in Milbank, Pickstock and Ward, *supra* note 51, at ch. 7; 'Sex After Natural Law,' *Studies in Christian Ethics* 16 (2003): 14–28.

120 Vincent W. Lloyd, 'Radical Celibacy: Towards a Christian Postmodern Sexual Ethic,' *New Blackfriars* 84 (2003): 230–41.

121 A not inconsiderable source. Not only were most books of the New Testament written within fifty years of his ascension by eyewitnesses to his life and the next generation, but in volume, the New Testament provides more words about his public ministry than any other contemporary historical source does for his historical contemporaries, including Augustus Caesar.

122 Especially Paul's 'sin lists': Rom. 1: 24–32; 1 Cor. 6: 9–10; 1 Tim. 1: 8–11.

123 This is my body. This is my blood: Matt. 26: 26–8; Mark 14: 22–4; Luke 22: 15–20.

124 Hélène Cixous, *Coming to Writing and Other Essays* (Cambridge, MA: Harvard University Press, 1991) at 129, cited in Ward, *supra* note 39 at 600.

12 The Re-enchantment of the World? Max Weber, Ernst Troeltsch, and Human Rights

CLINTON TIMOTHY CURLE

When I think about the intersection of law and religion today, my thoughts consistently return to the contemporary human rights project.[1] As a Christian, I find a number of shared elements between my religion and human rights, and I suspect that adherents of other religions would find similar convergences.[2] Like religions, human rights establish a normative framework to govern social life. This framework is set forth in the most authoritative way; rights are absolute and inalienable, and although they are guarded by the state they are generally considered to be higher than the state. When we enquire about the nature of this authority, we are confronted with the language of mystery. The absence of a generally agreed-upon philosophy of human rights does not disrupt their authority; on the contrary, it rests upon the bold affirmation of individual human dignity, presented as an article of faith. The philosophy of human rights, like Anselm of Canterbury's ontological arguments for the existence of God, is an exercise in 'faith seeking understanding.' Finally, there are a substantial number of shared practical goals between religion and the contemporary human rights project, centred on the alleviation of human suffering. Given these similarities, human rights discourse has tremendous potential as a site to think about the intersection between religion and law.[3]

Accordingly, I want to do two things in this essay. The first is to give an account of human rights as a manifestation of late-modern political and legal life. Max Weber will be our guide in this endeavour. I will focus on Weber's notion of 'disenchantment' as it is developed in his 'Vocation' lectures and *Economy and Society*.[4]

The second thing I want to do in this essay is explore the possibility of a rapprochement between the contemporary human rights project and Christianity, the latter being viewed as a partial remedy for the 'crisis of modernity' Weber describes.[5] With the help of Weber's bosom friend Ernst Troeltsch and his notion of 'compromise,' I will identify theoretical criteria that are a necessary precondition to any practical compromise between traditional religions and human rights. In fine, with the contemporary human rights project as my focal point, I will use Weber to think through the modern condition, and then look to Troeltsch for a strategy to negotiate the challenges given in that condition.[6]

It is not my intention to suggest that religion is the only possible answer to Weber's critique of the modern condition, or that one is forced to choose between either traditional religions or a soulless bureaucratized political machine. Rather, I am enquiring into the possibility of a rapprochement between Christianity and human rights, following the intuition that human rights have potential for functioning as a hinge between religions and politics, in the hope that this rapprochement could genuinely benefit both of these spheres of human existence.

I take my start with what Weber called the 'disenchantment of the world.' Consider Weber's famous lecture, 'Science as a Vocation.' What, for Weber, is the character of modern science? '[T]here are no mysterious incalculable forces that come into play, but rather that one can, in principle, master all things by calculation. This means that the world is *disenchanted*. One need no longer have recourse to magical means in order to master or implore the spirits. Technical means and calculations perform the service.'[7] Science, progress, and disenchantment are inextricably bound together. We possess a new way of knowing, which is scientific. The warrant for truth claims now resides in the adherence to the scientific method. The aspects of human life that are not amenable to this method are relegated to the realm of subjective values and do not qualify as truth. With this restriction on knowing comes a restriction on what can be known. Science cannot provide answers to questions of ultimate meaning, and intellectual rationalization, of which science is a part, cannot permit other sorts of ultimate answers.[8] Individuals committed to science must restrict themselves to immanent facts and avoid delving into questions of value as much as possible. As Weber states, 'the various value spheres of the world stand in irreconcilable conflict with each other,' and science simply cannot assist in making the choice between these spheres.[9]

This new age of science has severed us from the old exclusivity of the 'grandiose moral fervour of Christian ethics.'[10] We now understand ourselves as people with options regarding ultimate meanings, and simultaneously we understand ourselves as people who have no ultimate criteria by which we can choose between these options. Weber refers to this situation as a 'struggle that the gods of the various orders and values are engaged in':[11]

> We live as did the Ancients when their world was not yet disenchanted of its gods and demons, only we live in a different sense. As Hellenic man at times sacrificed to Aphrodite and at other times to Apollo, and, above all, as everybody sacrificed to the gods of his city, so do we still nowadays, only the bearing of man has been disenchanted and denuded of its mystical but inwardly genuine plasticity. Fate, and certainly not 'science,' holds sway over these gods and their struggles. One can only understand what the godhead is for the one order or for the other, or better, what godhead is in the one or in the other order.[12]

While science has subverted any claim to exclusive normativity in questions of ultimate value, it cannot itself provide answers to these questions. Science is only fitted to enhance humankind's control of external objects by calculation, to provide methods of thinking, and to help individuals attain clarity regarding their own conduct in the scientific sphere.[13] The 'struggle of the gods' cannot be resolved so long as we stay anchored in the immanent.[14] We each must simply choose our gods or demons, looking inward to discover our 'calling.' With regard to Christianity, Weber is explicit. We have two options: we can return to the Church and sacrifice our intellects to gain the comforts of a re-enchanted value sphere; or we can pursue intellectual integrity, meeting the scientific demands of the day in commitment to a god/demon, fully aware of the complete absence of rationale for this commitment in anything external to us.[15] As Weber concludes, 'each finds and obeys the demon who holds the fibres of his very life.'[16] This is the meaning of vocation for Weber: to bring some semblance of meaning, grounded in personal, inward commitment, into a disenchanted and objectively meaningless world.

At the political level, this modern crisis of meaning is felt most keenly when we ask questions pertaining to legitimization. Under what conditions is constraint acceptable? The discussion of laws is unavoidable. Indeed, the question of the legitimacy of laws is crucial to Weber. The reasons why are put forth in his 'Politics as a Vocation' lecture. For Weber, the state is understood as 'a relation of men dominating men, a relation supported by means of legitimate (i.e. considered to be legitimate) violence. If the state is to exist, the dominated must obey the authority claimed by the powers that be.'[17] Understood in this fashion, the very existence of the laws of the state give rise to crucial questions: 'When and why do men obey? Upon what justifications and upon what external means does this domination rest?'[18] Weber's answer is that the sole modern ground of legitimacy is 'legality,' by which he means 'a belief in the validity of legal statute and functional "competence" based on rationally created *rules*.'[19] All considerations outside the parameters of the strictly defined sphere of legal logic are excluded. This exclusion notably applies to ethical imperatives, ideals of social justice, and utilitarian considerations.[20]

These very exclusions, necessitated by the rationalization of law, lead to what Weber viewed as the modern problem of legitimacy. Simply put, the problem is that the expectations of parties under the law are oriented towards those notions that are formally excluded by a rationalized legal system. The legal system is unable to fulfil those expectations; confidence in the legitimacy of the legal system is shaken. Weber expands on this problem in *Economy and Society*:

> New demands for a 'social law' to be based upon such emotionally colored ethical postulates such as 'justice' or 'human dignity,' and directed against the very dominance of a mere business morality, have arisen with the emergence of the modern class problem ... By these demands legal formalism itself has been challenged. Such concepts as economic duress, or the attempt to treat as immoral, and thus as invalid, a contract because of a gross disproportion between promise and consideration, are derived from norms which, from the legal standpoint, are entirely amorphous and which are neither juristic nor conventional nor traditional in character but ethical and which claim as their legitimation substantive justice rather than formal legality.[21]

According to Weber, such a legal system leads to the 'iron cage' of rationality.[22] Three threats loom in such a society: a loss of individual freedom, the unchecked tyranny of bureaucratic power, and the end of the kind of heroic leadership that makes politics possible.[23]

Given the rootlessness of society in the wake of disenchantment and the inadequacy of formal rationality as a legitimizing principle, given the absence of criteria to answer questions of ultimate meaning and the consequent 'struggle of the gods' between value spheres, and given the irreconcilable tensions between the individual and bureaucracy, what can be said about human rights from a Weberian perspective?

A good starting point for this discussion is Weber's conclusion regarding Natural Law in *Economy and Society*: 'In consequence of both juridical rationalism and modern intellectual skepticism in general, the axioms of natural law have lost all capacity to provide the fundamental basis of a legal system ... The disappearance of the old natural law conceptions has destroyed all possibility of providing the law with a metaphysical dignity by virtue of its immanent qualities. In the great majority of its most important provisions, it has been unmasked all too visibly, indeed, as the product or the technical means of a compromise between conflicting interests.'[24]

Let us apply this assessment of law to the contemporary human rights movement. With an entirely immanent, disenchanted view of law, we cannot entertain any notion of a transcendent rationale for human rights. Further, when we pull off the mask of natural law conceptions, what we find in rights discourse is 'the technical means of a compromise between conflicting interests.' Put in the terminology of the 'Science' lecture, rights discourse forms the arena in which 'the battle of the gods' occurs. In the absence of an absolute principle to determine competing value claims, the only recourse is to contestation and compromise, ultimately decided by a combination of political expediency, consistency with past decisions, utilitarianism, popular opinion, philosophical liberalism, and the vestiges of religiously derived morality. In a Weberian light, rights discourse is the locus where our society is presently wrestling with its values.

Science, the only absolute framework we have in modernity, cannot answer these questions. The vast array of other belief structures do offer answers to these questions, but we have no way of choosing one over the other without privileging one of them. These issues were formerly answered by the 'metaphysical dignity' of the natural law, which (ideally) endowed all humans with dignity, bracketed state power with the fear of God, and fostered the notion of divine calling. The solution the modern West has produced to manage this challenge is human rights.

What the Christian religion formerly did for the West in making room for individual freedom, in providing some limits for state power, and in allowing for the possibility of powerful, non-submissive leadership, human rights now do for us.[25] But where Christianity provided a more or less monolithic solution to these threats in our history, human rights discourse is anything but monolithic. Rather, it comes to us as a dialogue, in most cases a contestation. We must allow the various accounts of the good to coexist, and sometimes to conflict, with each other in our society, and in this coexistence and conflict to hopefully arrive at a provisional societal consensus on the strongest 'gods and demons,' which will allow us to live together and have our science too.

Ultimately, the extension of Weber's thought that I have described paints a picture of law responding to the crisis of legitimization with human rights. There thus seems to be a radical incompatibility between the culture that is expressed in the modern human rights movement, understood as a product of disenchantment, and Christianity. The modern human rights culture is completely immanentist, which on first blush necessarily excludes all religious claims of transcendence of any kind. Furthermore, human rights discourse seems to function in society as a replacement for Christianity, making room within the 'iron cage' of rationalized society for individual freedom, democracy, and purposive action.

But religion is not going away. One of the primary deviations from Weber's disenchantment thesis is the persistence of religion in the twentieth century. Yet the disenchantment of the public sphere is undeniable. This raises a crucial question: is there any compatibility between the disenchanted civilization that is revealed in the human rights movement and traditional religions? The question is not merely of interest to religionists. The process of disenchantment, for Weber, is complicit with the loss of human freedom in the 'iron cage' of formal rationality. Can religion moderate the loss of 'spirit' in modern public life?[26]

In thinking through this question, I have found the work of Lutheran theologian Ernst Troeltsch indispensable. Ernst Troeltsch (1865–1923), professor of theology and philosophy at Bonn, Heidelberg, and Berlin, is generally recognized as a 'pivotal representative of the early twentieth-century "crisis in consciousness."'[27] Troeltsch and Weber were close friends, and Troeltsch was acutely aware of the challenge of disenchantment described by Weber.[28]

For our purposes, Troeltsch's most important publication is *The Social Teachings of the Christian Churches*, not least because it marks the beginning of his response to Weber.[29] This work was an enquiry into the social and ethical possibilities of Christianity today via a study of the sociological structures of religious organization.[30] Troeltsch identified three distinct sociological types of religious organization – Church, sect, and mysticism.[31] Because of his concern for the social and ethical possibilities of Christianity in the modern world, Troeltsch set aside sect and mysticism. Both are precluded by their very nature from having a direct effect on society, sect because of its insularity, and mysticism because of its interior and individualistic bent.[32] The Church type alone promises serious religious contributions to society.

How could such a contribution be made? Troeltsch argued that religion and society could influence each other via a process of *compromise*. This is an important concept for Troeltsch, and to understand it one must first appreciate his view of the Christian religion. Troeltsch saw a permanent and fundamental tension in Christian social ethics: Christ demands detachment from the world and self-giving love for God and humanity. The full expression of this ideal requires a new world – the kingdom of God, which Jesus proclaimed. But such a world is not yet available. The teachings of Christ must be blended with something this-worldly, which serves as a kind of interface between Christ and culture. Only in this way can serious social engagement occur. For Troeltsch, 'the history of the Christian ethos becomes the story of a constantly renewed search for this compromise, and of fresh opposition to this spirit of compromise.'[33] The great historical compromise in the West was the augmentation of Christianity with Stoicism, which produced the doctrine of natural law. This doctrine allowed for the existence of law, war, private property, and wealth accumulation within the framework of Christian ethics.[34] But the modern scene presents us with entirely new problems, to which the Church must respond afresh.[35] Troeltsch concludes *The Social Teachings* on a note reminiscent of Weber's 'Science' lecture, invoking the images of the ongoing battle, which is a necessary aspect of the modern condition: 'Nowhere does there exist an absolute Christian ethic, which only awaits discovery; all that we can do is to learn to control the world-situation in its successive phases just as the earlier Christian ethic did in its own way. There is also no absolute ethical transformation of material nature or of human nature; all that does exist is a constant wrestling with the problems which they raise ... Faith is the source of energy in the struggle of life; but life still remains a battle which is continually renewed upon ever new fronts.'[36]

Like Weber, Troeltsch recognized that the former harmony between nature and spirit that had existed up to the late medieval period, and which found its apogee in Thomism, was tottering. The scientific way of knowing, which in large part defined the modern mood, did not need faith, and in fact reduced faith to the status of phenomena and made it one of the objects of its enquiry.[37] In the modern ethos a new compromise is needed.

Where is this compromise to be found? Consider Troeltsch's response to Weber's 'Science' lecture.[38] Troeltsch agrees with what Weber says about science *qua* science, but disagrees with Weber's conclusions. Rather, Troeltsch makes the case for a compromising Christianity that does not 'simply push aside the practical conditions of life with disgust and scorn, but must take account of them and adjust to whatever is an inevitable part of the economic, social and political life forms of the times.'[39]

What, then, is 'an inevitable part of the economic, social and political life forms of the times' in our present context? Our answer today would surely include human rights. Troeltsch himself recognized the significance of rights for the late modern period and identified this as the likely ground of compromise between Christianity and culture. To explore Troeltsch's synthesis, we will consider the evolution of his treatment of human rights in his writings.

It is helpful to think of an early Troeltsch, a middle Troeltsch, and a late Troeltsch. The early Troeltsch, represented by his 1904 article 'Political Ethics and Christianity,' held that Christianity was the source of democratic ethical ideals, which for Troeltsch included the 'rights of man.'[40] The essence of the 'rights of man' was the independent value of the individual, a concept that finds its historical roots in the Christian idea of personhood. However, Troeltsch also held that these ethical ideals were not purely Christian, but were commingled with Stoic ideas of equality.[41]

In Troeltsch's middle period (1911–12) he identified the specific historical source of human rights in the freedom of conscience demanded by Christian mysticism through the sects.[42] Human rights are the secularized and amplified children of this original claim to individual liberty, which go far beyond Christianity. At this time Troeltsch regarded human rights and Christianity as basically compatible, Christianity's central task being to guard the original impulse towards human freedom.[43]

Troeltsch's late period (1922–3), which interests us most, shows a greater appreciation of the gap between modern culture and the Christian religion. Troeltsch still held onto a hope that there would arise a new compromise between the realm of politics and the realm of the spirit in the future, but now contended that this compromise was unattainable without first laying a new social foundation for it.

In 'The Social Philosophy of Christianity,' Troeltsch argued that the very idea of 'Christianity' as 'the universally-human or the common religious element in all Christian groups' is completely new, a product of the Enlightenment.[44] Prior to this there were Christian churches and Christian sects, and one could speak of 'Christendom,' but these terms all designated historically anchored phenomena. In contrast, 'Christianity' denotes an abstraction – the essence of what was found in the historical existence of the churches and sects. Troeltsch comments that this universal 'Jesus-religion,' which existed apart from church dogma, 'may have been and may still be a necessity for modern spiritual life.'[45] He continues:

> For, when considered as the generic concept and quintessence of the historical forms of life of the Christian churches, this new, universal 'Christianity,' existing apart from church and dogma, is a purely private or individual religion. It is the modern personal, individualistic religiosity, which corresponds on the whole to modern individualism. It approaches social problems with merely private charity or with very general humanitarian ideals of pacifism, philanthropy, justice, progress, and the dignity and rights of man. As a result, understanding is lost not only for the old Christian social philosophy but also, especially, for the concrete social significance and productive power of religion as such.[46]

The 'modern Christian mentality,' which accords with Troeltsch's mystical type described in *The Social Teachings*, lacks the ability to engage the sociopolitical realm, terminating instead in individualistic casuistry.[47] But this is the only form of religion that can exist within a disenchanted society. 'It is quite natural that religion has taken refuge in mysticism and sentimentalism. For religion does not know what to do with such a society.'[48]

Troeltsch's conclusion? Modern social ills are amenable only to secular and scientific political solutions. Religion at present can only address itself to generating a new ethos conducive to human flourishing. Should this ethos pervade society, it could provide the foundation for a fresh compromise between the Christian religion and Western civilization. Per Troeltsch:

> It remains true, of course, that such immense problems are not to be solved without moral renewal and deepening, without kindness and justice, without a sense of solidarity and a readiness for sacrifice, without a basically believing outlook on life and the world ... Self-restraint, consideration for others, a feeling for the solidarity of nations, and respect for human rights, must be inculcated in people's minds; and the spirit of obligation to a more-than-human truth and justice must be aroused. That is task enough in itself, without any need for religion to embroil itself in dilettante social philosophy or amateur social ethics. The spirit it can thus awaken will then on its own redound to the benefit of social and political reconstruction, which in turn will have more and more occasion to call for such a spirit. Then, perhaps, unanticipated new syntheses will be possible.[49]

It is clear from this quotation that Troeltsch regarded all that we normally associate with the contemporary human rights project – 'self-restraint, consideration for others, a feeling for the solidarity of nations, and respect for human rights' – as the ideal site to begin laying the groundwork for a new compromise.[50]

In fine, Troeltsch was not advocating a simplistic turn towards a radically individualized form of Christianity. Rather, he was pointing a way for the Church type to go, co-opting the essence of 'Spiritual Religion' within itself as it seeks to compromise with the modern world.[51] The difficulties inherent in this direction, however, are daunting. We might say that Troeltsch is caught on the horns of a dilemma. On the one hand, neither sect nor mysticism can generate any real or lasting influence on society. Their very nature is separatist (sect) or radically individualistic (mysticism). Only church structures are able to speak to culture as a whole, and to pursue the compromise with that culture which is the church's vocation. But on the other hand, the churches have presently exhausted the potentialities of the old compromise with natural law, and the only foreseeable compromise Troeltsch could identify was between the modern way and the mystical expression of Christianity. He hints at a future possibility of the churches returning to their mystical roots for fresh inspiration as they seek a new compromise. But this, for Troeltsch, was only a hope.[52]

Troeltsch's last published work, 'Politics, Patriotism, Religion,' is highly provocative on the potentials of this new compromise.[53] He admits that politics will always be a power struggle, springing from 'the natural constitution and the natural requirements of man.'[54] But we must also recognize that we humans do not live on this plane alone, even in our political activities, but that we are also spiritual. He writes: 'Indeed, politics have a meaning only as conditioning and bringing into being a material environment in which the life of the spirit can flourish. Nevertheless, for this very reason the latter realm cannot fail in its turn to react upon the former, and, after all the catastrophes brought about by naturalism, it sets to work again to make the realm of nature serve its ends.'[55]

We can apply this analysis to the power politics inherent in the contemporary human rights movement. The gamble for power that dominates all political action certainly includes human rights discourse. Weber provided us with a compelling account of this in his 'Science as a Vocation' lecture. But against this political struggle Troeltsch asserts the life of the spirit. Positing the spiritual nature of human beings as a working assumption, Troeltsch is able to reinterpret political struggle as a struggle for a purpose. That purpose is to create an environment in which the life of the spirit can flourish. It is a struggle for the necessary tools to attain meaning.

As Troeltsch remarks, 'many of us in Germany regard "compromise" as the lowest and most despicable means to which a thinker can have resort. We are asked to recognize a radical disjunction here, and to choose either *for* or *against*.' One is again reminded of Weber's 'Science' lecture. Contrary to this conclusion, Troeltsch sees both struggle and compromise as integral to the human condition:

> In the last resort life itself, both purely animal existence and our human life, a dualism of body and spirit, consists in a constant, persistently precarious compromise between its respective constituent elements. And it is from out of this dual human life and out of its compromise that the highest heights of religious personality and of religious interdependence arise and grow. And in this their growth and struggle they point to a Beyond where they will at last be wholly free from earthly obstacles. This is the lot of humanity: human life is a struggle not only for physical existence or for the recognition of men's social and political rights. It is primarily a struggle between the life of nature and the life of the spirit that rises above nature and yet remains bound to nature, even whilst it turns against it. And if the whole course of history is thus characterized by compromise, it is not likely that the thinker can escape it.[56]

What can we conclude from Troeltsch's treatment of 'the Rights of Man?' First of all, we perceive Troeltsch's consistent approval of these rights as promoting human freedom, which he, along with Weber, believed to be at risk in the modern era. Beyond this, Troeltsch is suggestive but ultimately ambiguous. The root of this ambiguity is Troeltsch's complex attitude towards the individual, mystical type of Christianity. The best ground for compatibility between rights and Christianity is found in a mystical expression of Christianity. But the individual nature of this mystical expression prevents Christianity from having a direct influence on political and social life.

However, his final lecture indicates that he saw within the struggle inherent in politics a higher purpose. The motivations behind these struggles were manifold, but ultimately there is a kind of spirituality that drives humans towards seeking meaning. This led Troeltsch to express hope that in the end, when politics runs its course, there will come a fresh synthesis of religion and culture – a new compromise between the life of the flesh and the life of the spirit. In Weberian terms, Troeltsch hoped for a re-enchantment of the world.

By the end of his life, Troeltsch believed that at present Western Christian thought had retreated into a mystical form whose interiority and individuality forestalled serious social engagement. But the energizing impulse of Christianity is preserved in just such individual mysticism, and because of this Troeltsch maintained a hope that a true compromise between Christian thought and modern culture could be achieved in the future. He felt that purely political struggles would always lead to the search for more than worldly power – that they would ultimately turn to the transcendent.

To sum up the argument so far: in seeking to plumb the potential for synthesis between Christianity and modernity's human rights discourse, we have uncovered two basic hermeneutical frameworks and directions for modern human rights, both of which go behind and beyond the rhetoric of the dominant discourse. The first interpretation is the one derived from Max Weber's theory of disenchantment. This reading understands human rights as the attempt of our society to sort out its values, and specifically to pursue the respective meanings of the individual, the collective, and the relationship of the individual to the collective. This is done in the only way possible in the absence of an absolute moral-metaphysical framework – it is done by contestation. We used Weber's metaphor of 'the battle of the gods' as a conceptual key to unlock the nature of the contemporary human rights project.

Under this reading, the relationship between human rights and Christianity is necessarily antagonistic. The radically immanent nature of human rights, and the fact that it acts as a functional replacement for Christianity in its attempts to discover or create meaning in society, automatically exclude Christianity as it is traditionally conceived, except perhaps as one of the contestants in 'the battle of the gods'; that is, as a claimant for religious rights and freedoms.

The second proposed direction for human rights we probed corresponded to Troeltsch's analysis of the potential for compromise between Church and Western civilization. Troeltsch helped us apprehend the problems inherent in such a compromise, as well as the potentials for such a compromise that are anchored in the nature of the religion that is given to us in the New Testament. We will now turn to the shape of this Troeltschian compromise within the context of the contemporary human rights project.

Criteria for Assessment

Recall Troeltsch's words from 'Politics, Patriotism and Religion': 'This is the lot of humanity: human life is a struggle not only for physical existence or for the recognition of men's social and political rights. It is primarily a struggle between the life of nature and the life of the spirit that rises above nature and yet remains bound to nature, even whilst it turns against it.'[57] In general terms, Troeltsch has given us the fundamental requirement for a compromise between the Christian religion and human rights, which might easily be extended to apply to other religions as well. The synthesis must remain responsive to both 'the life of the spirit' and 'the life of nature' in their present expression in our modern, pluralistic society. What Troeltsch meant by these two terms, 'life of nature' and 'life of the spirit,' is revealed in another quotation from the same lecture: 'The important thing to recognize is that, above the sphere of politics and the natural man's gamble for power, there rises a realm of the spirit, of religion, which unites individuals belonging to different nations by forces and motives of an entirely different order. In this way there arises a unity and interconnection among men that operates in continual opposition to the demands of mere political expediency, which, for all its veneer of intellectual refinement, remains at bottom so crude.'[58] Troeltsch uses the term 'nature' to refer to the necessities and exigencies forced upon us by the ethos in which we life. All that pertains to power in society, to competing and conflicting interests, is considered by Troeltsch to be 'the life of nature.' Clearly, Troeltsch looked to Weber's analysis to provide him with an account of the life of nature. Against these necessary, worldly considerations Troeltsch contrasts the 'life of the spirit.' This realm includes within it all that which seeks to rise above the 'crude' compulsory aspects of societal existence by way of lofty religious ideas, sentiments, and practices. These two realms are locked in perpetual struggle with each other. The real task, for Troeltsch, is to find a way to appease the demands of both realms.

In other words, the goal of Troeltsch's compromise is to arrive at a common way of being a good citizen in our sociopolitical context that is at the same time a way of being a good Christian. In the following subsections we will break these categories down into more usable criteria for our present context.

The Life of the Spirit

Just as Christianity must shape itself for compromise with human rights, so must this compromise shape itself for Christianity and the religious life in general. Troeltsch cited as his ultimate category this one feature: that ultimately the pursuit of political goals must function as a 'conditioning and bringing into being a material environment in which the life of the spirit can flourish.'[59] Without this, politics has no meaning.

Under this category, which concerns itself with the responsiveness of any compromise to Christianity in the modern era, Troeltsch has provided us with three points of reference that we may easily identify as criteria for compromise. The synthesis must derive from the Christian principles of human freedom and personality, it must emphasize the unifying aspects of 'the life of the spirit,' and it must allow Christianity to foster a common psychological atmosphere of human sympathy in society.

First, Troeltsch predicted that if there was to be a new synthesis of contemporary political culture and Christianity, it was to be organized around the Christian notions of personality, individuality, and freedom.[60] Troeltsch thought that this was the fertile bed of much that was truly emancipatory in the trajectory of modernity, particularly 'the Rights of Man.' Not only is there a high degree of conceptual affinity between the ancestor and its progeny, but Troeltsch maintained that religion served to guard the claims of rights against the rationalizing forces marshalled against them.

Second, Troeltsch understood Christianity not as an 'absolute' religion, but rather as the Western expression of a 'universal religious *a priori*.'[61] This enabled him to posit religion as a powerful source of unity, not conflict. However, such an approach towards religion must be deliberately pursued, lest religion drift in the opposite direction towards fundamentalism. This is not to say that any compromise must generate a syncretistic mash of all religions, but rather that it must actively seek to define the shared content of a spiritual perspective, a perspective that engages ultimate meaning. Christians must still be Christological, but in their interaction with the world they must seek peace, which necessarily involves, at a minimum, acknowledging the social and ethical value of other religions, if not their ultimate salvific character. At the same time Christianity must insist on this acknowledgment from other religions if a compromise between Christianity and human rights is to be pursued in a pluralistic setting.

Finally, Troeltsch insisted that one of the central tasks of religion in society was to promote what might be called human sympathy. This operates independently of any attempted compromise, but it is nonetheless a valid criterion, in that any compromise must allow Christianity to function in society in this way, and that this fostering of sympathy indirectly influences the ongoing development of the compromise. It follows that there must remain some critical distance between politics and Christianity. A synthesis can never be complete, but only partial, as Christianity must always point to a higher and ideal moral level that is unattainable in political reality.

The Life of Nature

What are the criteria for a synthesis regarding 'the life of nature?' For Troeltsch, 'nature' is defined in terms of the socio-political necessities forced upon us by the age in which we live. To contend for one's own interests against all others, to exercise power, to resist power – these are instances of 'the life of nature' for Troeltsch. Any synthesis between Christianity and human rights must appease these necessities as well as the lofty aspirations of the life of the spirit. What, then, are the marks of a synthesis on the side of nature? We have looked to Max Weber to show us the essential character of our present age. What are the sociopolitical demands forced upon us at the end of Modernity? Our analysis of human rights from the perspective of disenchantment provides us with three criteria for a synthesis. (1) It must maintain an immanent orientation; (2) it must maintain an endlessly contestatory stance towards the problems of value; and (3) it must function to restrict the power of rationalized forces in society from eroding individual freedom, democratic rule, and responsible leadership.

First, as moderns, Weber was correct in demanding of us that we fully acknowledge the radical immanence that our science leads us to, and to seek to act responsibly in this vacuum of moral guidance. This means that we must forego appeal to moral facts, and in the absence of moral absolutes restrict our discussion to values, the empirical statements of our internalized commitments. Any synthesis between Christianity and human rights must fully acknowledge that Christianity cannot be what it once was. It cannot be asserted as absolute, even if its adherents believe it to be. Empirical evidence of religious consensus is all that is allowed by the immanent nature of our way of knowing.

Second, because of the absence of absolutes, Weber pointed to the necessity of adversarial approaches to societal value formation. These contests are ongoing and endless. Individuals commit to values and fight for these values in the public sphere, notably through human rights discourse. The fusion of Christianity with this political situation will not hinder the adversarial nature of human rights discourse. The battles over what is justice and what is human dignity will have to be fought, regardless of whether Christianity is present or not.

Finally, recall Weber's threefold concern at the conclusion of *Economy and Society*. In the absence of a common moral absolute, how can our society resist the forces of rationalization so that individual freedom, democracy, and responsible leadership can be preserved? This concern forms the final criteria for any new synthesis; it must function as a bulwark against the manifold forces of rationalization in society. Specifically, it must address the political problems that accompany the condensations of power in immense bureaucratic, rule-governed systems. The need for function is all the more acute due to the rise of new forms of rationalization made possible by globalization.

Conclusion

We have come to the end of our exploration of the potential for a rapprochement between the contemporary human rights movement and religion. While Weber's theory of disenchantment would lead us to understand the contemporary human rights project as a replacement for religion, Troeltsch's concept of compromise raises the possibility of a synthesis between law, politics, and religion via human rights.

Troeltsch has given us the impossible but necessary task of attempting to bring together irreconcilable forces: the life of the spirit, understood in terms of lofty religious aspirations regarding the potential of humankind, and the life of nature, understood in terms of the sociopolitical necessities forced upon us by our circumstances and by the ethos in which we live. We discovered, with the help of Troeltsch and Weber, three criteria under each heading. Under the life of the spirit, we identified the demands for human freedom and personality, for unity and for sympathy. Under the life of nature, we identified the demands for an immanent orientation, for contestation, and for a restriction of rationalization. These are the minimum standards for a synthesis in our day. They are culture dependent, and might easily change in the future, but they are ours now.

The form that the life of nature takes in Modernity is so contrary to the life of the spirit that there is no hope for an easy compromise between the two in the present ethos. The above six criteria provide us with the essential conditions for a compromise between Christianity and Modernity. Any proposed compromise must address all of these forces. However, it is important to keep in mind that these forces are malleable. A compromise can and should shape these forces even as it appeases them. Troeltsch never anticipated a compromise that stands still.

Troeltsch predicted that the spiritual considerations most amenable to Modernity were those pertaining to human freedom and personality, unity and sympathy, and that there would be a turning towards such Christian notions despite the deep incompatibility between these notions and the life of nature from which they arose. But these spiritual notions are then enlisted in the service of the life of nature, being used to restrict the rationalizing forces that form the potentially oppressive power structures in modern society. This function, in turn, creates an environment in which the life of the spirit can flourish. Ultimately, the life of the spirit, if it is allowed to flourish, in turn poses a challenge to the domination of the life of nature. And so the compromise evolves.

The need of the day is not for an ultimate compromise within the bounds of these six criteria, but rather for a fresh start, a provisional compromise that will move beyond the present impasse between spirit and nature. The contemporary human rights project is the most likely site for this tentative and partial re-enchantment of the world.

NOTES

1 By 'contemporary human rights project' I mean that historical movement which began with the UN's ratification of the Universal Declaration of Human Rights in December 1948.

2 Although this essay takes up the relationship between human rights and Christianity, my hope is that there will be much here that followers of other religions would find relevant in their own attempts to reconcile faith with contemporary Western civilization.

3 The fall 1998 edition of the *Journal of Religious Ethics* was devoted to just this issue, and contains a number of excellent articles from various perspectives. See especially Louis Henkin, 'Religion, Religions and Human Rights,' *Journal of Religious Ethics* 26 (Fall 1998): 229–39; and Max L. Stackhouse, 'The Intellectual Crisis of a Good Idea,' *Journal of Religious Ethics* 26 (Fall 1998): 263–8. Henkin interprets the shared elements between religion and human rights as a replacement of religion by human rights; Stackhouse interprets the shared elements as a latent reopening of the law to transcendent concerns. I will explore both of these options in a general way via Weber and Troeltsch.

4 Why Weber? Weber was keenly conscious of the connections between politics, law, and religion. Via Weber's analysis, we can understand current human rights discourse in terms that render it capable of being discussed in a religious structure of understanding. By making the implicit secularity of human rights explicit, we avoid the radical conceptual disjointedness between religion and rights that tends to automatically reduce such discussions to simplistic either-or approaches.

5 A word should be said defending the theoretical nature of this investigation. Would it not be more useful to discuss the potentials of compromise between a particular Christian group and a particular aspect of the human rights movement? The justification for our approach is that a general theoretical enquiry is a necessary precondition to any concrete synthesis. This is due to the nature of religious communities. Religious communities regard themselves as fideistic communities, bound together by common beliefs. If they are bound together by various sociological and psychological forces, they are also bound together by a shared commitment to a set of doctrines, of more or less abstract ideas, which guide the interpretation of life. If abstract questions of religion and human rights are not plumbed, there is no hope of any lasting practical cooperation between human rights advocates and religionists. Religious discourse is explicitly un-pragmatic in its basic orientation; any coming-

together of religion and human rights requires a general theoretical validation, at least from the side of the religious.

6 Both Weber and Troeltsch have produced and provoked large bodies of literature. My goal here is not to provide a comprehensive review of these literatures, but rather to use the primary sources generated by Weber and Troeltsch as lenses through which we can see the potentials and limits for both law and religion in the context of human rights.

7 Max Weber, 'Science as a Vocation,' in *From Max Weber: Essays in Sociology* (New York: Oxford University Press, 1958), 129–56, at 139, italics added.

8 Weber's argument only makes sense if one interprets him to mean that science, as the dominant way of knowing, prohibits other claims to knowledge. That position is reserved for science in the modern world. The problem is that science, as the dominant discourse, is by its very nature incapable of resolving questions of ultimate value. As one commentator on Weber writes: 'Disenchantment in this respect diminishes the autonomy of intellect by withdrawing the imprimatur of scientific legitimacy from intellect's prime ambition: to show "the way to true being" by discovering the meaning of the world and guiding conduct in accordance with this meaning.' Rogers Brubaker, *The Limits of Rationality: An Essay on the Social and Moral Thought of Max Weber* (London: George Allen and Unwin,

9 Weber, 'Science as a Vocation,' *supra* note 7 at 147. This contestation between spheres is particularly acute in the case of salvation religions and 'the world.' Also see Max Weber, 'Religious Rejections of the World and Their Directions,' in *From Max Weber*, *supra* note 7, 323–59, at 328: 'For the rationalization and the conscious sublimation of man's relations to the various spheres of value, external and internal, as well as religious and secular, have then pressed towards making conscious the *internal and lawful autonomy* of the individual spheres; thereby letting them drift into those tensions which remain hidden to the originally naive relation with the external world.

10 'Science as a Vocation,' *supra* note 7 at 149.

11 *Ibid.*, 148.

12 *Ibid.*

13 *Ibid.*, 152.

14 *Ibid.*, 152–3. Löwith's comment on this point is germane: '*we here today* live in a world that has become reified through scientific technology while, at the same time, the objectivist rationality of science has liberated us from an adherence to universally binding moral and religious norms. Since the progress of science is unstoppable, it must be seen as a force

which destroys the authority of tradition. The value-judgments we ultimately make can therefore neither find support in tradition, nor claim scientific foundations; they are, whether we like it or not, a matter of personal decision.' Karl Löwith, 'Max Weber's Position on Science,' in *Max Weber's 'Science as a Vocation,'* ed. Peter Lassman and Irving Velody, trans. Erica Carter and Christopher Turner (London: Unwin Hyman, 1989), 138–56 at 145.

15 Weber's ambivalence towards a radical commitment to Christianity *contra* 'the world' is apparent in his conclusion to his lecture. He clearly takes the Sermon on the Mount, interpreted in simple and perhaps even simplistic fashion, as the essence of the Christian ethic, and sees this in radical opposition to the way of science, of progress. This comes out most clearly in a 'open letter' Weber wrote to the editor of *Die Frau* in February 1916: 'The position of the Gospels is absolutely unambiguous on the decisive points. They are in opposition not just to war, of which they make no specific mention, but ultimately to each and every law of the social world, if this seeks to be *a place of worldly 'culture,'* one devoted to the beauty, dignity, honour and greatness of man as a creature of this earth. Anyone unwilling to go this far ... should know that he is bound by the laws of this earthly world, and that these include, for the foreseeable future, the possibility and inevitability of wars fought for power, and that he can only fulfil the 'demand of the day,' whatever it may be, *within* the limits of these laws.' Max Weber, 'Between Two Laws,' in *Weber: Political Writings*, ed. Peter Lassman and Ronald Speirs (Cambridge: Cambridge University Press, 1994), 75–9 at 78.

16 Weber, 'Science as a Vocation,' *supra* note 7 at 156.

17 Max Weber, 'Politics as a Vocation,' in *From Max Weber*, *supra* note 7, 77–128 at 78.

18 *Ibid.*

19 *Ibid.*, 79. Under Weber's system, there are two other possible sources of legitimation: tradition and revelation from a 'charismatic leader.' Weber believed that disenchantment rendered the first impossible and the second highly doubtful. See Mark E. Warren, 'Nietzsche and Weber: When Does Reason Become Power?' in *The Barbarism of Reason: Max Weber and the Twilight of the Enlightenment*, ed. Asher Horowitz and Terry Maley (Toronto: University of Toronto Press, 1994), 68–96 at 89.

20 Of course, particular laws embody visions of utility and justice. Weber is referring to the legitimacy of the law in general. The validity of the legal system in a rationalized context has no other foundation but 'legality.'

21 Max Weber, *Economy and Society*, vol. 2, Guenther Roth and Claus Wittich,

eds., Ephraim Fischoff et al., trans. (New York: Bedminster Press, 1968), 886.

22 The 'iron cage' is Weber's best-known metaphor. Here is the quotation in full: 'This [modern economic] order is now bound to the technical and economic conditions of machine production which to-day determine the lives of all the individuals who are born into this mechanism, not only those directly concerned with economic acquisition, with irresistible force. Perhaps it will so determine them until the last ton of fossilized coal is burnt. In Baxter's view the care for external goods should only lie on the shoulders of the "saint like a light cloak, which can be thrown aside at any moment." But fate decreed that the cloak should become an iron cage.' Weber, *The Protestant Ethic and the Spirit of Capitalism*, trans. Talcott Parsons (New York: Charles Scribner's Sons, 1958), at 181.

23 Weber, *Economy and Society*, vol. 3, *supra* note 21, 1403–4.

24 *Economy and Society*, vol. 2, *ibid.*, 874–5.

25 The affirmation of the Christian religion's positive function in Western society should not be taken as an implicit denial of its complicity with various forms of oppression in the history of the West.

26 This is not to suggest that the sources of law are reducible to political struggle and religion. The question I want to address is the potential for a rapprochement between human rights and religion, and not the broader question of the sources of law.

27 James Luther Adams, 'Foreword,' in Robert J. Rubanowice, *Crisis in Consciousness: The Thought of Ernst Troeltsch* (Tallahassee: Florida State University, 1982), ix–xix, at x. Reflecting back on his life as an academic, Troeltsch himself claimed, 'for me the practical quest for the justification of religious commitment in the face of a naturalism that was carrying all before it always remained central.' From Ernst Troeltsch, 'My Books,' in *Religion in History*, trans. James Luther Adams and Walter F. Bense (Edinburgh: T. and T. Clark, 1991), 365–78 at 367.

28 See Marianne Weber, 227–8. Upon Weber's death, Troeltsch composed an obituary in his honour, writing: 'Concerning myself, I will only take note of the fact that for years I experienced the infinitely stimulating power of this man in daily conversation and that I am conscious of owing to him a large part of my knowledge and skill.' Ernst Troeltsch, 'Max Weber,' in *Religion in History*, *ibid.*, 360–4, at 362. On the specific reference of each author to the other in their major works, see Friedrich Wilhelm Graf, 'Friendship between Experts: Notes on Weber and Troeltsch,' in *Max Weber and His Contemporaries*, ed. Wolfgang J. Mommsen and Jürgen Osterhammel trans. D.R. McLintock (London: Allen and Unwin, 1987), 220–4.

29 Ernst Troeltsch, *The Social Teachings of the Christian Churches*, vol. 1–2, trans. Olive Wyon (New York: Harper Torchbooks, 1960).

30 Troeltsch's methodology was criticized strongly in some circles. A discussion of his methodology and the critical responses to it is beyond the ambit of this paper. For a helpful overview of these issues, see Benjamin A. Reist, *Toward a Theology of Involvement: The Thought of Ernst Troeltsch* (Philadelphia: Westminster Press, 1966), 25–30.

31 Troeltsch, *The Social Teachings*, *supra* note 29 at 993. Troeltsch's definitions of these types are not germane; it is sufficient for our purposes to recognize that each of these types led to a distinctive social ethic.

32 *Ibid.*, 1000–1.

33 *Ibid.*, 999. Reist, *supra* note 30 at 157, shows that, for Troeltsch, the term 'compromise' was free of negative connotations. Rather, it suggested a state of reciprocity or mutual benefit, so that whenever Christianity has a real influence on its worldly context, it also incorporates into itself a part of that context. In my opinion, Troeltsch's 'compromise' can be regarded as an extension of the Christian dogma of the Incarnation.

34 Troeltsch, *The Social Teachings*, *supra* note 29 at 1000.

35 'Today, however, in an entirely new state of civilization these earlier supplementary movements [wherein the supernatural and ascetic elements of Christianity were combined with an "ethic of civilization"] have become impossible. A new supplementary process, therefore, is necessary. In a permanent world the Christian Ethos cannot live and be entirely self-sufficing. The question is simply this: How can this supplement be shaped to-day? The answer to this question constitutes an imperative demand for a new Christian ethic.' *Ibid.*, 1001–2.

36 *Ibid.*, 1013. But to this he adds the very Christian addendum: 'the Kingdom of God is within us. But we must let our light shine before men in confident and untiring labour that they may see our good works and praise our Father in Heaven. The final ends of all humanity are hidden within His Hands.'

37 See Reist, *supra* note 30 at 20–5.

38 Ernst Troeltsch, 'The Revolution in Science,' in *Max Weber's 'Science as a Vocation,'* 58–69.

39 *Ibid.*, 64.

40 Ernst Troeltsch, 'Political Ethics and Christianity,' in *Religion in History*, *supra* note 27, 173–209.

41 *Ibid.*, 202–3.

42 See Ernst Troeltsch, 'Stoic-Christian Natural Law and Modern Secular Natural Law,' in *Religion in History*, 321–42, *supra* note 27, and *Protes-*

tantism and Progress, trans. W. Montgomery (Boston: Beacon Press, 1912), particularly 117f.

43 *Protestantism and Progress, ibid.*, 207.

44 Ernst Troeltsch, 'The Social Philosophy of Christianity,' in *Religion in History, supra* note 27, 210–34, at 216.

45 *Ibid.*, 217.

46 *Ibid.*

47 '[I]t accompanies [the world and society] as no more than a pervasive melody filling the inner life. In this way one can account for the social indifference and unproductiveness of modern Christianity, which run deep in both churchly and sectarian circles; hence the disjunction of the inner and the outer worlds. Meanwhile the old social philosophy of the churches has been forgotten to the point that it can no longer be understood.' *Ibid.*, 224–5.

48 *Ibid.*, 230.

49 *Ibid.*, 233–4.

50 On Troeltsch's commitment to human rights as the centre of this new ethos, consider these words: 'The theory of the Rights of Man – rights which are not the gift of the State, but the ideal postulates of the State, and indeed of Society itself, in all its forms – is a theory which contains so much of the truth, and satisfies so many of the requirements of a true European attitude, that we cannot afford to neglect it.' 'The Ideas of Natural Law and Humanity,' appendix I in Otto Gierke, *Natural Law and the Theory of Society: 1500 to 1800*, trans. Ernest Barker (Cambridge: Cambridge University Press, 1958), 201–22, at 220.

51 Bryce A. Gayhart captures Troeltsch's thought well when he comments, 'It is the task of the Church to strive continually to reconcile the [inner-worldly and outer-worldly ethic] in such a way that the voice of Christianity never loses its contemporary relevancy. It is, additionally, the task of the believer to seek to maintain the sociological significance of Christianity by refusing to relegate its authority only to the private, personal sphere. Although a compromise was not foreseeable in Troeltsch's case, it was no doubt a genuine act of faith on his part to believe that such a way eventually would be found. If the voice of the Christian communities in the modern world would avoid becoming "the last echo of a disintegrating Christian piety," then it must neither be assimilated to society or separated from society.' *The Ethics of Ernst Troeltsch: A Commitment to Relevancy*, Toronto Studies in Theology, vol. 53 (Lewiston, NY: Edwin Mellen Press, 1990), at 232.

52 Troeltsch's mixture of hope and despair regarding the affinities between

mysticism and modernity is overt in his conclusion to 'On the Possibility of a Liberal Christianity,' in *Religion in History, supra* note 27 at 355f.

53 Ernst Troeltsch, 'Politics, Patriotism, Religion,' in *Christian Thought* (London: University of London, 1923), 131–67. This lecture was intended to be presented to the London Society for the Study of Religion in March 1923. Troeltsch died before being able to deliver it, and it was published posthumously.

54 *Ibid.*, 159.

55 *Ibid.*, 161.

56 *Ibid.*, 165–6.

57 *Ibid.*, 166.

58 *Ibid.*, 160.

59 *Ibid.*

60 The concept of personhood in Christianity cannot be separated from the call to offer – and receive – selfless love. Personality comes alive when the individual awakens to God's love and is then enabled to love God and others. For our purposes, the crucial connection between love and human personality is the insistence on human choice. The concept of love that is given in Christianity requires free choice. This is implicit in the crucifixion story, where the Gospel writers record Jesus' 'moment of decision' in Gethsemane. The theme of human decision is amplified in the Pauline corpus, where it forms an elaborate pattern of tension and collaboration with the prior theme of God's decision. This pattern of tension and collaboration is inherent in the orthodox interpretation of Jesus; specifically, that Jesus revealed at an ontological level the true nature of God while at the same time being *the* paradigmatic human. In general, the assertion that to be fully human requires freedom from compulsion – i.e., the capacity to receive and give selfless love – is the most promising basis for a compromise between Christianity and the politics of human rights.

61 By 'religious *a priori*' Troeltsch meant to indicate an inherent religiosity displayed in human history and human nature. See Ernst Troeltsch, 'On the Question of the Religious *A Priori*,' in *Religion in History, supra* note 28, 33–45 at 35–6. Whether religions are reducible to this universal impulse is obviously contentious. But from the perspective of practical religious involvement in a pluralistic society, it would seem axiomatic that religions must speak with one voice in order to be heard in a non-oppressive fashion, and to speak with one voice requires finding some more-or-less common ground. Beyond practicalities, the very notion of compromise, which Troeltsch convincingly argues is inherent in Christianity, should also include within its ambit compromise with other religions. The New Testament records the beginning of a trajectory toward such an approach in the apostle Paul's speech at Athens (Acts 17:16f).

Contributors

Logan Atkinson, University Secretary and Associate Professor of Law, Carleton University

Marie-Claire Belleau, Professeure titulaire, Faculté de droit, Université Laval

Clinton Timothy Curle, Executive Director, World Hope International Canada, Halifax

Rebecca Johnson, Associate Professor of Law, University of Victoria

Diana Majury, Associate Professor of Law, Carleton University

Sophia Moreau, Assistant Professor of Law and Philosophy, University of Toronto

M.H. Ogilvie, Chancellor's Professor and Professor of Law, Carleton University

Alain Papaux, Professeur associé, Faculté de droit et des sciences criminelles, Université de Lausanne et European Academy of Legal Theory, in Brussels

Rémi Samson, Legal Counsel, Supreme Court of Canada

Neil C. Sargent, Associate Professor of Law, Carleton University

Brenda Carr Vellino, Associate Professor of English Language and Literature, Carleton University

Barry Wright, Professor of Law and Criminology, Carleton University